15⁰⁰

KING OF ROME

❦❦❦❦❦

Books by André Castelot

✤

KING OF ROME

QUEEN OF FRANCE

The King of Rome
by Däffiger

King of Rome

A BIOGRAPHY OF NAPOLEON'S TRAGIC SON

BY ANDRÉ CASTELOT

TRANSLATED FROM THE FRENCH
BY ROBERT BALDICK

HARPER & BROTHERS PUBLISHERS
NEW YORK

To My Mother

I envy him, for glory awaits him, whereas I had to run after it! . . . To take hold of the world, he will only have to stretch out his hands. . . .

NAPOLEON

Contents

A group of illustrations will be found following page 116.

Foreword

Once Upon a Time

The story begins like a fairytale. . . .

Once upon a time, so they say, there was a young Austrian girl—one pictures her as a blue-eyed blonde—who, one day in 1957, was curious enough to go and look inside a big trunk full of old papers standing in a corner of the attic in the family mansion which she had just inherited. One can imagine her surprise and wonder when she lifted the lid, for inside the trunk, carefully arranged, classified, wrapped in paper or bound in boards, there was a mass of letters—over eight thousand, in fact—which had been addressed to her great-great-grandmother. . . .

The importance of her find will be appreciated when I add that this distant ancestor of hers was the Empress Marie Louise.

The girl—who is directly descended from Napoleon's second wife and General Neipperg—started examining her treasure trove, which included, among other documents, 119 letters, 68 of them in French, from the Duke of Reichstadt to his mother; 86 letters addressed to Marie Louise by her father, the Emperor Francis II; 310 letters from her sister Leopoldine, Empress of Brazil; 168 letters from the Empress Maria Ludovica written in French to her beloved stepdaughter; and 870 letters—also written in French—from Count Maurice von Dietrichstein, tutor to Napoleon's ill-fated son—reports which in their continuity form a veritable biography of the Eaglet.

All those who had served, watched over, cared for and loved the sometime King of Rome were there, gathered together in the old Austrian attic: his preceptors and "officer-supervisors"—Foresti, Hartmann, Moll, Obenaus; his doctors—Frank and Malfatti; his mother's friends—Countess Lazansky (700 letters), Victoire de Lorraine, *née* Folliot de

Créneville, the Duchess of Montebello, Countess Scarampi. Finally, there were the letters from his Austrian relations: from his great-uncles, the Archdukes John, Rainer, Louis; from his great-aunt, the Queen of Saxony; from his grandmother, the old Queen of Naples; from the Empress Caroline Augusta, the fourth wife of sensual Francis I; from his uncles, the Archdukes Francis, Charles and Leopold; and from his aunts, the Archduchesses Sophia, Maria Elizabeth, Maria Clementine. Not forgetting Metternich, the *deus ex machina* of the drama.

For Marie Louise lived at Parma, and every week couriers traveled the road to Parma with news of the child whom politics and her own selfishness had forced her to abandon.

News of this discovery spread throughout the world and a mammoth sale was arranged to take place at Munich on April 29 and 30, 1958. It seemed as if a mass of documents of incalculable historical interest was going to be broken up and lost to sight in countless private collections. Since the French government was not rich enough to buy the letters, cables were exchanged organizing funds to which Corsicans all over the world promised to contribute. And then news came which brought comfort to lovers of the past and disappointment to collectors. The Austrian government banned the sale, and the letters took the road to Vienna, where they were deposited in the state archives. However, on February 27, 1958, the Eaglet's letters and those addressed to Parma by Dietrichstein, representing an eighth of the total collection, were sold at Munich. Only the letters written by Napoleon's son tempted the buyers.

Two years before, I had begun writing this book, and the excitement which these events aroused in me can be imagined.

At present Marie Louise's archives are not accessible to scholars, and Countess Coreth informs me on behalf of the Oesterreichisches Staatsarchiv that they will remain inaccessible for a long time to come.

Fortunately the house of Karl and Faber of Munich, in order to attract buyers to the first sale, which did not take place, had had printed a voluminous catalogue reproducing *in extenso* the text of several hundred documents and publishing thousands of extracts from letters specially concerned with the Eaglet's life. It will be readily understood that this remarkable work, for which Herr Karl Hartung was responsible, has been immensely useful to me.

Then again, a fortnight before the date fixed for the sale, the House of Charavay of Paris put on show for four days a considerable number of documents, including, besides the 119 letters from the Duke of Reichstadt, the letters from the Empresses Maria Ludovica and Caroline Augusta, those written by Dr. Malfatti and General Hartmann, and an appreciable number of Dietrichstein's reports. M. Michel Castaing, the director of the House of Charavay, kindly allowed me to make a copy of these documents, and I should like to express my profound gratitude to him here. I should also like to thank M. David, who has translated for me all the letters in German, notably those written by the Duke of Reichstadt from 1816 to 1827 (from 1827 until his death, Napoleon's son resumed the use of his native tongue) and those written to his daughter by the Emperor Francis in 1814 and 1815.

It was in 1932 that there appeared Octave Aubry's moving biography and the extremely well-documented work by the Austrian historian the Baron de Bourgoing, an authority whom one cannot but consult if one wishes to write the life of the poor Eaglet. Following on Édouard von Wertheimer's important discoveries at the beginning of the century, the Baron de Bourgoing, pursuing the same course as Wertheimer, published in the *Revue des Études Napoléoniennes* the *Notes and Observations* of the Duke of Reichstadt's preceptor-supervisors. He used for his works the rough drafts of some of Dietrichstein's reports to Marie Louise, of which we now possess nearly all the originals.

Since then, other documents of even greater importance have been made public. First of all the letters from Napoleon I to Marie Louise, published in 1935; next Captain Moll's *Journal*, which appeared in France in 1947 and which provides us with a day-to-day account of the last two years of the Duke of Reichstadt's life; and then the documents belonging to M. Glauco Lombardi which were published in the *Revue des Deux Mondes* in 1938 and 1939 by the Baron de Bourgoing and Jean Hanoteau: the private diary kept by Marie Louise in 1814 and seventeen letters from Napoleon's son to his mother.

In 1945 the *Revue de Paris* gave us the moving memoirs of the Comtesse de Montesquiou, the King of Rome's governess. The importance of this text, which has not been used by previous historians, will be appreciated in due course.

Then, most important of all, Marie Louise's letters to Napoleon were exhumed in 1955 from the King of Sweden's archives: letters which are used here for the first time and which throw a definitive light on what has been called Maria Louise's treachery. This correspondence, of capital importance to our subject, was unavailable to Frédéric Masson, Édouard Gachot and Octave Aubry, and, more recently, to Jules Bertaut, the pamphleteer Jean Savant and Marie Louise's remarkable biographer Mme. Raymonde Bessard.

Finally, mention must be made of the letters of Marshal Maison, Louis Philippe's ambassador in Vienna, which were made public only in 1957 by the *Revue des Deux Mondes*.

Apart from consulting this mass of documents, which completely alters the picture we had of Austria's little prisoner, I have also gone through the Malmaison documents exhibited at Bois-Préau, and above all I have engaged in research at the Archives Nationales, where, like Frédéric Masson before me, I have been able to discover more unknown details about my hero's life at the time when he was heir to Europe.

In order to avoid burdening the pages of this biography with footnotes, I have consigned all my sources, old and new, to the back of the book.

I have adopted here the method I used for my book on Marie Antoinette: as far as possible, I have tried to follow the chronological order of events instead of dividing the work into a series of chapters devoted to my hero's education, his mentality, his health, the French prince or the Austrian archduke. . . . It seems to me that this makes it easier to follow the life and development of him who bore successively the names of King of Rome, Prince of Parma, Napoleon II, Prince Francis Charles and Duke of Reichstadt.

A. C.

Part One

＊

THE KING OF ROME

Part One

THE KING OF ROME

1

The Beautiful Heifer

*Austria has presented a
beautiful heifer to the Minotaur.*

THE PRINCE DE LIGNE

ON TUESDAY MORNING, March 13, 1810, it was cold and raining. While the bells rang out and the cannon thundered, the people of Vienna massed on the Graben and the Kärntnerstrasse watched an extraordinary cavalcade pass by, led by Prince Paar, Grand Master of the Imperial Post. It consisted of eighty-three carriages drawn by four, six or eight horses, in which there sat in state grand master, grand mistress, ladies-in-waiting, chamberlains, aulic councilors, doctors, surgeons and chaplains. Over three hundred people were leaving the capital in this procession. And at their head rolled a heavy golden coach in which a girl was trying to hide her tears.

The fair-haired Archduchess Marie Louise, eldest daughter of the Emperor Francis I of Austria, formerly Francis II of Germany, was being given in marriage to Napoleon, who had already twice entered the city as a conqueror and had carved up the Habsburg empire with his sword. But anything was better than living those tragic hours all over again. Anything, even this fantastic marriage, this immense sacrifice imposed by the conqueror on the Viennese aristocracy and

3

its leader—anything, even the shameful knowledge, for the bride-to-be, that she was nothing but a last resort. For everyone knew that Marie Louise had been chosen only because the Tsar Alexander had refused to give his sister in marriage to the French upstart.

To the people of Vienna these affronts were of small moment. What did an archduchess matter when the monarchy was in peril? Some lighthearted citizens jokingly inquired whether Marie Louise would henceforth call herself Mme. Buonaparte. Others, of a more solemn disposition, asserted that Europe was about to witness the blessing of a bigamous union, an adulterous consummation. In God's sight, was not Napoleon still bound to Josephine? The Officiality of Paris might have annulled the marriage, but only the Vatican had the right to undo princely unions. So if a son was born to Napoleon and his second wife, that son would be a bastard. . . .

This was what the poor nineteen-year-old Archduchess could have heard as she rode through the streets of Vienna, if she had not been shut up behind the thick windows of the coach drawn by eight horses which was bearing her to the sacrifice. Tears fell from her china-blue eyes and trickled down her plump and rosy cheeks. Her mouth tightened to hold back her sobs, a mouth marred by a pendulous lower lip—the famous Austrian lip which the Habsburgs had proudly handed down from generation to generation since the time of Philip the Fair and Charles V, and which had survived the introduction of countless new strains of blood. "Ugly rather than pretty," said Metternich when describing the girl he was handing over to the Minotaur. "She has a beautiful figure, and with a little titivation and dressing up she will look most pleasing."

Sitting beside the Archduchess, her former governess, Countess Lazansky, tried to comfort her. But what could she say? For ten years now, the French leader had personified the bloodthirsty people who had guillotined the fiancée's great-aunt, Queen Marie Antoinette. For nearly five years, the victor of Austerlitz had appeared to be the Devil incarnate, Antichrist. At the end of 1805, when Marie Louise was not yet fourteen years old, she had been obliged to travel over seven hundred miles through frost and snow to avoid falling into the hands of the soldiers of "the French Ogre." In the course of this appalling journey, she had taken on trust all the lurid tales that she was told about the French—that in the Tyrol "they had burned priests alive," while Napoleon himself had killed two of his generals "with his own hands" because they had fled from the Archduke Charles's troops at Aspern. The future Empress had shown her loathing for the man by calling the fleas that infested the wayside hostelries "napoleons" and by letting her brother Francis Charles burn one of her dolls, telling everyone that he was roasting "the Corsican." Not that this had prevented the Emperor of the Revolution from bringing the old Austrian monarchy to its knees, so that little Marie Louise was left with no other resort than prayer.

"We hope for great things from God," she sighed, "who has surely not forgotten us and will not refuse us His protection. Victory will go in the end to Papa and there will certainly come a time when the usurper will be laid low. Perhaps God has permitted him to go so far in order the better to cut off his retreat and bring about his downfall."

But the usurper was to go farther still! A few years later, in fact, in 1809, "Antichrist" stood once more before the gates of Vienna, with troops who according to Marie Louise had "made war like regular Huns." And once more she had been forced to take flight, this time in the rain, saddened by the news that "the Krampus"—the Austrian name for the horned devil—had installed himself again in her beloved Schönbrunn. Soon peace was being negotiated and Austria being carved up again. It was rumored that Napoleon was going to visit the Imperial family at Erlau, where they had taken refuge. Marie Louise had shuddered at the idea:

"I assure you that the sight of that person would be a worse torture for me than any martyrdom."

The interminable procession was now wending its way through the suburb of Mariahilf, where the houses were decked with tricolors. For the previous day, when the religious marriage had been celebrated by proxy in the Augustinian church, with the Archduke Charles, the victor of Aspern, taking Napoleon's place, those three revolutionary colors had become those of the Archduchess Marie Louise of Austria. . . .

Two months before—she could not help thinking about it today—Marie Louise had merely shrugged her shoulders at the news her piano teacher had brought her: that Napoleon, having just repudiated Josephine, was thinking of asking her hand in marriage. "He must be mistaken," she wrote to her best friend, Victoire de Pontet, Countess

Colloredo's daughter, "for Napoleon is too afraid of a rebuff and too eager to do us further injury to make a request of this sort, while Papa is too kind to force me to act against my wishes in a matter of such importance."

However, feeling a little uneasy, she had written to her father:

> The many proofs you have given me of your kindness and affection encourage me to venture to tell you something which I would have preferred to postpone until your arrival at Ofen, but the latest news makes it necessary for me to open my heart to you unreservedly. I have read in today's newspapers of Napoleon's divorce. I must tell you, dear Papa, that this news troubles me deeply. The thought that it is not impossible that I should be one of those whom he might choose to be his second wife impels me to inform you of something which I confide to your paternal heart. With your customary kindness, you have repeatedly assured me that you would not compel me to marry against my will, and since I have been at Ofen I have had occasion to meet the Archduke Francis. In him I find all the qualities required to make me happy. . . .

For her cousin, who was twelve years older than herself, Marie Louise had felt a *Jugendliebe* which made her heart beat wildly. How pleasant it would have been to reign with him one day over the peaceful little duchy of Modena, presenting him every year with another child! But now, alas, this romantic archducal dream had been shattered by "the Krampus."

The long bridal procession was now passing Schönbrunn, and memories of her childhood came crowding in on the Archduchess. She recalled the summer days spent gathering herbs, chasing butterflies and pursuing a white rabbit which had been allowed to escape— to be precise, a white doe rabbit, for all male animals were kept strictly out of the archduchesses' sight. And then, later on, the rides on horseback through the Vienna woods with her governess, Countess Colloredo—her beloved *comtine* who was to watch over her for seven years and whom she called her *mamma*. Her real mother, the prolific Maria Theresa of Bourbon-Sicily, was too busy, night and morning, satisfying her husband's tyrannical temperament to show her numerous offspring the slightest affection.

One cannot, in fact, blame Marie Louise for getting over her mother's death as quickly as she did—for Maria Theresa had finally died in harness, in 1807, after an ill-fated seventeenth pregnancy. Moreover, her father, who could not live without a woman by his side, had married again, his third wife being his cousin Maria Ludovica of Este.

The young Empress was only four years older than her stepdaughter, and on this Tuesday, March 13, she had wept copiously on seeing off the Archduchess:

"How can I describe my feelings," she wrote to her, "as I saw your coach leaving, taking my thoughts and my heart with you on your journey? I did not feel equal to coming to the foot of the stairs—you will forgive me, dear Louise—in such a cause. . . ."

Thinking of this same "cause" which was leading him to sacrifice his daughter, the Emperor Francis had gone on ahead and was waiting for the procession at St. Pölten to give a farewell kiss to the victim of politics . . . and his own weakness. "Papa is too kind to force me to act against my wishes in a matter of such importance." But Papa had found it impossible to be kind. It was said, not without justice, that he had "a political heart." And then, how could he oppose his new minister, Herr von Metternich, who had succeeded Count Stadion only a few months before?

Count Klemens Lothar, future Prince von Metternich, who was also to be found in the cavalcade following the new Ariadne, was all smiles today. A triumph for his policy of peace, this shameful marriage was a practical illustration of the famous report he had submitted to the Emperor on the previous August 10, three days after his nomination as Minister of State: "Whatever the final peace conditions may be, the result will still be the same: our only hope of security lies in adapting ourselves to the triumphant French system. . . . My principles are immutable but no one can fight against necessity. . . . Accordingly we must confine ourselves, once peace has been concluded, to a policy of shifts and evasions, of flattery and compliance. Only in that way have we a chance of prolonging our existence until the day of reckoning, that is to say the day of general deliverance."

Fortunately for him—and in spite of the fact that he had been "intoxicated with the idea of peace"—he had not had to put his signature to the degrading Treaty of Vienna.

"I will not negotiate with that diplomatic mountebank," Napoleon had declared.

If Marie Louise had only known! If she had only known that, a few weeks before, the "diplomatic mountebank's" wife had played the procuress on her behalf! Metternich had been ambassador in Paris, and when he had left his wife had stayed behind. She had been instructed by her husband to "see how the land lay" and find out whether Napoleon, yesterday's enemy, was prepared to marry the little Archduchess.

Incredible though it may seem, Countess Metternich's mission had been greatly facilitated by none other than the Empress Josephine, who, as she reported to her husband on January 3, had told her at Malmaison:

"I have a plan which is now occupying my attention to the exclusion of all else, and which must succeed if I am to feel that the sacrifice I have just made has not been in vain: it is that the Emperor should marry your Archduchess. I talked to him about it yesterday and he told me that he had not made up his mind yet; but I think he would if he were sure that you on your side would agree."

Josephine had added that the Emperor was to lunch with her that same day, and that she would speak to him again. However, Napoleon failed to come to a decision. He was still thinking of marrying the young Russian grand duchess, but the Tsar was far from enthusiastic and was keeping him waiting for a reply. There was no lack of good excuses: his sister Anna was of the Orthodox faith and was much too young to become a mother. Throughout the month of January, Alexander said nothing. Finally, on February 6, 1810, Napoleon received a message from his ambassador Caulaincourt: the Tsar was hedging again. The next day Schwarzenberg, the Austrian representative in Paris, was summoned to the Tuileries to be told that the Emperor had chosen the Archduchess Marie Louise to be his wife. The luckless diplomat asked for time to advise his Court, but was given to understand that this was out of the question. All he could do was to explain apologetically to Metternich: "Considering the Emperor Napoleon's character, it seems clear to me that if I had shown the slightest hesitation he would have abandoned this project in favor of some other. . . ."

That same evening the French people were informed: "A marriage will take place between H. M. the Emperor Napoleon, King of Italy, Protector of the Confederation of the Rhine and Mediator of the Swiss Confederation, and Her Imperial and Royal Highness Mme. the Archduchess Marie Louise, daughter of H. M. the Emperor Francis, King of Bohemia and Hungary."

"Austria," quipped the Prince de Ligne, and the Parisians after him, "has presented a beautiful heifer to the Minotaur."

The aforementioned King of Bohemia and Hungary still had to be acquainted with Napoleon's decision: as for the "beautiful heifer," she was the negligible quantity in this equation. Taking care to appear disinterested, Metternich did his best to persuade Francis I to send his daughter to the sacrifice.

"In the life of a State," he told the Emperor, "as in the life of an individual, there are times when an outsider has no right to put himself in the place of the person responsible for making a decision, especially when that decision cannot be reached by cold calculation. It is for Your Majesty alone to consult his obligations as an Emperor and as a father before acting in one direction or another."

Francis remained silent for a moment and then replied:

"I intend to leave the decision to my daughter. I shall exert no pressure on her, since I want to know what her feelings are before throwing my duties as a monarch into the scale. Go and see her, and then come back and tell me what she said to you. I shan't tell her that you are coming, as I don't want to appear to be trying to influence her decision."

This is Metternich's story. But what trust can we put in these all too impressive explanations destined for posterity?

"M. de Metternich," said Napoleon, "is admirably fitted to become a statesman, he is such a good liar!"

It seems unlikely that Marie Louise's father gave way quite so quickly, especially as Count Hohenwart, the Archbishop of Vienna, had told him:

"Until I have seen the authentic documents emanating from the French civil and religious authorities on which the nullity and invalidity of the Emperor Napoleon's marriage are based, I cannot acquiesce in his union with the Archduchess Marie Louise."

Otto, the French ambassador, had refused to communicate the findings of the Officiality of Paris to this "old man under the control of *émigré* priests," but had condescended to certify in writing that the

Emperor's union had been duly and properly annulled because, when it was celebrated, "the most essential formalities required by the laws of the Church and recognized at all times in France had been neglected." This was a little vague, but the Archbishop had been obliged to submit. And the Viennese Chancellery, much to its relief, had been able to inform Paris that "the difficulties had been removed," a somewhat naïve declaration, as Viktor Bibl has pointed out, "since nobody in Paris had given the matter a thought." Already Marshal Berthier, Prince de Wagram, had been instructed to proceed to Vienna as ambassador extraordinary—and incidentally advised, as a matter of tact, to use his other title of Prince de Neuchâtel.

As for the most interested party, her reply had been worthy of one of Corneille's characters:

"I desire only what duty commands me to desire. When the interest of the State is at stake, I must abide by that and not by my feelings. Please ask my father to consult his imperial obligations and not to subordinate them to considerations of my personal interest."

Here there can be no question of a reply arranged by Metternich. A few days before, the young Archduchess had written:

"If misfortune requires it, I am ready to sacrifice my personal happiness for the public good, in the conviction that true happiness lies in the performance of one's duty, even to the prejudice of one's inclinations. I do not wish to think about it any more, but my spirit is prepared to endure this doubly painful sacrifice."

She was now conscious of having become a national heroine, "the Angel of Peace" as the King of Saxony had called her a fortnight before. And on this Tuesday, March 13, to save her father, the monarchy and the Austrian people, and to spare her country a third invasion, she would have been prepared to go to the stake. She even thought herself capable of playing a part in international politics, and, at St. Pölten, throwing herself into her father's arms, she tearfully assured him: "I shall work for your happiness and for mine."

On March 16, the official "delivery" was to take place at Braunau, a little Austrian town which marked the frontier of the Confederation of the Rhine.

It was here that the adventure really began which was to make the little Archduchess the mother of the heir to the great European Em-

pire . . . and the heroine—despite herself—of the most astonishing epic
of all time. An epic from which, as it happened, Marie Louise would
one day dissociate herself so completely that she would end up by forgetting all about it. . . .

All the ceremonial had been copied from the delivery of Marie
Antoinette. Because on May 7, 1770, in the wooden house built for
the occasion on an island in the Rhine, the Prince de Poix had watched
Marie Antoinette through a keyhole as she left the Austrian rooms and
entered the "delivery room," M. de Bausset, the palace prefect, had to
do likewise. He later admitted: "I had brought a gimlet along with me
and bored several holes through our drawing-room door." Courtiers
jostled each other to take a look through these holes: the women, it
seems, were the most inquisitive. Caroline Murat, Queen of Naples—
who had taken the throne of Marie Louise's grandmother—Mme.
Lannes, Duchesse de Montebello, and the Comtesses de Luçay, de
Montemart and de Bouillé wanted to be the first to see their new mistress. The men—the Comte de Beauharnais, gentleman-in-waiting, the
Bishop of Metz, chaplain, Prince Borghese, master of the horse, the
Comte de Ségur, sergeant, the three chamberlains and the two equerries—followed after. All of them were thus able to see Marie Louise,
in her heavy dress of figured brocade, seated on her gold brocade
throne, and the women had to admit that her hair was "admirable" and
that her feet were exceptionally tiny.

But now the Comte de Seyssel, the Austrian master of ceremonies,
arrived and knocked at the French door. The procession formed up and
entered the room. There followed the prescribed bows and curtsies, the
reading of the acts, the ritual introductions and embraces, and the first
farewells to the Austrian Court which brought the ceremony to an
end.

Before arriving at Braunau, Marie Louise had passed the soldiers of
the Friant and Pajol divisions, those soldiers of whom their new sovereign had said the year before that "their cruelty and sacrilege would
bring down Heaven's curse upon their heads." Bells rang out, drums
beat a tattoo, artillery salvos shook the air: Marie Louise had become
a Frenchwoman. A little later, from the "palace" of Braunau, a few
houses knocked into one, she was to write to her father:

> I am thinking of you all the time and I shall always think of
> you; God has given me strength to endure the shock of separation

from all my Austrian friends. I put my trust in Him alone. He alone can console me in the performance of my duty, in this sacrifice which I am making for you. I arrived at the French camp today at two o'clock, after resting for a while in the Austrian quarters. I no longer had any idea what I was doing while I was kissing the hands of the people who were bidding me farewell. I could not help shivering, and I was so depressed that the Prince de Neuchâtel wept in sympathy. I turned toward him and all my companions left me. Heavens, what a difference there is between French women and Viennese women! The Queen of Naples kissed me and behaved in a very friendly way to me, but I do not trust her; I suspect that something other than the desire to serve me inspired her to make this journey. She took me to the French camp, where she spent two hours helping me to dress. I assure you that I am now as well perfumed as any French woman.

Napoleon was using every possible means to win his wife's affection. The new Empress's trousseau, which had been put on show in the "palace," was a cascade of dresses and lingerie, of Kashmir shawls decorated with huge palms or English fichus supplied by Herbaut of the Rue Neuve-Saint-Augustin or Corbie of the Palais-Royal. Tessier of the Rue Neuve-des-Petits-Champs had delivered twelve dozen pairs of silk stockings, and the shoemaker to the Empress (Josephine) fifty pairs of shoes. Marie Louise scarcely glanced at these wonders and turned her nose up at the fans studded with hundreds of brilliants and emeralds. Everything she was to use from now on—apart from her chamberpot with its agate base—would be in gold or silver-gilt, down to her bidet and her syringe, her earpick and her tongue scraper. The Emperor would give her a dress allowance of 480,000 francs a year, and 120,000 francs for her privy purse.* Josephine's dress allowance was only 360,000 francs, but then she was always in debt.

In the modest "palace" of Braunau, thirty servants, including ten footmen from Paris, fussed around her—not counting her ladies-in-waiting and her serving women. The food was worthy of the Tuileries and over two tons of meat would be consumed on this one occasion. The pikes, burbots and carps had been brought on March 3 from Strasbourg, and through being kept on ice were still in good shape.

* Approximately $280,000 and $70,000 in 1960.

But what did all this matter to Marie Louise?

"Heavens," she wrote to her father, "but how my mind harks back to the days I spent with you! I assure you, dear Papa, that I am inconsolably sad."

Terrible weather, an appalling lunch at Günzburg and the redoubtable stammering of the Bavarian Prince Royal—who thought fit to make a long speech—did nothing to improve matters.

But later, riding toward Munich and Strasbourg in a carriage furnished by her imperial fiancé and built specially for the occasion, along roads lined with firs and strewn with clover, Marie Louise began thinking about her marriage. Setting aside those stories of the Krampus, what did she know about the man who had become her husband? She already had three letters from him. The Emperor had written them in his own hand, with great care—and this represented a considerable effort on his part—calling her "cousin" in the first and "sister" in the second and third. And if they were undeniably formal in character, they were also as full of charm as they were of . . . spelling mistakes:

"Are you I wonder sympathetic enuff to understand my feelings on hearing everybody speak so highly of your person and of the noble qualities which have earned you the adoration of all my peoples?"

She replied—obviously without weighing her first words very carefully: "How I should love to be a laurel in order to come closer to you. . . ." Laurels won on the Austrian battlefields . . .

She also possessed a portrait framed in twelve large brilliants which he had sent her.

"He has a handsome face and a noble bearing," she had told Countess Lazansky, her companion on this present journey.

What else did she know about him?

The week before—on Tuesday, March 6—she had subjected the French ambassador to a lengthy interrogation over dinner.

"Will Your Excellency permit me to display a little curiosity? It gives me so much pleasure to talk about things French."

"I am entirely at the disposal of Your Imperial and Royal Highness."

"First of all the arts. Is the Napoleon Museum close enough to the Tuileries for me to be able to go there often to study the treasures and antiquities it contains?"

"Madame, the two palaces are next to each other."

"Does the Emperor like music?"

"Very much indeed, especially opera. . . . He has some highly cele-brated Italian singers."

"Could I take lessons in the harp, an instrument of which I am exceedingly fond?"

"His Majesty will always esteem it a pleasure to make himself agreeable to Your Highness."

"The Emperor is so good to me; I wonder if he would allow me to have a botanical garden?"

"Compiègne and Saint-Cloud would both lend themselves to a project of that sort."

"Monsieur, I have been told that Fontainebleau has some extremely wild and beautiful scenery; I know of nothing more fascinating than a beautiful landscape."

"In natural beauty, Fontainebleau surpasses everything that has ever been painted or written."

The conversation had ended with these words:

"I hope the Emperor will show forbearance to me. I don't know how to dance the quadrille; but if necessary I will hire a dancing master."

At Compiègne, waiting for his wife to arrive, Napoleon for his part was already taking dancing lessons. And, paradoxically enough, it was the Queen of Holland, Josephine's daughter, whom he had asked to teach him.

"From now on I shall have to unbend a little. This severe, solemn manner of mine won't appeal to a young woman. She is sure to like the pleasures of her age. Come now, Hortense, you who are our Terpsichore, teach me how to waltz."

Josephine's daughter burst out laughing, but the Emperor insisted and she had to obey. Napoleon had probably done no dancing since his days at the Military Academy, where—if we are to believe the Duchesse d'Abrantès—he had created the impression of a Puss in Boots.

"Our dancing master," the Emperor used to relate, "had advised us to practice waltzing with a chair in place of a lady. I never failed to fall over with the chair I was clasping amorously in my arms, break-ing it under me. The chairs from my room and the rooms of two or three of my friends all went the same way, one after the other."

This time too, the result was pitiable.

"I'm too old for it," declared the Emperor. "Besides, it isn't as a dancer that I should try to shine."

He could not keep still, and kept going to see the apartments that had been prepared for the new Empress, where dresses, lingerie and shoes copied from originals sent from Vienna were already waiting for her. One day he picked up a "remarkably small" shoe, and gave his valet a playful tap on the cheek with it.

"Look at that, Constant—there's a shoe that promises well. How many feet have you seen as small as that, eh? Why, you could hold it in your hand!"

He was like a drunken man, "drunk with impatience, drunk with happiness." Wagram and Austerlitz seemed to have intoxicated him less than this marriage to a granddaughter of Charles V.

"I'm providing myself with ancestors," he said.

Napoleon was also providing himself with a family that included Louis XVI and Marie Antoinette, who by this extraordinary match became the bridegroom's great-uncle and great-aunt.

Although an Italian woman—Mme. de Mathis—was giving him nightly occupation, and would go on doing so until the very eve of the new Empress's arrival, he continued to write letters to the Archduchess that were impatient and already almost amorous in character:

> How happy I shall be to see you and to tell you of all the affection I feel for you! The telegraph told me yesterday that you had caught cold. I beg you to take care of yourself. This morning I have been hunting; I am sending you the first four pheasants I killed as a token of the loyalty I owe the sovereign of all my most secret thoughts. Why cannot I be there in the page's place to take the oath of allegiance, with one knee on the ground and my hands in yours? But accept it in imagination. In imagination too I cover your beautiful hands with kisses. . . . Farewell, Madame. The idea that you are talking about me and thinking of me delights me. But then, you are only being fair, for I think of you often, Louise.

Louise! She was no longer "Madame," "Sister" or "Cousin." And the couriers, whose every journey cost three hundred napoleons, were submitted to an eager interrogation.

"Now tell me frankly, what did you think of the Archduchess Marie Louise?"

"She is charming, Sire."

"Charming tells me nothing. Tell me now, how tall is she?"

"Sire, she is about the same height as the Queen of Holland."

"Good. And what of her complexion?"

"Pale, Sire, with very clear coloring like the Queen of Holland."

"So she looks like the Queen of Holland?"

"No, Sire."

The Emperor sighed.

"It's the devil of a job to get a few words out of them. I can tell that my wife's ugly because not one of those young rascals could bring himself to say that she was pretty. Still, provided she's good-natured and gives me some strapping sons, I'll love her as much as the greatest of beauties."

That in fact was the whole question.

"It's a womb I'm marrying!"

"What is the latest age at which one can still become a father?" he had asked Corvisart. "I'm only forty, but does a man of sixty who marries a young woman have children?"

"Sometimes, Sire."

"And a man of seventy?"

"Invariably," answered the doctor with a smile.

Never, perhaps, had any man wanted to outlive himself as much as Napoleon. As soon as he had taken possession of the imperial throne, his chief preoccupation had been founding a race, creating a new dynasty, forging the first link in a long chain.

Josephine having given proof of her fertility with Eugène and Hortense, Napoleon had imagined for a long time that he was incapable of procreating. Remembering the adoption of Octavius, the new Caesar had turned to his clan and chosen as his heir the eldest son of Louis and Hortense—the first male born of his race. He had a strange feeling for the boy he called "little Napoleon," regarding himself both as his uncle and as some sort of grandfather—for were not Eugène and Hortense to some extent his own children? The Emperor used to take the child to see the Guard on parade, teased him and joked with him, and had him taught to ride a pony until he was ready for the horse he had promised him. It was with this boy in mind that in the *Family Statutes* of March, 1806, he made the education of the Imperial Princes his special province. But on December 13 of the same year, the birth of little Léon, "son of Demoiselle Eléonore Denuelle, aged twenty, of independent means, and of a father unknown," gave hope to the "father unknown." It was Josephine who was sterile! He could transmit life—he could outlive himself! And when at Finckenstein he learned of the death of little Napoleon Charles, carried off by croup on May 5, 1807, at The Hague, his grief was no longer that of a father and head of a dynasty. The idea of divorce had already occurred to him. However, since "Demoiselle Eléonore Denuelle" had also shown Murat certain special favors, Napoleon still had his doubts. And even when the beautiful Pellapra assured him, a little later, that the daughter she had just brought into the world was his, Napoleon remained only half convinced. He knew the extent of her popularity. . . .

It was at Schönbrunn that Napoleon finally attained absolute certainty: Mme. Walewska was pregnant. This time there could be no possible doubt, for his "Polish wife" was above suspicion. And so he made up his mind to repudiate Josephine, to whom, strangely enough, his second marriage would owe so much.

"It's a womb I'm marrying!"

At Compiègne, during these waiting days, all that he saw in his union with the Archduchess was the fecundity of the Habsburgs and the Lorraines—Maria Theresa had had sixteen children, the Emperor Francis thirteen, Maria Caroline of Naples seventeen—and he never gave a thought to the number of archdukes and archduchesses who had died mad, consumptive or in infancy, and whose little coffins thronged the burial vault of the Capuchin church—even though, one night in 1809 when he was occupying Vienna, he had paid a torchlight visit to the Habsburg crypt. What mattered to him now was not the problem of heredity but the need to provide ancestors for his future heir, who on his mother's side would be descended twice over from Henri IV and once from Louis XIV, and would be the great-nephew of Louis XVI and Marie Antoinette. The child would not be usurping the Bourbons' position but simply succeeding them.

Already, even before the marriage had been consummated, he had begun planning his son's empire. By the *senatus consulte* of January 30, 1810, Italy was taken back from Eugène and the prerogatives granted to his brothers and their heirs were abolished in favor of the Emperor's direct descendants. What was more, the *senatus consultum* of February 17, 1810, created the title of King of Rome. That of King of the Romans had previously been nothing but an honorific distinction, so the Emperor took care, in the same *senatus consultum*, to carve the Papal States up into departments named after the Tiber and the Trasimene. And finally, on March 16, the King of Holland "ceded" several provinces to the French Empire.

On Tuesday, March 27, the cavalcade, still in pouring rain and changing 122 horses at every posting station, was dragging its way along toward Soissons, where it was to halt for the night. The future Empress was dozing. She was finding it hard to stomach not only the lavish meals, of which the menus are preserved to this day in the National Archives, but also the hundreds of triumphal arches, garlands, cantatas, girls with bouquets, speeches, artillery salvos and peals of bells which she had had to suffer with a smile since leaving Braunau twelve days before. With her all the time was Queen Caroline, who, in her anxiety to impress "the little girl" was behaving odiously, something which was well within her competence. At Munich, ostensibly on Napoleon's orders, she had sent Countess Lazansky home. "My fiancé," Marie Louise wrote to her father, "could not have asked a greater sacrifice of me, though I suspect it is not he who is to blame."

Liebe Mamma had replied:

"Her prompt return greatly surprised me . . . but then, such is the fate of all princesses, and when one decides to embrace the married fate one must have the courage to break away, if necessary, from everything one held dear in order to devote oneself entirely to one's husband. He alone should rule over your heart, and I feel sure that that is what you said to yourself when Lazansky left you. . . ."

And she added in all seriousness:

"How sweet it is for a thinking person to submit to the will of a husband destined by Providence. . . . May he be the sole object of your affection."

However, as Maria Ludovica had guessed, Maria Louise was at this moment "a prey to the liveliest anxiety," for the next day she was at last to meet her husband, five miles beyond Soissons, in a tent erected close to the farm of Pontarche.

"Are we going to have the Braunau ceremonial all over again?" she had asked with some trepidation.

Queen Caroline had reassured the girl, not without a certain malignity: in a tent erected for the occasion—it cost 689 francs 50 centimes—the Archduchess had "simply" to throw herself on her knees at the Emperor's feet and recite a little complimentary speech to him which the poor child never stopped rehearsing from then on. As her father had written to her on the 17th—the letter would reach her only at Compiègne—she shared with him "the consolation of having done their duty."

The rain went on falling. Suddenly the two hussars in blue and mauve who were riding at the head of the cavalcade signaled to the carriage to stop. They were in front of the little church of Courcelles. A footman hurriedly opened the carriage door and lowered the folding steps. Marie Louise had no time to ask any questions, for at the very same moment the duty chamberlain—M. de Seyssel—shouted:

"The Emperor!"

Napoleon stood before her and embraced her: Napoleon in a dripping gray frock coat—the coat he had worn at Wagram and had donned again on this occasion "out of vainglorious coquetry" since he was about to conquer Vienna once more. . . .

The prescribed program of events was turned topsy-turvy by the Emperor's impatience . . . the impatience of a schoolboy in love. Sitting down opposite the two women, he blurted out:

"Madame, it gives me immense pleasure to see you."

In spite of the unlovely toque crowned with waving ara feathers which Marie Louise was wearing, his first impression of her was extremely favorable. Marie Louise was just the "fine strapping lass" he had been looking for. The eyes were too protuberant—but a very pretty sky-blue; the nose too long—but it gave the face an air of nobility; the chin already a little heavy—but it went very well with the fleshy lower lip; as for the bosom, it was full and high as fashion demanded. The general effect, if not one of grace, was at least one of pink and white freshness. And then Marie Louise had delicate hands and feet—much to Napoleon's delight, for he loathed what he called "vulgar offal."

For her part, the girl was pleasantly surprised. The "Krampus" had considerable charm, especially when he smiled and laid himself out to please.

Soissons! The calvacade pressed on without stopping. The Emperor was in a hurry to reach Compiègne.

There, the court hastily gathered together in the state rooms. An Austrian diplomatic courier—the Comte de Clary et Aldringen, grandson of the Prince de Ligne—has left this picturesque account of the arrival:

At last, about ten o'clock, a mud-stained page arrived with the news that they were getting very near. People started bustling about; the staircase was covered with carpet; and the kings and queens took up their positions at the bottom. The courtyard of the château was lit up. There were orchestras everywhere and torches in abundance. Suddenly a tremendous noise was heard, and the drums started rolling. Marshals, generals, equerries, chamberlains and pages came galloping up, followed by three or four carriages drawn by six horses driven at full speed, and finally an eight-horse carriage containing Their Majesties and the Queen of Naples. Some beautiful, though rather sad, music performed on wind instruments greeted them. I saw the Empress leap nimbly down from her carriage, embrace the whole family straight away, and go up the staircase led by her little husband. . . . As she is half-a-head taller than he is, she carried it off very well. . . .

It was not a wedding but an abduction. Moving at the double, and cutting short presentations, bows and curtsies, Napoleon urged the Empress to go to her apartments. While Mme. de Montebello—her lady-in-waiting—and Mme. de Luçay were showing her the way, the girl remarked:

"For such a formidable warrior the Emperor is very charming and very gentle; I think now that I shall grow to be very fond of him."

On entering her apartments, Marie Louise decided that the Emperor was all the more charming in that she found there the canary she had left behind in Vienna, her little dog which Caroline had sent home with Countess Lazansky, and a tapestry she had left unfinished in her room in the Hofburg. A table was laid for three, and the Emperor, Marie Louise and Caroline dined merrily, while the Court discussed the arrival and criticized the somewhat awkward and embarrassed attitude—yet how could it have been otherwise?—of the new Empress. Why, they asked, go to the trouble of hunting out a princess brought up on the steps of a throne if she was to prove unequal to the task before her? They knew nothing of the Viennese Court's middle-class simplicity, of its flower-picking expeditions, or of the balls at which they might have seen Marie Louise dancing a two-step with a cook's son on the Emperor Francis's birthday. Court etiquette, an old Spanish legacy, only held sway on ceremonial occasions, and there was no daily ritual in Vienna.

While the courtiers joked and gossiped downstairs, a real comedy was being enacted on the floor above. Napoleon was consulting his uncle Cardinal Fesch. First of all, was he married? Most certainly, he was told, according to civil law, but perhaps not entirely according to canon law. Could a sacrament be administered by proxy? That was a debatable point. But Napoleon had no intention of convening an ecclesiastical council, and that very night, without waiting for the religious ceremony which was only due to be celebrated the following Monday in Paris, he decided to go straight into action. The Emperor would not be sleeping, as etiquette required, at the Hotel de la Chancellerie. . . .

We know what followed from Gourgaud, to whom Napoleon recounted the scene at St. Helena on August 30, 1817.

First of all he asked Marie Louise what advice her father had given her.

"He told me that as soon as I was alone with you I should do whatever you told me to, and that I should comply wholeheartedly with your every demand."

"When you are alone I shall come to you."

Caroline was instructed to give her the customary advice, but found that "they had already told her all about it in Vienna." Then Napoleon, naked underneath his dressing gown, his body soaked in eau de Cologne, returned to Marie Louise. "I came along," he said later, "and she laughed happily all the time."

The next morning, the Emperor went around slapping everybody on the back, and told his aide-de-camp:

"My dear fellow, when you get married, pick a German woman: they're the best in the world, sweet and good-natured, and as fresh and innocent as roses."

As for Marie Louise, she wrote to her father:

"Ever since my arrival here, I have been with him nearly all the time, and he loves me dearly. I for my part am deeply grateful to him and I respond sincerely to his love. I find that he gains considerably by close acquaintance; there is something very captivating and forceful about him which it is impossible to resist. . . . I cannot thank God enough for granting me such great happiness, and you, dear Papa, for not listening to my entreaties at Ofen."

The Archduke Francis was well and truly forgotten; and for another four years Marie Louise would remain under the spell cast by her "captivating" night at Compiègne.

2

❦

The Austrian Womb

"AH, BUT SHE'S a beautiful princess!" exclaimed an onlooker as he watched Marie Louise making her entry into Paris on Monday, April 2. "A proper beauty! And it touches your heart to see her riding in her carriage with her old governess."

The "old governess" was in fact none other than Napoleon himself, the naïve Parisian having been misled by the Emperor's yellow complexion, his "Spanish" costume of gold-embroidered satin, his cloak sprinkled with golden bees, and above all his black velvet hat studded with eight rows of diamonds and topped with three white feathers. According to Marie Louise's first lady-in-waiting, this ridiculous hat had been "put on and taken off several times," and "a good many positions" had been tried before it bore any resemblance to a piece of masculine headgear. The final effect, as we have seen, was anything but successful, yet the Emperor seemed to be delighted with his appearance. When he entered the Square Room of the Louvre, which had been converted into a chapel for the occasion, Chancellor Pasquier was "struck by the air of triumph which permeated his entire person. His face, normally serious, was radiant with joy and happiness. The ceremony, celebrated by Cardinal Fesch, did not last very long, but afterward we were astonished to see that the Emperor's face, so happy a little while before, had become somber and threatening. What could have happened, we wondered, in this short space of time?"

What had in fact happened?

As soon as he set foot in the Square Room, Napoleon had seen that, out of twenty-seven cardinals invited, only twelve were present. The Italian prelates, who were then in forced residence in Paris—their master, Pius VII, being himself a prisoner at Savona—had chosen to stay at home, thereby showing their disapproval both of the findings of the Officiality of Paris and of Napoleon's second marriage.

"I shall never forget the withering look he shot at the vacant arm-chairs," wrote the Austrian diplomat Lebzeltern. "A whole red line was missing from the magnificent if theatrical decoration of his chapel. This look of his foreshadowed many violent storms to come."

"The fools!" muttered the Emperor. "I see what they want to do: they want to cast doubt on the legitimacy of my race and undermine the foundations of my dynasty! The fools!"

A letter from Fouché to the Minister of Cults reveals that Napoleon thought of charging the absent cardinals with conspiracy against the state, but this threat was never carried out. For the moment, he simply had the recalcitrant prelates turned out of the Tuileries when they came to the official reception two days later. Their carriages having been sent away, they could be seen wandering about in the Cour du Carrousel, dressed in their scarlet robes.

The attitude taken up by the Italian prelates—an attitude which the Vatican was likewise to adopt, four years later—would serve Metternich's purposes admirably in the future, enabling him to convince his master's daughter that her marriage to Napoleon was null and void. But on this April 2, 1810, it was in Austria's interest to assume the opposite position, to turn her sacrifice to good account and pander to the conqueror. In the evening, in a Paris ablaze with light, the Chancellor stepped onto the balcony of one of the state rooms in which the banquet had been held, holding a glass of champagne in one hand, and cried out like a herald:

"I drink to the King of Rome!"

A surprising toast to come from the lips of the chief minister to the ex-Emperor of the Holy Roman Empire, who, before his coronation, had—like his forefathers—borne the title of King of the Romans . . .

But it needed more than that to astonish the Parisians. The common people watched the show without any great enthusiasm, even though they had been gorged with food and drink: nearly five thousand pies, over two thousand legs and shoulders of mutton, a thousand head of poultry, three thousand sausages, and wine flowing from the fountains. But as Napoleon explained in philosophic mood:

"I've spoiled the Parisians so much with the unexpected and the impossible that if I married the Madonna herself it wouldn't surprise them."

Learning how to play the oldest game in the world, Marie Louise—who was not her father's daughter for nothing—had fallen head over heels in love with her instructor. She used the *tu* form of address with him, and called him "Nana," "Popo," or—if he left her for a few hours —"my naughty love."

"Your Majesty is well placed to hear all about the battles in the recent wars," suggested Countess Lazansky.

As if Marie Louise cared! All that she thought about was love.

"I have nothing to fear from Napoleon," she said; "but I am beginning to think he is just a little afraid of me."

In her letters to Vienna, she never stopped talking about how happy she was. "You will understand," she told her father, "when you come to know the Emperor personally."

"Your letters from Compiègne dated March 29," he replied, "and even more so that from Paris dated April 3, have filled me with pleasure, for they tell me that you are happy and content."

Marie Louise had also confided in her beloved Countess Lazansky, who replied on April 20:

> The confidences with which Your Majesty has honored me are extremely precious to me, since they bring me the assurance of her happiness. I beseech Heaven to make it perfect by granting all her wishes and those of her august spouse. By now Your Majesty will no longer have any doubts on this point, for it is not impossible that She should have become pregnant during the first days of her marriage. . . . I hear too that the Emperor was agreeably surprised to find her far superior to the descriptions which had been given him. Your Majesty has had the same pleasant surprise, and I can readily believe in all the qualities which She has discovered in Him, these offering me a surer guarantee of her happiness than all the glory He has won to this day.

Napoleon had indeed been "agreeably surprised," and he had even allowed himself to be infected by the neophyte's enthusiasm. After being in love with what Frédéric Masson called "an ambitious fantasy," he was now really and truly in love with the daughter of the Caesars.

"He loves her so much," Metternich informed his master, "that he cannot conceal his feelings for her, and all his habits are subordinated to her desires."

As a matter of fact, not *all* his habits.

"The Empress didn't approve of getting out of bed at night," Napoleon told Bertrand in after years, "even to answer Nature's call. She had got into the habit of never having a fire in her bedroom, which was annoying for me as I always used to get up during the night. Perhaps that was what stopped me, a score of times or more, from going to the Empress's room. Now a good lady-in-waiting would have told her how annoying a thing like that could be, because it was just a silly little habit she could easily have got out of. The Duchesse de Montebello didn't behave at all well. She was a woman entirely lacking in breeding. . . ."

Marie Louise's whining voice sometimes got on the Emperor's nerves. She was very much a hypochondriac at the time—the best customer the imperial pharmacy had, as the account books show. She was forever complaining about her health, all the more so as she ate like a horse and never stopped guzzling cakes, a practice that brought on frequent attacks of indigestion—attacks so frequent, indeed, that Napoleon imagined that his wife was pregnant less than a month after the "captivating" night at Compiègne. Corvisart, who was called in at once, chose to attribute his patient's aches and pains and vomiting to overindulgence in her favorite cream tarts rather than to the Emperor's conjugal prowess. More than a little annoyed, Napoleon sent for the famous obstetrician Baudelocque. He was of the same opinion as Corvisart, and placed an immediate ban on cream tarts, which, combined with excessive hydrotherapy—Marie Louise loved soaking herself in hot water—constituted, he declared, "an indisputable obstacle to fertilization."

On Sunday, April 28, the two monarchs set off on a visit to the French provinces of Belgium and Holland. They had scarcely arrived at Laeken before the local army doctor, a certain Jouan, was called in to attend to Marie Louise, who was suffering from violent stomachache. Jouan, more at home when he was dealing with soldiers, and influenced in the bargain by the Emperor's tendency to take desire for reality, stated authoritatively that the Empress was "expecting an heir" and risked having a miscarriage if she ventured to continue her jour-

ney. Marie Louise, who was well aware that she had simply been in-
dulging a little unwisely in the delights of Belgian cooking, staged a
faint, apparently in a typically feminine attempt at revenge for "the
useless mental torment which this erroneous judgment was inflicting
on her husband." The threat of a bleeding brought her back to consciousness, and the very next day, every trace of her indisposition having disappeared, the imperial cavalcade set off at noon for Antwerp.

The following Sunday, arriving at half-past ten at night at Bois-le-
Duc, the Empress suffered another indisposition, which was cured all
the more rapidly in that Jouan, who had been left behind at Breda,
did not catch up with the imperial party until two in the morning. His
carriage had overturned on the way, he had lost all his drugs, and he
arrived in the middle of the night, covered in mud from head to foot.
However, Marie Louise apparently took this fresh attack of indigestion
to be an early sign of pregnancy, for three days later she wrote to
Vienna from Middelburg: "I already have hopes, though too vague
to be worth mentioning."

At nine o'clock in the evening of Friday, June 1, after thirty-six
days of journeys, receptions, speeches and reviews, husband and wife
finally arrived at Saint-Cloud. "Tired out" though she was by the tour,
Marie Louise still had no regrets, for as she told Vienna: "It would
hurt me too much to spend even a day apart from the Emperor." She
had no difficulty in following the advice given her by Maria Ludovica.
Forced by a tyrannical husband to travel to Prague in the course of a
serious illness, the Austrian Empress recommended "self-sacrifice" as the
supreme source of happiness: "Mention traveling to me, and all I can
say is: undertake it with a brave heart, if such is your husband's desire. . . . I find it perfectly natural that, with the Emperor's permission,
you should have decided to accompany him; a woman is never happier
than when she is with her husband. . . ." It should be added that she
herself submitted gladly to all her husband's demands, even spending
her days writing him utterly unprintable erotic letters in order to keep
alive a flame which had no real need of a Vestal's attentions.

For his part, when he heard that his daughter was back in France,
the Emperor of Austria sent her this advice: "Look after your health,
and avoid anything which might jeopardize the all-important object
of having children." His hopes were soon to be fulfilled, for on July 2,
1810, Marie Louise was at last able to announce: "I am now doubly
happy because the doctor assures me that I have been pregnant since

last month. God grant that he is right, for the Emperor is full of joy at the news. He has already forbidden me to go dancing or riding any more. . . ."

"You may imagine," replied Francis, "the joy I felt on hearing that you were pregnant, not only because of the importance of the circumstance in itself, but also because of the comfort it will have afforded your husband and the affection I feel for you. You have done well to give up dancing and riding, but take care also to avoid anything which might frighten you, for my late wife lost several children in that way. . . ."

By the time she received this letter Marie Louise was indeed expecting a child—but she was only a few days' pregnant. To quote Dr. Ganière:

> Corvisart somewhat shamefacedly informed the Emperor that he had made a mistake with regard to the vital dates and only in August had Her Majesty entered the second month of her pregnancy, a fact which postponed the arrival of the imperial offspring until some time in the middle of March. In mitigation of his error the doctor could point to various extenuating circumstances. In the first place, he was as yet only very imperfectly acquainted with the young Empress's constitution and could not know that her menstrual periods were extremely irregular and likely to give rise to misinterpretation. Then again, it should not be forgotten that the Court was in the grip of a veritable "maternity psychosis" by which it was difficult to remain entirely unaffected. In any event, no one blamed Corvisart for letting himself be influenced by this obsessive atmosphere, since knowing for certain that Marie Louise was pregnant was more important in everyone's eyes than knowing the exact date of her delivery.

There was an even more important consideration: would Marie Louise give birth to a son? The Empress herself had no doubt on this point: "We are quite certain that it will be a boy. If it should happen to be a girl, I fear she would be given a cold welcome." As for the Emperor, he did not seem to regard the possibility of having a daughter at all seriously: if the child were a girl, she was to be called the Princess of Venice, but Napoleon thought of nothing but the King of Rome. As Metternich told his master: "He is in indescribably high spirits. . . ." In this mood he went on planning an empire for Napoleon

II. The Hanseatic ports were given French names; Holland was divided into eight French departments; the republic of Valais was called the department of Simplon and annexed to the Empire. France was to stretch from Hamburg to Rome. The empire swallowed up nations, provinces and kingdoms, turning into an enormous hybrid monster, doomed to die one day of morbid hunger. A European empire could have endured, but a centralized empire—it would take the fastest courier a fortnight to cross it from end to end—carrying in itself all the elements of self-destruction, was bound to collapse in time. Not that the idea ever entered Napoleon's head: he believed in the future and stability of the gigantic edifice. Once he had bedded the plump young Archduchess, he never stopped dreaming about his son's empire, the "grand empire" that was to prove his own undoing. Excited by the mere presence of the waiting cradle, drunk with power, and dazzled by an ambition that had become paternal in character, he strode on like an automaton toward the final cataclysm. The prospect of fatherhood had blinded him to even the most elementary realities. Imagining that the Emperor Francis would become his stoutest ally, and believing in the sincerity of the man he called "one of the dearest members of my family," Napoleon put his trust in "the piety, honesty and good faith of the Emperor of Austria." This he admitted with a sigh at St. Helena —when it was too late to do anything but acknowledge that "that marriage of mine, that trap covered with flowers, was the ruin of me."

That marriage and its natural consequence . . . As Frédéric Masson has pointed out, "he should have known, after the 1809 crisis, that if his family system were submitted to a fresh test, it was bound to result in a catastrophe." By a cruel paradox, this "fresh test" was to be the arrival at the Tuileries of the King of Rome, the climax of Napoleon's superhuman career.

The great event which was to "gladden the hearts" of the people of Europe from the North Sea to the Adriatic had to be prepared for with scrupulous care.

The Emperor himself gave the news "with infinite satisfaction" to all the bishops, at the same time ordering them to offer up "special prayers." Prelates who failed to show sufficient delight or who prescribed prayers for their flocks which were considered "unsuitable"—or even downright unseemly, like the Bishop of Nantes's offhand orisons —were given a sharp rap over the knuckles. The Central Consistory likewise called for prayers to be said in all the Israelite temples in the Empire, and expressed the hope that "the fatherly heart of our beloved monarch Napoleon may quiver with joy as he beholds in his offspring a worthy heir to his throne and his glory."

As early as October, Ségur, the grand master of ceremonies, was hard at work gathering information about the pomp and circumstance which had attended royal births over the past 150 years, from the birth of the Grand Dauphin, Louis XIV's son, to that of Louis XVI's elder son. The same file in the Archives shows us to what lengths M. de Montalivet, the Minister of the Interior, was prepared to go in flattering the Emperor, whom he reminded in all seriousness that at the birth of Sesostris, the son of Amenophis the Great, all the Egyptian children born on the same day were taken to Court to be brought up with the Pharaoh's successor. . . .

While arrangements were being made for the forthcoming *Te Deums,* illuminations, bonfires, processions, almsgiving, free performances, artillery salutes and firework displays across the length and breadth of the 132 imperial departments and the various vassal states, Ségur was trying his best to answer the questions the Emperor kept firing at him.

"Will the King of Rome's carriage be drawn by six horses or eight?"

"By eight, naturally."

"Will he be addressed as 'Sire' and 'Your Majesty'?"

"Certainly, since that was how the King of the Romans was addressed."

It was the future governess's prerogatives that gave rise to the most discussion. As it was feared that they might have an adverse effect on the privileges enjoyed by Mme. de Montebello, Marie Louise's lady-in-waiting, with whom the new Empress was positively infatuated, Napoleon made the following ruling:

When the governess is with the Children of France, nothing can separate her from them. They walk immediately behind the Emperor, and on such occasions the governess gives place to no one, not even the princesses. Without the Children, she takes precedence over all the ladies of the Court, but she does not occupy the position assigned to the lady-in-waiting by her duties. Thus if she accompanies Their Majesties' procession to the chapel, she walks immediately behind the princesses. At Court entertainments, she sits in the high officials' box; at the Emperor's table, on His Majesty's right; at social gatherings, on the first chair in the row to the right of the Emperor.

Who was going to take on this heavy responsibility?

On October 22 Napoleon appointed as governess to the King of Rome—or, to be more precise, governess to the Children of France—the wife of the Baron de Montesquiou, Count of the Empire, President of the Legislative Assembly and Grand Chamberlain. She did not accept the appointment lightheartedly. "I hesitated, frightened at the thought of so unfamiliar a life and so great a responsibility, and of all the obstacles which injustice, envy, hatred and the uncertain future could put in my way in the course of this new career."

Forty-six years of age, she was a Le Tellier de Louvois by birth, and the blood of the Noailles and the Gontauts flowed through her veins. Napoleon had singled her out because, one Friday at Trianon, invited to sit at the imperial table and put on the Emperor's right, she had refused to eat meat. This had made a deep impression on him. "She is a woman of rare merit," he said later, and when she came to be sworn in he told her:

"Madame, I am committing the destinies of France to your care. Make a good Frenchman and a good Christian of my son, for the one cannot go without the other."

Then the Countess took her oath:

"I swear obedience to the Constitutions and loyalty to the Emperor. I promise to serve, assiduously, devotedly and in all the duties of the office which His Majesty has conferred upon me, the Children which it shall please His Majesty to entrust to my care; to comply strictly with the orders which He gives me and to see that all the ladies and other persons put under my command carry out their duties efficiently; to employ economically and in His Majesty's interests the monies which are assigned to me; to carry on no foreign correspondence; to have no connection with foreign princes and to accept no presents from them, and if anything prejudicial to their safety or the service of His Majesty or the Children of France comes to my notice, to inform His Majesty of it without delay."

A veritable ministry came into being of which Mme. de Montesquiou was the all-powerful head. If the honors attached to her position were considerable—she became the second lady of the Empire—so were the obligations. She was never to leave the imperial offspring; she was to sleep in his bedroom; she was to superintend all his meals. Paid an annual stipend of 40,000 francs, she would have at her disposal two deputy governesses—the Comtesse de Boubers-Bernatre and pretty Mme. de Mesgrigny; three children's nurses—Mmes. Soufflot, Darnaud and Froment; three cradle-rockers—Mmes. Marchand, Legrand and Petit; two mistresses of the wardrobe and two maids. The "masculine" household consisted of a gorgeously dressed general staff: a first equerry —the Baron de Canisy; two ordinary equerries; a secretary with a sword at his side, a gold-laced coat of blue and a three-cornered hat with a black feather; a secretary to the governess; two ushers in green cloth coats and scarlet jackets; two grooms of the chambers in green, red and gold, with red waistcoats; four valets; a house steward and a carver dressed in green, white and silver.

The most important matter to be decided was the appointment of the physician in ordinary and the surgeon in ordinary who "were to visit the Children of France every day, give an account of their visit to the governess, never leave the place where they were residing, and follow them on all their journeys."

After a brief struggle over matters of precedence between Corvisart and Mme. de Montesquiou, Dr. Bourdois de la Motte and the child specialist Dr. Auvity *père* were appointed. There remained the question of the physician-vaccinator. On February 28 Corvisart put forward the name of Dr. Husson, a doctor at the Hôtel-Dieu and the vaccine hospital and "the author of several dissertations," but Mme. de Montesquiou objected in the following terms:

"I have no observations to make on the choice of M. Husson, a person of whom I have never heard, but I wonder if it is necessary to have a special doctor for such a simple operation, which seems to me to lie within the competence of the physician and the surgeon who have already been appointed."

For all that, Corvisart had the last word.

Marie Louise was still blissfully happy. *Liebe Mamma*, who had never succeeded in becoming a mother, wrote to her on November 1: "I can imagine your happiness on feeling the child stir within you." And at the end of the same month she said again: "I can guess at the sweet exultation one must experience on becoming conscious of a living creature inside one's body." But when Marie Louise expressed her intention of feeding the little king herself and asked Maria Ludovica for advice, the latter described the idea as "majestic folly" and added:

> I would recommend it to any mother who was in good health and who was able to devote herself entirely to this sacred duty. But for you who are in a position to find a wet-nurse in perfect health and irreproachable character from whom one can count on extremely healthy milk; for you who by your rank and station are obliged to carry out innumerable duties; for you who rightly wish to accompany your beloved husband whenever possible on his travels or when he goes hunting, I should imagine that a good wet-nurse would be preferable. Naturally, everyone's opinion is subject to the supreme judgment of the Emperor himself, with whose wishes you should comply in every particular; and even if he should allow you to decide on this point, you should subtly discover his unspoken preference and abide by it.

Napoleon decided on the "good wet-nurse" recommended by his mother-in-law.

Three wet-nurses had in any case already been shut up in the "detention establishment" at 14 rue de Rivoli, under the supervision of a deputy governess. It was a Parisian woman from Chaillot, plump Marie Victorine Auchard, the twenty-four-year-old wife of a publican, who was finally chosen.

Already—toward the end of 1810—Mme. de Montesquiou had begun worrying about the cradles. At least two were required. The first, ordered from the shop *À l'Enfant de France,* can still be seen at Bois-Préau. Made of elm root, it had two uprights crowned with Victory heads, "mat-gilded, copied from the antique"; the nacelle was decorated with laurel leaves and lined with green fabrics; it cost 3,000 francs. The second, made of yew, with its legs in the shape of an X, cost twice as much and looked like a little monument; there were bas-reliefs representing the Tiber and the Seine, and the canopy was surmounted by plumes and a bronze eagle "to adjust the curtain." And on March 3 the City of Paris for its part presented the Emperor with the third and most famous of the cradles, designed by Prud'hon, made by Thomire and Odiot, and decorated by Roguet: the cradle which would be sent one day to Vienna. No one who has seen it, even in reproduction, could ever forget this monstrous lump of silver-gilt, overloaded with bees, palm leaves, ivy leaves and laurel leaves, and representing the inevitable Tiber and the no less inevitable Seine receiving the King of Rome from Mercury's hands. The whole thing rested on four cornucopias with genies leaning against them, one holding Hercules' club and the other a pair of scales. An eaglet perched with half-open wings on the poop of this little ship gazed anxiously at the heavy winged Glory which was wobbling unsteadily on top of the World, at the same time trying to hang on a laurel wreath in imminent danger of falling and far too big for a child's head. The price: 152,289 francs for the silversmiths and 6,000 for Prud'hon.

Mme. de Montesquiou also ordered some nursery tables—on which the child's diapers would be changed—and countless utensils: bowls, basins, warming pans, mugs, chamberpots, syringes and bedside lamps. All these things came from the establishment of one Biennais, at the sign of the Purple Monkey, and were made of silver-gilt, which Mme. de Montesquiou thought was going a little too far.

At noon on February 14, 1811, a cohort of solemn individuals led by a grim-faced auditor to the Conseil d'État—the "Inspector of Accounts relating to Crown buildings and furniture"—called on Mlle. Minette, linen draper, of 30 rue de Miromesnil, who submitted to their expert examination forty-two dozen diapers priced at 7,812 francs, twenty dozen vests, twenty-six dozen nightgowns costing 9,000 francs, fifty dozen pilches, twelve dozen fichus and handkerchiefs, and twelve dozen nightcaps, all trimmed with Valenciennes, Brussels and Mechlin lace. Every one of these items was marked with a star, the King of Rome's emblem, and some were also stamped with a bee and a royal crown. The commission felt and fingered, the auditor to the Conseil d'État delivered himself of an opinion, the others voiced their approval, and a report was drawn up to the effect that "the prices quoted by Mademoiselle Minette appear to be reasonable."

The same operation took place before approval was given to the child's fourteen long dresses in blue or pink satin, marceline and percale, trimmed with Valenciennes lace and embroidered with stars or Greek designs. The entire collection cost 40,402 francs, which was not exorbitant, considering that the layette for Louis XVI's elder son came to the equivalent of 284,795 francs and that intended for the future Louis XVII to 246,786 francs.

Over a month before the Empress's confinement, the layette had been installed in the "Child of France's" ground-floor apartments, which had once been occupied by the Duc de Frioul and whose windows looked out on to the Carrousel. The bedroom was green and gloomy, with green walls, gray-green curtains with gold fringes, and chairs, armchairs and stools covered in green and trimmed with gold braid. The rest of the furniture—highboys and a chest of drawers in elm, and a table and washstand in oak—was overlaid with marble and gilded bronze. Green too, "with gold trimmings," was the bed on which the cradle was to rest. A plume of white feathers was the only cheerful note in this civil-service décor.

On the mantelpiece stood a clock which represented the Muse of History leaning against an old merestone. The plinth, of course, was green—"May-green," to be more precise. This clock, fitted with a striking mechanism and a calendar into the bargain, would count out the first hours of the little King's life.

In the drawing room there was another clock, this time "in architectural bronze," decorated with "genies of the sciences reclining on clouds." This second room, with its walls hung with blue damask, was somewhat less gloomy—even though the settee, the two easy chairs and the eight armchairs were covered with Beauvais tapestry—but the child was to spend very little time in it. As for the other rooms, they consisted of a dining room, a study and a closet.

The Emperor did not intend this to be anything more than a temporary home for his son. On Monday, January 28, 1811—the 23rd, according to Bausset—he stopped unexpectedly in front of a house built on the Chaillot heights, facing the Champ de Mars and directly in line with the Pont d'Iéna, which was then in process of being constructed. Alfred Nettement, the owner's son, wrote later:

He was returning from the hunt with his suite. Since no warning had been given of his visit, no notice was taken for a long time of the bell ringing at the garden gate, which, giving as it did on the outer boulevard, was a long way from the house. When it was realized that the Emperor was outside, the servant instructed to open the gate panicked and took the wrong key, thus keeping Napoleon waiting even longer and adding to the impatience of his suite. Finally my father arrived with the key just as they were sending for a mason to knock down part of the wall, to enable the Emperor to enter our property like a real conqueror, through the breach. . . . As there were three steps leading from the outer boulevard into the garden, the whole suite dismounted; only the Emperor rode down the steps. In spite of the impatience which the enforced delay outside our gate had caused him, he spoke graciously to my mother, who had gone forward to welcome him. Perhaps she owed this kindly reception in part to the answer she was able to give to the question the Emperor put to every woman he met:

"How many boys have you got?"

My mother had three. All three of us were brought along, and were put practically under the horse's head. The youngest of us was four years old, the eldest ten. After all these years, I can still feel the gaze the Emperor directed at us, that piercing gaze which seemed to go right through you like a sword.

"When they are old enough," the Emperor said to my father, "you must send them to a military academy."

Napoleon admired the magnificent view from the house and, returning on February 2, decided that this should be the site for the King of Rome's palace, a colossal monument with a frontage a quarter of a mile long and a park which was to take in the Bois de Boulogne and stretch as far as the Arc de Triomphe. On February 15 the architect Fontaine called in his turn on the Nettements and told them: "This certainly is a handsome property, and the view is priceless—so we shan't put a price on it."

The compensation he offered them was so absurdly low that the Nettements refused to go. Their house was demolished for all that, and work was begun on the foundations of the Babylonian palace.

In the meantime, Marie Louise was getting ready for the great event. Her confinement trousseau had been delivered, and also an extraordinary bed which had cost 120,000 francs and which was entirely covered with bee-sprinkled Alençon lace—a bed so extraordinary in fact that Marie Louise preferred to be confined in her marriage bed, which she had brought from Saint-Cloud. She was now terrified of the cold, and so had the bed surrounded with screens in green *cannetille*.

Napoleon, who went to see his wife several times a day, gave his approval to these changes. Marie Louise spent her time drawing, writing to her Austrian relations, reading, and turning her ear inside out

—a trick which was apparently a specialty of hers. Napoleon had provided her with so many ladies-in-waiting and laid down such a strict code of etiquette that for the former archduchess life at the Tuileries was rather like life in a harem. She was almost always in a dressing gown, and this worried Maria Ludovica, who wrote to her: "It upsets me to think that you spend your mornings in muslin dressing-gowns; I hope they are elegant and I hope too for your sake that your husband does not mind this waiting period. . . ."

Napoleon did not mind at all, for he had resumed his relations with Mme. Walewska. Luckily for her, Marie Louise knew nothing of this. She was blissfully happy, as she told her father yet again. He replied:

> I note with great satisfaction that you are in good health, that you are happy and content, and that you recognize that I was right, two years ago, not to give in to your requests. I am happy to think that I did my duty at that time, and even happier to see that God has now rewarded me for it. In making you happy, your husband makes your father happy too, and for this I beg you to thank him most sincerely. Let us thank God for your good health; I look forward to a safe delivery, and whether the child is a boy or a girl I shall be content. But take good care of your health, especially during delivery, and in the course of your pregnancy take regular but not excessive exercise; above all, avoid falls or journeys over very bumpy roads. . . .

Marie Louise followed this advice, and went for only a single outing in a carriage, across the Monceau plain, before March 4. During the last fortnight of her pregnancy, "enormous and anything but imposing," according to one witness, "with a placid, expressionless face," and leaning on Mme. de Montebello's arm, she went for walks along the riverside terrace overlooking the swollen waters of the Seine. To reach the terrace, she had to make her way through crowds of people, who came so close that one day a woman shouted to her:

"Don't you worry, mother—it'll be all right. I should know—I've got eight kids of my own!"

"Coral red," the Empress turned round and waved to the woman, but the Emperor hurriedly arranged for a covered way to be built so that his wife could get to the terrace without being seen.

It was Antoine Dubois who had been appointed to deliver the Empress, but Marie Louise scarcely knew him and swore only by Corvisart, whom she was forever plying with questions, "insisting that he should specify the sex of the child she was carrying, and repeating over and over again that so eminent a doctor could not possibly be in ignorance of such an important detail." Dr. Ganière, to whom we owe this information, adds that Napoleon was just as anxious as his wife: "He was so agitated and disturbed that the First Physician was never allowed to leave the Palace without first going to give him an account of his latest findings. The Emperor, obsessed by the description of disastrous cases of which he had heard, submitted him to lengthy interrogations and made him describe the mysteries of Nature time and again. Corvisart provided the required explanations and commentaries patiently enough, but he could not restrain himself from telling his friends that the Empress was 'a weakling' and that he was surprised at 'the great warrior's fears over such a trifling matter.' "

The "trifling matter" began in the evening of March 19.

That evening there was to be a small entertainment at the Tuileries in honor of the Grand Duke of Würzburg, the Emperor Francis's brother and the former and future Ferdinand III of Tuscany, who had arrived in Paris two days before to be present at his niece's delivery. For the past twenty months—ever since the Battle of Znaïm, five days after Wagram—there had been no fighting in Europe. The Imperial Court spent its time merrymaking and had stopped looking like an elegant bivouac. Evening dress was stipulated more often than uniform, and gold lace took precedence over gold braid.

The guests were gossiping in the drawing rooms and wondering how soon the great event would be. It was true that the Empress was complaining of feeling out of sorts, but then that was nothing new. Her backache had not prevented her from receiving her uncle and the Austrian ambassador a little while before, not to mention Josephine's son Eugène de Beauharnais.

It was seven o'clock and preparations were being made for the evening's entertainment. Soon Marie Louise would make her appearance, taking little steps and leaning on her husband's arm. . . . But then, all of a sudden, the door leading to the Empress's apartments opened, and the Court saw Mme. de Montebello, "not yet dressed," going to see the Emperor.

It was going to be that night!

The prescribed ceremonial was well known to everyone: "When the Empress feels certain pains indicating that her delivery will not be long delayed, the lady-in-waiting will go to see His Majesty. On her arrival, she will take orders from H.M. the Emperor and advise the princes and princesses of the Family, the princes and grand dignitaries, the grand officers of the Crown, the ministers, the grand officers of the Empire, and the ladies and officers of the Household. All these persons will go to Her Majesty's apartments dressed as for Mass on Sunday. The ladies will be in court dress. . . ." The ladies were already, but the men who were in evening dress rushed home to change into whatever uniform or costume was laid down by etiquette.

In her bedroom, Marie Louise, who had just been afflicted with "unbearable pains in the back," was walking up and down, leaning on the Emperor's arm. Looking on were Mmes. de Montebello, de Luçay and de Montesquiou; two first ladies—Mmes. Durand and Ballant; two chambermaids; the accoucheur Dubois and the surgeon Auvity. Now and then the Emperor left the room and went into the Salon des Grâces to join Madame Mère, the Grand Duke, Viceroy Eugène, Prince Borghese, Julie, Pauline and Hortense, as well as the two doctors Bourdier and Yvan who were holding themselves in readiness to rush to Marie Louise's bedside.

Everyone waited.

In the Salon du Billard there were the two grand dignitaries—Berthier and Cambacérès—who were to make out the birth certificate. In the Empress's drawing room there were the ministers and grand officers. From time to time a cry could be heard uttered by the Empress.

At ten o'clock Corvisart made his appearance. According to him there was no hurry, and he calmly went off to bed. The pains continued to be quite severe until two in the morning, and then eased off. The Emperor was far more agitated than he had ever been on the eve of a battle, while Dubois sat quietly behind a little table on which he had arranged his instruments in meticulous order—a sight which poor Marie Louise found anything but reassuring.

Napoleon asked Dubois: "Well, Monsieur?"

"Sire, we are waiting."

"Have the pains been severe?"

"Sire, we are at present in a period of calm."

Dubois was seriously displeased. He was usually helped by one Mme. Lachapelle, but the presence of a midwife at the Empress's bedside would have been contrary to etiquette. The accoucheur had insisted, but Bausset, the Palace Prefect, had remained inflexible . . . and explicit:

"We'll give her a five-hundred-franc gratuity, but right now she can go to hell!"

In the drawing rooms, the Court went on waiting. "It was an amusing sight in every respect," wrote the Queen of Holland, "with women flirting, men dozing, ministers twiddling their thumbs, the Emperor looking anxious, and all this going on around tables on which wine and chocolate were being served." Comte Krasínski, of the Light Horseguards, was heard betting a thousand ducats to a hundred that the child would be a boy. But weariness gradually took hold of the Court, and here and there people dropped off to sleep, much to the indignation of the watching ushers.

At five in the morning Marie Louise herself fell asleep. At six, Corvisart, the only person who had had any rest, made out a report for the gazettes: "Her Majesty the Empress felt the first pains of labor at about eight o'clock yesterday evening. The pains became less frequent during the night and today have practically ceased. H.M. is in the best of health."

From the middle of the night, the great bell of Notre-Dame and the bells of countless parish churches had been inviting the people of Paris to pray for a safe delivery. At the palace, the Emperor got into his bath—a bath of boiling water, as usual. He had been in it a quarter of an hour when a white-faced Dubois came into the room. He seemed to have lost the power of speech.

"Well?" said the Emperor. "Is she dead?"

And, as he told Gourgaud at St. Helena—explaining that he was so used to great events that the news of them never affected him at the time, but only later—he added:

"If she's dead, we'll bury her!"

Dubois finally managed to open his mouth.

"No, Sire, but the waters have broken too soon—something that happens only once in a thousand times, if then."

"Well? What are you going to do about it?"

"I shall have to use the forceps."

"Good God. Is there any risk involved?"

"I shall have to treat one of the two, the mother or the child, more carefully than the other."

"Then look after the mother. With the mother I can have another child."

Napoleon had already got out of the bath, scarcely giving Constant the opportunity to dry him.

"Nature is no respecter of persons. Act as if you were attending an ordinary housewife of the rue Saint-Denis—as if it were a cobbler's son you were bringing into the world."

What had happened? "Labor had become so much quicker and so violent as to produce a premature rupture of the membranes. To make matters worse, the child was awkwardly placed—hip first, it seems—and the contractions of the uterus, in spite of their increased frequency, proved entirely ineffectual."

When Marie Louise saw Dubois and the Emperor coming back together she started screaming louder than ever. It was worse still when they told her that she would have to change to another bed so that the forceps could be used.

"I'm being sacrificed for my son!" she cried.

"She screamed dreadfully," said the Emperor later. "I am not a tenderhearted man, but it upset me to see her suffering so much."

Mme. de Montesquiou kept telling her that the same thing had happened twice to her and that everything had been all right in the end—but all in vain. As for Dubois, he was utterly panic-stricken and refused to operate unless Corvisart was present. At this Napoleon lost his temper.

"But what can he tell you that you don't know already? If it's a witness you want, you've got me here. So let's have no more shilly-shallying, Dubois. I order you to deliver the Empress."

Finally, however, Corvisart, who had possibly gone to bed again, reappeared and held the Empress, together with his colleagues Bourdier and Yvan, while Dubois, assisted by Auvity, operated. "The Duchesse de Montebello," said the Emperor later, "stood there like a fool all the time." He himself waited, his heart pounding wildly, in the adjoining dressing room.

At last, at twenty past eight, after twenty-six minutes of labor, the child was born feet first, "skilful manipulation of the forceps disengaging the head."

Napoleon came into the room, cast only a cursory glance at the newborn child lying on the carpet—according to an eye-witness, he thought it was dead—and gave all his attention to the Empress, whom he clasped in his arms. No one thought of attending to the principal character in this historic scene, who did indeed appear to be dead. Mme. de Montebello brought up the question of etiquette: the Prince had to be presented by his governess to Chancellor Cambacérès, who had just come in, "so that he might verify His Majesty's sex." "Corvisart," recounted the Emperor in after years, "sent her packing."

But finally the First Physician picked the baby up, dipped it in a bath of warm water, slapped it gently all over, blew a few drops of brandy into its mouth, and wrapped it in hot towels. And after seven long minutes, the newborn child uttered its first cry.

The Emperor turned round, took the baby and gave it to Marie Louise.

"My son!"

But she was not allowed to keep him for long. Mme. de Montesquiou was at last able to show the child to Chancellor Cambacérès, Duke of Parma, who had the birth certificate made out in the Empress's drawing room by the Secretary of State to the Family, Regnault de Saint-Jean-d'Angély.

"It is my intention," declared the Emperor, "that my son shall bear the names Napoleon, Francis, Joseph and Charles."

Francis in honor of his grandfather and godfather the Emperor of Austria—represented by the Grand Duke of Würzburg; *Joseph* in honor of his second godfather, the King of Spain; *Charles* in honor of his paternal grandfather, Charles Bonaparte.

Napoleon signed first, followed by Madame Mère, the Grand Duke, Prince Eugène, the Emperor's sisters, Hortense, Berthier, and last of all Talleyrand, who signed his name as Charles Maurice, like a sovereign.

The usher threw open the double doors, and the whole Court saw the child in Mme. de Montesquiou's arms, with the two deputy governesses, the Colonel of the Guard, the duty equerry and a plumed and gilded suite behind them.

The usher then took one step forward and shouted:

"The King of Rome!"

Napoleon, beside himself with joy, had gone back to his apartments, after giving the famous order:

"My pages and the hundred and one guns!"

And to his valet he said:

"Well, Constant, we've got a strapping boy! Kept us waiting too, the young devil!"

He went to the window. The pages were already bearing the news to the four corners of the capital. The cannon began to thunder. It had been arranged that twenty-one guns would be fired to tell the Parisians of the birth of a princess, a hundred and one for the birth of the King of Rome. All over Paris people stood at their windows or on their doorsteps. There was an extraordinary silence.

The city held its breath and counted. . . .

"I was in bed with Angeline," wrote Stendhal in his journal for March 20, 1811. "The cannon woke us up at ten o'clock. It was the third gun; we greeted the twenty-second with transports of delight. At our nineteenth, which was the twenty-second for everybody else, we heard people cheering in the street. . . ." The twenty-second gun set off a veritable explosion of gladness, "a long-drawn shout of joy," as even Mme. de Boigne, an enemy of the régime, had to admit. "To us," wrote that most popular of the Ultras, the Baron de Frénilly, "the twenty-second gun sounded like the crack of doom, for it seemed to spell death to the House of the Bourbons."

The enthusiasm of the people of Paris was amazing, delirious, indescribable. Hats were thrown up in the air. Complete strangers shouted to each other, spoke to each other, embraced each other. "My friends and I hurried over to the Tuileries," wrote a medical student called Poumiès de la Siboutie. "The streets were already crowded; the workers were leaving their work, the shopkeepers closing their shops; there was an atmosphere of frantic joy, of intoxication. When we arrived, the quays, the Carrousel and the garden were packed with people singing, dancing and giving deafening cheers."

Hidden behind a curtain, Napoleon listened and watched from one of his windows, while tears of joy ran down his cheeks.

3

The King of Rome

AT HALF-PAST TEN in the morning a huge *caroline* rose majestically from the Cour du Carrousel, to the cheers of the crowd. It was Mme. Blanchard, the famous aeronaut, carrying the news by air to a waiting world . . . though in the event the balloon's journey came to an end at Saint-Thiébault, near Lagny, in the department of Seine-et-Marne.

Luckily the semaphores had begun jerking their arms up and down—at the modest cost, for the whole Empire, of 4,048 francs 11 centimes—and on the very same day, March 20, Brussels, Antwerp, Lyons and Strasbourg learned of the birth of their future master. At the end of each semaphore line, couriers set off at a gallop to take the news still farther. Nice only heard it on the 24th at seven in the evening, Florence on the 23rd, The Hague in the evening of the 22nd and Amsterdam on the 21st. At Parma, the chief town of the department of the Taro, a courier from Turin arrived in the afternoon of the 22nd; the bells started ringing immediately, and in the evening the city was illuminated and took on its gayest holiday appearance. Dernieri, the porter at the palace of Parma and Colorno—where Marie Louise would live one day—carried away by the general enthusiasm, decorated the windows "spontaneously and without orders" with seventy-two white wax candles weighing over two hundredweights and costing 1,110 francs 95 centimes—a sum which the reckless porter would have some difficulty in recovering. On the 23rd work stopped, and bread and wine were distributed to the people; on the 24th the bells of Parma rang out again, a hundred and one guns shook the air, and in the evening there were more illuminations and shouts of "Long live the Emperor! Long live the Empress! Long live the King of Rome!"; on the 25th a *Te Deum* was sung and a subscription fund was opened for the poor.

I have lingered a little at Parma, whose princely title the newborn child would one day bear, but in every town and city in the immense Empire there were similar displays of joy and enthusiasm. In Rome it was the guns of the Castel Sant'Angelo and the bells in all the steeples and campaniles that announced the event to the Pope's former subjects; and for the birth of its "King" a thousand bonfires blazed in the Eternal City.

Across 132 departments people shouted: "Long live the King of Rome!" in Italian, German or Dutch. From the Baltic to the Adriatic there was an endless succession of illuminations, torchlight retreats and *Te Deums*. The peasants left their fields, the artisans their workshops.

Never in the course of history had the birth of a child been celebrated on such a scale.

This is to say nothing of the celebrations in the vassal states. The Westphalian, Bavarian, Rhenish, Swiss, Polish, Illyrian, Neapolitan and even Spanish cities—though these last with less enthusiasm—decorated and illuminated their streets to the sound of bell and cannon.

At Florence the townspeople gathered around great bonfires to celebrate, while the Prefect of Perugia "chose this moment of general joy" to invite six prelates at Foligno who had not yet taken an oath of loyalty to the Emperor to remedy the omission—and they agreed "with deep emotion."

At Vienna the news of the birth of the Emperor Francis's grandson was known as early as the evening of March 23, thanks to Major Robebeau, who had ridden several horses to death to bring it from Strasbourg, in three days. The Austrians, it seems, were delighted. "You should have seen the joy and gladness of the people of Vienna," wrote the Archduke Francis Charles to Marie Louise. And Countess Lazansky, for her part, wrote to her former charge on March 26: "I can imagine the jubilation the event will have caused in Paris from the general delight which was felt here; the news spread rapidly throughout the city, and I can say with assurance that everyone, great or small, was overjoyed."

It is said, however, that a lady at Court murmured behind her fan: "Bah! In a few years we shall probably be educating the little King of Rome here out of charity!"

Liebe Mamma likewise rushed to her writing table: "I can feel your happiness at being a mother, at hearing your son's first cries. . . . You are now more of an expert than I, dear Louise, and you could act as my teacher, for alas I know nothing about childbirth. Do not imagine that I am envious. . . . Papa having several children, I can submit to the sacrifice with a certain courage, though sometimes with a sigh of regret."

The courier set off again for Paris on the 26th, taking with him this letter too from the Emperor Francis:

> I am entrusting these few lines to today's courier to congratulate you from the bottom of my heart on your happy delivery. Any child would have given me joy; the birth of a son can only add to that joy, on account of your happiness and satisfaction, and your husband's. My dearest wishes have been fulfilled, and at the moment I am waiting impatiently for further news of yourself and your child. I enjoin the greatest prudence on you, above all in the first ten days but also for six weeks, since your health in the future—as you well understand, so you tell me—depends on this. I therefore rely on you. I am well, your brothers and sisters too. I envy my brother for being close to you, and for having been with you on such a momentous occasion.

Unfortunately the Emperor's brother had not been present at the actual delivery; he had remained in the Salon des Grâces . . . and ugly rumors had already begun circulating. Yet when the birth had taken place there had been present in the bedroom, not only the four doctors, but also Mmes. de Montesquiou, de Montebello and de Luçay, the six first ladies in their uniform amaranth dresses—hence their nickname of "the red ladies"; the five first chambermaids—known as "the black ladies"; a nurse—Mme. Blaise; and two maids. That would appear to be a sufficient number of people to exclude any possibility of deception. However, Napoleon would have cause to regret not having invited the Grand Duke of Würzburg into the room.

The slander alleging a fake delivery eventually reached Hartwell, and the ears of the man who, ever since the official announcement of

Louis XVII's death, had styled himself Louis XVIII. He merely shrugged his shoulders.

"So now the *Napoleone* family have a baby!" he remarked. "Whether it sprang from the unfortunate Archduchess's womb or was brought into her bedroom through the door doesn't matter a jot to me. A good many people regard the event as of great importance. I am not of that opinion, and this is my argument: if God has damned the world, then Bonaparte will not lack a successor, but if, on the contrary, the divine wrath abates, all the brats on earth cannot save the temple of iniquity from destruction."

Pending the day when the King of France of Navarre would sit heavily—though also wittily—on Napoleon II's throne, the former Comte de Provence, in this spring of 1811, was the only person to hold this opinion. Everyone else thought like Napoleon as he stood daydreaming beside his son's cradle—this son of whom he was so proud:

"I envy him, for glory awaits him, whereas I had to run after it! I shall have been Philip; he will be Alexander. To take hold of the world, he will only have to stretch out his hands."

Everything seemed to indicate that the Emperor was right and Louis XVIII wrong. The great imperial machine, started up by the Comte de Ségur as soon as the child was born, began working in the evening of the same day, March 20, on the occasion of the private baptism celebrated in the chapel, pending the ceremony at Notre-Dame.

At nine o'clock in the evening the grand master of ceremonies went to fetch the Emperor and the King of Rome. The procession formed up, the orchestra at the head of the great staircase started playing, and the ushers led the way, followed by the heralds at arms, pages carrying torches and ceremonial stewards. Then, in slow procession, there came the household officers, the master of ceremonies, the King of Rome's officers, the Emperor's equerries, the chamberlains, His Majesty's aides-de-camp, the palace governor, the grand officers, the baptismal witnesses, the grand dignitaries and the princes of the family. Finally little Napoleon appeared, carried by Mme. de Montesquiou. He preceded his father, followed by the Colonel of the Guard. The princesses and their ladies brought up the rear.

At the door the chaplain offered holy water to Napoleon, who went and sat down in an armchair. This was laid down by protocol in this somewhat obscure text: "The Emperor, on his knees, will pray, then H.M. will present the child for baptism. The governesses will uncover the head of H.M. the King of Rome. His governess will present the King of Rome's head to His Eminence, who will pour baptismal water onto it in accordance with the prescribed rite."

Everything happened as planned, and to the sound of the *Te Deum* the little King was accompanied back to his apartments by "His Majesty's service": one of the Emperor's aides-de-camp, four chamberlains, two equerries, a master of ceremonies and four pages carrying their torches.

Even now the unfortunate baby was not allowed to have his evening feeding in peace, for the grand chancellors of the Legion of Honor and the Crown came and laid the grand cordon of their orders before him. And then, by way of a lullaby, three batteries repeated the performance they had given that very morning and fired off a hundred guns.

The theaters were determined to make their contribution to the celebrations. On March 20 the Variétés put on *The Good News, or The First Arrival*. At the Vaudeville there was a show called *The Hundred Guns,* and *The Semaphore News* was billed for the next day at the same theater. The Ambigu was rehearsing *Hope Fulfilled,* and the Opéra Comique promised *The Cradle* for the 23rd.

Paris was illuminated, cold meat was given away at open-air buffets, and the fountains were once again running with wine. As they drank—and as they fought to fill their mugs—the people sang:

> *Et bon, bon, bon*
> *C'est un garçon*
> *Vive Napoléon!*

A few dandies passed proudly by, dressed in an excremental brown known as *caca roi de Rome,* the new color every self-respecting male had been wearing since the morning. And that evening all the non-commissioned officers of the 1st Regiment of the Guard—the veterans of Austerlitz and Wagram—cut off their mustaches as soon as they got back to barracks, to make a pillow for the King of Rome.

The next day the Senate delivered a harangue to the Emperor seated on his throne:

"Grant, Sire, that we may not distinguish between our tender respect for the son of Napoleon the Great and the sacred obligations which bind us to the heir to the monarchy. . . ."

Napoleon "granted," and the senators, who three years later would cheerfully vote for their master's deposition, left him with the assurance of their "unshakable loyalty." They then went to do obeisance to the King of Rome, the President of the Legislative Assembly—M. de Montesquiou—taking the opportunity to harangue the Governess to H.M. the King of Rome, alias Mme. de Montesquiou: "We appreciate, Madame, the choice which had been made of your person to watch over his first years. . . ."

Mme. de Montesquiou replied in fitting terms to her husband, while the little King, who "had just been sucking eagerly at his nurse's breast," slept in his silver-gilt cradle, flanked by his deputy governesses, two chamberlains, four equerries and a guard. The Council of State followed on the heels of the Senate. More speeches. All the other official bodies—the Supreme Court of Appeal, the Audit Office, the Imperial Court, the Municipal Corps, the Institute, the Metropolitan Chapter—after seeing the Emperor, did homage, fortunately in silence, before the little King. The representatives of the University, who likewise kept quiet while doing obeisance, were highly vexed at being cheated of their harangue. They had expressed their pain and disappointment to His Majesty. Was it not the University which "would educate the King of Rome's subjects"? Had not the Rector harangued Louis XVI's son in his cradle, with the words: "Monseigneur, you have long been the object of our longings, you are now the object of our hopes. . . ."

It so happened that the venerable professor was still alive. His speech too could be used again: it would be sufficient to substitute *Sire* for *Monseigneur*. . . . But Napoleon had remained inflexible.

In the meantime, the greatest names in France were being entered into the registers kept at the door of the first drawing room of the Grand Apartment. A chamberlain was stationed there to give visitors the latest news of the little King, solemnly informing them on the 22nd for instance that "His Majesty had suffered a passing attack of griping pains such as was inevitable at his time of life. . . ." And the secretary of the Chamber wrote down the visitors' names . . . the same names that would be found on similar registers nine years later, on the occasion of the birth of the Duc de Bordeaux, the Bourbon heir to the throne.

Josephine did not call at the Palace, but sent her ex-husband a charming note in which this sentence stands out: "My sacrifice has not been in vain." Napoleon replied:

"My dear, I have received your letter, and thank you for it. My son is big and healthy. I hope he will come to some good. He has my chest, my mouth and my eyes. I hope he will fulfill his destiny."

Dubois was given a hundred thousand francs "as a mark of satisfaction." A few months later he would be made a baron, with a coat of arms depicting "a she-wolf proper suckling a child," a heraldic allusion to the birth of the King of Rome. Corvisart for his part received twenty thousand francs, Bourdier twelve thousand, Yvan six, and Mme. de Montebello—for standing there "like a fool," to quote Napoleon— porcelain to the value of thirty thousand francs. In order to maintain the tradition of the French royal house on the occasion of a prince's birth, a considerable sum—a hundred thousand francs—was distributed to people owing money to wet-nurses for suckling-time. Thus 2,526 fathers and a few unmarried mothers received sums ranging from twenty-two to fifty-two francs. Another sum of a hundred thousand francs was made over to the pawn office, so that objects on which small loans had been advanced could be redeemed.

From April 13 to 18, in accordance with a scrupulously established protocol, Marie Louise, stretched out on her chaise-longue, received a succession of grand dignitaries, ministers, princes and princesses and their households, diplomats, cardinals and ladies of the Court. On the 19th the churching took place, very simply, in the dining room, which had been transformed into a chapel for the occasion. The first chaplain officiated, and only members of the Empress's household were present. The very next day the Court left for Saint-Cloud, where the little King soon came to join his parents. He was installed on the ground floor, in a room overlooking the garden. Mme. de Montesquiou had had one of the cradles taken to Saint-Cloud by four men carrying it in turn, two at a time. For future occasions, however, the governess would have a folding iron cradle made which would be far more convenient. The curtains, naturally enough, would again be in the inevitable green. . . .

In her joy at being a mother, Marie Louise had forgotten the pain she had suffered in the course of her delivery. Moreover, she had been told of the order the Emperor had given Dubois at dawn on March

20, to "save the mother," and had begun to think that it was not just "a womb" that he had married. She wrote to her father on April 13:

> You cannot imagine the full extent of my happiness. I had never dreamed that I could experience such great joy. And since the birth of my son, my love for my husband has increased, if that be possible. I shall never forget the tokens of affection which he has given me lately, and I am moved to tears when I think about them. They would bind me to him forever if his fine qualities had not done this already long ago. . . . I am sending you a portrait of my son. It is a good likeness and does not flatter him, and I feel sure you will notice the resemblance to the Emperor. He is very strong for five weeks and can hold his head up straight without a pillow. When he came into the world, he weighed nine pounds and was twenty inches long, and he has grown since then. He is very healthy and spends all day in the garden. . . .

The whole Austrian imperial family sent their congratulations to Marie Louise. She had been handed over to the Minotaur and had done precisely what was expected of her. Everyone regarded the little King as a pledge of peace given to Europe. Marie Louise herself wrote to her elder brother—the future Emperor Ferdinand: "We cannot thank God enough . . ." while her Uncle Joseph, Palatine of Hungary, congratulated her on this happy event "which will tighten the bonds linking two great empires and consolidate the happiness and tranquillity of Europe." The Queen of Saxony, on receiving the medallion struck in honor of the little King's birth, described the child as a *Trutscherl,* which in popular Viennese signifies a plump young turkey. Leopoldine—Marie Louise's favorite sister—found him not only plump but also "pretty and healthy-looking." And she added: "I can imagine how much he must have suffered when he was vaccinated." This vaccination was in fact a great event in the baby's life. A few cases of smallpox having been reported in Paris during the month of May, six doctors promptly met in conference in the wet-nurses' lodging, with Corvisart in the chair. Husson decided to "take some vaccine from a ten-month-old girl who had recently been immunized" and to inoculate three of the nurses' children with it. Every day, as the records show, the faculty came to see how scarification was progressing, and on the 10th they picked out the child who seemed to offer the best guarantee of safety. The next day the little patient was taken to Saint-Cloud, and there, while the Court held its breath, Husson respectfully made three incisions in both the King of Rome's arms, into which he introduced a drop of vaccine. Throughout the operation, the child who would soon be known as the Eaglet lay in the arms of his nurse, a pretty, fresh-faced girl in a ruched bonnet, and placidly went on feeding. Every morning the cohort of doctors bent gravely over the royal cradle to study their young patient's reactions. The expected pocks appeared earlier than usual, producing a certain restlessness on May 21, 22 and 23. By way of a check, it was decided that three children should be inoculated with a drop of the little King's vaccine, and the vaccines of these privileged babies used for the inoculation of thirty-nine other patients, in order to confirm the success of the imperial vaccination. "H.M.'s restlessness abated." On May 31 his scabs fell off as expected and he was given a purgative, a subtle mixture of peach blossoms and chicory syrup, lovingly prepared for him by the First Pharmacist. The same day the proud and happy doctors made out their report, to which they complacently attached the scabs from the royal pocks. It is not known whether these were sent to Alençon, which the Emperor and Empress reached that day on their way back from Cherbourg. The fact remains that Husson received the sum of six thousand francs for having treated his royal patient so successfully.

Napoleon and Marie Louise were reunited with their son on Tuesday, June 4, at Saint-Cloud, where the child spent part of the day in a tent "of striped Brussels twill" erected in the little park. Meanwhile preparations were being made for the 9th, when the greatest ceremony of the imperial reign was to take place: the baptism of the King of Rome, a ceremony which was possibly even more important than the Coronation, since the Emperor saw it as a "dynastic enthronement."

The godfathers were to be the Emperor of Austria, represented by his brother, the Grand Duke of Würzburg, and King Joseph. But the latter, as a king, refused to give precedence to the former Grand Duke of Tuscany, although it had been decided, on August 22, 1810—contrary to the etiquette of 1804—that "an emperor, a king or an elector shall have precedence over His Majesty's brothers." Würzburg, representing the Emperor of Austria on this occasion, was bound to be given precedence over the King of Spain. Joseph stood firm on this question of protocol, declined the honor which had been offered him, and decided to attend the baptism as a mere king.

Madame Mère was the first godmother, and she raised no difficulties, but the Queen of Naples, nominated as second godmother, declined like Joseph, lamenting over "the cruel and irreparable privation imposed on her by the state of my health." The Murats and the Emperor were not on the best of terms. There was talk of joining the Kingdom of Naples to France, and indeed, since the birth of the King of Rome, it seemed quite likely that all the feudatory kings would be replaced by super-prefects. In short, Caroline preferred to stay in Naples, where she would play the Regent, while Murat, who had not been invited to the baptism, went to Paris.

At five o'clock in the afternoon of June 8, on the eve of his baptism, the little King left Saint-Cloud with his suite. On his arrival at the Place de la Concorde, he was greeted by a salute of a hundred and one guns from a battery of six cannons on the terrace of the Tuileries Garden. The child would be waked up the next morning by a similar din, to which would be added the sound of the great bell of Notre-Dame and all the bells of the city. At five in the afternoon, more artillery salvos announced his departure from the Tuileries for Notre-Dame. "For the first time," said the *Journal Officiel*, "all were able to see the august child, whose royal name was about to be consecrated by religion. The effect produced by his appearance was indescribable: there was an uninterrupted shout of *Long live the King of Rome!* along his entire route."

In point of fact, the Parisians did not shout at all as the magnificent procession went by. They were accustomed to dining at five o'clock, and the time chosen for the ceremony upset their daily routine. What is more, it was rumored that there was going to be a shortage of flour, for the drought threatened to produce a disastrous harvest. Soon people would start wondering where they were going to find the thirteen hundred bags of flour the bakeries needed every morning, and the people of Paris, in accordance with a time-honored custom, had already stripped the grocers' shops of dried vegetables.

The start of this food crisis—which would reach its climax the following winter—was scarcely calculated to put the average Parisian in a mood for enthusiasm. And yet the glittering golden procession which made its way from the Place de la Concorde to Notre-Dame, between a double row of troops lining the boulevards and the Rue Saint-Denis, was a splendid sight. People blinked their eyes to avoid being dazzled.

First of all came a squadron of the Guard, the gendarmerie, the 2nd Dutch, the 1st Polish, the Mamelukes and the light cavalry. A symphony in blue and white, in red and gold; a riot of bearskins and multicolored plumes; a blaze of gold braid, stripes and bullions. After the Commandant of Paris and his staff, and after the heralds at arms— a swaggering, glittering cavalcade, studded and spangled with gold— there followed twenty-four six-horse carriages inside which one could distinguish more of the inevitable gold, but also feathers, silver embroidery and silk of every color: the masters of ceremonies, the grand officers, the grand eagles, the chaplains, the ladies of the palace and the princes and princesses in even gaudier trappings than usual, with their equerries on either side. Then at last there came the hero of the day, the little King, in the Empress's carriage, which had been specially refurbished for the occasion. Lying in Mme. de Montesquiou's lap, the child was wearing a dress of English point lace against which the grand cordon of the Legion of Honor stood out in vivid contrast. The two deputy governesses and the nurse sat opposite. Bunches of gold and white pages, like those that clung to the Coronation coach, hung on at the back and the front as best they could. On either side rode an equerry and a general.

There was a pause in the procession.

Then Napoleon and Marie Louise appeared in the Coronation coach. With them, a whole world went by. A meticulously ordered world of marshals, generals, equerries, grand officers, aides-de-camp and staff officers disposed around the coach. The Emperor was not dressed in the best of taste. He had put on his plumed velvet hat again, with a coat and cloak in red velvet, gold braid and white breeches. The Empress was wearing a white dress that sparkled with diamonds. There were diamonds everywhere it was possible to put diamonds. There were perhaps rather too many. . . .

Other carriages followed, flanked by valets and troopers, and the Guard brought up the rear. It was not until seven o'clock that the head of the procession reached Notre-Dame, where state officials, senators, archbishops, and diplomats, in all 7,220 guests, had been waiting for two hours.

To music from the orchestra conducted by Le Sueur above the altar, the procession moved up the brilliantly lit nave with solemn dignity. After the heralds at arms, the pages, the chamberlains and the grand officers came "the child's regalia." The taper, with its velvet sheath decorated with thirty-one bees and twenty-four roses, was held by Mme. Berthier, Princes of Neuchâtel and Wagram. The chrisom—

a magnificently embroidered veil—was carried by Princess Aldobrandini and the salt cellar by the Comtesse de Beauvau. The Duchess of Dalberg, the Comtesse Vilain XIII, and Mme. Soult, Duchess of Dalmatia, shared the godparents' regalia among them: the silver-gilt bowl, the towel and the ewer.

In front of the little King walked the Grand Duke of Würzburg, Madame Mère and Queen Hortense, representing the second god-mother, Queen Caroline. The child, carried by Mme. de Montesquiou, was attended by his deputy governesses. Behind them came the nurse and Marshal Kellermann, duc de Valmy, who had the signal honor of bearing the train of the child's cloak, five ells of ermine-lined cloth of silver which had cost 3,800 francs. The Marshal was to be given a snuffbox valued at 20,000 francs for his trouble. The whole group walked beneath a canopy surmounted by 180 ostrich plumes and four aigrettes hired from one Widow Dathy, "feather-dealer and florist."

The Emperor and Empress followed beneath two more plumed canopies, and between them Joseph, King of Spain; Jerome, King of Westphalia—both "dressed as French princes"; Eugène, Viceroy of Italy; Prince Borghese and the Grand Duke of Frankfurt. There was only one princess in the procession: lovely Pauline. Élisa was away and Julie pleaded illness.

After the *Veni Creator,* Cardinal Fesch came down to the altar rail, where the godfather, the godmother and Mme. de Montesquiou—still carrying the little King—were standing.

"What child dost thou present to the Church?" he asked.

"A son," replied the Emperor Francis's brother.

"What doth he ask?"

"Baptism."

"What name dost thou give to this child?"

"Napoleon."

Would the Grand Duke of Würzburg remember this response, one wonders, when his brother later changed the little King's name to Franz?

After the exorcism, the Cardinal pulled gently at the child's swad-dling clothes.

"Ingredere in templum Dei."

In front of the baptismal font, which had been placed beside the thrones where the sovereigns were now sitting, the following dialogue was exchanged:

"Napoleon, dost thou renounce Satan?"

Madame Mère and the Grand Duke replied together for the child: "I do renounce him."

"And all his works?"

"I do renounce them."

"And all his pomps?"

"I do renounce them."

The holy oil was placed on the little King's chest and shoulders.

"Napoleon, dost thou believe in God the Father Almighty, Creator of heaven and earth?"

"I do believe."

"Dost thou believe in Jesus Christ, His Son?"

"I do believe."

"And in the Holy Ghost?"

"I do believe."

The veil was put in position, the taper lit, the two little pieces of material in the shape of a cross placed on the infant Napoleon's head, and nothing remained but the reading of the Gospel according to St. John.

Mme. de Montesquiou then handed the child to Marie Louise, who held him up for all to see while the principal herald, one Duverdier, stepped forward and shouted three times:

"Long live the King of Rome!"

The acclamations of the congregation echoed through the cathedral and grew louder when Napoleon, after kissing his son three times, was suddenly overcome by emotion, and, drunk with joy and pride, his heart beating wildly, raised the little King high above him, as if to show the people the future sovereign of the Western Empire.

The *Vivat* rang out. Mme. de Montesquiou, after making a deep curtsy before the Emperor, withdrew with the King and his suite. By eleven o'clock they were back at Saint-Cloud, while Napoleon and Marie Louise were arriving at the Hôtel de Ville for the baptismal banquet. There the entire Court and all the guests sat, faint with hunger, and watched the eleven imperial and royal personages eat. Captain Coignet, then a sergeant in the Grenadiers, has left us a picturesque description of these grandiose meals which Napoleon had copied from the ancien régime:

The master of ceremonies called out: "The Emperor!" He appeared, followed by his wife and five crowned heads. I shouldered and presented arms; then I was given the command to order arms. I was standing in front of my squad, facing the Emperor; he sat down first and motioned to the others to take their places. When the crowned heads had sat down, the table was cleared and everything disappeared: the carvers were at work in an adjoining room. Behind each king or queen stood three footmen, one pace apart; the others served as links with the carvers and passed the plates, never doing more than turn round to take them; when the plate got as far as the sovereign, the first footman offered it to him, and if the sovereign shook his head the plate disappeared; another one immediately took its place. If the head did not move, the footman placed the plate before his master.

Since the food had been well cut up, each person took his roll, broke it and started eating, without using a knife. After every mouthful he used his napkin to wipe his mouth, so that soon, behind every chair, there was a pile of napkins which had been used only once.

Nobody said a word. Each person had a carafe of wine and a carafe of water in front of him, and nobody poured out for his neighbor. They ate and drank as they wished, and accepted or refused food with a nod or a shake of the head. Nobody was allowed to say anything except when the sovereign master spoke to his neighbor. This may be imposing, but it is not at all gay.

Meanwhile, since the beginning of the afternoon the Champs-Élysées had been turned into a vast fairground. There had been a lottery for food, with five hundred winning tickets out of a thousand; and later cold meat was given away—2,400 pies, 1,200 sausages, 900 tongues, 600 legs of mutton and 900 chickens—"for which," says an eye-witness, "people fought like savages." Similarly there was something like a pitched battle to get near the twenty-four fountains of wine. Four orchestras played continuously, while the traditional amusements—seesaws, whirligigs, greasy poles and ring games—drew big crowds. The fairground shows proved just as popular, from Mlle. Garnier at the Carré Marigny, who "executed graceful postures, performed acrobatics on horseback at the greatest possible speed, and concluded with the famous pistol shot," to Mme. Saqui by the Allée des Veuves—now Avenue Montaigne—with her remarkable troupe of tightrope performers consisting of her husband, her father, her sisters, her brothers, her brothers-in-law and her children. There was also Séraphin's shadow theater. Préjean's scientific experiments, the more amusing experiments of one Duhamel—carried out while his daughter "executed character dances"—Dupont's "picturesque and mechanical views" and Olivier's card tricks. The Parisians could also watch a display of Numidian trick riding and lance-and-saber dueling at a tournament composed of six "squadrons" of five horses, or go and admire the performing stag Tephis, which "after various exercises carried out to the sound of musket fire, climbed Vesuvius while it was in eruption."

A firework display in the Place de la Concorde brought the evening to a close: a display "divided into three acts, each consisting of emblematical and allegorical patterns arranged with the utmost ingenuity."

On June 16 there was a ball at the Tuileries, preceded by a great banquet in the Salon de la Paix attended by deputies from all parts of the Empire. "A few of us women of the Opposition were there," records Mme. de Boigne, "and we had to admit that it was a magnificent sight. It was the only such occasion on which I have ever seen all the men in evening dress. Uniform was forbidden, and our old soldiers looked extremely self-conscious. When the Emperor arrived, followed by his suite, he had to cross the room to reach the dais at the far end. He led the way, walking so quickly that everyone, the Empress included, almost had to run to keep up with him. Though it detracted from the dignity and grace of the occasion, this bustling advance at the double had a conquering air about it that became him well. It was the grand manner in a new style. He certainly seemed superior to all the magnificence around him. He was wearing just an ordinary uniform, alone among all those men in splendid evening dress, and this made him even more conspicuous and struck the imagination more forcibly than all the gold braid in the world could have done."

A week later, on Sunday, June 23, the last of the baptismal celebrations was held in the brilliantly illuminated park at Saint-Cloud. The trees had been festooned with 9,000 fairy lights and 2,400 colored lanterns. Eight orchestras of fifteen musicians each played continuously, and there were more lottery buffets weighed down with food for which four thousand winning tickets had been sold. Beside the Château, German peasants danced waltzes on "a delightful lawn," and crowned a bust of Marie Louise with flowers. Here and there in the groves of the Bas-Parc, audiences applauded Mme. Saqui's twelve tightrope performers, Auguste's ten tumblers, Dupont's fantoccini and "picturesque views," Séraphin's silhouettes and the magic lantern of the Théâtre des Transparents. But the two chief attractions of the evening were undoubtedly the Guard's firework display on the Seine, representing a naval battle with the King of Rome's palace "in a fiery apotheosis," and another balloon flight by Mme. Blanchard. "Surrounded by firework stars," writes an eye-witness, "she seemed to soar in a fiery chariot to immense heights." Not content with throwing "stars" into the air, she bombarded the crowds below with copies of an "aerial poem" entitled *The Messenger from Iris, or the Astronomico-historical Vision.*

The authorities had spent 8,530 francs on watering the road from Paris to Saint-Cloud—needlessly as it happened, for suddenly a storm of tropical intensity blew up. Napoleon and Marie Louise were listening to *The Village Fête,* an entertainment by Étienne, set to music by Nicolo, and performed by the combined companies of the Opéra and the Opéra-Comique. Sheltered by their canopy, the sovereigns were unaffected by the rain, but the courtiers were soon dripping wet. "The poor musicians," Constant tells us, "were soaked to the skin and could not get a sound out of their instruments, whose strings had been stretched or broken by the rain; it was time to call a halt."

There followed, in the midst of a torrential downpour, a fantastic rout, an indescribable scramble. Three hundred thousand people fought their way to the waiting carriages, whose drivers ignored their masters in favor of anybody who was willing to pay a few hundred francs to get back to Paris. Deluged with rain, "the crowds of pedestrians and carriages formed a compact mass which moved along at walking pace, to the accompaniment of cries of pain, oaths and imprecations."

Finally, on June 27, Prince Schwarzenberg, the Austrian ambassador, arrived in great state at Saint-Cloud to invest the little King, on behalf of his imperial grandfather, with the grand cordon of the Order of St. Stephen. On July 1 Marie Louise thanked her father in the following terms: "My son is very strong and happy for his age. I think he will soon have a tooth. Permit me, dear Papa, to kiss your hand in gratitude for the magnificent present you have given him."

The only present he would keep when everything had collapsed around him . . .

And now nothing remained but to pay the bill for this extraordinary baptism: a bill amounting to 1,896,652 francs.

4

*

"The Little Fellow"

aria Ludovica)

HIS FIRST PLAYTHING was a plume, the plume of a sergeant of
the Guard, Sergeant Coignet, which the child, still in his nurse's arms,
noticed one day on the terrace at Saint-Cloud. He stretched out his
little arms toward the red feathers gleaming in the sun.

"Come here, sergeant," said Marshal Duroc.

> I bent down [wrote Coignet in later years] and the child started
> pulling my feathers out. The Marshal said:
>
> "Let him do as he pleases."
>
> The child was delighted, but my plume was ruined. I looked a
> little sheepish. The Marshal said to me:
>
> "Give it to him. I will see to it that you get another."
>
> The lady-in-waiting and the nurse burst out laughing. The
> Marshal said to the lady:
>
> "Give the prince to this sergeant and let him carry him."
>
> I held out my arms to take the precious burden: everyone
> crowded around.
>
> "Well?" said the Marshal. "Is he heavy?"
>
> "Yes, sir."

59

"Go on, walk up and down with him; you are strong enough to carry him."

I went for a turn round the terrace. The child stroked my feathers and took no notice of me. His clothes hung a long way down and I was afraid of falling. But I was happy to be carrying such a child. I gave him back to the lady, who thanked me, and the Marshal said to me:

"Come and see me in an hour's time."

An hour later the future Captain Coignet was given a voucher for two plumes. One, said Marshal Duroc, was for Sundays.

"I can see you," Maria Ludovica had written on June 4, "holding the little fellow in your arms, and I envy you that joy. . . ."

In imagining her stepdaughter holding "the little fellow" in her arms, *liebe Mamma* was deceiving herself, for like all royal mothers of her time, Marie Louise loved her son at fixed hours. Mme. de Montesquiou brought him every day to her bedroom—one might almost say to the gynaeceum, since it was impossible for any representative of the male sex to approach Marie Louise. She would look at the child, but did not dare to touch him. Faced with that fragile little body, she felt cold, and far from motherly. Later on, when he kissed her, she would wipe her cheek in disgust. . . . It is true that she did the same with her husband, and this did not prevent her from loving him.

"Come now," the Emperor said to her one day. "Give the child a kiss."

"I don't know how anyone can kiss a child," she replied.

She would soon hand the baby over to his nurse and immerse herself in the day's newspapers or her voluminous correspondence. After all, she had so many uncles, aunts, cousins, brothers and sisters to whom she had to write on their name days, wedding anniversaries or other occasions. . . . "The child grew bored," Constant tells us, "and the governess took it away. At four o'clock it was the mother's turn to visit her son: Marie Louise would come down to the King's apartments, bringing some embroidery with her at which she worked absent-mindedly. Twenty minutes later someone would come and tell her that M. Isabey or M. Prud'hon had arrived for her drawing or painting lesson. And the Empress would then return to her own apartments."

On several occasions the Emperor, who was in the habit of paying secret visits to his first wife, had told Mme. de Montesquiou that Josephine would like to see the little King.

"But that would distress the Empress so much that I can't bring myself to give you the necessary instructions."

"Let me see to it, Sire. Just give your approval to what I intend to do."

"Very well, but be careful how you go about it."

The very next day [writes Mme. de Montesquiou in a recently discovered text] I sent M. de Canisy to Malmaison to tell the Empress Josephine that I knew of her desire to see the King of Rome, and that we should be going for a drive to Bagatelle the following Sunday, at half-past two. She replied to the effect that she was delighted and that she would be the first at the meeting place. To keep our plan a secret, I had arranged with M. de Canisy that as we got into the carriage I should say to him that I left the choice of a route entirely to him. A little later, I told him that if the child needed to stop, we should go to Bagatelle. And at Bagatelle we eventually arrived. When we drew up in the court-yard M. de Canisy, a look of surprise on his face, came and told me that the Empress Josephine was there. I replied:

"Now that we are here, we cannot go without seeing her: that would be unseemly."

She was in the little room at the back. She had us admitted immediately. She went down on her knees before the child, burst into tears and kissed his hand, saying:

"Sweet child, one day you will know the extent of the sacrifice I made for you. I rely on your governess to help you to appreciate it."

After spending an hour with the child and myself, she asked if she could see the people who were then in attendance on the young King. She was as gracious as she always was, and spoke so kindly to the nurse that as we were getting into the carriage the woman said:

"Lawks, but that one's got a kind heart! She's said more to me in a quarter of an hour than the other one has in six months."

The little King's real mother was undoubtedly Mme. de Montesquiou, whom the child was to call *Maman Quiou* or *Maman Mont*—the first words he spoke. She was present whenever he was fed, and later would always sit beside him at mealtimes. She used to take him to see his father at lunch, which Napoleon took under the great chestnut tree in the park. The Emperor was entranced by his son. He would sit the child on his knees, and, to the despair of the governess, try to get him to eat or else put his glass to his lips, laughing at the faces he pulled when a drop of wine pricked his tongue. "One day," writes Méneval, the Emperor's secretary, who witnessed the scene, "he offered him a morsel of food from his plate, and when the child opened his mouth to take it, he drew it away. He wanted to go on with the game, since it amused him, but at the second attempt the child turned his head away. His father then let him have the morsel, but he stubbornly refused it."

This surprised Napoleon, and Mme. de Montesquiou had to explain to him: "He doesn't like being tricked. He is proud and sensitive."

"Proud and sensitive!" exclaimed the Emperor, kissing the child. "Splendid! That's how I like him!"

Maria Ludovica gave her approval:

"I am glad that, quite apart from his happiness at the birth of a son, the Emperor enjoys playing with the child. This is the best of occupations for those who write a great deal."

From September 23 to November 11, 1811, Marie Louise saw nothing of her son. She had joined her husband at Antwerp on September 30, and they had traveled together through the Low Countries and part of Rhenish Germany. "You were right in thinking that I should be happy to see my son again after two months away," she told her friend Victoire de Créneville on her return. "The emotion I felt can be experienced but cannot be described. I found him stronger, with four teeth, and able to say *Papa*, but thinner and pale as a result of teething."

The child was indeed having trouble with his teeth. When he was ten months old, four back teeth came through, but not his incisors. Meanwhile he was being taught to walk with the help of trolleys made by one Bouillier, a carpenter at Saint-Cloud. Maman Quiou did her best to keep him amused with a variety of toys. For New Year's Day, 1812, the cabinet-maker Cacheleu made him a set of skittles in polished yew wood, a mahogany truck fitted with a silver bell, a ninety-piece collection of doll's furniture, a three-octave piano with ivory keys, some teetotums in carved mother-of-pearl, and a woolly lamb made of wood, standing on brass casters, and wearing a gold-and-velvet collar with silver bells.

Dressed in a percale bonnet and a Levantine-blue box coat which concealed the ribbon of the Legion of Honor, he was taken for regular drives along the boulevards and in the Bois de Boulogne. His six-horse carriage was escorted by a troop of light cavalry. He went out in all weathers.

That winter, on February 22, 1812, Marie Louise moved, much to her delight, from the Tuileries to the Élysée, where the garden was closed to the public. The little King joined his parents there on the second floor. His apartments were furnished just as severely as at the Tuileries. Everything—consoles, tables, chest of drawers—was in mahogany. The bedroom walls were—inevitably—green, and all the chairs were covered in green *cannetille*. Only the sky-blue sofas struck a soft note in this far from childlike room. It was at the Élysée that he was given his first birthday presents: a splendid drum fitted with bells, a Polish lancer, a Chinese puzzle, a boxwood top, and a clock bird of his which had been carefully repaired, for it had taken to refusing to come out of its locket and sing.

On April 8 another move took place, this time to the Château de Meudon, whose healthy air had once been recommended to Marie Antoinette's eldest son. Here a detachment of twenty infantrymen watched over the little King. It was a small guard, but the Paris garrison had been reduced to its minimum strength: every man capable of bearing arms had been dispatched to the Russian frontier, which was soon to witness "the beginning of the end." . . . It was at Meudon that the Emperor intended to establish what he called the Maison d'Éducation des Princes, and already a library of forty thousand volumes had been installed there, together with maps, vases depicting some of the Empire's monuments, and a table service with instructional views painted on the plates. The little King was also given a magic lantern with forty-three colored slides telling the story of the Bible. Since he was not yet sixteen months old, this was just as premature as the course of geography lessons which it was planned to give him with the aid of a globe discovered at Meudon, a globe which had belonged to Louis XVI's son. On this globe, incidentally, the frontiers of the European states were to be made mobile. A sage and elementary precaution for a son of Napoleon . . .

It seemed likely that the little King would be the only boarder at the Maison d'Éducation des Princes. The Faculty strongly advised the imperial couple against having any more children; according to the doctors, Marie Louise was incapable of bearing the strain of childbirth a second time. In later years Mme. Neipperg would show how wrong they were. . . .

On Saturday, May 9, 1812, Napoleon and Marie Louise left Saint-Cloud for Dresden, after a touching farewell scene with the little King, who had considerable difficulty in saying *Pa-pa*.

"You lazy fellow!" exclaimed the Emperor. "Why, at your age I could already give Joseph a drubbing."

At Dresden the Emperor met his father-in-law again and made the acquaintance of *liebe Mamma*.

Napoleon embraced the Emperor [Maria Ludovica told her mother later], made as if to do the same to me and kissed my hand. Then he went into a bedroom, the doors of which were closed behind us, and stood there for a quarter of an hour, engaged in small talk. . . . After that the Empress arrived in gala dress, covered with jewels, and accompanied by her entire retinue. I went to meet her. Although she was pleased to see her father again, the presence of so many people and trouble with her dress led her to assume that air of embarrassed frigidity which is common to them all and which annoys me intensely. Pretending not to have noticed it, I embraced her warmly, for I was sincerely moved. I took her into my room and shut the doors, and we began chatting together on a settee, oblivious of everything but the joy of being reunited.

The Emperor did his best to captivate his young mother-in-law, showering her with compliments and courtesies, but all in vain.

"He talks a great deal," she reported, "and has a habit of asking questions. One can avoid the questions, but not the answers. I became aware that he was doing it on purpose and I cut him short—so short indeed that the conversation never recovered."

Francis, seeing Napoleon take precedence over him, lead the way to the dining room, sit at the head of the table, and keep his hat on when he, Francis, was bareheaded, was utterly dumfounded.

"*Das ist ein ganzer Kerl!*" he exclaimed.

During their stay at Dresden, the imperial couple received a whole correspondence concerning the weaning of the King of Rome. The couriers galloped from Paris to Dresden and from Dresden to Paris to keep their master fully informed as to this important matter. On the very morning of his departure, the Emperor had ordered Corvisart "to do whatever he thought fit in this connection, on his own responsibility." That was a Saturday. On the following Wednesday the First Physician went to Meudon. "I informed the Governess of the unlimited authority with which the Emperor had invested me, and, after conferring with MM. Bourdois, Auvity and Dubois (the first two not being of a definite opinion), I suggested weaning the child. The Governess refused to agree to this without first writing to the Emperor for permission. I pointed out that His Majesty had given me the most complete and categorical authority, but she took no notice."

Corvisart happened to be on intimate terms with Mme. de Montebello, and, since the two ladies could not stand one another, that was a sufficient reason for Mme. de Montesquiou to differ in opinion from the First Physician. The governess then asked the three doctors who advised against the weaning to draw up a report to that effect, and this document was sent to Dresden without Corvisart's knowledge.

"In medical matters," replied the Emperor, "I have complete confidence in my First Physician Corvisart."

Mme. de Montesquiou had to give in, and told Corvisart that "the obstacles had been removed."

"Note the word obstacles!" he wrote to Mme. de Montebello. "Who, may I ask, put them there in the first place?"

The following Wednesday—June 3—Corvisart, full of his own importance, went once more to Meudon and summoned his three colleagues—although, as he later pointed out, "the Emperor's authorization left me free to dispense with their services."

"Gentlemen," he said, "I ask you, on your honor and in all conscience, to say whether the King can be safely weaned without further delay."

"Yes," they replied.

"We went to the King's apartments," writes Corvisart. "I gave instructions that he was to be weaned. There was another attempt to put off weaning him for a few more days, but I insisted . . . and weaned he was."

On June 7 Corvisart wrote to Mme. de Montebello: "You can inform His Majesty that the King of Rome has been completely weaned; since last Wednesday he has not seen his wet-nurse and has consequently stopped being suckled. I believe he is all the better for it. I saw him yesterday. He is perfectly happy; he is eating, drinking and sleeping splendidly; and his teeth are coming through."

While Napoleon took the road to Moscow, Marie Louise spent a month with her father, who had written to her: "I shall not keep you longer than your husband wishes, for you belong to your son and to the country in which you are established."

In Prague she dazzled everyone with her style of living. "She makes do with a hundred and fifty valets," wrote Mme. de Montet. "The Emperor of Austria has two." People considered that her appearance had improved: "Her figure has become very graceful, in other words quite unrecognizable. . . ." She showed everyone her son's portrait.

"I can see a warlike look in his eyes," declared the Prince de Ligne.

"Oh, no," said Marie Louise. "He is as quiet and peaceable as I am."

"It would be a queer thing," concludes Mme. de Montet, to whom we owe this anecdote, "if Napoleon's son turned out to be a mild little man!"

Marie Louise got back to Saint-Cloud on July 18, 1812, to find a letter from the Emperor in which he wrote: "I envy you the joy of seeing the little King again; give him a kiss from me. He will have grown a lot. Tell me if he is beginning to talk."

Alas, no, he was not talking, and this worried his mother. The child also had great difficulty in walking, as the Empress remarked in her letters to Vienna. "I can understand your anxiety," replied her uncle, Archduke Louis, "if he keeps falling down. But that is the best way for him to learn to walk, and it will also accustom him to taking knocks at an early age."

Gérard was then putting the finishing touches to his portrait of the little King. It was anything but a good likeness; indeed, as Frédéric Masson has justly remarked, it was a portrait of Napoleon seen as a child, even down to the famous lock of hair. After seven days on the road, the painting reached the Emperor in his bivouac inside a hollow square formed by the Old Guard. It was the eve of the Battle of the Moskva. He made no attempt to hide his impatience while the canvas was being unpacked in front of him. When at long last he was able to see the picture, he promptly declared that it was a masterpiece.

"My son is the most beautiful child in France," he told Rapp.

All day long, the portrait stayed on a chair.

"Gentlemen," said the Emperor to his officers, when they came for general orders, "if my son were fifteen years old, you may be sure he would be here in the flesh and not just in a painting."

Before going the round of the bivouacs, as he always did on the eve of a battle, Napoleon took a last look at his son's portrait and said: "Put it away. It is too soon in life for him to see a battlefield."

A week later the picture was hanging in the Emperor's bedroom in the Kremlin. On his bedside table was the miniature painted a month before by Aimé-Thibaut, depicting the child riding a sheep. He had received it at Smolensk, considered it a remarkable likeness, and would never agree to being parted from it. He was to take it with him to St. Helena.

Marie Louise stayed on at Saint-Cloud. She felt no anxiety whatever about Napoleon's Russian campaign. On September 13 her father had written to her from Baden:

"Up to now the Emperor has conducted his present venture with his customary success, so that if the Russians should be stubborn enough to hold out, everything should soon be over."

On October 20, after a drive beside the Seine, the child started coughing. His doctors met at once and prescribed powerful medicines to cure him. They also mentioned the advisability of returning to the Élysée. Already, three days before, Mme. de Montesquiou had given orders for the little King's drawing room and bedroom to be padded from the wainscoting to the floor—stipulating a sky-blue cloth this time instead of the traditional green. The same month, fireguards were put in front of all the fireplaces.

On October 23 the château was wrapped in fog, but this did not prevent Marie Louise from going for a walk in the park with her beloved Montebello. Suddenly, about eleven o'clock, the two young women saw Prince Aldobrandini, the Empress's First Equerry, coming toward them down the great avenue of chestnut trees, white-faced and out of breath.

"A revolution has just broken out in Paris!"

It was Ferniot—a noncommissioned officer in the château guard—who had given the alarm. He had heard the news from a friend of his living at Chaillot. Marie Louise—who never for a moment forgot the

fate of her aunt Marie Antoinette—rushed back to the château, and
carriages were hurriedly ordered to take the Empress and the little
King to Saint-Cyr. The Comte de Beauharnais put the "garrison" under arms: 25 troopers, 42 infantrymen, 17 gendarmes and 26 sappers.
A total of 110 men. So the servants were armed with the Emperor's
own guns. . . .

At a quarter past eleven an aide-de-camp—M. de Verdun—arrived at
a gallop shouting: "Everything's all right! It's all over!"

He carried a letter for Marie Louise from the Minister of War. She
tore it open and read:

MADAME,

An event occurred this morning which need cause Your Majesty
no alarm. The former generals Malet and Lahorie, in a fit of madness, succeeded in leaving the places where they were being held
under arrest, used their uniforms to trick certain detachments of
the National Guard, and, at their head, armed with a counterfeit
proclamation by the Senate, arrested the Minister of Police and
wounded General Hulin. However, they themselves were soon
arrested and the matter ended there.

In the circumstances I have decided to send some detachments
of the Imperial Guard to stand by Your Majesty and the King of
Rome. I beg Your Majesty not to entertain any misgivings. M. de
Verdun, my aide-de-camp, will deliver the present letter to Your
Majesty and enlarge, if need be, upon the details it contains. . . .

M. de Verdun was submitted to a barrage of questions, which he
answered to the best of his ability. It was General Malet who had
planned everything in the nursing home where he was being held on
account of various abortive plots in which he had been involved. This
time, his plot had been infinitely more cunning than its predecessors.
He had worked out a plan to escape from the nursing home, don his
uniform again, and tell the troops of the Paris garrison that Napoleon
was dead, killed by a bullet outside Moscow. With the help of fake
orders and counterfeit proclamations establishing a new government,
he had hoped to be able to take over the Prefecture of Police, the
Hôtel de Ville, Army Headquarters and all the Ministries.

But what of his accomplices?

Here Malet had had a stroke of genius. He had decided to recruit accomplices *in spite of themselves,* by picking enemies of the Empire and getting them to believe in Napoleon's death and the creation of a new government. Where would he find them? Where else but in prison? Malet had thought first of all of General Lahorie—Victor Fanneau de Lahorie—who was being held in the Prison de la Force, probably unjustly, for complicity in the Moreau conspiracy. He had also resolved to secure the services of another prisoner, General Guidal, who was accused, with greater justification, of having tried to sell Toulon to the English for thirty thousand francs.

Accompanied by two confederates, one disguised as a police inspector and the other as an aide-de-camp, Malet had turned up at half-past three in the morning at the Popincourt barracks, where everything had gone according to plan. It never occurred to a single officer that, once Napoleon was dead, Napoleon II automatically became Emperor of the French; and when Malet asked for an escort to accompany him to the Prison de la Force to free Lahorie and Guidal, the escort was promptly provided. The two puzzled generals, nonplused by their sudden release, found themselves in the prison office, face to face with Malet. The latter embraced Lahorie, whom he had not seen for eighteen years, and Guidal, whom he had never met before, was introduced to him. Without further delay he told them what had happened and informed them that their orders were to arrest the minister Savary, Pasquier the Prefect, Desmarets the Head of the Sûreté, Chancellor Cambacérès and Clarke the Minister of War. Guidal and Lahorie did not seem to be at all dismayed by this ambitious program. Napoleon's death had released them from prison, and as enemies of the régime it was perfectly natural that the new government should give them immediate employment. Besides, they had seen so many changes since 1792. . . .

"I thought I was living through another 18 Brumaire," said Lahorie afterward, "and I followed Malet as I had followed Bonaparte then."

An hour later Pasquier, Savary and Desmarets had taken the two generals' places in the cells of La Force. It was considered unnecessary to put the Prefect of the Seine, the Comte Frochot, in prison, since he had handed the Hôtel de Ville over with the greatest courtesy and alacrity.

And so the conspiracy followed its course, conducted by men who had no inkling of the truth and who played their parts all the more naturally because of that. Once the machine had been started, it ran smoothly and well. Mounted orderlies of the 10th Cohort arrived at the Minimes and Courtille barracks with documents signed by Malet ordering the appropriate regiments to take arms and to occupy, in the name of the new government, the Palais-Royal, the Quai Voltaire, the Senate, the Treasury and the principal gates of the city, while the main body of troops was to assemble in the Place Vendôme, where Malet himself was operating. Everyone obeyed, even Colonel Rabbe, the commanding officer of the Paris Guard. The result was that at a quarter to ten on that Friday morning, October 23, Malet was in control of three-quarters of Paris. Once the conspirators had taken care of Cambacérès and the Ministry of War, there would have been nothing left to do but to collect the Empress and the King of Rome at Saint-Cloud. The surprising thing is that the only man that day who bungled the part he had allotted himself was . . . General Malet. At Army Headquarters in the Place Vendôme, he was arrested by the adjutant and his chief of staff, who knew him of old and guessed the truth as soon as he appeared on the scene. Lahorie and Guidal too were soon apprehended, but the conspiracy, though decapitated, went merrily along for all that. The troops Malet had set in motion continued to act on the orders he had given them. The consequence was a series of comical misunderstandings, and the whole affair turned into a farce. For instance, the authorities had considerable difficulty in finding Savary, who had been "mislaid" in one of the Paris prisons. But the most amusing incident of all was undoubtedly Baron Pasquier's return to his prefecture. The sentries thought he had escaped and tried to arrest him again. But the prefect managed to slip through their fingers, took refuge in a pharmacy, borrowed a wig and a dress from the chemist's wife, and in this disguise, so it is said, escaped from his pursuers.

Marie Louise found it hard not to smile when Cambacérès, who arrived soon after M. de Verdun, told her the whole story. And Queen Hortense, who came to hear the news, found her "in the best of spirits."

"What could they have done to me?" she asked with bland innocence. "Am I not the Emperor of Austria's daughter?"

Cambacérès, more than a little annoyed, retorted "acidly": "Upon my word, Madame, Your Majesty is fortunate indeed to be able to view events so philosophically. Your Majesty is no doubt aware that it was General Malet's intention to put the King of Rome in the Foundling Home?"

But on that particular morning Marie Louise never gave a thought to her son. Nor, for that matter, did any of the state officials. As Frochot, the Prefect of the Seine, put it the day after the conspiracy: "Nobody ever thinks of the dratted King of Rome!"

It was precisely this forgetfulness that wounded Napoleon more than anything else. In the carriage bringing him back at full speed from Russia, he was forced to face the fact that the Revolution had killed, not only a monarch, but also the principle of hereditary monarchy.

"Among all those soldiers and officials who were told that I was dead, not a single one thought of my son! The Minister of War, who is always telling me about his devotion to duty, didn't even put his boots on to go round the barracks administering the oath of loyalty to the King of Rome!"

And what of Malet?

"Malet is a lunatic!" Napoleon said later. "You have to be crazy to imagine that putting the police out of action and deceiving a few soldiers and a prefect for three hours is enough to overthrow the government, when there's an army of two hundred thousand men outside the country and not a single accomplice in the government or in the departments. He's just a fool who wanted to go down in history in front of a firing squad, but what he's done has shown me something I already suspected anyway—that there's not much trust to be put in others."

And he cast the same reproach in his ministers' faces on December 19, the day after his return to the Tuileries:

"Your oaths, your principles, your doctrines! You make me tremble for the future!"

What had gone wrong? In the hope that, in imitation of the old royal cry, people would shout: "The Emperor is dead! Long live the Emperor!" he had gone to great pains to follow in every particular the customs of the *ancien régime,* not only for his son's birth but also for his education and the composition of his household. Better still, he had made his heir not a dauphin but a king, a sovereign comparable to the King of the Romans, a title borne both by the Emperor of the West before his coronation and by his acknowledged heir. To do that, he had revoked with a stroke of the pen the gift his "predecessor" Charlemagne had made to His Holiness the Pope. He had arranged for a baptism at Notre-Dame, a ceremony which, by its pomp and splendor, was intended to prove the definitive establishment of the Napoleonic dynasty at the head of a homogeneous empire whose people, living in what had become French departments, would gradually lose all sense of having once been Dutchmen, Italians or Germans. And yet . . .

"Nobody ever thinks of the dratted King of Rome!"

It must be admitted too that that morning when Malet succeeded, almost single-handed, in gaining control of three-quarters of Paris, nobody thought of the "Empress-Queen" either. Once Napoleon was dead, the Empire automatically collapsed. He might marry the daughter of the Caesars and provide his son with ancestors, but for all that the little King would never inherit the Empire. That escapee from a nursing home and his comic-opera conspiracy had proved that beyond a doubt.

The Emperor, however, decided to try and avert the inevitable by having the Empress and above all his son crowned during his lifetime. The Pope was the only person who could conduct a ceremony of that nature since—as Malet had shown—it was essential to try and revive the concept of the Divine Right. But Pius VII was a prisoner at Fontainebleau, stubbornly refusing to bow to the Emperor's demands and abandon his right to appoint bishops. He would have to be coaxed and wheedled, first of all into agreeing to a new Concordat. The *commediante* tried charm and then threats. "Pressed, hustled and harried by Napoleon," writes Mme. B. Melchoir-Bonnet, "and no doubt fascinated too by the Emperor's charm and his cunningly presented arguments, Pius VII looked in vain for help from his cardinals, who were quite content to leave matters as they stood. The lonely old man could not hold out much longer. After a few days' discussion, he finally accepted a compromise which, it was expressly stated, was to 'serve as a basis for a definitive agreement.'" This agreement was signed on the evening of January 25. The Pope surrendered his right of appointment. In exchange, Napoleon, in somewhat imprecise terms, envisaged surrendering Rome to its sovereign.

Marie Louise, who understood nothing of what was happening, gave her father the good news: "Today the Emperor settled the affairs of Christendom with the Pope. The Pope seems to be very happy; since early this morning he has been very gay and in high spirits, and he signed the agreement a quarter of an hour ago. I have just been to see him and found him in the best of health. . . ."

In fact he was neither in the best of health nor happy about what he had done. Assailed by remorse, he was tortured by the thought that he had "acted against the interests of the Church." He felt that he had failed in his duty and he did not dare to say Mass any more.

So far Napoleon suspected nothing. On his return to Paris he informed the Privy Council of the proposed *senatus consultum* on the Empress's regency and the coronation of the King of Rome. The latter ceremony could have taken place on March 7 or, better still, on the 20th, Napoleon II's second birthday. But the Pope showed so little eagerness that it was postponed. Wisely, as it happened. On March 24, Pius VII retracted, refused to sign the new Concordat and, by the same token—there was no longer any point in asking him—made it clear that he was not going to "confirm the Corsican's descendants in the imperial dignity."

The King of Rome would never be crowned.

Indifferent, one imagines, to all the fuss being made about him, the little King went on growing and was soon taken out of his merino dresses. He seems to have recognized his father on his return, and Marie Louise was able to reply in the affirmative to *liebe Mamma,* who had written to her on January 16, 1813:

"You owe me lots of interesting details about the reception your dear little friend gave his Papa. Did he recognize him, did he shout *oho!* and did the Emperor find he had grown and changed? What a happy moment it must have been for you to take that sweet child in your arms. . . . How I wish you could show him to me too: I should so enjoy kissing him, and then too I should try to amuse him. . . ."

She shared this ambition with Leopoldine, who also longed to "frolic and play" with her little nephew. The child was now playing with some new toys Cacheleu had just made for him: five wooden guns with velvet fittings, a tricolor flag, a small racket with some shuttlecocks to go with it, and a silk ball adorned with stars. As a boy, he showed a certain contempt for the four hundred pieces of equipment in his toy kitchen, as also for the "food and fruit on a series of pewter dishes."

He was soon to have two real merino sheep trained by the Franconi brothers, the famous circus proprietors, to trot like ponies and to draw a delightful little carriage "lined with gray velvet, mounted on flexible springs, decorated with paintings and speckled with bees" which his aunt the Queen of Naples had given him. With a page holding the sheep's bridle, little Napoleon would go driving in this carriage along the Terrasse du Bord de l'Eau, cheered by the passers-by. He was cheered too whenever his father sent him and his suite for a drive along the boulevards and the main streets of the capital. As the situation of the Empire deteriorated, the Emperor saw fit to show his son to the people of Paris as often as he could. He would be at one of the château windows on March 1 to see the fatted ox, and again on the 5th to watch the Guard on parade. Napoleon took the child in his arms and carried him along the ranks of lancers and grenadiers, riflemen and dragoons. The boy smiled and stretched his hands out toward the plumes and decorations.

"He seems to know that these good fellows are all old friends of mine," said the Emperor, who never missed an opportunity to add to his legend.

At this time the little King was usually dressed in a green suit with gold buttons, or a purple jacket, or else a jacket in white kerseymere. When it was cold he wore a vest in bright velvet. For his second birthday, which was celebrated at the Petit Trianon, he was given, among other toys, a papier-mâché horse with a fringed velvet shabrack and a set of skittles . . . not to mention a dozen balls. The same day Maria Ludovica wrote asking her stepdaughter for news of her son, "whom I imagine as sweet-natured and handsome in the last degree; tell me what progress he is making. Everything about the little fellow is a source of delight to me."

Alas, the "little fellow" was now in his third year of life and still finding it hard to express himself. This backwardness of his was the despair of his mother. "If your son is not talking," wrote the Emperor Francis, "that is not a matter of great concern, but it may be due to the fact that he wants for nothing and his every wish is anticipated."

There was certainly no denying that the little King was a spoiled child. He would often fly into temper, and this indeed was his chief failing. The Archduchess Leopoldine wrote to her sister: "I hear that your son has been suffering from a fever brought on by a fit of temper. You will forgive me if I find that hard to believe, but if it is true then he must be very headstrong and full of life. . . ."

He was undoubtedly full of life, and this made his silence all the more difficult to understand. Accordingly in May, 1813, Mme. de Montesquiou chose the son of one of the "red ladies"—young Albert Froment—to be the little King's playmate. The two boys got on splendidly, fighting all the time, and one day when Froment had hurled little Napoleon to the ground, the latter said as he got up:

"If they'd seen you do that! . . . But don't be frightened, I shan't tell."

He was soon talking freely, and Marie Louise, who had become Empress-Regent for the duration of the German campaign, was able to report good progress to her husband. He replied from Liegnitz on May 28: "I am happy to see that my son has started talking and is pronouncing words properly. Everything you tell me about him fills me with a desire to see him, and I hope that on my return he will be talking very well indeed."

His return! Alas, that would not be until November, and then he would only see the little King for two and a half months. In the meantime he fought to save his son's empire. The campaign against Prussia and Russia opened on May 1 and, marked by the victories of Bautzen and Lützen, had lasted only a month. On June 4 an armistice had been signed which gave Austria time to take sides with the Emperor's enemies. On June 26, at Dresden, Napoleon received a visit from Metternich, who came ostensibly as an arbiter but in reality as a future belligerent, ready to sacrifice without a moment's hesitation both Marie Louise's future and the destiny of his master's grandson.

This momentous encounter, this historic duel began with a question from Napoleon: "Do you bring war or peace?"

But the Emperor did not give the Austrian Minister time to reply.

"So you want war, do you? Well, you'll get it. I've destroyed the Prussian army at Lützen, I've beaten the Russians at Bautzen, and now you've decided that it's your turn I'll make an appointment with you in Vienna. Men are really incorrigible: experience is wasted on them. I've restored the Emperor Francis to his throne three times, I've promised to remain at peace with him as long as I live, and I've married his daughter. I told myself at the time that I was a fool to do that, but I did it and now I'm regretting it."

Metternich, to whom Berthier had just been saying: "Don't forget that Europe needs peace, and France needs it more than anyone else," said that he brought peace.

"And what do you mean by peace?" shouted the Emperor. "You mean plunder, don't you? You want Italy or Brabant or Lorraine. Well, I'm not giving up an inch of ground! I'm prepared to make peace on the basis of the *status quo ante bellum.* . . . I may even give part of the Duchy of Warsaw to Russia; but I shan't give you anything because you haven't beaten me, and I shan't give Prussia anything because she's betrayed me. If you want West Galicia and if Prussia wants some of her former possessions, that can be arranged, but only if you're willing to pay compensation to my allies. It cost me two hundred thousand men to conquer Illyria; if you want it you'll have to expend the same number. . . ."

Metternich remained silent, "plaster-faced" as the Tsar used to say.

"The fact is that you want Italy, Russia wants Poland, Prussia wants Saxony and England wants Belgium and Holland. You're all just longing to hack the French Empire to pieces. Oh yes, all I have to do is evacuate the half of Europe I still occupy, withdraw my legions behind the Rhine, the Alps and the Pyrenees, and entrust my uncertain future to the generosity of the enemies I've just beaten in battle! . . . How do you expect me to face the French people if I do that? The Emperor Francis is strangely deluded if he imagines that in France of all places a broken throne can offer protection to his daughter and grandson. . . . *Ah, Metternich, how much did England pay you to make you turn against me like this?*"

These last words were not reproduced by Metternich in his *Memoirs,* and we know about them only through Maret, who confided them to Fain.

The Emperor showed the Minister his maps, in an attempt to convince him of his strength.

"I'll make another appointment with you in Vienna," he said. "Next October."

"I have seen your troops," said Metternich quietly. "They are just children. You have killed off a whole generation. What will you do when these boys have disappeared?"

The Emperor flared up: "Monsieur, you are not a soldier. You know nothing of what goes on in a soldier's heart. I've grown up on the battlefield, and a man like me wouldn't give a damn for the lives of a million men."

He threw his hat to the ground and strode up and down the room, irritated beyond measure by the cold irony with which Metternich contemplated the hat lying on the floor. Suddenly Napoleon picked it up and, going over to the Minister, said: "Tell me, Metternich, don't you think I was a fool to marry an Austrian princess?"

"Since you ask me my opinion, I think that Napoleon the great conqueror made a mistake."

"So the Emperor Francis is prepared to turn his daughter too off the throne of France?"

"Sire, the Emperor of Austria takes nothing but the good of his empire into consideration and will act in its interests without paying any attention to his daughter's fate. He is first and foremost a sovereign and will not hesitate to sacrifice his family for his empire's good."

There was an oppressive silence. Then Napoleon replied quietly: "What you have just said doesn't surprise me, but only serves to convince me of the gravity of my mistake. When I married the Austrian Archduchess I thought I should be able to give new life to the past by linking it with modern times, by coupling Gothic prejudice with present-day enlightenment. I was wrong, and today I can see how wrong I was. My mistake may cost me my throne, but I shall bury the world under the ruins!"

The scene was over. Napoleon accompanied the Minister to the door, and there he stopped and put his hand on Metternich's shoulder.

"Tell me now, you won't fight me again, will you?"

Metternich, who had always been so obsequious with the Emperor, gave him "a haughty look." And his thin lips shaped the words: "You are done for, Sire! I thought as much when I came here, and now I am certain of it."

Immediately afterward Metternich wrote to his friend Hudelist: "Bonaparte is finished."

It was the truth, yet Napoleon could still inspire awe. On Thursday, July 22, Maria Theresa of Austria, Queen of Saxony and the Francis of Austria's sister, who saw the Emperor nearly every day at Dresden, wrote to her niece Marie Louise: "Anyone who decides to try conclusions with him is making a great mistake . . . for there never has been and never will be a genius comparable to his. . . . He is never still for a moment, moving fast and appearing where you least expect to see him. . . . It is astonishing to see what he attempts and achieves in a short time, physically and mentally. And yet he is in a very good humor, at his happiest when he is thinking and talking about you. I hope he will not put on any more weight. He has lost the olive complexion he used to have and now he has a fresh, healthy look. . . ."

Anyone who decides to try conclusions with him is making a great mistake . . .

But this in no way deterred the Queen's brother from declaring war on his "beloved son-in-law" a few days later, on Wednesday, August 11.

Marie Louise, who was on her way home after spending a few days with the Emperor at Mainz, heard the news from her father and her husband at the same time. Both men tried to soften the blow and to reassure the unfortunate woman, who saw her son's father and grandfather about to fight each other.

"Keep calm," wrote the Emperor Francis on August 11, the very day the armistice was broken. "The war we are waging is totally unlike any other; it is purely political. I shall never be your husband's enemy and I hope that he will never be mine."

"Do not take your father's behavior too much to heart," wrote Napoleon for his part. "He has been led astray by Metternich. I want you to be very brave."

Marie Louise wrote in reply to her father:

"The Emperor would have a poor opinion of me if he were not well aware of the feelings I entertain for you. Likewise you would have a poor opinion of me if what I desired above all else were not the happiness of the Emperor and my son."

As Jules Bertaut has remarked, this woman, who is generally regarded as having been stupid and insensitive, found the right words that day and the right tone. But that, unfortunately, would not always be the case.

At Cherbourg, to which she had to pay an official visit—for she was now Regent of the Empire—she lost nothing of her melancholy. "We are really most unhappy," she wrote in her diary. "When you are tired you have to hold a reception; when you want to cry you have to laugh; and even so nobody so much as sympathizes with you!" However, on August 31 good news arrived: Napoleon had won the Battle of Dresden—the last of his victories.

"Papa Francis had the good sense not to turn up," he wrote. "I gave a thorough trouncing to Prince Schwarzenberg and the Emperor Alexander. Papa Francis's troops have never been worse; they are ill clad, practically naked. I have taken twenty-five thousand prisoners, thirty colors and a good many guns. I am going to send you the whole lot."

She returned to Paris on September 5 to carry on with her work—work with which, on her husband's orders, she associated her son. It was important that the people should see them as often as possible, and Napoleon had ordered public entertainments and country dances. Yet nobody felt in the mood for dancing. For the past three years a harvest of men had been gathered three times a year.

Already, in his parents' absence—during the journeys to Mainz and Cherbourg—little Napoleon had begun his royal apprenticeship. He had held Court on Sundays, and Chancellor Cambacérès, Monge, Senator Clément de Ris and Marshals Moncey and Lefebvre had solemnly come and kissed his hand. The weekly report stated in all seriousness that "the young ladies from a private school" had been "admitted to the hall which His Majesty had deigned to cross." His duty done, he quickly returned to the toys he had been given on August 15, the Emperor's birthday: a magnetized boat, a rocking horse and a dwarf horse, not to mention a doll "which could be undressed" and which he doubtless ignored. Soon after her return home, his mother gave him *Stories for My Son, Science in Miniature, The Children's Magazine* and *The Glorious History of the French Nation.* The text of this last book was read to him—he was not yet three years old—while he looked at the pictures over and over again. He would take the book to Vienna the following year and talk about it for hours with his Austrian tutors.

When he was naughty he was punished by being forbidden to put on one of his uniforms, for a whole series of outfits had been made for him, ranging from that of a Polish lancer to a mounted grenadier. He wore them proudly with the diamond-studded star of the Legion of Honor.

"Your son," Marie Louise told Napoleon on September 29, "has made me promise to give him a cap like those worn by the mamelukes of the Guard; he has a passion for things military and we shall soon see his bedroom filled, not with toys, but with all sorts of soldierly equipment."

This touched Napoleon, and undoubtedly won his approval. Yet this same "passion for things military" was to prove the Emperor's undoing. This month of October, 1813, was the month of Leipzig, of the Battle of the Nations in which, for all his soldiers' heroism, Napoleon's power was crippled by the blows struck by "Papa Francis," the Tsar, the King of Prussia and Bernadotte. And soon Murat, in the hope of becoming "the Bernadotte of the North," would likewise abandon his old master, Jerome Bonaparte would try to bargain with the Allies, and Louis would lay claim to Holland "on condition that he was left at liberty to negotiate with Europe."

Communications between Marie Louise and her father had not yet been severed. The Emperor Francis suggested that his daughter should send her letters by way of the outposts.

> My replies [he wrote on December 12, 1813] will reach you by the same route. I have proved that I am convinced that your husband and I can understand each other and live in peace by giving you to him in marriage, and I prove it again every day by praying for peace. But that does not depend on me . . . in any event, whatever happens, I shall never forget that your husband's wife is my daughter and that your son is mine too. . . . I note that your son is well and showing great promise; I am delighted to hear it, and from my own experience I can imagine the pleasure he affords you. May God grant me the joy of holding him in my arms one day, and you will see what I shall make of him, though without spoiling him. . . .

The rough draft of this letter is in Metternich's hand. As for Marie Louise's reply, it was dictated by a Napoleon who was staking everything on a final throw. Thus the dialogue begun at Dresden went on:

> You cannot imagine how sad I am to think that you should be engaged in a war against the Emperor, your own son-in-law, when you are both endowed with dispositions which should make you friends. . . . May God grant us peace very soon. The Emperor wants peace and so does everyone here; but peace cannot be concluded without negotiations, and at present there appears to be considerable reluctance to negotiate on your side. I feel sure that this is the fault of the English.

On the 20th the Emperor Francis replied:

> Your letter of December 12 reached me yesterday and I am pleased to see that you are well. Thank you for your New Year greetings. . . . I send you my own heartfelt good wishes. As for peace, believe me when I say that I want it just as much as yourself, as the whole of France and, I hope, as your husband. There is no happiness or salvation except in peace. My ambitions are modest, and I hope for a solution which will ensure a lasting peace; but in this world of ours hope is not enough. I have con-

siderable obligations to my allies, and *unfortunately the question of the peace which I hope we may soon enjoy is very complicated. Your country has upset all the old ideas;* whichever way one approaches the question, there are well-founded grievances and prejudices to be overcome. That is not to say that I have the affair any the less at heart for that, since peace is my dearest wish, and I hope that we may very soon bring all our side together. There is no ill will in England, but great differences of opinion, and there must inevitably be a certain delay before the matter can be broached—but then God's will will surely be done. The news you give me of your son affords me considerable pleasure. . . .

In spite of the war between their two countries, *liebe Mamma* went on writing to her stepdaughter, thanking her for the dresses she had managed to send her, inquiring after "the little fellow," expressing an interest in "his prattle," and asking Marie Louise if she was teaching him "a few words of German."

From the Tuileries, "a palace in which already it seemed as though someone had died," the Emperor tried to convince France that she was exhausted only because "she imagined that this was the case." It was an impossible task. As a contemporary, Poumiès de la Siboutie, remarked, "Napoleon's popularity was at its lowest ebb." A pall of gloom hung over the palace, and the only sign of life came from the King of Rome with his childish high spirits. Napoleon had seen nothing of him from April 15 till November 9; he had left a dumb child and had come home to a delightful little chatterbox. The boy would often escape from his apartments and go and see his father at work in his study. But the usher, whom Napoleon had forbidden to admit the child without his governess, would bar the way. Then the little boy would stamp his foot and raise his voice.

"Sire, I cannot admit Your Majesty."

"I am the little King!"

"But Your Majesty is alone."

Fortunately Mme. de Montesquiou would appear on the scene.

"Open the door to the King!" the child would say.

And the usher would throw open the double door and announce: "His Majesty the King of Rome!"

One day he burst in at the end of a meeting of the council of ministers, and, ignoring the distinguished persons taking leave of their master, went straight to his father and kissed him. Napoleon frowned in disapproval.

"Sire, you have not greeted these gentlemen."

Little Napoleon turned round and blew kisses to all the dignitaries. The Emperor gathered him up in his arms.

"Well, gentlemen, nobody can say that I neglect my son's education."

Already, just after the Malet affair, he had thought about finding a tutor for the "little fellow." He had spoken to Caulaincourt about it, and had mentioned several names—Daru, Molé, Pasquier—without stopping at any one of them.

"Aren't you rather at a loss, Caulaincourt, for someone to suggest, even among the people we have just been talking about?"

Caulaincourt had to admit that he was right.

"But what about Fontanes?" he asked.

"Fontanes is too much the man of letters. He is a magnificent orator, but he is entirely lacking in those far-reaching ideas, those sweeping political and administrative concepts which go to the making of a statesman. And then again, he has sung my praises so often that the public would be sure to say that I had picked my favorite courtier to be my son's tutor."

Mme. de Montesquiou, left in sole charge of the little King's education, brought him up to the best of her ability—and as we have seen, this was anything but easy. She had taught him to say his morning and evening prayers on his knees and to add:

"Dear Lord, inspire in Papa the desire to make peace for the good of France and the happiness of us all."

One evening Napoleon heard this prayer. He smiled and said nothing. Peace? He would be only too glad of it.

"In three months' time we shall have peace," he told the Legislative Assembly. "Our enemies will have been routed or I shall be dead."

As Talleyrand was to remark one day to Charles X, the Emperor had forgotten the third possibility: the post-chaise.

Before putting on his Italian boots and taking command of his troops, Napoleon sent M. de Beaumont to see the Pope at Fontainebleau. The Emperor was prepared to hand back his States to His Holiness. Why? M. de Beaumont explained quite frankly to Pius VII:

"Holy Father, I have come to inform Your Holiness that since the King of Naples has concluded an alliance with the Coalition, one of whose objects appears to be the union of Rome with his States, His

Majesty the Emperor and King has decided that it would be in conformity with the basic policy of his Empire and in the interests of the people of Rome to return the Roman States to Your Holiness. He would prefer to see them in the hands of Your Holiness rather than in the hands of any other sovereign, whoever he might be."

In return the Emperor hoped that the Pope would reconsider his decision of the year before. He reckoned without the powers of resistance inherent in the old man's body.

"God knows," said the Pope, "how many tears I have shed over the so-called Concordat which I was misguided enough to sign. I shall bear the mark of my anguish and remorse as long as I live, and that is a sure guarantee that I will not be tricked a second time."

His only desire now was to return to Italy.

"It may be that my sins have made me unworthy ever to see Rome again, but you may be certain that my successors will recover the States which belong to them by right."

Henceforth little Napoleon was a king without a kingdom.

5

✣

The Imp

THAT SUNDAY, January 23, there were seven or eight hundred officers waiting in the vast Salle des Maréchaux on the first floor of the center pavilion of the Tuileries. The Emperor had summoned them here, but they had no idea what was expected of them. In whispers they exchanged the latest news. The Allies, striking across Alsace and Switzerland, had crossed the Rhine and were advancing into Lorraine. It was said that they were at Saint-Dizier and that the Marshals had already abandoned the town. For the past fortnight a guard had been mounted at the gates of Paris. It was rumored that the Emperor never stirred now from his study. King Joseph and Napoleon had made it up; the former King of Spain had just installed himself in the Luxembourg and his brother had appointed him Lieutenant-General of the Empire for the duration of the campaign. Worse still—everyone was talking about it—he had appointed him Commandant of the Paris National Guard. That was a present the people of Paris could well have done without. The only one of the Emperor's brothers who was worth anything at all—Lucien—had quarreled with him. The other three were plumed and gilded nonentities. At least Jerome was an amusing comic-opera monarch, and Louis with his rheumatism was an object of pity. But Joseph . . .

"The Emperor!"

Everyone saluted. The master did not stop, but went on to the chapel to hear Mass. Not until twenty minutes later did he return to go round the vast circle several times, saying a few words to the legion commanders. Once again Marie Louise was late. At last she arrived with her suite and Mme. de Montesquiou holding the King of Rome in her arms. There was profound silence, broken by the clear, warm tones of the Emperor's voice:

"Gentlemen, part of the territory of France has been invaded. I am going to take my place at the head of my army, and with the help of God and my brave soldiers I hope to throw the enemy back across the frontier."

"I hope to throw the enemy back. . . ." He only hoped! This was a kind of language he had never used before. It was true, of course, that never before had such a tidal wave of enemy troops converged on the heart of France. Through the breaches made at Strasbourg and Basel—and later at Bayonne and in the north—the allied armies were pouring into France and would soon spread right across the country.

In a somewhat theatrical manner Napoleon then took the Empress and his son by the hand and said: "If the enemy approaches the capital, I entrust to the courage of the National Guard the Empress and the King of Rome . . . my wife and my son. . . ."

A few officers left the ranks to kiss the hands of their Emperor and the little King. All of them—even those who were opposed to the military dictatorship which for ten years had lain heavy on the shoulders of France—all of them were moved.

The Emperor had retired to his study. Tomorrow he would leave Paris to trace his finest campaign on the pages of history. Tonight he burned his papers and then bent over his maps, calculating how, with a few handfuls of men, he was to deal with over two hundred thousand Allied troops who would be joined by another hundred thousand in a few days. Meanwhile the little King played beside him on the carpet with his father's "maneuver pieces"—little jagged pieces of wood in different colors representing battalions, regiments and divisions.

And the Emperor pondered the problem of how to stop both Blücher and Schwarzenberg with a mere fifty thousand men: Blücher and his Silesian army of seventy thousand men who had crossed the Rhine and were moving into Lorraine; Schwarzenberg with his Bohemian army of a hundred and thirty thousand men who had come through Switzerland and were advancing toward the plateau of Langres. Not to mention a second Austrian army, or those two renegades: Bernadotte and his Swedes and, later, Murat and his Neapolitans.

The child went on playing, ruining his father's skillful maneuvers . . . but the Emperor smiled tenderly and put his army back in position.

"Fifty thousand men!"

He preferred to think only of the two hundred thousand soldiers who had penetrated into France. There would be time later on to deal with the rest who, ensconced behind the Rhine, had not yet ventured to cross the frontier. Fifty thousand men against two hundred thousand!

"But fifty thousand men and myself makes a hundred and fifty thousand!"

Once again his son had disarranged the battlefield. However, as Méneval later recorded, "such was the Emperor's presence of mind and his affection for his son that he remained unmoved whenever his maneuvers were disturbed, and without showing the slightest annoyance, he would set out his pieces all over again."

"I'm going to beat Papa Francis!"

He repeated this claim the next day to Marie Louise, who never stopped crying. The scene took place after dinner. The Empress and Hortense were warming themselves by the fire, which Napoleon was feeding continuously with bundles of papers. Every time he came near the fireplace he kissed the young woman.

"Don't be sad. Have faith in me."

And turning to his stepdaughter and sister-in-law, he added with a smile: "So the people of Paris are scared, Hortense? Already seeing Cossacks, are they? Oh, they haven't got here yet!"

A few minutes later, throwing another packet of documents into the fire, he took his wife in his arms and said: "Don't cry. Have faith in me. Do you think I've forgotten how to fight? I shall come back soon."

"But when?"

"That, my love, is God's secret."

The sun had not yet risen on January 25 when the Emperor, before throwing himself into his berlin, went on tiptoe to take a last look at the curly-headed little King, asleep in his bed.

He would never see him again. Never.

While the Pope, traveling in a chaplain's carriage, was slowly making his way to Rome to resume possession of his States—little Napoleon's sometime kingdom—the Emperor was still fighting to save his son's inheritance. With a series of blows of the ax, as Louis Madelin put it, directed at Champaubert, Montmirail and Vauchamp, he cut the Russian and Prussian armies to pieces—but, thanks to reinforcements from Belgium, the pieces soon came together again behind him. He was obliged to strike again, this time pursuing the enemy as far as Laon.

The day after Napoleon's departure, informed by his mother that his father "would not be back for some time," the little King burst into tears, and, according to a letter from Mme. de Montesquiou to the Emperor, "promptly started praying to God to keep you safe and ensure your speedy return." Finally, on January 27, the first letter arrived from the Emperor at Châlons. "Your son behaved delightfully this morning," wrote Marie Louise. "When I told him that I had news of you he shouted: 'King very happy,' and he pulled at my hand, saying: 'Let us go and see Papa.' He thought you were really there, and when we explained that it was just a letter he started crying; fortunately at his age sad impressions fade quickly, for in the evening he was as gay and impish as ever."

This letter from Marie Louise—like all those she wrote to Napoleon*—is instinct with love for her husband. She only came to life when the courier dismounted in the courtyard of the Tuileries, shouting "Good news!" "If you could see how ill-tempered and unhappy I am," she wrote, "after a day without news of you, you would have pity on me." And on the 31st she complained:

I almost feel tempted to pick a quarrel with you for not writing to me for two days; it really is too bad of you. If I did not know how busy you were, I should not forgive you. I beg you to send me regular news of yourself, just a word to say that you are well, and I shall be satisfied. Today I need that reassurance more than ever, for it is one of those days when I look on the dark side of everything. Since you went away all my days have been like that; I should like to be able to see nobody, and I am so sad that I am unfit for human society. I know that I will not recover my composure until you return.

Two days later she felt happier: Brienne had been recaptured.

* The letters from Marie Louise to Napoleon written in 1814 have only recently been discovered and have not been used before.

But these letters have something more to tell us: they show that Marie Louise was beginning to take an interest in her son, now that he was no longer an infant at the breast. Since the Emperor's departure ten days before, Mme. de Montesquiou had got the King of Rome to learn "The Grasshopper and the Ant" and half of "The Fox and the Crow" by heart. The Empress had him recite the two poems to her and could not help laughing, for what he reeled off was sheer "gibberish" of which she could not understand a single word.

The Empress's awkwardness and indifference were now things of the past, and when she went to her son's apartments to watch him being washed and dressed—something she did much more often than before— the child was in the seventh heaven of delight. He kept on kissing her and insisted on her tying his shoelaces. She for her part was just as happy, and longed for peace to come quickly so that her husband might, like herself, "enjoy him at leisure." "You have seen so little of him," she sighed, "since he was born."

He had indeed spent no more than a few months with his "little imp." But that did not prevent him from thinking of the boy. In his letters—notes scribbled in the interval between two encounters—the words "a kiss for the little King" recur like a leitmotiv. The smallest details of his son's life had the power to move him, and Marie Louise was well aware of this when she wrote to him:

"Your son is as good as ever and has asked me to tell you that he has eaten all his spinach. That may not appear very interesting to you, but it is great news for him as it means that he has conquered an aversion."

She had had a little National Guard uniform made for him, with a three-cornered hat adorned with a tricolor cockade and a magnificent white plume. The boy wore this uniform for the first time to go to Mass on January 30. He strutted about, very proud of himself, but when he heard shouts of "Long live the King!" he burst into tears. The "imp" drew his little sword and declared:

"I shall use this to defend Papa against his enemies."

He was forever thinking about his father.

"I have had a dream," he told his mother when he awoke on February 4. "I went to see Papa at Châlons and I asked dear Papa to come back quickly and he came back with me."

"You see how much he thinks about you, even when he is asleep," wrote Marie Louise, telling the story to her husband. "This love he bears you makes him dearer than ever to me.'

On the Tuileries floor the child, in imitation of the Emperor, "was capturing lots of Cossacks and Bashkirs . . . making prisoners and bringing back booty." He played at being a soldier "like Papa," wrote Marie Louise, "giving battle" and making "magnificent cavalry charges on his papier-mâché horse"—the horse on which he would have liked to install Mme. de Montesquiou, "imagining that this would give her immense pleasure." He was also in the habit of beating a drum his mother had given him, and once "nearly missed his dinner as a result." "I have never known a child reveal military predilections so early in life," sighed the Empress. "He takes greatly after you, but I do not think that he can ever be as perfect as you are."

At a time when her husband had the whole of Europe to contend with, was sleeping two or three hours a night, living on horseback in a temperature of eighteen degrees below freezing point, and eating when he had time, Marie Louise felt the need to acquaint him with all her minor ailments. In the course of the first three weeks of February she complained of sciatica in the right leg on the 2nd, of backache in the morning of the 6th and rheumatism in the evening, of "an illness lasting several days" which began on the 13th, of stomach-ache on the 9th and 14th, of migraine on the 12th, 15th and 21st, of a cold on the 19th and 20th, of a fever on the 20th, a cough on the 22nd. . . . And this by no means exhausted the catalogue of her ills. She was well aware that they were utterly insignificant—indeed, she admitted as much—but she complained about them to the Emperor for all that, without even realizing that she was doing so. "I never mention them to him," she declared in all sincerity, in one of the letters she wrote at this time to her favorite, Mme. de Montebello.

She also kept her father fully informed of the state of her health—for the correspondence between Francis and his daughter continued to pass through the outposts, in spite of the mobility of operations. On February 9 the Emperor of Austria replied:

> Your health, so you tell me, is still not satisfactory, and you are not feeling well. This causes me great concern, and I should very much like to contribute to your recovery, but I cannot see any way of doing so. The situation in France and especially in the occupied provinces is familiar to us; let it be enough for you to know that, for your husband and your child, you are the supreme

source of happiness; *in me you have a tried and trusted father and friend and I shall never distinguish between your fate and the fate of your dear ones;* but I am the only one to hold this view; not only can nobody share it, but all the others have cause to entertain diametrically opposed feelings. Things in this world have changed considerably, and I hope that you will never forget it. Only if we remember this fact can we hope to achieve a happy solution to our problems. . . .

If the Emperor of Austria, on that February 9, 1814, could envisage a "happy solution," the same could not be said for Paris. The fighting at La Rothière and Brienne had gone against the French, and Napoleon was retreating. The capital was beginning to panic, and Parisians were burying their bold and sending women and children into the country for safety. Madame Mère, so Marie Louise told her husband, was "dying from fright." People were spreading alarmist rumors. "For some days now," wrote Marie Louise on the evening of the 9th, "there has been a big crowd outside your son's windows, trying to see whether he is still here or not." The Parisians' fears were justified. That same day, King Joseph had received a letter from his brother ordering him to send his wife and son away if the Allies reached the outskirts of Paris.

In the midst of all this agitation, the little "imp" went on living the life of a child. "He is wonderfully healthy and happy, and as fresh as a rose. He plays and drills a lot. . . ."

Marie Louise wrote this on February 10. The same day the Emperor won the victory at Champaubert: "My dear Louise, *Victory!* I have destroyed twelve Russian regiments, taken six thousand prisoners, forty guns and two hundred ammunition wagons, captured the Commander-in-Chief and all his generals and lost fewer than two hundred men. Have the Invalides cannon fired and the news published in all the theaters."

The good news reached the Tuileries while Joseph, accompanied by the little King, was reviewing the grenadiers of the National Guard. The boy was wearing his uniform and his three-cornered hat, which he raised in a graceful salute, to be greeted by rousing cheers. The ceremony made him so excited that he could neither eat nor sleep afterward. The same day that Marie Louise sent these details to her husband, the Emperor won the victory of Montmirail. A sixty-gun salute gave the news to the people of Paris and the Tuileries witnessed another parade. Naturally enough little Napoleon attended this ceremony too, which made him "naughty all day." As Marie Louise explained to the Emperor, "when there is a parade no one can do anything with him, he goes to bed late, and he is bad-tempered with everybody for the rest of the day."

The Empress had threatened to write to his father, but the boy had retorted as all children do in such a case: "I don't care!"

"You can see from that," sighed Marie Louise, "what a very docile nature he has!"

He was dictatorial, stubborn and disobedient; he often said: "I want"; he stamped his foot. He behaved, in fact, like a thoroughly spoiled child, but that was scarcely surprising when everyone called him "Sire" or "Your Majesty." Poor Mme. de Montesquiou had a difficult task on her hands. One day, when the child was stamping and screaming with rage, she quietly gave instructions that the shutters facing the Carrousel were to be closed. Little Napoleon stopped short in surprise.

"I love you too much," explained Maman Quiou, "not to want to hide your anger from everybody else. What would they say, all the people you will probably rule over one day, if they could see you like this? Do you think they would want to obey you if they knew you were so naughty?"

The boy threw himself into his governess's arms.

"Do you think they heard me? Oh, I'm sorry, Maman Quiou, I won't do it again."

His good nature touched his governesses' hearts and they were extremely indulgent with him. When, at lunch, he knocked over his mother's water jug or her glass, everyone laughed. "When he hears someone whispering something, he wants to know what it is straight away, and he gets angry when he is not told. . . ." But no one thought of reprimanding him for his curiosity. It was as much as they could do to prevent him from eating everything he could see on the Empress's table. And after making an appalling din in his mother's dressing room and turning all her things upside down, he disarmed everyone by saying:

"I love Papa with all my heart."

It needed very little to forgive him. "He is becoming an awful imp," reported Marie Louise, "but he has a heart of gold. . . . He has been dreadfully stubborn all day, but we refused to give in to him, and now, after saying lots of stupid things, he has had to obey. This evening he has promised to be very good; the child really has a very good heart." All who saw him playing with Mme. de Montesquiou's granddaughter had tears in their eyes: "He is so funny when he tells the little girl: 'Dear Aline, I adore you' and then takes her into a corner to kiss her. I do believe he is passionately in love with her."

On the evening of the 19th he called her "my dear love." Every heart promptly melted, and his tantrums were forgotten. . . . Besides, he was not feeling well that day. It was just a slight fever, but the next day Corvisart was called in. He diagnosed a cold in the head and held the weather responsible: the thermometer was registering twelve degrees of frost. "He is still a little unwell this evening," wrote the Empress, "and did not want any dinner; but he is very cheerful and is playing happily with a set of prints of French and Russian soldiers, the kind they sell on the quays, which I gave him as a present. He has given Albert the enemy soldiers and kept the others for himself."

By the evening of the 22nd the cold was no better. Corvisart was sent for again and declared: "If he weren't a king, no one would take any notice of a cold like this."

For all that, Maman Quiou decided to wrap the child's head in a madras kerchief, of which he was not a little proud. He told everybody he met: "I'm a Colonel in the Lancers, and I was wounded in the head in my last battle."

On the 24th the Faculty discovered that the royal cold had "gone to his chest" and in accordance with the therapeutics of the time prescribed ipecacuanha syrup—"not to make him vomit, but to clear the phlegm." The next day he was afflicted with toothache—"but there is no cure for that," said his mother, "since it comes from a decayed tooth. Dubois talks of pulling it out, but we shall never be able to persuade him to agree to this operation, seeing that when we suggest just putting some cotton wool in the tooth he utters dreadful screams."

The toothache disappeared and the boy started going out again. However, for the parade held on the 27th, he was made to keep his bonnet on underneath his three-cornered hat and muttered angrily: "The little King doesn't want to look like a baby."

A baby who was incidentally something of an actor and who enjoyed seeing people panic over him. "Your son is in good health," Marie Louise told her husband the next day, "although he recently claimed to be suffering from toothache. We have discovered that very often he complains of feeling ill when there is nothing really wrong with him, but as soon as I told him that going out was bad for the teeth and we should have to deprive him of that pleasure, his toothache vanished all of a sudden, and there was no mention of it this evening."

As this correspondence shows, Marie Louise had become a true Frenchwoman, to the point of rejoicing over her husband's victories: "It is wonderful that you should retain the advantage day after day, and I am so pleased. We have now grown quite accustomed to your victories, but there remains one which I should like to see, and that is the victory you must win over Prince Schwarzenberg." Schwarzenberg, who was in command of Papa Francis's armies. . . . When he had heard of the first Prussian reverses—at Brienne and Saint-Dizier— Schwarzenberg had jeered at Blücher and Alexander, who in his opinion had drunk too much champagne and had "maneuvered like pigs." Now the Austrian commander had been driven back at Montereau and had had to withdraw as far as Troyes and Chaumont. But he would return.

The former Archduchess seemed to have entirely forgotten her native land. "Now it is the Austrians' turn," she wrote. "I hope they will be beaten like the others, and that you will force them to make peace quickly; they richly deserve to be punished. The item which pleases me the most in your letters is the assurance that you are well, and fortunately I find it in them all. Paris is delighted with the good news you have sent us; everyone looks more cheerful, and those who were badly frightened have become positively lion-hearted."

On the evening of the 19th, the Emperor received at Montereau a letter from the Empress together with her "comfit-box," which had been decorated with a portrait of the King of Rome by Isabey. The little King had abandoned his toys; he was shown kneeling in prayer, his hands folded together, his head bowed. Before setting off the next day, the Emperor dictated the following letter to Champagny, Intendant-General of the Crown: "The Empress has sent me a little portrait of the King of Rome saying his prayers which strikes me as extremely interesting. I want Denon to have it engraved with this caption: *I am praying for my father and for France.* If this can be done in forty-eight hours, it should have a good effect. . . ."

The engraving reached him at Arcis on the 27th. He was very pleased with it and wrote that he wished further copies to be made "in which the King of Rome should be dressed in the uniform of the National Guard."

Finally, on March 1, while he was in full pursuit of Blücher, he ordered a courier to be sent to Troyes "with this pretty present." To Troyes because the Emperor Francis was there and Napoleon apparently hoped that his heart would be touched by a picture of his grandson praying for his father. But the picture had no effect whatever —probably because the child was obviously also praying for the defeat of Papa Francis's troops. Nor was the Emperor of Austria moved by the arguments put forward by Caulaincourt at the Congress of Châtillon, which had opened without waiting for the cessation of hostilities. The Congress achieved nothing in the end. How indeed could Napoleon agree to abandon all the conquests of the Revolution? How could he even consider leaving nothing to his son but Louis XVI's inheritance? He persuaded his wife to write to Francis: "It is bad policy to try to force us to accept a shameful and dishonorable peace which could not possibly endure. Here everyone is ready to die rather than accept such conditions. Imagine my position, dear Papa, if there were a battle so terrible that I could not go on living afterward. I beg you therefore, dearest Papa, to think of me and my son."

But Marie Louise's father was not to be swayed:

> I hope that your husband will soon bring the war to an end. *Any peace which, reducing the power of France to limits in keeping with the strength of the other Great Powers, procures for your country that peace on the high seas which it has lacked for so long is honourable, useful and, therefore, acceptable.* . . . Consequently, if the Emperor wants peace, he must do what is necessary to obtain it. *The greatest service you can render your husband, your son and your present homeland is to support my views and my advice, which I offer in a genuinely friendly and even fatherly spirit.* I have been ruling now for twenty-two years and your husband will do me the justice of admitting that no one has ever spoken to him more frankly than I have, under all circumstances.

Marie Louise sent her husband a translation of these lines, but she made the mistake of also showing the letter to King Joseph. He thoroughly approved of the Emperor Francis's views. He too wanted

Napoleon to make peace at any price, even if it meant agreeing to the 1792 frontiers. Perhaps he tried the effect of his charm on the Empress, in an attempt to win her over to his point of view, for in a letter tinged with jealousy Napoleon wrote to his wife:

Everyone is turning against me; am I to be betrayed by the King as well? That would not surprise me, nor would I find it more than I could bear. The only thing which could shake me would be to discover that you had had relations with the King of which I was ignorant and that you were no longer what you used to be for me. Beware of the King; he has a bad reputation with women and a greed for power which first affected him in Spain. If you wish to please me instead of making me unhappy, show none of my letters, your father's letters or your replies to the King, and keep him at a distance. I have been informed that the King had conceived the senseless and culpable idea of persuading people to petition me for peace. If that were true, it would annoy me greatly, it would benefit no one, and it would damage the interests of France. Why do you not tell me of these things? Once again, safeguard your secrets and your person against the King, if you have my peace of mind and happiness at heart. All this makes me a little sad; I stood in need of comfort and consolation from those nearest to me; I am accustomed to their causing me nothing but annoyance, but for you to follow suit would be unexpected and unbearable for me.

Deeply moved by these, the first reproaches her husband had ever addressed to her, Marie Louise replied:

My dear love, I received your letter of the 12th last night at half-past twelve. I would have replied to it straight away had I not been suffering from a severe chill accompanied by a violent headache. Now that I feel better, I am writing to you at once to say that I was grieved to think that you could imagine that I trust the King more than you and that I should tell him things I kept from you. I hope you do not really believe that, for if you did it would make me dreadfully unhappy. Be sure on the contrary that I love you dearly, and that I should like to find a way to give you proof of my love. I am annoyed with myself for having mentioned my father's letter to the King: I translated some sentence or other for him in order to reassure him, as he had completely lost his head. . . .

All that mattered to her was her husband's love. On March 20, her son's birthday, her mind went back three years to that morning of March 20, 1811, when the Emperor had agreed to sacrifice his new-born child.

I thought about you today. It is three years since you gave me a touching proof of your love which I can never recall without being moved to tears, so it is an important day for me. I am sure you have thought a little about your son and me. He sends you a kiss; he is quite well, except that he still suffers from toothache from time to time—but that is due to decayed teeth which are bound to go on troubling him. He has been delightful all day long. He has made a few good resolutions, and says that now that he is three he is always going to be good. Everyone thinks him wonderfully good-looking and much stronger. He is very happy because I have given him lots of books and toys and his uncles and aunts have given him lots too. . . .

The day before, he had pestered his mother to tell him what his birthday presents were, and Marie Louise had finally given in.

"You can see that I am not very strong-willed," she explained to her husband. "And so I have decided to spoil him as much as I can for a few more years."

Napoleon celebrated his son's third birthday by recapturing Arcis-sur-Aube from Schwarzenberg's Austrians. Giving his wife news of this battle—the last victory of the campaign—Napoleon was unwise enough to reveal his plans: "I have decided to make for the Marne in order to push the enemy farther back from Paris and to get nearer to my fortresses." Reinforced by the French garrisons which had remained in Germany and which would have come to meet him, the Emperor would have attacked the enemy from the rear and cut his lines of communication. But unfortunately the courier was captured by the Cossacks. Blücher had the letter translated, forwarded a copy to Schwarzenberg and then, with scrupulous gallantry, sent the original to its addressee, with a bunch of flowers.

The Austrian general might well send Marie Louise a bouquet, for the captured letter told him all he wanted to know about Napoleon's plan of campaign. The Allies immediately decided to mass their forces at Châlons and move toward Saint-Dizier to attack the little French army. But in the meantime a letter from Savary to Napoleon was intercepted, begging the Emperor to return at once to Paris, where the royalists were busily plotting his overthrow. Alexander succeeded in persuading the Austrians and Prussians to abandon their pursuit of Napoleon and to march on the capital, which was defended only by Marmont and Mortier with their army corps and by the National Guard.

Paris guessed what the Allies were planning to do, and panic gripped the Tuileries. The "little imp" kept coming across groups of people talking in whispers, and his sleep suffered as a result. He cried and tossed about in his bed, and when he was asked to describe his nightmare the following morning he simply replied: "I dreamed about dear Papa. . . ."

He was pressed to say more, but in vain. "We were unable to get a word of explanation out of him."

That evening, while his little King was sobbing in his sleep, Napoleon was courting death on the battlefield of Arcis by "going to meet the enemy fire halfway."

The child heard nothing now but talk of mail being captured or held up . . . and for him everything was an excuse for a game. "He has been busy all day," wrote Marie Louise in the evening of March 24, "making believe that he was a courier and that he was bringing you news of your armies and bringing us letters from you. . . ."

On the 27th there was another parade—the last French review that Napoleon's son would ever see. It lasted three hours, much to the boy's delight. The news reaching Paris on the 28th was dramatic. The enemy had reached Claye and Meaux, and it was even said that the Cossacks had occupied Bondy. The day before, Marie Louise had urged Mme. de Montebello to send her children to the country. The Council met at the Tuileries, with Marie Louise in the chair. King Joseph was there, with Chancellor Cambacérès, Lacépède, the President of the Senate, Clarke, the Minister of War, Savary, the Minister of Police, Champagny and, inevitably, Talleyrand. What was to be done? Clarke proposed that the Empress and the King of Rome should leave the capital. Most of the members of the Council opposed the idea. It cannot be denied that if Marie Louise had been in Paris to throw herself into her father's arms, and to welcome the Tsar and the King of Prussia in her capacity as Regent, the restoration of the Bourbons would have been a difficult task. She would not have been a refugee—as she was to be a month later at Rambouillet—begging for help and protection for her son, but a "government" with which the Allies would have had to reckon and negotiate. The reign of Napoleon II would doubtless have been regarded as the only possible solution. On the other hand, could not the fight go on? If the capital were defended, every narrow street would become an obstacle, and it would take days of fighting to overcome them all. All that was needed in fact was a breathing space of a few hours, for as Napoleon was to say at the Cour de France, on the evening of March 30:

"If I had arrived four hours earlier, I could have saved the situation."

The majority of the Council—and even Talleyrand, who wanted to play the regency card—spoke in favor of remaining in Paris. Cambacérès on the other hand recommended leaving. A vote was taken: the Empress and the little King were to stay. It was then that Joseph stood up and read out a letter from Napoleon dated February 8:

If, as a result of circumstances which I cannot foresee at the moment, I fell back on the Loire, I should not allow the Empress and my son to move far away, because one or the other of them would undoubtedly be abducted and taken to Vienna. This would be all the more certain to happen if I were no longer alive. If I were to lose a battle and be killed, the news would reach you before my ministers. Send the Empress and the King of Rome to Rambouillet; order the Senate, the Council and all my troops to gather together on the Loire; leave the Prefect or an imperial commissioner or a mayor in Paris. . . . It is in the country's interest that the Empress and the King of Rome should not remain in Paris, because the country's interest is inseparable from their persons and I have never heard of any sovereign since the beginning of time allowing himself to be taken prisoner in an open city. If I remain alive, I must be obeyed, and I have no doubt that I will be obeyed; if I die, then the honor of the French people demands that my son as ruler and the Empress as regent avoid capture and withdraw to the last village with their last soldiers. . . . Once the Empress and the King of Rome were in Vienna or in enemy hands, you and all who continued to resist would be treated as rebels. As for my personal opinion, I would rather see my son's throat cut than see him brought up in Vienna as an Austrian prince; and I think highly enough of the Empress to feel sure that she shares my opinion, in so far as a mother and a woman can. . . . I have never seen a performance of *Andromaque* without pitying the fate of Astyanax outliving the rest of his house and without thinking that it would be better for him not to survive his father.

There was a dramatic silence. Then Savary and Champagny begged Marie Louise to take no notice and to remain at the Tuileries, pointing out that the letter was seven weeks old. But Joseph stood up again and, like an evil spirit, took another letter from Napoleon out of his pocket. He had received it on March 16.

In conformity with the verbal instructions I have given you and the spirit of all my letters, you must under no circumstances allow the Empress and the King of Rome to fall into the enemy's hands. I am going to maneuver my troops in such a way that you may be without news of me for several days. If the enemy advances on Paris in such strength as to render all resistance impossible, send the Regent, my son, the grand dignitaries, the ministers, the grand officers of the Crown, the Baron de la Bouillerie and the Treasury in the direction of the Loire. Do not leave my son and remember that I would rather he were in the Seine than in the hands of France's enemies. The fate of Astyanax as a prisoner of the Greeks has always seemed to me to be the unhappiest fate in history.

The master had spoken; they could only obey. As a matter of form another vote was taken. The Empress and "Astyanax" were to leave, but part of the government was to remain in Paris. This was madness. If the Regent and the little King were to go, everyone should have gone. The Council were making sure that they suffered all the disadvantages of their decision while depriving themselves of the advantages.

At midnight, as Talleyrand was getting into his carriage to return to his house in the rue Saint-Florentin, he remarked: "So that's the end of that. They had a good hand and they threw it away."

At the same time Marie Louise was writing to her husband:

The Council is only just over: it is after half-past twelve. After lengthy discussion it was finally decided that I should leave, and that tomorrow morning at the latest. . . . I must confess that I am entirely against this idea; I am sure that it will have a dreadful

effect on the people of Paris, depriving them of the will to resist
which they would otherwise have had. The National Guard will
do nothing whatever, and when you arrive to rescue us you will
find the capital in the enemy's hands. But you told me that I
should follow the Chancellor's advice, and I shall do so on this
occasion because I do not want to expose my son to danger.

During the night Marmont sent the following note from his forward positions:

The enemy is gaining ground; we may be surrounded this evening.

At dawn, ten big green berlins were standing in the Cour du Carrousel. But no one was prepared to give the order to go, the order to
ring down the curtain on this play which had lasted ten long years.
Everyone knew that once they had crossed the threshold of the Tuileries they would be nothing more than fugitives. Marie Louise hoped
that something would happen to avert the irreparable. Early in the
morning, after a sleepless night, she took up her pen again:

God's will be done, but I am sure that you will not be pleased,
for this will utterly unman the National Guard and tomorrow the
enemy will be in Paris. It is said that he has made no progress
during the night, but that he has sent out guerrillas in the direction of Rambouillet; apparently it is considered better to be
captured by the Cossacks than to remain quietly in Paris! But
everyone has lost his head except myself, and I hope that in a few
days you will tell me that I was right not to want to leave the
capital for fear of fifteen thousand cavalrymen who could never
have made their way through the streets. I am extremely vexed at
the idea of leaving, for this will cause you immense inconvenience,
but they have pointed out to me that my son is in danger, and I
did not dare oppose them after seeing the letter you wrote to the
King. So I entrust myself to Providence, convinced that no good
will come of this.

She had already put on a hat for the journey when she received a
deputation from the National Guard who begged her to remain in
Paris with the little King. The weak young woman threw herself into
an armchair and burst into tears:

"Dear God, let them decide, let them put an end to this agony!"

At ten o'clock, at the earnest entreaty of Clarke, who was afraid of seeing a band of Cossacks arrive at any moment, the order was finally given, but then little Napoleon refused to leave his apartments. Marie Louise was summoned to the rescue. The child was in tears, clinging to a chair and crying: "Let's not go to Rambouillet, it's a horrible château; let's stay here. I don't want to leave home."

The scene dragged on. At first they tried reasoning with him.

"I don't want to go away," he replied. "And since Papa isn't here, I'm the master."

In the end it was decided to use force. Canisy picked the boy up, but the little imp—as Marie Louise told the Emperor the same day—"hung on to the doors and chairs, sobbing all the time."

Finally the boy was put into his mother's carriage. "The poor little thing was quite touching," she told her husband; "he was twice as affectionate with me as usual." "Three or four score onlookers," writes Méneval, "watched this melancholy procession in a gloomy silence, much as one would watch a funeral procession; and indeed, what they were witnessing was nothing less than the funeral of the Empire. They gave no outward sign of their feelings; not a single voice was raised to mark with some expression of regret the bitterness of this cruel separation. If anyone had felt inspired to cut the horses' traces, the Empress would not have left. She passed through the gateway leading out of the Tuileries courtyard with tears in her eyes and death in her heart."

The King of Rome was followed by Mme. de Montesquiou and Mmes. de Boubers and de Mesgrigny, his equerry, M. de Canisy, and his personal physician, Dr. Auvity. His pages occupied a huge "gondola" drawn by eight horses. Then came the coronation coaches covered with canvas. Inside, thrown haphazardly onto the white satin cushions, could be seen the spare saddles and harness. Finally, bringing up the rear and rolling noisily over the cobblestones, came the wagons containing the crown jewels, the coronation robes, the imperial sword, the plate, the silver-gilt table service . . . and the Treasury: thirty-two little barrels of gold.

Of the whole gigantic State stretching from Hamburg to Naples and from Warsaw to Brest, nothing remained but this gilded travesty of an epic.

When they carried off the little King by force, on that rainy morning of March 29, 1814, they robbed him of his Empire.

"I want my soldiers," said the Eaglet, when he arrived at Rambouillet, "so that they can fight the Russians."

Shortly before ten o'clock, Marie Louise received news from Paris. King Joseph advised her to leave Rambouillet as soon as possible and make for the Loire. For the first time since the Hundred Years' War, Paris was on the point of falling to the enemy. The Queen of Westphalia and Madame Letizia had now joined the Regent; the next morning would see the arrival of King Louis. "He was so frightened," reported Marie Louise, "that he wanted us all to take refuge in a fortress. I opposed the idea. He has lost his head so completely that he is quite embarrassing."

The next morning the little King "made as much fuss about leaving Rambouillet as he had about leaving Paris." The cumbersome procession moved off. At Maintenon, where they stopped for the "imp" to have a drink of milk, a letter from the Emperor was delivered to Marie Louise, dated the 28th but written in fact on the 29th. He was at Bar-sur-Aube and making posthaste for Paris. "I shall soon be with you. . . ."

At the Prefecture of Chartres the child's sorrows were forgotten: "He is happier this evening and amusing himself as best he can without any toys." King Joseph and King Jerome, who had left Paris at about five in the afternoon, arrived during the night. It was not Napoleon's wife, the Regent of the Empire, that they had come to join, but their sister-in-law, the victor's daughter, who might be able to protect them.

That same night—about ten or eleven o'clock—Napoleon passed through Juvisy and arrived at the Cour de France, only to learn that Paris had capitulated.

"They can't do anything right when I'm not there!" he exclaimed as he strode angrily up and down the road. "They didn't use the National Guard, who, given a little encouragement, would have defended the fortified points well enough while the troops disputed the approaches. They had more than they needed to hold out for forty-eight hours at least and give the army time to arrive. They had over two hundred guns and provisions for a month—ten times more than they needed to hold the city, if only they had shown a little energy. Joseph lost me Spain and now he has lost me Paris. And the loss of Paris means the loss of France."

Above all, the loss of Paris meant the loss of Napoleon II's empire —the only thing which could still be salvaged from the wreck. For Napoleon himself it was all over, but he was the only one who did not appear to realize this.

"I am getting my army together near Fontainebleau," he wrote to Marie Louise. "I suffer at the thought of what you must be suffering."

His letter reached Marie Louise at three in the morning of April 1, in a wretched inn—the Hôtel de la Poste—at Châteaudun. "Fortunately your son had a good room: that was all that mattered to me. He is in the best of health and is crying at the moment for some toys to play with. Heaven knows when I shall be able to give him some!" The hapless Court spent the night camping in torrential rain. In the morning the rain stopped and passers-by could see Marie Louise and her son walking about in the hotel garden. The child was throwing pebbles into the little river Loir.

The halt at Vendôme was more agreeable. The little King and his mother spent the night in the Marquise de Soisy's house, now the subprefecture. The Emperor was directing the retreat from Fontainebleau, and the Empress was instructed to make for Blois instead of Tours, as had been originally decided. At ten in the morning the heavy coronation coaches lumbered off, with the people of Vendôme gaping in astonishment at the silver-plated wheel hubs.

It is only twenty miles from Vendôme to Blois, but the journey took no less than nine hours. "The road had not been finished," writes one of the Empress's ladies-in-waiting. "Most of the carriages, especially those which were most heavily laden, sank into the mud. It needed the combined strength of all the horses to pull some of them out." A spring broke under the imperial carriage. And finally, as a last straw, the convoy took the wrong road, found itself at Oucques, on the road to Orléans, and had to turn back. By this time it was no longer a procession but a rout. Marie Louise was visited by girlhood memories of the Austrian court fleeing from the French. Now it was Austrian troops from whom she was running away.

The Château de Blois was full of English prisoners and wounded, so since Saturday morning the Prefect, Baron Christian, had been getting the former bishopric and present prefecture ready for the imperial party. It was seven in the evening when a courier announced that the procession was approaching. A crowd gathered in the square. Night was falling when a great rumbling of carriages was heard, and soon the first coach drew up in front of the prefecture. Amédée Thierry, who had come to watch with his father, wrote later:

> A head poked out of the window. I just had time to see a face lined with fatigue and a tousled mop of fair hair underneath the hood of a gray cloak.
> "Her Majesty the Empress," said my father, taking off his hat.
> It was already too dark and we were too far away to see what followed. In the light of the lanterns we could make out a few shadowy figures, one of which was carrying a child in its arms. There were two or three timid shouts of "Long live the Emperor!" Christian, whom we could recognize by his glittering uniform, came out onto the steps. He obviously intended to make a speech, but he was robbed of the opportunity of doing so, because the new arrivals disappeared inside the prefecture and the doors were promptly closed behind them.

"So Napoleon's done for at last," said a voice in the dark. "The nightmare is over!"

Before going to bed, at ten in the evening of April 2, Marie Louise wrote to the Emperor: "Your son sends you his love. He has stood the journey wonderfully well and is full of gaiety. He is at a happy age and I often envy him. He is a delightful traveling companion and not at all troublesome; indeed, he is so sweet and lovable that even people who do not know him very well are drawn to him."

The Court settled down as best it could. The presence of "all these princesses and kings" created "appalling congestion." Yet there was a return to the Tuileries routine, and the next day, April 3, a banquet was held at the "palace." "Today at five o'clock I received the local authorities," wrote Marie Louise, "and as they had asked to see your son, I took him with me. They thought him the loveliest child they had ever seen; he had just woken up, so that he had a magnificent color. He is in the best of health and has been taking the air all day on a terrace adjoining his rooms; this has done him a great deal of good."

She begged her husband to write to her as often as he could:

> I need to have news of you regularly to sustain my courage, which is at times in danger of deserting me; it is true that ours

is not a happy situation, and as I love you more than anyone else I am deeply concerned about you. But I do not want to talk to you about such melancholy matters, as I know that it must distress you and you have no need of additional vexation. I conclude therefore by assuring you that there is no one in the world who loves you as much as

Your faithful and affectionate Louise

On July 19, 1821, learning of Napoleon's death, she was to write to her childhood friend Mme. de Créneville: "I have never experienced any kind of strong feeling for him. . . ."

6

✣

The Prince of Parma

IT WAS IN PARIS that the King of Rome's fate was to be decided. The proclamation issued by Schwarzenberg before the Allies entered the capital was directed solely against the Emperor: his son could therefore come to the throne. In the afternoon of April 2, the Tsar Alexander made this clear to Napoleon's envoy Caulaincourt. If the Emperor were "far away and could neither wield influence nor create anxiety in Europe," then the candidature of the King of Rome would meet no opposition. The Allies stated positively that they had no intention whatever of imposing on France "either a government or a sovereign she had not chosen herself."

Napoleon had little or no faith in this solution. The only possible choice, in his opinion, lay between himself and the Bourbons.

I am not going to cling to the throne [he told Caulaincourt]. Born a soldier, I can become an ordinary citizen again without complaining. My happiness does not lie in pomp and grandeur. I wanted France to be great and powerful; I want her to be happy above all else. I would rather abandon the throne than sign a shameful peace. I am glad that they would not accept your conditions, for I should have been obliged to agree to them, and both France and History would have reproached me with this act of weakness. Only the Bourbons would be pleased with a peace dictated by the Cossacks. Talleyrand is right: they are the only ones who can accept the humiliation being inflicted on France today, for they have nothing to lose. They find the country just as they left it. . . . The Austrians are the same as ever: cowardly and contemptible. When I was a conqueror they came and begged me to marry an archduchess, telling Narbonne and Berthier that it was the Emperor's favorite daughter, the apple of his eye, that they were offering me. And now that she is in trouble, they leave her in the lurch.

However, remembering his father-in-law's religious sentiments, he still hoped that "Papa Francis" would shrink from turning his daughter and his grandson off the throne. Surely, he thought, the Austrian Emperor would be able to stand up to Metternich, who, as he was well aware, wanted to bring about his downfall. After all, an archduchess as Regent of France could be considered a triumph for Vienna. The poor wretch clung pathetically to this idea as night fell over the château.

Shortly before noon the next day, in the Cour du Cheval Blanc, he reviewed the Friant Division of the Old Guard and the Henrion Division of the New Guard which had arrived at Fontainebleau the day before. The Emperor's voice rang out loud and clear, echoing from one end of the vast courtyard to the other:

"Soldiers, the enemy has taken possession of Paris. We must turn him out. Unworthy Frenchmen, *émigrés* whom we had pardoned, have donned the white cockade and joined our enemies. The cowards will pay for this fresh outrage. . . . Let us swear to conquer or die; let us swear to enforce respect for this tricolor cockade which, for the past twenty years, has accompanied us along the road to honor and glory!"

A great shout went up: "Long live the Emperor! To Paris! To Paris!"

This scene was repeated the next day, after the ceremony of the changing of the guard. But the Marshals of France, who had welcomed defeat with a certain satisfaction, were about to come on to the scene. They were not yet thinking of the Bourbons. In their opinion, the accession of the King of Rome seemed the only way of saving the Empire and their own emoluments, since the Senate had just voted for the deposition of Napoleon.

Legend has it that Ney and the defeated Marshals strode like conquerors into their master's study and demanded his abdication. But according to Napoleon's description of the scene to Caulaincourt, they maintained a dignified and respectful attitude:

"They said nothing, but I could see that they were in favor of abdication. They think it just means substituting one man for another.
The fools don't see that their salvation and the salvation of France
lies in me, that what they have been offered is just bait to catch them,
that my son cannot guarantee anything, and that he is being used in
a treasonable plot to ruin the country. The first step is to strip the
father of all his power. . . ."

However, "dignified and respectful" though they might have been,
the Marshals had made it clear to the Emperor that if he went on
fighting it should only be to impose the King of Rome on the Allies.
Napoleon bowed to their arguments.

"Leave for Paris immediately," he told Caulaincourt. "You know my
plans. If I win, we shall have an honorable peace. . . . But if I lose
the battle, poor France will be humbled and humiliated. As for myself, I repeat that I want nothing."

But after a short silence he added reflectively: "Will they accept
my son?"

They would pretend to accept the son of course, but only in order
to get rid of the father more easily: Napoleon had no illusions on this
score. So it was without much hope for the future that he handed
over to Caulaincourt, Ney and Macdonald the document to which he
had just put his signature—his conditional abdication:

> The foreign Powers having declared that the Emperor Na-
> poleon was an obstacle to the re-establishment of peace and the
> restoration of the integrity of the French territory, faithful to his
> principles and to his oaths to do everything in his power for the
> happiness and glory of the French people, the Emperor Napoleon
> declares that he is prepared to abdicate in favor of his son and to
> deliver the act of abdication in due and proper form in a message
> to the Senate as soon as Napoleon II is recognized by the Powers,
> likewise the constitutional regency of the Empress. On this con-
> dition the Emperor will immediately retire to whatever place shall
> have been agreed upon.
>
> Given at our Palace of Fontainebleau, April 4, 1814.
>
> *Signed:* NAPOLEON

The Master of the Horse and the two Marshals set off for Paris
while the Guard and the Emperor's little army—sheltered by Marmont's

army corps, which was keeping watch between Fontainebleau and Paris—got ready to fight for Napoleon II. On the way, the three men stopped at the headquarters of Marshal Marmont, Duke of Ragusa, whose corps still numbered twelve thousand men, and informed him of the decision which Napoleon had just made.

"The Emperor abdicating?" exclaimed General Bordesoulle, who was in command of Marmont's cavalry. "Well, Marshal, that saves us a lot of trouble!"

Ney, Macdonald and Caulaincourt pricked up their ears. What did Bordesoulle mean by that? Marmont was obliged to explain that the day before, April 3, he had been studying the *Kaiserlichs'* outposts through a spyglass, from a window in a house in Essonnes, when he had been told of the arrival of "a Russian emissary" from Chevilly, bearing this letter from Prince von Schwarzenberg:

> I have the honor of sending Your Excellency, through a trust-worthy intermediary, all the official papers and documents required to acquaint Your Excellency with the events which have taken place since you left the capital, as well as an invitation from the members of the provisional government to embrace the true cause of France. I urge you, in the name of your country and of humanity as a whole, to give your sympathetic attention to these proposals, which are intended to put an end to the shedding of the precious blood of the brave men under your command.

The "Russian emissary" was in fact a former aide-de-camp of Marmont's—Charles de Montessuy—disguised as a Cossack down to the knout he carried in his hand. Among the other documents he had brought for his old commander was the proclamation to the army issued by the provisional government which the Senate had set up on April 1: "You are no longer the soldiers of Napoleon. The Senate and France as a whole release you from your oaths."

Instead of informing the Emperor, Marmont, this same morning of April 4, had replied to Schwarzenberg that he "was prepared to leave the Emperor Napoleon's army, together with all his troops," on condition that he was allowed to retire to Normandy and that suitable provision was made for the Emperor "in a circumscribed locality." Once the letter had been sent off, he called his generals together in order to settle the details of this wholesale desertion. Souham, the senior divisional commander, had welcomed the idea; the others, as Marmont readily admitted, had accepted it more or less unwillingly. The most violent opposition had come from Bordesoulle, who had accused the Marshal of throwing open the road to Fontainebleau and leaving the Emperor to the enemy's mercy. But as he confessed to the Emperor's envoys, Marmont had stood by his decision: the defection was to take place that very evening.

"Have you signed anything?" asked the dumfounded Caulaincourt.

"Not yet . . ."

"Then you can come with us! On our way through Chevilly you can tell Schwarzenberg that you are breaking off negotiations."

Marmont agreed and, before setting off, handed over command of the 6th Corps to General Souham, forbidding him to carry out any troop movements during his absence but adding: "As soon as I have gone, you will muster the troops and inform them of the Emperor's abdication."

He took care not to specify that the abdication was conditional and in favor of Napoleon II. In any event, Napoleon's decision was supposed to be kept secret until the Allies had accepted his conditions.

In Paris the negotiations at Talleyrand's house seemed to begin well. The first question the Tsar asked the four plenipotentiaries was whether the Emperor had agreed to abdicate.

"Yes, Sire, in favor of his son."

Alexander listened carefully to what they had to say, "discussed everything, only raising objections about matters of small importance," and finally declared: "I'm no supporter of the Bourbons. I don't know them. I shall lay your proposals before my allies and give them my support. I too am in a hurry to make an end of it all."

He then dismissed the three emissaries, asking them to return at noon the next day.

"By then I shall have had time to consult the King of Prussia and the allied ministers."

In the evening of the 4th—in spite of Talleyrand's intrigues and in spite of the attitude of the imperial authorities who had suddenly turned ultra-royalist—the odds on Napoleon II improved slightly. Lunching together at Ney's house at half-past eleven the following morning, the Emperor's plenipotentiaries did not shut their eyes to the difficulties which faced them, and yet remained hopeful of success. Just as Caulaincourt and the three Marshals were getting ready to go and keep their appointment with the Tsar, an officer arrived and asked to speak to the Duke of Ragusa. The Marshal went out and came back a few moments later, "white-faced and scarcely able to speak": Marmont's army corps, under General Souham's orders, had crossed the Austrian lines during the night and gone over to the enemy.

"I am utterly dishonored. Souham has disobeyed orders, betrayed his trust: he has gone over with the whole 6th Corps. . . . I would give my right arm to undo what has happened."

"Why not your head?" shouted Ney. "It wouldn't be too much."

What had happened was that in the Marshal's absence Souham had opened a letter from Headquarters addressed to Marmont which stated that "it is the Emperor's wish that you should present yourself at the Palace of Fontainebleau at ten o'clock this evening." A few minutes later Gourgaud had arrived to confirm the order, whereupon Souham and the other generals had fallen into a panic. In fact Napoleon knew nothing of their plans and had simply summoned *all* his corps commanders to Fontainebleau. But Marmont's divisional commanders had assumed that the Emperor had been told of their intended desertion.

"The Marshal has taken flight!" Souham had exclaimed. "I'm taller than he is by a head, and I've no desire to be shortened!"

If they were to escape the Emperor's wrath, they would have to go over to the enemy. Even Bordesoulle had admitted this to be true. And at dawn the whole 6th Corps had defected, passing between two lines of enemy troops at the present.

The road to Fontainebleau was open, and henceforth Napoleon could no longer lay down conditions.

Marmont was livid with rage.

"What a disgrace! All is lost! I am going to join my troops to try and undo the damage. . . ."

Later Marmont would regard the incident in a less tragic light and accept readily enough the congratulations that would be addressed to him, but at the time he seemed to be genuinely anxious to repair the irreparable. Alas, it was too late. The damage had been done, and could not be undone.

Ney, Macdonald and Caulaincourt kept their appointment for all that, though with death in their hearts. The Tsar appeared to know nothing as yet of what had happened.

"Let me tell you again that the allied sovereigns have no desire to impose a government on France which she would find unsuitable. Yet various senators and men of note who have had nothing to do with recent events regard the restoration of the Bourbons as the most sensible solution, the one which would reconcile all points of view."

"Sire," replied Caulaincourt, "the Emperor has only abdicated in favor of his son. France and the army will never renounce the imperial dynasty, which is a far surer guarantee of every interest!"

An argument developed and once again Caulaincourt had the impression that, having brought down the Eagle, the Tsar, who had no love for the Bourbons, was prepared to agree to the Eaglet's candidature. But suddenly the door opened and an aide-de-camp came in to announce the arrival of an officer sent by the Commander-in-Chief.

"What does he want?" asked Alexander.

"To tell you, Sire, that the Duke of Ragusa's army corps came over to our side this morning."

The aide-de-camp had spoken in Russian, but Caulaincourt, who had been French ambassador to St. Petersburg, had understood.

"Bad news," he whispered to Macdonald, as the Tsar went across to the aide-de-camp. "We are lost: he knows everything!"

All was lost in fact. The Tsar promptly informed the plenipotentiaries that the Allies refused to negotiate "either with the Emperor or with any member of his family." All that was left to Napoleon was unconditional abdication. Marmont's treachery had destroyed the last chance that remained to the King of Rome, that April 5, 1814, of mounting the French throne. As Caulaincourt wrote to the Emperor the same day: "In a word, the sovereigns of Europe, in their implacable hatred of Your Majesty, are taking advantage of the treachery of a few Frenchmen to exclude the son from power just as they have already sought to exclude the father, and it must be admitted that this coalition policy is also Austrian policy."

The next day, April 6, the senators—officials appointed by the Emperor—declared "Napoleon Bonaparte to have forfeited the throne." Then the senators joined the deputies in "freely summoning to the throne Louis Stanislas Xavier of France, brother of the last King." The *Moniteur* of the same day published letters from the Generals adhering to King Louis XVIII. Napoleon noted the signatures of Jourdan, Augereau, Maison, Kellermann, Lagrange, Oudinot, Latour-Maubourg, Milhaud, Belliard. . . .

Caulaincourt, who was back at Fontainebleau, heard him heave a sigh.

"I find it humiliating to see men I have raised so high sink so low. . . . What must the allied sovereigns think of all the notabilities of my reign? I take anything that injures the reputation of France as a personal affront, I have grown so accustomed to identifying myself with my country."

Around the defeated master everything was collapsing: his marshals, his generals, even his servants were taking flight and galloping toward Paris. That evening—for the third time—Caulaincourt set off for the capital. His mission this time? To wind up the Empire's affairs. To obtain settlements and indemnities. To beg for the island of Elba for the man who had held sway over all Europe. To ask if Tuscany might be given to his wife and son.

"One other thing," Napoleon had said. "Have them send some Austrian and Russian generals, or even an Englishman, to watch over the Empress and ensure her safety. See to it that they have orders to place themselves at her disposal, to follow her and protect her, and to enforce respect for her and also for her Court and her baggage if she comes to join me. Inform the Empress when they have agreed to do this. And tell Schwarzenberg that it is disgraceful that the Austrians should show so little concern for their Emperor's own flesh and blood."

In this palace in which he had received the Pope and six kings, Napoleon wandered about like a lost soul, suffering from "the most appalling melancholy" and saying nothing. He fell, says his valet, into "a kind of stupor, to the extent of seeing nothing that was happening around him." If anyone spoke to him, he made no reply. What is more, "nothing in his face, which I studied attentively," Constant tells us, "led me to suppose that he had heard me."

The attitude he was to adopt toward Marie Louise and his son was just as passive. On April 7, sending a commonplace letter to Blois, he did not dare to tell the Empress of his unconditional abdication.

The same day—and not the 9th, as previous historians have always stated—the Emperor Francis wrote to his daughter:

All that I can say to you is that whatever happens I shall always be a father to you, to your child, and consequently to your husband as well, since he has made you happy. *If you and yours are looking for a refuge you will find it with me.* I cannot say more than that; as regards the other wish concerning your son, it is natural for a mother to expect help in its fulfillment, but I doubt if it will be possible for me to give much help, since I have certain obligations toward my allies.

Had Marie Louise already written to her father asking him to save the Empire for her son? We cannot tell. In any event, this same April 7, the Empress was still unaware of the magnitude of the disaster, for those around her had entered into a conspiracy of silence. She had only one desire, and that was to join her husband. She declared that she would feel "braver and calmer" if she could be at his side, sharing his fate and comforting him in his misfortune. She even hoped that she might be useful to him "in some way or other."

It cannot be denied that if he had summoned his wife and son to Fontainebleau, the Emperor would have remained a power to reckon with. Already, if the King of Rome and his mother had been at his side on April 2, it would have been infinitely easier to bring about the accession of Napoleon II. Caulaincourt's hand would have been immeasurably strengthened by the presence at Fontainebleau of the Empress and her son, and he would certainly have been able to obtain Tuscany for his master's wife. But it appeared that Napoleon wanted to leave the decision entirely to Marie Louise. He would not prevent her from coming to join him at Fontainebleau, but on the other hand he would not order her to come. This was leaving a clear field to Austria—and to Mme. de Montebello.

It was also playing with fire. If Marie Louise decided to go and see her father, there was a danger that the malleable archduchess would fall once more under the influence of her environment, since for years she had regarded the Emperor Francis as the paterfamilias whose decisions no one would think of questioning. Napoleon was well aware that his wife was made of wax. He knew that the Austrian ruler would be able to do what he wanted—or rather, what Metternich wanted—with his daughter. As for the King of Rome, his fate in that case could only be the fate of Astyanax. Why then did he throw away what at the time was his trump card: his position as the Emperor of Austria's son-in-law? Perhaps the explanation of his attitude is to be found in a report written by the Prussian General Walburg-Truchsess, one of the allied commissioners who accompanied the fallen Emperor, a fortnight later, to the Isle of Elba. According to Walburg-Truchsess, Napoleon was suffering from a "gallant malady" for which he doctored himself under the very eyes of his "enforced companions." Questioned about this, the Emperor's physician had replied that his imperial patient had contracted the disease in Paris the previous winter. And a "gallant malady" was a treasonable offense which the archduchess would certainly not have forgiven, despite—or because of—the violent and exclusive passion which she still felt, even now, for her "naughty love."

Personally, I find it hard to accept this explanation. It does, however, throw light on the events of the next five days.

Whatever the truth of the matter, Napoleon could no longer conceal his present situation from Marie Louise. On the 8th he sent Colonel de Galbois to her with a letter announcing an "amenistice" and the imminent arrival at Blois of one of the Tsar's aides-de-camp, who had instructions to escort Marie Louise to Fontainebleau. He then appears to have taken fright at the idea that the Empress might take him at his word, for he added: "But I sent word that you were to stop at Orléans, as I am on the point of leaving. I am only waiting for Caulaincourt to finish arranging matters with the Allies." He told his wife that he was to be given sovereignty over the Isle of Elba and that he had hoped to obtain Tuscany for her and their son, "since that would have enabled you to spend as much time with me as you wished and to live in a pleasant country likely to prove beneficial to your health. But Schwarzenberg, acting on your father's behalf, refused. It seems that your father is our worst enemy. I do not know what has been decided. It vexes me to have nothing left to offer you but a share in my misfortune. I would have taken my life if I had not thought that to do so would only add to your unhappiness."

Marie Louise's eyes filled with tears. She found it hard to believe that she was no longer Empress and that her father could behave so cruelly. Poor Marie Louise! Her troubles were only just beginning. . . .

Colonel de Galbois then showed her the document which Napoleon had signed two days before: "The allied powers having declared that the Emperor Napoleon was the only obstacle to the restoration of peace in Europe, the Emperor Napoleon, faithful to his oath, declares that he renounces the thrones of France and Italy for himself and his heirs, and that there is no sacrifice, even that of life, which he is not prepared to make in the interests of France."

"But this is impossible!" she exclaimed. "Impossible! My father would never allow this to happen, for when he placed me on the French throne he repeated to me twenty times that he would always maintain me on it, and my father is a man of his word."

She wanted to go to Fontainebleau straight away with her son. Their place, she said, was at the Emperor's side.

"I want to go to him now! I shall be happy anywhere, provided I am with him!"

She secretly ordered a carriage in which she intended to slip away with her son and Colonel de Galbois. It was at this point that Mme. de Montebello intervened. Hearing of the Empress's decision, this woman who owed everything to the Emperor chose to play the Bourbons' game. Urging the Empress to wait for the Tsar's aide-de-camp, with whom she could travel in safety, and reminding her that she was responsible for her son's life, she succeeded in postponing her mistress's departure. She had gained a breathing space, but there was no time to lose. Shuddering at the idea of having to go into exile, Lannes's widow sent M. de Champagny off to see Schwarzenberg and warn the Austrians of what was afoot.

The morning of April 8—Good Friday, 1814—witnessed Marie Louise's greatest tribulation. She had only just agreed to wait for the arrival of the Russian officer mentioned by Napoleon when King Joseph and his brother Jerome came on the scene. But here it would be best to allow Marie Louise to speak for herself, since we now know, thanks to her, exactly what happened in this fearful scene. Better than any commentary, the Empress's stumbling words and staccato phrases reveal the anguish and distress she felt as she wrote to her husband:

> The King came to see me and urged me to throw myself into the arms of the first Austrian corps I met. He said that they would come with me, that that was their only hope, that the Emperor of Austria would provide for them, and that I ought not to consult you when there was no time to lose and you might not approve of such a step. I replied that I considered that it would be an act of treachery on my part, that as long as there was breath in my body I would keep faith with you, that in any event I could not be certain that the Austrian Corps from Lyons had not been won over by the Russians, and that I had no desire to throw myself on their mercy. He said that those were poor arguments, and the King of Westphalia said that they would force me to go. So I agreed to go to Rambouillet, fully determined to go no farther. But just as he was about to give orders for our departure, the

*Empress Marie Louise
by Gérard*

Birth of King of Rome
by J.-B. Isabey

*Sergeant Coignet carrying the
King of Rome
after the painting by J. Le Blant*

Culver Service

*The King of Rome
after a painting by Gérard*

Bettmann Archive

Marie Louise and the King of Rome
by Gérard

The Emperor and the King
after a painting by Steuben

Comtesse de Montesquiou
by J. Lebrun

Prince Metternich
after a painting by Lawrence

Francis I, Emperor of Austria
after a painting by Kupelwieser

Schönbrunn

officers of the Guard came into the courtyard and declared that they would not allow me to be taken away, that they were ready to let themselves be cut to pieces for you, your son and myself— that they knew that your brothers wanted to take me to the Austrians and that they would not agree to this unless it was on your orders or mine, and that if your brothers were afraid, then they only had to take themselves off; they said too that they would rather die than abandon your son. We calmed them down and they went away extremely pleased with what they had accomplished. I then told the King that I would not go, that everyone agreed with me and that I would await your orders; this made them very angry, but I do not care; I am above that sort of thing. I therefore await your orders and beg you to send for me.

The writing of these lines had done nothing to allay the feverish agitation which had taken hold of her. For the first time she thought of taking refuge with her father in the event of Czernicheff and his Cossacks arriving at Blois and preventing her from traveling to Fontainebleau. In the same mood of hysterical anxiety she wrote to the Emperor Francis asking for asylum in Austria for herself and her son. "All that I want is to be able to live quietly and bring up my son somewhere, no matter where, in your States. Heaven knows that I shall warn him never to entertain any ambition."

Was she already thinking of leaving her husband? Possibly she was, but after these few hours of depression she would be just as sincere in the course of the following days when she swore that there was only one thing she wanted—to join Napoleon. That same April 8 saw the arrival at Blois of Count Shuvalov, the Russian aide-de-camp who was to accompany Marie Louise to Fontainebleau the next day. The appearance of the Russian general—who was accompanied by M. de Saint-Aignan, a commissioner of the provisional government—was taken by the ministers and leading members of the imperial court as the signal for departure. There was a headlong rush to the town hall to obtain passports which were then taken to Count Shuvalov to be endorsed.

Meanwhile the Empress sent for Bausset.

"Monsieur de Bausset, are you willing to perform yet another service for me?"

"Command, Madame, and you may depend on me to obey."

"In that case, you are to leave for Paris this evening. You will no doubt find my father the Emperor there and you will hand to him a letter I am about to write. You will then go to Fontainebleau with another letter for the Emperor Napoleon. I for my part hope to go there too, for it is my duty and my desire to be near him. Go and make the necessary arrangements and come back for my dispatches at eight o'clock this evening."

She then wrote to her husband and her father. To the former she announced her departure for Orléans, the first stopping place on the road to Fontainebleau. As for Francis, he was asked to intercede with the Allies on her behalf.

"I am not asking you to intercede for him—for Napoleon," she explained, "but for me and my son, and especially for the latter. I am convinced that you do not want the Isle of Elba to be his sole inheritance. I am convinced that you will stand up for his rights and make better provision for him than that. I only wish that you could see him, this unhappy child who is innocent of all his father's errors. He does not deserve to share such a sorry fate. I am convinced that you will champion his cause and also mine."

For the first time we find Marie Louise talking of her husband's "errors." . . . As Octave Aubry remarked, "the Bonapartes' clumsy approach had aroused the archduchess in her." The atmosphere around her was scarcely calculated to sustain her courage. Mme. de Montebello was in a vile temper, and at lunch, just before the departure for Orléans, she went so far as to exclaim:

"The sooner this is over, the better I shall like it! Oh, to be sitting quietly with my children in my little house in the rue d'Enfer!"

Marie Louise's eyes filled with tears. "That was cruel thing to say to me, Duchess."

The procession set off—this time without the coronation coaches, which had been laid up at Chambord. This was a wise precaution as it happened, for at Beaugency the convoy was held up by a party of Cossacks. They had already surrounded the Treasury when Shuvalov rode up and restored order. Only the wagon containing the Empress's hats and bonnets was pillaged.

In the late afternoon of Saturday, April 9, the National Guard of Orléans stood lining the streets all the way from the city gates. The silence which greeted Marie Louise's arrival was so offensive that an officer was heard to shout:

"Cry *Long live the Empress,* you swine!"

There were a few pitiful shouts here and there. The procession finally came to a halt in front of the monumental doorway of the bishopric, the imposing seventeenth-century building where Marie Louise and the King of Rome were to be lodged. Preceded by the Prefect of the Loiret, the Empress climbed the great stone stairs and shut herself up in her rooms.

Orléans was in the midst of an interregnum. Out of regard for Marie Louise's susceptibilities, the city pretended to be still under imperial rule, while the rest of France—with the exception of Fontainebleau—was already a kingdom. The King of Rome, in his little sailor suit, played in the courtyard of the bishopric. Clutching a wooden sword in one hand, he held a review of the young pages in his escort.

A certain Dudon arrived on behalf of the provisional government to collect the diamonds belonging to the Crown. The operation was carried out without either courtesy or consideration. Dudon went so far as to ask for a "slave necklace" of pearls which the Empress was wearing and which the Emperor had given her. Marie Louise made no protest, but simply took off the necklace. The wrecker went on to abstract even the Emperor's handkerchiefs. When he had gone there was no silver left, and the Empress's party had to borrow plates, forks and spoons from the Bishop.

What was Marie Louise to do? Mme. de Montebello kept urging her to abandon her husband's cause and seek refuge with her father, while on the other hand the Emperor's faithful followers exhorted her to take the road to Fontainebleau. But Napoleon still made no move, and his orders were vagueness itself. It was a cruel dilemma for a woman who had never in her life made the smallest decision. True, four years before, she had agreed to be handed over to the Minotaur, but all that she had had to do was accept a ready-made decision. Now she found herself mistress of her fate and she was completely at a loss:

"I do not know what to decide. I am living on nothing but my tears. I can understand the people of this country hating me and yet it is not my fault; but why did my father marry me off if this is what he was planning to do? . . . I am all alone and can only put my trust in Providence. I would have done better to have accepted its guidance when it inspired me to become a canoness, instead of coming to this country."

The next day, April 10—Easter Sunday—Anatole de Montesquiou, aide-de-camp to the Emperor and Maman Quiou's son, arrived at Orléans at seven in the morning, bearing two letters from the Emperor written the night before. It was too early for Marie Louise to receive him, so after going to see his mother, the young officer—he was twenty-four—went to pay his respects to Mme. de Montebello. She received him in bed, wrapped in a great cashmere shawl which "brought out the whiteness of her complexion." Simpering and smirking at the young man, she began by talking about the cold she was afraid of catching in that bleak bedroom devoid of curtains and hangings. Then at last she asked the question that was burning her lips:

"Well now, what of the Emperor? How is he? . . . Is he dead?"

"Dead?" exclaimed the aide-de-camp. "Not a bit of it. On the contrary, he is in excellent health and has asked me to give news of himself to his family."

"You mean to say he isn't dead? You are quite sure? But when did you leave him?"

"At seven o'clock last night."

"So at seven o'clock last night he still wasn't dead? Yes, but since then . . . Do you think he is going to commit suicide?"

"Commit suicide? No. He accepts misfortune and good fortune with the same sublime equanimity."

Somewhat taken aback by this conversation—as he reveals in his recently discovered memoirs—Montesquiou went off to see King Joseph, who also received him in bed and declared. "Well, it's all over. Now all we want is the King of France to allow us to go on living in France as ordinary citizens. He is a wise and thoughtful prince. May he bring happiness to his people. . . ."

At the Paschal Mass celebrated by Cardinal Fesch, the young officer saw for the last time Madame Letizia, who had repeated her famous *Pervided it lasts!* so often that she seemed less surprised than anyone else by the change in the family fortunes. Beside her sat her three sons, the three kings without kingdoms, Louis, Joseph and Jerome, and the latter's wife, the admirable Catherine von Württemberg, who was to remain faithful to her husband. The whole family would scatter next day like a flight of sparrows. Marie Louise had not attended the Mass. Failing to obtain an audience of her, Anatole de Montesquiou delivered the letters he was carrying to Mme. de Montebello. Marie Louise opened the first letter. The Emperor was being anything but helpful:

"You will have arrived this morning at Orléans," he wrote to this woman who was waiting for precise directives. "You can stay there, if you are traveling with your own horses. If you are using post horses and can come here, you are free to do so. . . ."

Napoleon was well aware that Marie Louise and her son were traveling with their own horses, but he was obviously still in no hurry to see them. Marie Louise understood this perfectly, and in her reply, after assuring her husband that she loved him and that her only desire was "to be able to console him," she announced that she was going to write to her father to ask if he would receive her. She now no longer asked her husband's permission: "I have decided not to go away with you before seeing him. I am convinced that I can exercise considerable influence upon him, to your son's advantage. If I cannot see him for several days, I shall join you later, with better news, I am sure, than you might imagine, for you cannot have any doubt of my tender affection for you or of the devotion with which I shall endeavor to console you. I repeat, my love, that I have decided not to leave without seeing my father: I believe that that is my duty and also in the interests of both you and my son." However, feeling somewhat apprehensive of the Emperor's reaction to this repeated affirmation of her intentions, she added this postscript: "If you will allow me to go and see my father, I am sure, or almost sure, that I can obtain Tuscany."

In the absence of precise instructions from Napoleon, can one blame her for deciding to go and see the Emperor Francis before taking the road to Fontainebleau or the Isle of Elba?

Montesquiou finally succeeded in obtaining an audience with Marie Louise at eight o'clock in the evening. The interview took place not in the Empress's study but in her drawing room in front of a score of ladies sitting in a circle. The few ministers who had not fled to Paris were there too, and also—"as a crowning insult," writes Anatole de Montesquiou—General Shuvalov, aide-de-camp to the Emperor of Russia. "She was standing in front of the fireplace. It was there that she spoke to me, with all eyes and ears attending to us. In the coldest of voices she asked me: 'How did you leave the Emperor? Do you think he will commit suicide?'"

Montesquiou "shuddered" at the question and raised his voice so that everyone there should hear his reply:

"Have no fear, Madame, I am sure that he will not commit suicide, for who could avenge him better than he himself? Only a weakling takes his own life, and the Emperor is even greater in misfortune than when he occupied the first throne in the world."

Marie Louise looked embarrassed and after glancing at the other people in the room said: "But he is going to the Isle of Elba. I have done what I could to join him, but it was impossible. I am very sorry. Are you going to the Isle of Elba?"

"Yes, surely. This is the moment for the Emperor's true friends to prove their affection for him."

Marie Louise registered the reproof and hurriedly replied:

"I too shall be going to join him on the Isle of Elba. I want to and I must. I know that I shall not be happy there, but that is of no importance. I shall be doing my duty."

She appeared to be deeply moved but, writes Montesquiou, "I should have liked to think it was by her husband's fate and the fate of her son."

Later that evening she sent another courier to Napoleon with a letter repeating how essential she thought it was for her to visit her father. "He has a kind heart, he will be touched by my tears, and your lot will be improved, for although you will have to stay on the Isle of Elba, you will also reign over the territories they will probably give us, and by that I mean Tuscany." Pleading her cause and looking for an excuse, she thought that she had found one in her chronic ill health. Was she once again falling a victim to her imagination when she told the Emperor that she was "spitting blood" and that she needed "rest and medical attention"? Whatever the truth of the matter, she went on:

I shall not be able to rest until I know and see you to be happy and contented and resigned to your sorry lot. That is the only happiness I desire apart from that of knowing that you love me. But I have great expectations of the approach which I have made to my father, and so it is with considerable impatience that I await permission to go and see him. I love you and kiss you with all my heart.

Your faithful LOUISE

Orléans, April 10, 1814.

P.S. This evening I saw M. Anatole de Montesquiou, who made me more eager than ever to join you. I hope that you will be happier than Fate would appear to wish.

The surprising thing is that Napoleon too seemed to believe in the desirability of a meeting between father, daughter and grandson, failing to realize that Francis would never allow the others to rejoin the outlaw. Caulaincourt, who was still in Paris, wrote in astonishment: "I cannot understand how the Emperor could delude himself to such an extent."

He had seen Metternich, who had stated categorically: "The Empress must only be considered as an archduchess or a princess and the King of Rome as a prince."

The Emperor of Austria shared this opinion. As for giving Tuscany to his daughter and his grandson, that was quite out of the question. That territory was to revert to his brother Ferdinand, Grand Duke of Würzburg and godfather to the King of Rome, who had been dispossessed of it and would not resume his title of *Grossherzog von Toscana*. Parma? That was out of the question too. The Archduchess ought to be content to return to Vienna with her son. . . . In the end, however, thanks to the intervention of the Tsar, who was revolted by the Austrian attitude, Caulaincourt succeeded in having the following article incorporated in the Treaty of Paris: "The Duchies of Parma, Piacenza and Guastalla shall be given in absolute sovereignty to H.M. the Empress Marie Louise, to be handed down to her son and his heirs in lineal descent. The Prince, her son, shall henceforth bear the title of Prince of Parma, Piacenza and Guastalla."

On the morning of April 11, Napoleon sent his wife the news, concealing his despair and pretending to be pleased to see his "little King" lose 132 departments and the crowns of Italy, the Low Countries and the Confederation of the Rhine, to become the heir to an "object" of 400,000 souls and three or four million francs in revenue: the sometime department of the Taro. "You will at least have a house and a beautiful country to go to," he told his wife, "when you grow tired of living on my Isle of Elba and I become a bore, which is sure to happen when I am older and you are still young."

In the bishopric of Orléans the news spread rapidly, and without the slightest irony the little Court came to "offer its congratulations to

H.M. the Duchess of Parma, Piacenza and Gustalla." Even now it seems that the new Duchess of Parma—in the absence of clear instructions from her husband—was still undecided about her future . . . to Mme. de Montebello's consternation. But the lady-in-waiting found an ally in the person of her friend Corvisart—"that swine Corvisart," as the Emperor was to call him at St. Helena—who was dismayed at the thought of following his august patients to the Isle of Elba. When Méneval, at the Emperor's request, asked him if the climate of the Isle of Elba would be beneficial to Marie Louise, the First Physician threw up his hands and declared that "he was convinced that the climate of that island would prove baneful to her." He condemned out of hand "all the mineral waters of Italy" as powerless to remedy the Empress's ills, for which he "strongly recommended" a cure at Aix-en-Savoie. One can imagine the reactions of the Empress—who already believed that she had one foot in the grave—on being told that the Mediterranean sun would be "baneful" to her. And just then, on this same Easter Monday, a reassuring letter from Metternich arrived at Orléans. Her Majesty was welcome to go to Rambouillet, where she would see her august father once more. Everything would be arranged for the best. Princes Esterházy and von Liechtenstein were on their way to Orléans to escort her. She was to take heart again.

And soon the two Austrian princes were indeed standing there before her, bowing respectfully and pressing her to accompany them. Marie Louise hesitated . . . and this time gave the order to go.

Seeing preparations being made for a journey, the new Prince of Parma became very excited.

"I want to go," he shouted. "I want my carriage. I want to go home. I want to go and see my Papa."

Mme. de Montesquiou tried to calm him down: "How impatient you are, little King. You can see that we shall be going very soon now."

But the child, shaking his curly head, went on repeating: "I want to go, I want to go."

The scene was the courtyard in the late afternoon. Some townspeople came up and asked Mme. de Montesquiou if they might kiss the "little King's" hand.

"Yes," replied Maman Quiou. "Yes, you may."

One lady—who had once pressed her lips to Louis XVII's hand—

knelt down and held the boy's hand for several moments while he went on stamping and shouting: "I want to go and see my Papa. I want to go."

At last all the horses had been put to the carriages and the carriages moved up. The old lady heard Mme. de Montesquiou say to a footman:

"Will you kindly put some biscuits beside me ready for tonight, so that I can give him one as soon as he asks; you know what he is like, he hates waiting. And may I have something I can give him to drink straightaway, so that he doesn't have to wait?"

There was a hint of fear in Maman Quiou's voice as she thought of her little charge's difficult temper. . . .

Before getting into her berlin, Marie Louise sent word to her husband that the two Austrian princes were making her leave "immediately" for Rambouillet. "I told them that I could not go without your consent, but they said that they could not wait for it, and that if I wanted to go away with you without seeing my father, they would use every means in their power to prevent this happening. I therefore thought it best to yield with a good grace. I am dreadfully unhappy at having to leave like this without seeing you; the idea plunges me into such despair that I do not know what to do. . . ."

She could not bring herself to recognize the incomprehensible passivity of the Emperor's attitude toward her as a fact. She imagined that he was angry with her and decided to forestall his reproaches: "Do not be angry with me, my love. I cannot help it, I love you so much that it breaks my heart. I am so afraid you might think I am plotting against you with my father. . . ." She already felt guilty. Yet at this point Marie Louise was absolutely sincere—her letters prove that at Orléans, on this Easter Tuesday of 1814, she longed to be reunited with the outlaw, but wanted to see her father first.

After talking to the Emperor Francis's envoys, the first faint doubt entered her mind. Would they allow her to join her husband afterward?

> They would have to be quite heartless [she wrote] to try and prevent me from coming to you, and even if they wanted to, I assure you they would never succeed. I want to share your misfortune, I want to care for you, to console you, to be useful to you, to allay your sorrows. I feel that I need to do all this if I am to go

on living, if I am not to succumb to this final blow. Your son is fortunate in that he cannot realize the full extent of his misfortune, poor little fellow, and only you and he can make life bearable for me. I am taking him with me, as I think that he will touch my father's heart, and I will bring him to you afterward, for I want to live with you. The more they want to part me from you, the more I feel the need to be beside you to care for you. Whatever happens, you may be sure that there is no one who loves you and feels for you as tenderly as I do. . . .

The carriage wheels had scarcely started turning before she realized that she and her son were prisoners. In the middle of the night—the night of April 12-13—on the road from Orléans to Rambouillet, she scribbled this message in pencil: "They have orders to prevent me from joining you, and even to resort to force if necessary. Be on your guard, my love, we are being duped. . . ."

That same night of April 12-13, though he had still to receive the Empress's last two letters, Napoleon guessed what had happened.

He committed suicide.

After swallowing the poison which Dr. Yvan had long ago prepared for him, he told Caulaincourt in a voice broken by hiccups:

"I can see that they are going to separate me from the Empress and my son. . . . In a little while I shall be dead. Tell the Empress that I only regret losing the throne because of her and my son, of whom I would have made a man worthy of governing France."

He then ordered Caulaincourt to take from his bedside table a letter which he had just written to the Empress.

"You will give it to her when I am no more."

The Master of the Horse picked up this letter which Marie Louise was destined never to read:

Fontainebleau, the 13th at 4 in the morning

My DEAR LOUISE,

I have received your letter. I approve of your going to Rambouillet, where your father will be joining you. It is the only consolation left to you in our misfortune. For the past week I have been waiting impatiently for this moment. Your father has been misguided and cruel to us, but he will be a good father to you and your son. . . . Adieu, my dear Louise. I love you more than anything else in the world. My misfortune affects me only in so

far as it hurts you. All your life you will love the most affectionate
of husbands. Give my son a kiss. Adieu, dear Louise.

All my love,

NAPOLEON

Had the poison lost its potency, or had he taken too strong a dose?
We cannot tell. . . . In any event, he was violently sick, and by the
time morning came he was out of danger.

"I am condemned to go on living," he said.

The letter Marie Louise had written on the 12th, before getting
into her carriage—it reached him on the afternoon of the 13th—gave
him the courage to face life once more. Did his thoughts turn at that
moment to the "little King"? And was he sincere when he said with a
sigh to Caulaincourt:

"My son is going to be an archduke. Perhaps that is better than
being Emperor of France."

Marie Louise had arrived at Rambouillet in tears. There were Russian soldiers mounting guard around the château. The Emperor Francis
was not there and was not expected for another three days. The Empress had indeed been "duped." The thought of being unable to write
every day to her husband and of not having a letter from him when she
awoke in the morning was "unbearable," and the message she sent him
that same April 13 was still warm with passion. She was "disgusted"
because there was "not a word" about the fallen Emperor in her father's
letters. She repeated that "not for anything in the world" would she go
to Austria with her son; her place was at her husband's side. If she
was forced to take the road to Vienna—the possibility had already occurred to her—it would be "a blow" from which she would never recover. "I love you too much for that."

For the moment only one consolation remained to her, and that
was her son. He seemed happy to be back at Rambouillet. "He really
is a sweet child," she wrote. "He grows more delightful every day. He
has no intention of giving the Emperor of Austria a pleasant welcome,
and I am afraid that nothing we may say will change his mind."

Meanwhile the "Prince of Parma" was doling out sweets to the
children of the town. When the box was empty he sighed: "I should
like to give you some more, but I haven't any left: the King of Prussia has taken all I had."

Asked about his toys, he answered angrily: "King Louis XVIII has taken them all from me!"

This was true in a way, since they had been left behind at the Tuileries.

Someone tried to explain to him that he "was not a king any more."

"I can see that," he retorted. "I haven't any pages now."

The latter, following the example set by the "grownups," had disappeared between Blois and Orléans. . . .

The thought of her approaching interview with her father was causing Marie Louise considerable anxiety. Hour by hour she grew more afraid of being "duped" and prevented from joining her husband. She was somewhat reassured when she read the letter the Emperor Francis had written to her from Troyes on April 12, and which had not been drafted by Metternich. Her father issued no orders, and seemed to be leaving her complete freedom of action. "Let me know if there is anything you need . . . *also if you intend leaving for my States,* so that I can arrange for my troops to provide you with an escort." Unfortunately he added: *"Follow Metternich's advice to you in every particular,* for he is my most loyal servant and my very good friend. . . . He will certainly take good care of my daughter and grandson. . . ." He would indeed take good care of them, doing everything in his power to prevent them from escaping. Marie Louise suspected as much and—on April 14—she seemed determined not to yield, even to force. She had refused to go and meet her father at Trianon, preferring to wait for him at Rambouillet, where it would be easier for her to receive him as a sovereign. Here at least she was still at home.

Even at a distance, nothing of the drama seemed to be lost on Napoleon. He too had suddenly realized that without his wife and son he had "no real leverage," as Metternich was already triumphantly explaining to his friend Hudelist. On April 15 he finally lost patience and ordered his wife to join him with the former King of Rome, "so that we may set off together for that land of sanctuary and repose, where I know I shall be happy, provided you can make up your mind to be happy too and forget all worldly greatness." But it was too late: the Emperor of Austria had announced that he was arriving on the 16th, and Marie Louise was obliged to wait for him.

Maman Quiou was trying in the meantime to prepare her charge for his first meeting with "Grandpapa"—and finding it no easy task. The boy stamped his foot angrily.

"He's Papa's enemy, and I don't want to see him!"

Mme. de Montesquiou reasoned with him and finally succeeded, with some difficulty, in calming him down. He was standing quietly beside his mother on the steps in front of the château when the Emperor Francis's carriage drew up. Greeting her father in German, she rushed forward and thrust her son into his arms. The little Prince politely kissed his hand. His grandfather, touched by the sight of his fair curls, blue eyes and archducal features, murmured: "Yes, he's got my blood flowing in his veins."

The governess promptly removed the boy, who, as a parting comment on his grandfather's solemn face and pendulous nose, declared: "Maman Quiou, Grandfather doesn't look very nice, does he?"

Until 1955 it was thought that the interview between father and daughter, at which Metternich was present, went off smoothly—most affectionately, says Viktor Bibl—and some historians, using Rovigo's *Mémoires,* the Marquis de Bausset's correspondence and above all Queen Hortense's *Souvenirs,* have made quite a touching story of it. But now all these suppositions have been destroyed by the discovery of the letter which the Empress wrote to her husband that very evening:

> My father arrived just two hours ago. I saw him straight away, he was very kind and affectionate toward me, but that was cancelled out by the most appalling blow he could possibly have dealt me: he forbids me to join you, or to see you, or even to accompany you on the journey. In vain I pointed out that it was my duty to follow you; he said that he did not wish it, and that he wanted me to spend two months in Austria and then go on to Parma, and that from there I could go and see you. This last blow will be the death of me; I can only hope that you can be happy without me, for I know that it is quite impossible for me to be happy without you. I shall write to you every day and think about you all the time. . . . I am so miserable that I just do not know what to say to you. I beg you again not to forget me and to believe that I shall always love you and that I am terribly unhappy. I send you a kiss and I love you with all my heart.
>
> Your faithful and loving Louise

How are we to reconcile this letter, which is patently sincere, with Queen Hortense's memoirs? For Josephine's daughter asserts that the day before, Marie Louise had asked her, in a frightened, tearful voice: "Do you think my father will force me to go to the Isle of Elba?"

And this calls forth a fine show of indignation from Hortense—the woman who, in her mother's home at Malmaison, welcomed the victors like old friends. No, so far Marie Louise had not betrayed her trust. In the letters she wrote during the week she remained at Rambouillet, she never stopped complaining about her fate and even "plotting" against her father in order to join Napoleon.

"I have already prepared my plan of campaign," she wrote, "and if you promise not to say a word about it when you write to me, I will tell you all about it. I am going to Austria now, because my father has set his heart on it, and I can see that if I did not go he would take me there by force. . . ." From Vienna she would go immediately to take the waters, and from the spa she would slip away to the Isle of Elba. True, the Emperor Francis had stated "most emphatically" that after taking the waters she would have to go back to Vienna, but "I did not press that point, because for the moment I think it is useless opposing a plan which, in spite of everything, I would never let him carry out when the time came, but I do not want to seem too set on it just now, so I beg you not to mention it, because that would ruin everything."

However, she confided her intentions to the Tsar, stressing her desire to join Napoleon so insistently that Alexander—so Marie Louise reported to her husband—exclaimed: "But, Madame, no one is going to prevent you, though you may be making a mistake in going to the Isle of Elba."

Before leaving, he asked the Prefect of the Palace: "Monsieur de Bausset, will you please take me to see the little King?"

It was with "death in her heart" that Marie Louise had received the Tsar, even if her father later told her that she had "made a conquest of him." But her ordeal was not over yet. Metternich, who was anxious to show the French people that their former Empress had embraced the allied cause, insisted on her receiving the King of Prussia. "He is very awkward by nature and rather brusque in manner," the Emperor Francis told her, "but he has a kind heart. Besides, he has had a very unhappy life." Marie Lousie heaved a sigh and resigned herself to being gaped at as if she were a strange animal in a zoo. As it happened, the King of Prussia was mercifully brief and took care not to talk to Marie Louise about "anything which might have been displeasing to her." He too wanted to see the "little King" and went off to stare at the child.

While Marie Louise was writing to the Emperor about her interview with the Tsar, who had thought the Prince of Parma was "wonderful," Anatole de Montesquiou arrived from Fontainebleau with a letter written by Napoleon on the eve of his departure. The young officer was received by Marie Louise. This time she was alone, and it was in a voice broken with emotion that she asked for news of the Emperor.

"I do so wish I could have joined him."

"Well, Madame," said the aide-de-camp, very daring, "why didn't you do so when the roads were still open?"

"I couldn't. But I still intend to join him."

"If you couldn't go to him when you were a sovereign, how can you do so now that you are a prisoner?"

She flushed at the question.

"I am the Emperor of Austria's daughter, which might perhaps be considered sufficient reason for submitting to his authority. I cannot be reunited with my husband at the moment, but I shall be later."

Anatole de Montesquiou shook his head sadly and went off to see the former King of Rome. As soon as he saw his governess's son, the boy rushed to meet him.

"Monsieur Anatole," he shouted, "how is Papa? Do you know, Monsieur Anatole, I can't wear the lancers' uniform any more, I can't wear the grenadiers' uniform any more, I can't wear the cavalrys' uniform any more. I have to dress like the enemy. . . ."

And he burst into tears in the young officer's arms.

That same day, Napoleon had taken leave of his Guard and since eleven in the morning had been traveling toward his cabbage patch at Portoferraio.

The Empire was dead.

The documents relating to the winding-up of the King of Rome's household, though drawn up on paper bearing the imperial letterhead —paper which was still being used at the end of June, 1814—were enclosed in files on which some clerk or other had written the words "Buonaparte's son." This was probably the same clerk who a month before had written "His Majesty the King," following the example set by his superiors. For the whole Napoleonic bureaucracy was soon marching in step again, referring to the Emperor without the slightest irony as "the head of the government which existed at the time." The Empire had turned royalist, but Marie Louise still wore a medallion portraying her husband, and the imperial machinery went on working around the former Empress and her son. In spite of several cases of desertion and an unavoidable reduction in expenditure, sixty-four people—including forty-three servants—remained to accompany them on their long journey and stay with them in Austria. Even at Schönbrunn, service, etiquette, habits and mealtimes would remain just as they had been at the Tuileries. The servants would go on wearing the imperial livery, and for many months to come the doors of the twenty-four carriages of H.M. the Duchess and H.H. the Prince of Parma would continue to bear the coat-of-arms of Napoleon.

Mme. de Montesquiou naturally remained faithful to the child whom she still regarded as her little King. Mme. Soufflot—"Toto" to the child—shed her "red lady" uniform to become a deputy governess. Her daughter Fanny, a girl of fifteen, came with her. Similarly, Gobereau, the valet, brought along his son Émile, who was to be the Prince's little playmate. The cradle rocker, Mme. Marchand—or "Chanchan" as the Prince called her—came too, just as her son, the Emperor's valet, accompanied his master to the Isle of Elba: they were a family to whom loyalty was second nature. One of the "second ladies," Mme. Petitjean, and another lady of the wardrobe remained in the Prince of Parma's service. Marie Louise was attended by the Baron de Méneval, the Marquis de Bausset, Mmes. de Brignole and de Hurtaut-Castener, Mlle. de Rabusion, General de Saint-Aignan, the equerry Caffarelli, and two recalcitrant travelers who had not yet summoned up the courage to desert but who would be the first to leave what they called the "courtlet": Mme. de Montebello and Dr. Corvisart. On April 23 the caravan set off for Grosbois, the first stopping place, where Marie Louise and her son were greeted by the Emperor of Austria. Berthier, the master of the house, had withdrawn to the little Château de Marolles adjoining Grosbois. In the evening he came and paid his respects to the Emperor Francis, but that exhausted the civility of the man who had asked for Marie Louise's hand in marriage and had gone to fetch her from Vienna. When the former Empress asked him the next morning to spend the day with her, he replied that he was afraid he had to go and see "Monsieur"—Louis XVIII's brother and the future Charles X.

Meanwhile a few more loyal supporters of the Empire arrived from Paris, including the Comtesse de Noailles, *née* Talleyrand-Périgord and the wife of Napoleon's Chamberlain, who appeared in a hat somewhat tactlessly trimmed with a bunch of lilies. Caulaincourt came too, and "with a heavy heart" kissed the hand of the former little King.

"He grows more intelligent every day, and is as fresh as a rose," Marie Louise told Napoleon on April 26, writing from Provins, the next stopping place. "He enjoyed himself tremendously at Grosbois with my father, who seems passionately fond of him: this pleases me very much, but I shall only be really happy the day I can see you again."

The Prince had "enjoyed himself tremendously" and, as Marie Louise also informed her husband, was "delighted at the idea of going on a long journey"; but we know from a letter from Mme. de Montesquiou to the Emperor that he never stopped asking for his father and complained that "all the traveling he was doing did not bring him any nearer to him." The governess had decided to stay with the child for another six months—in fact, she was to stay much longer—but even while she was writing this letter, on the morning of April 29, she was dreading the "moment of separation." The child sensed this, and would not let his beloved Maman Quiou out of his sight: "As he has noticed that a good many people have already left him, he is afraid that I might do the same."

Marie Louise was there, but she was traveling in another carriage and scarcely saw anything of her son except at stopping places. "I had hoped," sighed Mme. de Montesquiou in a letter to the Emperor, "that our unhappy circumstances would bring mother and son closer together, but nothing has changed in that respect. The friend [Mme. de Montebello] is keeping up her part to the end, devoting all her time and energy to it. It cuts me to the quick, and I shall never become reconciled to the poor child's unhappiness." Before sealing her letter, she slipped inside a lock of the "Prince's" hair. Maman Quiou no longer dared to call him, as she used to, "the little King." . . .

Across the burned and ravaged countryside, littered with stinking corpses between Provins and Troyes, the long caravan, led by the Austrian General Kinsky, whom Francis had sent to take charge, wended its way, marking time, stringing out, getting bogged down, and finally reaching Vesoul on May 1. There, as at Dijon, Austrian troops lined the streets, and in the evening Marie Louise was obliged to receive her father's officers. She wrote in her diary: "The sight of them is a source of distress to me; one can see in their eyes the joy they feel over their victory; I have a distinct impression that they enjoy seeing me suffer at leaving poor France, and for this reason I find them odious."

On Monday, May 2, after spending the night at Parma, the Prince of Parma left France forever. A cloud of dust greeted the exiles at the Swiss frontier: it was the Austrian cavalry and that of the Confederation coming to bid the Empress welcome. But they and the crowd of onlookers had eyes only for the new Prince of Parma, who stood at his carriage window waving to them.

The people of Basel were massed in front of the Maison Bleue belonging to Councilor of State Pierre Visher-Sarasin, where the former Empress was staying. Marie Louise picked her son up and showed him the crowd. An eye witness has left us a description of the boy's eyes, big and blue "like his mother's," and his pretty "ash-blond" curls, and goes into ecstasies over his delicate features. But he records that his complexion was rather pale and yellowish. The child had in fact been "out of sorts"—so Marie Louise told Napoleon—"but Corvisart said it was because he was eating too much cold meat during the day, so now we stop to let him take some soup. He is growing extremely intelligent and talks wonderfully well; everyone who sees him admires him, they consider him a very handsome child."

Often, like a moving antiphon, the little boy would repeat the question he had been asking ever since they had left Orléans: "Why won't they let me kiss Papa any more?"

"Pray give a very loving kiss to my son," the Emperor had written from Fréjus on April 28, just before leaving French soil. Marie Louise questioned the courier, who told her about the incident in which the Emperor had been involved on Monday, April 25, and which she recorded as follows in her diary:

"His journey was uneventful as far as Provence, where some wretched peasants threw stones into his carriage. He was forced to take horse and disguise himself in order to avoid them."

And she added:

"How cruelly affected he must have been! I blame myself for not following him. Am I deserting him too? Dear Lord, what must he think of me? But I will go and join him, even if I should be eternally unhappy. . . ."

Metternich and Mme. de Montebello had not won yet. . . .

The caravan left Basel on May 4 for Schaffhausen, and the journey began to assume the character of a tour. Much to the delight of the Prince of Parma, they saw the Rhine waterfalls, the Lake of Zurich and Lake Constance. But as they came nearer to the Tyrol, the little French court grew anxious. That province had been taken from Austria after Austerlitz, very much against its will, and given to Bavaria. Count Kinsky was therefore afraid that, to show their loyalty to the Habsburg monarchy, the Tyroleans might "commit impertinences" toward Marie Louise's suite. This was also Francis's opinion, for on May 4 he wrote to his daughter:

"As for the journey across the Tyrol, do not undertake it if there is any unrest in the country, for although I do not think they can do anything to you, your presence might lead to violence or the loss of human life, and that would be unpardonable."

But Marie Louise had already made up her mind: "I have enough courage not to alter my itinerary, and my Gentlemen approve of my decision. I am convinced that the Tyroleans will not do anything to us."

The citizens of Innsbrück merely showed their desire to become Austrian once more by giving a delirious welcome to "His Majesty's august daughter, who acquired deathless rights to her country's gratitude by an act of self-sacrifice rarely equaled in the annals of history." Her entry into the city took place on May 12 at eight in the evening. Shouting for joy, the Tyroleans unhitched the horses from Marie Louise's carriage and the Prince of Parma's, and took their places. "This is reducing men to the level of animals," noted Marie Louise in her diary, but no doubt her son was amused. The child was enjoying the journey and had already begun to forget his sorrows.

Marie Louise was now no longer a fallen Empress whose husband had been defeated returning to her native land, but the Emperor Francis's daughter making a triumphal entry. A warm welcome was also extended to the "little Napoleon" with the face of an archduke. In the entrance hall of the palace there was a portrait of the great Maria Theresa and her son Joseph II, then about ten years old; and everyone exclaimed at the resemblance between the Prince of Parma and his great-great uncle. M. de Bausset lifted the child up so that he was on a level with the picture, "and from that moment there was no longer any doubt about the likeness."

On May 15 the party set off for the Austrian frontier. "I am coming back to you, my beloved country," wrote Marie Louise in the diary which no one else was meant to see, "but with such bitter feelings! Why have I been forced to undertake this journey? Why am I being exposed to every kind of humiliation and self-reproach? Why did not the people of Paris cut the traces of my carriage like the loyal Tyroleans? What a heart-rending fate mine is—to slip out of the Emperor's hands and leave poor, unhappy France! Only God knows the extent of my misery! Oh, when I think how weak and powerless I am in this whirlpool of intrigue and treachery!"

Letters began to reach her from her family. *Liebe Mamma* had burst into tears on hearing about "the rendezvous at Rambouillet." She felt for her stepdaughter, who was in a "dreadful situation," but the warmth of the welcome she was preparing for her would console her. "Coming here, you will find yourself among people who adore you, whose only occupation will be to allay your sorrows. . . ." She would be free to follow her "penchants" and see no one she did not want to see. "Oh, Louise, you know how I feel," sighed Maria Ludovica. She hoped that she might be reunited with Marie Louise "on the high road, in your carriage, so that we may give free course to our emotions without any witnesses."

This hope was fulfilled in every particular on Saturday, May 21, at a stopping place between St. Pölten and Siegartskirchen, ten miles from Vienna. It was eight in the evening when the procession arrived at the castle of Schönbrunn. A great crowd had gathered outside the gates, more to see "little Napoleon" than to greet the Ariadne who had escaped with her life from the Minotaur's embrace. Cheers marked the appearance of the child, whose beauty conquered every heart. A police officer noted in his report "the indescribable enthusiasm aroused by the beauty and charm of this Prince," while tenderhearted Viennese ladies "dissolved into tears." The carriages drew up at the foot of the staircase on which Marie Louise's sisters and aunts were waiting to greet her. One and all fell on her neck, uttering squeals of joy and congratulating her with tears in their eyes, "just as if," writes Méneval, an ironic witness of the scene, "she had escaped some danger from which they were delighted to see her emerge safe and sound."

The Archduke Charles, the Emperor's brother and Director General of Engineering and Fortifications, considered the boy "a pretty, fair-haired, blue-eyed child, but with the features, the look, the stubbornness, the character and the mind of his father." He was the only person of this opinion. The young archduchesses looked at their little nephew and admired what they saw. He was the very image of Marie Louise, they said.

"Not a bit of it," she replied testily. "Those are the Emperor's features; and he has all his father's expressions and mannerisms."

She was still wearing the medallion decorated with her husband's portrait, and she invited her sisters and aunts to compare father and son. None of them felt any desire to do so, but all of them considered "little Napoleon sweet and handsome." "Well brought up. Something could be done with him" was the Archduke John's comment.

But that was the question. . . . What were the Austrians going to do with the boy who had become their prisoner and hostage?

7

✤

Astyanax

"ALL THAT WAS NEEDED to complete my misfortune was to become grandmother to the Devil!" Thus commented Queen Maria Caroline of Naples on the marriage of her granddaughter Marie Louise to Napoleon.

Napoleon's collapse had not brought the old Queen back to her throne. Murat, as the price of his treachery, was allowed to remain in possession of the Kingdom of Naples. This paradoxical situation disgusted Mme. de Montesquiou, who suggested to the Queen that she should go to Paris and ask the King of France for his support.

"Oh dear no!" retorted Maria Caroline. "They say Murat is planning to go to Paris. You wouldn't want me to meet him and dance a chaconne with him, would you?"

Pending the time when Murat would betray his new allies, the Queen went on living in her little residence at Hentzendorf, which was linked by an avenue with Schönbrunn. Often, in the early days of what Marie Louise regarded as her "exile," she would take her son to see his great-grandmother. Marie Antoinette's sister—she was only sixty-two at the time, but the suffering she had gone through made her look like a little old crone—would bend over the child's curly head and murmur softly: "Little Monsieur . . ."

She found him adorable.

"Madame," she confessed to Mme. de Montesquiou, "when he isn't there, I tell myself that I can't possibly love him, his father has caused me so much suffering. But as soon as I see him again, all is forgotten."

Liebe Mamma felt much the same way.

"He is a child of surprising beauty," she told the Emperor, who was still in Paris. "His appearance made a disagreeable impression upon me, for he resembles his father in every respect."

The people of Vienna were incapable of such subtleties. In this summer of 1814, gazing at the child was one of their favorite occupations on Sundays, when the park at Schönbrunn was open to the public. While they were highly critical of the ex-Empress, who "seemed to talk and behave as if Napoleon were still on the throne of France" and "showed a preference for everything that was French," "Little Bonaparte" sent them into raptures. It was a pity of course that Napoleon was his father, but they soon forgot that as they recognized in this blue-eyed, fair-haired child the blood of their beloved Habsburgs. "The Prince of Parma," states a police record, "continues to be the object of the affection and curiosity of the public"—though they considered the marshal's hat adorned with white plumes which he had been given to wear "ridiculous and even grotesque." But this did not prevent them from cheering "little Napoleon," who apparently stamped with joy whenever this happened. Sometimes, no doubt when he had had enough, he would shout: "Close the gates!"

A memory of life at the Tuileries.

Some English ladies came to see him. "He was playing soldiers," writes Mme. de Montet in her memoirs; "they obligingly acted as the enemy, he pretended to fire at them, they pretended to be hit and fell to the ground, and he went into transports of joy. . . ."

One day a certain Lady Clair tried to kiss him. The Comtesse de Brignole intervened. "Madame, one should only kiss the Prince's hand."

Accustomed to this sort of homage, the "Prince" extended his little hand and Lady Clair impressed a kiss on it. Recounting the incident afterward, she called it "a piece of impertinence on the part of the younger Napoleon."

One day *liebe Mamma* brought along the young Archduke Francis, Marie Louise's twelve-year-old brother, and the two boys were told to go and play together.

"I'm not going to play with a French boy," declared the Archduke.

Utterly astounded, the little Prince shouted: "Mamma, tell them to take this horrid boy away!"

Although he would often say: "I'm not a king any more! I'm not a king any more!"—sadly or gaily as the mood took him—the Prince of Parma was a happy child. Surrounded by his governesses and chambermaids, and served as he had been at the Tuileries by valets and liveried footmen, he cannot have found living at Schönbrunn very different from spending a few days in the country at Rambouillet or Fontainebleau. Every day after lunch, Mme. de Montesquiou would take him to see his mother, and he would be given one of the hundred different varieties of cake that were served to Marie Louise. Then he would go and play in the Archduke John's Tyrolean garden, climb up to the arcades of the Gloriette, or go and see the rare plants in the hothouses.

There was only one shadow on his happiness: his toys were still in Paris.

"The wicked old King has taken all my toys," he would say. "But he will have to give them back to me!"

The "wicked old King"—Louis XVIII—did just that, and one day the child saw the big packing cases from the Tuileries being carried into his bedroom.

"Ah! He was scared!" he said proudly.

His servants unpacked a round morocco case containing a broken silver rattle, two cavalrymen, a milkmaid and her cow, a tiny mahogany tumbril, a miniature billiard table, a troll-madam, a carillon, some toy stables, a bow, two big wooden horses, a hussar, a clockwork grocer's shop, a little water carrier's cart in crystal, a mountebank and a mandolin-playing Turk driven by clockwork, a grenadier, a dragoon, a hundred and fifty mineralogical specimens, a bird-organ in steel and mother-of-pearl, and finally twenty-five volumes "relating to the education of children." The silver-gilt dressing set and the famous cradle presented by the City of Paris arrived shortly afterward.

This was the entire fortune of the King of Rome.

No one at the time suspected that this was so. Everyone was convinced that Austria would not have the cruelty to separate mother and child and that "His Highness the Prince of Parma" would go and live in the duchy which he was one day to inherit. Marie Louise had not changed her plans. A fortnight after her arrival she had written to her husband describing her solitary life. "Tormented by care, and loving you more devotedly than ever," she wrote to the exile, "I am spending whole days in despair at being unable to see you. . . . Your son, on the other hand, is delightfully gay; he has never been in better health and is greatly admired by everyone who sees him. He talks about you a great deal, he is becoming very sensible, he keeps asking me 'when we are going to see Papa,' I should love him to have his wish granted soon."

The same day—June 5, 1814—she wrote to him again, recounting the "dreadful things" people were saying about her at Court: "A plot is being hatched there to prevent me from going to the spa, and they are even trying to take the Duchy of Parma from me so that my family can round off its possessions; they say too that the ideal thing would be to find some means of preventing my son" etc., etc., etc.

She was extremely wrought up in the morning of the 5th and thought of sending her son straight to Parma with Mme. de Montesquiou, but at five in the afternoon, when she wrote her second letter, she decided to take him with her to the spa. She was all the more distraught in that, ten days after her arrival at Schönbrunn, her beloved Montebello had deserted in her turn and gone back to Paris with Corvisart—though promising to join Marie Louise and her son at Aix.

Only one woman in the Austrian entourage had no illusions, and that was Maria Caroline of Naples. One day when, in her presence, the "little Monsieur" asked for news of his "dear Papa," the old Queen told him: "You will never see your Papa again."

Marie Louise promptly clasped her son in her arms, squeezing him tight and angrily repeating: "You will see him again, I swear it, you will see him again!"

It seems probable that Maria Caroline only replied as cruelly as she did in order to rouse her granddaughter and make her realize that the Corsican's son was already a prisoner. Did understanding begin to dawn on Marie Louise when, on June 15, two stages away from Vienna, she met her father on his return from France and joined him in his carriage? Francis set his face against his grandson's departure. His daughter was free to go and take the waters at Aix, but the Prince of Parma was to remain at Schönbrunn. Francis had one powerful argument: Louis XVIII could not be expected to see the son of "M. de Buonaparte" staying on French soil without a certain displeasure . . . and fear. But Marie Louise defended her plan so vigorously that Francis finally said: "Write to your husband and tell him what I have advised you to do; if he does not approve, then you can take your son with you."

When Metternich learned of this rash promise, he must have shaken his head sadly over his master's imprudence.

However, Marie Louise waited until June 22, that is to say a week after her father's return, before writing to Napoleon. In any event, the Emperor's reply could only reach her in Savoy, since in her letter of the 22nd she told her husband that she was leaving "this prison of Vienna" for Aix on the 29th.

Napoleon replied on July 3: "I think you should come as soon as possible to Tuscany, where the waters are just as good and of the same kind as those of Aix-en-Savoie. That will have every advantage. I shall hear from you more often, you will be able to have your son with you and you will be causing nobody any anxiety. Your visit to Aix offers nothing but disadvantages. If this letter finds you there, stay for only one season and come to Tuscany for your health."

This letter was not delivered to Marie Louise until August 10. It was too late then to leave for Tuscany! The reply she sent her husband was still full of tenderness: "I beg you to write to me often; it is one of the few pleasures left to me to enjoy at the moment; and above all, Dearest, never doubt my tender devotion, no one loves you or ever will love you better than I do. I kiss you and love you with all my heart."

She had already sent him a lock of her hair for his birthday . . . and she was embroidering tapestry covers for him "for a little drawing room. There will be a sofa, an armchair, a stool and four chairs." A week later she gave him news of the boy who had been their "little King":

> Your son is wonderfully well. I met someone yesterday who saw him a week ago; he left him cheerful and very happy. The Emperor of Austria is crazy about him; he goes to see him every day, and I feel sure you will think it a good idea to try and encourage him to be fond of him. He can already read fluently, and is growing into a delightful child. I can scarcely wait for the moment when I shall be able to bring him to you.

Marie Louise's sister Leopoldine kept her fully supplied with news of her nephew, whom she described as "life incarnate." The little Prince seems to have been very fond of the future Empress of Brazil. She found this "very flattering" and could have "played with him for hours on end." "Yesterday I had a delightful experience," she wrote on July 31, "for he called me and I had to go and join him in the garden, where he told me a story of which I did not understand a word, as he had a big croissant in his mouth."

On the 30th the Emperor Francis had returned from a short absence and had found his grandson "cheerful and lively." The child could already say a few words in Italian, and the Emperor, so the young Archduke Francis Charles told his sister, had given him "several toys from Upper Austria." "I for my part," he went on, "wanted to give him a pet squirrel, but as it might have escaped from the little garden by way of the espaliers, I had to set it free in the pheasantry."

He had also made a conquest—a much more difficult one—of Mme. Lazansky, Marie Louise's *Aja*, who "could not weary of admiring him." On the other hand the child had given an ill-tempered reception to the King of Saxony, his father's sometime ally.

Writing to her granddaughter on August 22, Maria Caroline of Naples told her that the "little Monsieur" had been to see her three times, and that he had been "very charming, quiet and well behaved; may God give you in him every consolation a mother can receive." On the morning of September 7 Marie Antoinette's sister stopped outside Mme. de Montesquiou's window and called her. When the governess opened the window she said:

"Madame de Montesquiou, bring my great-grandson to see me tomorrow morning. I have something that will amuse him."

There would be no tomorrow for the old Queen. At twelve o'clock that night she died of a stroke. On the 10th the body lay in state on a sheet of silver cloth, dressed in a black taffeta gown and a lace bonnet and ruff. A little casket containing her entrails had been placed at her feet, and on a velvet cushion on her right were displayed the order of the Starry Cross, a pair of gloves and a fan. "This was an old custom," Mme. de Montet tells us.

Some time before she died, looking sadly at the "little Monsieur," she had asked Mme. de Montesquiou: "What about his mother? What is she doing here? And what is the point of that big portrait of her husband she has hanging from her neck if she doesn't keep his picture in her heart? Why isn't she on the Isle of Elba?"

"But Madame, she isn't the mistress, and they refused permission."

"Refused permission? Oh, come now! Refused permission? But what difference does that make? You escape. I would like to have seen them try to prevent me from joining my husband in the old days! . . . Hasn't she got sheets in her bed and curtains in her room? You escape out of the window. There was a time when she ought not to have become his wife—and that was my opinion, as you may well imagine—but now that she is his wife, she must go on being his wife."

Napoleon himself was convinced that Marie Louise and his son were going to arrive soon on the Isle of Elba. He had already had apartments prepared for them in the Palazzina dei Mulini, where he had taken up residence on the very day that they had arrived at Schönbrunn. On the drawing-room ceiling he had had a "Conjugal Constancy" painted—a picture of two doves separated by clouds "but joined by a ribbon whose knot was drawn ever more tightly the farther they moved apart." "Your apartments are ready for you," he had written to his wife on August 18, "and I look forward to seeing you before the vine harvest." His thoughts were constantly with his son, and he seldom was without his snuffbox decorated with the portrait of the "little King." One day, when he was talking to Pons de l'Hérault, the snuffbox slipped out of his hand; he picked it up in alarm and gave a sigh of relief when he saw that it had not been damaged. "I should have been most upset if my little boy's features had suffered from my clumsiness. I have something of a mother's tender love for him—a great deal, indeed—and I am not ashamed to admit it."

He was no longer the founder of a dynasty thinking of his heir, of the first link in the chain of Napoleons, but an unhappy father who was perpetually preoccupied with the fate of his captive son.

"The poor little devil," he would mutter to himself.

One day he was looking through some engravings which had arrived from Rome. When he came to a portrait of the little King, "I cannot adequately describe," writes Pons, "the emotion the Emperor put into the words *My Son!* This heartbreaking picture is ever present in my mind." The Emperor then withdrew to his bedroom and only returned to the drawing room half an hour later, in a state of profound depression.

Every day he expected to receive news of the imminent arrival of the "poor little devil" and his mother. He had sent a Polish officer—Colonel Teodor Lanczinski—to Aix to beg his wife to come and join him. The officer had arrived on August 17 or 18 at an inopportune moment, for Marie Louise had just received the following letter from her father:

You may rest assured that I shall do all that I can for your happiness and your son's happiness, and hence for the good of everything that belongs to you. As for your person, all I ask is that you should observe our agreement, that is to say to return to Vienna and, as long as the Congress is in session, not to go to Parma or the neighboring States, for by going there prematurely you could only harm yourself and your son without obtaining any real advantage. You know that I wish for nothing but your happiness, and if I speak to you like this, you can be sure that it is not without good reason. Your presence close to us during the Congress may be more necessary to you than you imagine: you can trust your father in these matters, as indeed in everything as long as God grants me life and breath.

In this same letter—for the first time—the Emperor mentioned the presence at Aix of the Austrian general whom Metternich had chosen to act as Marie Louise's escort and attendant: "I note that you are satisfied with Neipperg, which does not surprise me."

The General had been given precise instructions: "Count von Neipperg will endeavor to divert the Duchess, with all necessary tact, from the idea of making a journey to the Isle of Elba, a journey which would deeply grieve the fatherly heart of His Majesty, who has the tenderest regard for the welfare of his beloved daughter. He will not hesitate to use all the means in his power to dissuade her from any such idea. . . ."

One of these means consisted of trying, in between "stimulating" showers and glasses of watery milk, to seduce the malleable Archduchess, who had been starved of love since the beginning of the year. Louise was attracted by Neipperg's swashbuckling appearance. A bandage over his right eye—a sword thrust had made him half-blind—gave him a certain piratical air which was not unpleasing to women. He very quickly became an amusing and indispensable companion for Marie Louise. At the same time she kept receiving letters from *liebe Mamma* encouraging her to make Neipperg her *directeur de promenade*. Intrigued by the situation, the Austrian Empress even went so far as to ask her stepdaughter, on August 8, whether the irresistible general "advised her to hitch up her skirts when climbing up steep mountain slopes"—a question which had a certain piquancy in view of subsequent events. These "subsequent events" came as no surprise. Mme. de Montebello, who had joined Marie Louise at Aix, had done her best to put the young woman on her guard. "I talked and talked," she wrote later, reminding the ex-Empress of their stay together at Aix, "until I nearly drove Your Majesty crazy with my efforts to warn you of the danger to which I saw that you were exposed!"

Already fascinated by Neipperg, Marie Louise no longer showed the same impatience to join the prisoner at Elba. Replying to the Emperor's letter, which she had received on August 17 or 18, she took refuge behind her father's advice and wrote:

How happy I should be if I could join you as soon as I had my son with me! I had given orders for him to be sent here when I received a letter from my father asking me to go back to Vienna for the Congress, where my son's interests are to be discussed; it seems that the Bourbons are campaigning to have Parma taken away from me. . . . In spite of all this, you can trust my determination to come to you; it will give me the courage to brave all obstacles, and unless they use force I shall certainly be with you soon, though I do not know yet how far they will go. I feel miserable not to be with you already on your happy island; it would be paradise for me. Do trust me: I should tell you frankly if it were I who were putting difficulties in the way of my going—you know me well enough for that—and I beg you not to believe everything they may tell you on that score. I shall try to leave as soon as I possibly can.

She protested too much, and her words no longer had the ring of truth. Napoleon guessed what was happening and, even before the Polish officer's return, he dispatched a second emissary on August 20: a certain Captain Hurault, the husband of one of Marie Louise's attendants. He arrived in Savoy at the beginning of September, a few days before Marie Louise's departure. He carried a letter from Napoleon insisting that the Empress should set off without further delay for the Isle of Elba. She could go and see her son later: the road to Vienna—or Parma—could pass through Portoferraio. If her Austrian entourage tried to stop her, she was to take flight: Hurault would see to everything. This time Napoleon was tired of waiting, and his letter, which has unfortunately been lost, was written, so it appears, in an almost threatening tone. Marie Louise promptly revealed to Neipperg the precise nature of the Captain's mission . . . and with this revelation began her betrayal of Napoleon. Even supposing that she wanted to join the Emperor—and this was no longer the case—and that, faced with the possibility of doing so, she did not want to leave her son, she should never have betrayed her husband's plans. Marie Louise was French no longer and no longer belonged to Napoleon: she had turned Austrian once more and would soon belong to Neipperg. For Neipperg had his reward a few days later—on September 27 to be exact—in the course of an excursion on the way back to Vienna. The ex-Empress and her "guardian angel," caught in a violent storm near the chapel of William Tell, were obliged to put up for the night at the Golden Sun inn. That night the amorous and love-starved Marie Louise gave herself to Neipperg.

As soon as she arrived in Vienna, she wrote in a remarkably off-hand tone to Mme. de Montebello: "Just imagine—during the last days of my stay at Aix the Emperor sent me one message after another urging me to go and join him, to set off on an escapade with nobody but M. Hurault, and told me to leave my son in Vienna, saying that he was perfectly happy there and that he did not need him. I thought this was really too bad and I told him frankly that I could not come just now. . . . I shall not go to the Isle of Elba for the time being, and *I shall never go* (for you know better than anyone else how little I want to), but the Emperor is really so casual, so irresponsible!"

The Emperor Francis had been lucky . . . and he said so quite shamelessly.

"Thank heavens," he exclaimed, "I picked the right kind of escort!"

No one saw anything reprehensible in Marie Louise's behavior. As Méneval remarked in a letter to his wife: "They are ready to tolerate anything provided she forgets her husband and even her son."

Neipperg had succeeded in awakening Marie Louise's senses, or at least in proving himself a better lover than Napoleon. The ex-Empress took after her father, the amorous Emperor who was now in the process of wearing out his third wife. Soon Marie Louise would be afflicted with nymphomania, and it is to this affliction that we must look for the explanation of the behavior which earned her the condemnation of history. But she had another excuse. On her return to Vienna she learned that the Papal Nuncio was secretly circulating a document purporting to prove that, since the marriage between Josephine and Napoleon had not been properly annulled, the union of Marie Louise and the Emperor of the French was null and void. And with remarkable naïveté the Vatican suggested that, as the Empress Josephine had just died at Malmaison, H.M. the Duchess of Parma should have her marriage to the sovereign of the Isle of Elba validated by receiving the sacrament of holy matrimony. The document concluded: "Posterity will pay tribute to the most upright and generous of sovereigns for sacrificing his daughter for his people's sake, but she will ask why, having been deceived by the monster [Napoleon], we aggravated the scandal by continuing to recognize the innocent victim as the spouse of a monster whom, from the Catholic point of view, she could only marry now that he is truly a widower and free to contract another union."

Marie Louise was astounded, then horrified. So, according to the Pope, she had been nothing but the "monster's" concubine and her son was just a natural child, a bastard! Soon after her return, Cardinal Consalvi—Napoleon's favorite drudge—had several conversations with Marie Louise on the subject. Marry Napoleon all over again? That was out of the question, all the more so as care had been taken to inform the young woman of the arrival on the Isle of Elba, on September 1, of Countess Walewska and her son. Nor had any attempt been made to conceal the Emperor's previous infidelities from her. Bausset had actually said in front of her, in her drawing room: "The Emperor had all the Empress's ladies in exchange for a shawl; Madame de Montebello was the only one who held out for three."

"Have you forgotten in whose presence you are speaking?" exclaimed Marie Louise in a fury.

When Mme. de Montebello heard about the incident from the ex-Empress, she was much more philosophical.

"What you tell me about M. de Bausset," she wrote to her imperial friend, "does not annoy me in the least. . . . Nothing that comes from a source like that is worth troubling about. . . . What does disturb me, however, is the impression I gain of the democratic manners people are permitting themselves in Your Majesty's presence. What can your drawing room be like for people to dare address you in such a way?"

The general tone of Marie Louise's drawing room was certainly not that of the Tuileries. Be that as it may, one fact emerged from the controversy stirred up by the Nuncio: Marie Louise wanted to have nothing more to do with Napoleon. On the other hand, Neipperg's victory was not yet complete. The Golden Sun incident had not developed into a proper liaison. Marie Louise had given herself to the one-eyed general, but she went on fighting against any stronger feeling and against the imperious demands of her temperament. Her son still occupied the first place in her heart, and she had been overjoyed to see him again. On October 13 she wrote to Mme. de Montebello:

I found my son bigger and more handsome; his hair now falls in curls over his shoulders, and you will remember what a lovely color it is. What is more, his mourning clothes suit him wonderfully; I had some made for him with long sleeves because I was afraid that the cold might affect him. He talks very clearly and spends several hours every day alone in my room. My *amour-propre* suffered dreadfully on the day of my arrival. I had wondered a great deal about the way he would greet me. I came in, and he allowed me to kiss him. General Neipperg came in, and my son ran up to him, dazzled by his colorful hussar's uniform. There was no way of getting him to think of anything else; I must confess that this caused me considerable chagrin and mortification. However I did not hold it against him, because since then he has been perfectly charming to me.

And three days later:

If only you knew how much fonder I grow of the poor child with every day that passes; he well merits it, because he is very sweet, very good, very charming; he loves me more every day; we have lunch together now; we see a great deal of each other during the day and when the weather permits I take him for a walk; you can see that I am very much taken up with him.

On November 2 she wrote:

My son is wonderfully well; he has begun going out in all weathers: that is a victory which I had to fight for and which I finally wrested from Mme. de Montesquiou. He thrives on it too; he is growing stronger and his complexion is much fresher. Yesterday he was terribly funny when Mme. de Montesquiou was unwise enough to say that she was very fond of M. de Sekingen; he flew into a dreadful temper, stamping and weeping and shouting: "I don't want you to be fond of him; I'm the only one you should be fond of." That promises well for the future. If he goes on like that, I shall be glad to be his mother and not his wife.

"If I had not got my son," she wrote on November 20, "I should be content with any position which guaranteed me, if not a happy future, at least a peaceful one. But for his sake I want to have a State; I do not want him to be able to reproach me in time for not looking after his interests; I owe him this as a mother, and I shall know no rest until he has Parma, or at least an indemnity equal in value to the territory, population and revenue."

On December 14 she reported that the day before "he told me that he was going to elope with me next year, that he was going to leave Maman Quiou and marry me, and that the only wife he wanted was his Mamma; I think this is the nicest declaration of love I could ever hope to receive."

She spoiled the child, sending to Paris for lead soldiers, a little cannon, a kitchen, a set of tin furniture and a house "which you can build yourself," because in Vienna, so she said, toys were "awful and very expensive."

As one might imagine, Neipperg did not abandon his advantages; he was always present and even became the Eaglet's playmate. On December 20 Marie Louise wrote to Mme. de Montebello:

> My son is wonderfully well; we often go for walks together; the weather is as fine as it was in September and the buds have started coming out again; there are even leaves on some rose bushes. I let my son run about while I sit somewhere in the sun to get warm. He frightened me yesterday by falling against a desk and getting a big lump and a graze on his forehead; I felt quite ill, because apart from the fright he gave me I had the mortification of being told by Mme. de Brignole and Count Neipperg that it was nothing and that if I went on coddling him like that I should turn him into a milksop. I still feel frightened when Count Neipperg is playing with him; they play such rough games that I am sure he will do him an injury one of these days. . . . They are the best of friends, and never a day passes but they spend an hour or an hour and a half before dinner playing together.

All these letters were full of sighs and lamentations. Resisting Neipperg's advances in response to Mme. de Montebello's exhortations was a difficult matter.

"In the meantime," she wrote on November 26, "I am exceedingly sad at heart. Your prophecy will not be realized this time. I feel more certain every day that it is for life, and that is dreadful because I shall never give way to my feelings in this respect. May God preserve you from a similar situation."

The constant presence of Neipperg at her side drove her to distraction. At the mere sight of him she fell a prey to "countless different sensations" which she "fought" to the best of her ability, so she said, but which had "already cost me many tears."

Mme. de Montebello went on advising her from a distance not to give way to Neipperg's blandishments.

"Yes," she replied, "with time, courage and health I hope to conquer a feeling whose existence I am reluctant to admit to myself and which will change to friendship. You can set your mind at rest on that score."

The lady-in-waiting congratulated her on her resolve, but added: "All the same, Madame, the consciousness of your strength must not be allowed to make you too proud to avoid danger; Your Majesty may assert that you only noticed the danger you know of late in the day, but I shall go on thinking that you did not want to see it. . . . At all events, the greater the danger you faced, the greater is Your Majesty's merit and the more I must congratulate you on your victory. . . ."

It was a brief victory. Neipperg resorted to extreme measures: on December 18 he threatened to blow his brains out to prove his despair, and Marie Louise felt her resolve weakening.

A little later she confessed to Mme. de Montebello: "I have been unable to do otherwise than put my trust in the General; how else could he manage my affairs? He has handled them so well that I must admit I have vowed a grateful friendship for him which will last the whole of my life. Forgive me if I say no more to you on this score; I have done my best to convince you of the honesty and sincerity of his feelings; you refuse to believe in them, but you will not convince me of the contrary. . . ."

More of a mistress than a mother, she would henceforth live only for the embraces of her beloved general.

A thousand-gun salute opened the Congress of Vienna a fortnight before Marie Louise's return to Schönbrunn. Days and nights passed in a succession of triumphal entries, receptions, balls, popular festivals, banquets, ballets, galas, picnics, more balls—masked, this time—hunts, lotteries, living pictures, and monster beats at Laxenburg. After a day's hunting one could go and listen to the Seventh Symphony or *Fidelio* conducted by Beethoven, a stocky, broad-shouldered Beethoven, a stone-deaf Beethoven who was the only person who could not hear his magnificent music. . . . And the cycle of dinners and balls went on, with waltzes and more waltzes.

Dancing was all that mattered for the moment. There would be plenty of time later on to stitch together again a Europe that had been torn up into French departments. The kings and princes were on holiday. Sometimes, it is true, when they had supped too well, their thoughts turned to the man before whom they had often bowed and scraped, the man whose hat they had picked up whenever he dropped it. The sight of Bonaparte's son playing under the trees at Schönbrunn or of Marie Louise leaning on her lover's arm in the anterooms of the Hofburg was proof that the nightmare was over. But the same sights also reminded them of the Tuileries and the not-so-distant past when they had been degraded and humiliated to the point of giving an archduchess in marriage to the son of the Revolution, to the point of smiling as they saw their finest cities turned into French prefectures. Some among them had even been obliged to hand a *real* princess or a *real* prince to be bedded by a member of the tribe. . . . But these shameful memories belonged to the past. All that remained was a beggarly ex-Empress—she had lost her high-and-mighty airs of Paris and Dresden—a poor child without a name, and an outlaw with the beginnings of a paunch, playing the monarch, planting his vines and attending to his saltworks while English cruisers mounted guard over his comic-opera "kingdom."

Vienna could waltz with an easy mind. Vienna could watch the Emperor Francis dancing a polonaise with Lady Castlereagh or throwing himself into a country dance with Lady Matilda. Vienna could smile freely at the sight of sad-faced Castlereagh yawning his head off, yawning so much indeed that Metternich found himself following his example. What did it matter if the Congress was making no progress? There was so much gossip to be exchanged: for instance, it was said that the King of Denmark had fallen in love wlth a pretty little *grisette*. There was the Grand Duchess Catherine talking about the art of fortification with breathtaking expertise, or poking fun at the old-fashioned Marquis de Montchenu, who had come specially from Paris to claim an indemnity for forage dating back to the Seven Years' War! It was so delightful to forget about the war, and even about the Congress, to put on a disguise, to go for a stroll in the Prater, to admire the finest horses, the finest diamonds, the finest dresses in the world. There was always something amusing to see, whether it was the living game of chess at the Countess Zichy's or M. de Talleyrand having his hair dressed while his valet sprinkled his club foot with vinegar—"a scene well worth the trouble of a visit." The Tsar's ablutions too had a certain originality, for he required an enormous block of ice every morning in order to wash his face and hands. Tireless souls determined to miss nothing in the way of gala evenings could go to the Princess von Metternich's on Monday, the Princess Trauttmansdorff's on Thursday and Countess Zichy's on Saturday, while people with good digestions could go every evening to M. de Talleyrand's, where the pretty Comtesse de Périgord presided over the best table in the whole Congress. Two other attractions were immensely popular: the aeronaut Krakowsky above the rooftops waving the flags of all the nations, and the sledges which took you out to the Vienna Woods. "Picture to yourself," wrote Marie Louise to her beloved Montebello, "thirty-two golden sledges drawn by horses loaded with embroidered housings, bells and plumes, and warmly but elegantly clad ladies in the carriages themselves; it was a delightful sight; after crossing a large part of the city we arrived at Schönbrunn, where there was dinner and an entertainment, and we returned by torchlight with big snow-flakes falling; I thought of you while enjoying this rather chilly outing."

The ex-Empress avoided the Congress, although one evening she watched a reception through a window concealed in the ceiling of the great ballroom, the same room in which the festivities in honor of her marriage had been held four years before. Foreign potentates called on her, but they were obviously amused to find her footmen still wearing the imperial livery of France. They were no less amused to see her driving about with Neipperg in carriages whose doors and harness still bore the Napoleonic coat of arms. Not everybody laughed, however, and when the ex-Empress drove to see the Tsarina on December 2, the crowds showed noisy disapproval. Marie Louise had to give orders for Napoleon's arms to be replaced by her monogram. The Congress talked of nothing else for three days.

Isabey, who had come to Vienna to paint the great men gathered there for the Congress, was asked for a portrait of "young Napoleon" —the portrait which, seven months later, the Emperor Napoleon would take with him to St. Helena. The child was posing in the uniform of a hussar, with the cross of the Legion of Honor on his chest, when the footman announced Field-Marshal Prince de Ligne. The first time the conqueror of Belgrade had sent in his name, the little Prince had anxiously asked: "Is he one of the marshals who betrayed Papa? If he is, I don't want to see him."

It had been explained to him, though not without difficulty, "that France was not the only country in the world that had marshals." Since then the old Prince had often come to see the child. On this particular day, as soon as the boy saw him coming in behind Maman Quiou, he jumped off his chair and ran into his old friend's arms. The Prince was accompanied by the Comte de Lagarde, whom he introduced as "a Frenchman."

The boy held out his little hand. "I like Frenchmen," he said.

"He was really the most handsome child one could imagine," wrote the Comte de Lagarde later. "His resemblance to his grandmother Maria Theresa was astounding. His angelic profile, the brilliant whiteness of his complexion, the fire in his eyes, and his beautiful fair hair falling in great curls over his shoulders provided Isabey with the most charming of models."

While the two visitors were admiring the portrait, "an astonishing likeness," the boy fetched a box of wooden hussars who, "mounted on moving bases, could execute all the movements of a regiment."

"On parade, Prince!" shouted the old Field Marshal.

The regiment was promptly set out in battle order. The Prince de Ligne drew his sword.

"Attention!"

The young Prince immediately "straightened up, as solemn as a Russian grenadier," and took up his position on the left wing of the regiment. A succession of commands were then carried out "with the same promptitude and solemnity." An hour later, driving toward Vienna, the old Field Marshal sighed and said to his companion:

"When Napoleon was at Schönbrunn arranging for the occupation of Vienna and drawing up his plans for the memorable Battle of Wagram; when he paraded his victorious regiments in those huge courtyards, he was far from imagining that the ruler whose fate he held in his hands would one day hold as hostages the son of the victor and the daughter of the vanquished. In the course of my long career I have seen much glory and much misfortune, but nothing comparable to the story whose last chapter we have just enacted."

Some time before, the boy had told the Prince how he had seen General Delmotte's funeral procession go by and how wonderful it had been.

"I shall give you something much more satisfying soon," the old Prince had said with a smile; "because a field marshal's funeral is the most magnificent thing you can see of that sort."

And on December 13, 1814, the little Prince of Parma did in fact see the procession go by, followed by ten thousand troops, that was taking his old friend to his last resting place.

On January 1, 1815, the Emperor's valet Marchand went into his master's bedroom at Portoferraio, to be greeted with the question: "What are you giving me for the New Year?"

"I can only express the wish to see Your Majesty reunited with the Empress and the King of Rome."

Napoleon looked at him with tears in his eyes and sighed: "The poor child!"

And to Commissioner Campbell he declared: "They have taken my son away from me just as they used to take the children of the vanquished to adorn the trophy of the victors. Nothing more barbarous has been perpetrated in modern times."

Meanwhile, for New Year's Day, Marie Louise had written her last letter to the Emperor:

I hope this year will be a happier one for you; at least you will be at peace on your island and you will live there happily for many years to the joy of all who love you and are devoted to you as I am. Your son sends you a kiss and asks me to wish you a happy New Year and to tell you he loves you with all his heart; he often talks about you and is growing taller and stronger in the most astonishing way. He has been rather out of sorts this winter; I consulted Frank straight away and he completely reassured me by saying they were only passing attacks of fever; and indeed he recovered almost at once. He is beginning to know Italian fairly well, and is learning German too; my father is treating him with the utmost kindness and affection. He seems to be very fond of him and spends a great deal of time playing with him. . . .

What a lot had happened in a year! Nearly twelve months had gone by now without her seeing her husband, and her married life already seemed to have been blurred by time. On this morning of January 1 the little French colony crowded into the gallery after Mass to wish her a happy New Year. The child they still called "the little King" ran to Méneval's arms and hugged him hard. The afternoon and the next day the "poor child" spent with his mother. "We were busy yesterday and today," she wrote, "making our New Year calls, in which he acquitted himself with all his usual boyish charm; I felt touched and proud at all the compliments the people paid him as we went by; you know what severe judges they are, but my son conquered them with the way he waved to them." The crowds shouted: "Long live the Duke of Parma!" . . . which made some people shrug their shoulders. Would the prisoner of Europe, they asked, ever reign anywhere, even in Parma? And they smiled maliciously at the King of Bavaria's account of the call he had paid on "little Napoleon." Not in the least intimidated, the child had apparently asked "when he was going to join his Papa" and had declared:

"Saint-Cloud is nicer than Schönbrunn and I like French soldiers better than Austrian soldiers!"

He would have to get used to the Vienna Woods and the white uniforms of the Austrian army, for it seemed unlikely that he would be allowed even to go to Parma with his mother. There was even some doubt whether the ex-Empress herself would be able to take possession of her "object of four hundred thousand souls." The Treaty of Paris had promised her the Duchy, but the Spanish Bourbons, the former rulers of Parma, Piacenza and Guastalla, were plotting behind the scenes and claiming the territory for the son of the former Queen of Etruria. As Méneval observed, "the claims put forward by the Court of Spain were by no means displeasing to the allied sovereigns, who felt certain misgivings at the prospect of having Napoleon's wife established in Italy. They provided material for fresh arguments which were successfully employed to persuade her to appear indifferent if not hostile to the Emperor's interests. She was given to understand that any suspicion of complicity with him would deprive her forever of the advantages which Austrian benevolence could afford her, and the loss of which would harm not only her but also the Austrian Empire. These considerations, expounded with great skill, the fear instilled into the Empress that she might hurt her father, for whom her respect grew in proportion to the sterile affection which he displayed for her, the impossibility of ever being reunited with the Emperor, and the Austrian way of thinking which, so to speak, beset her on all sides, left her weak and defenseless."

The most ardent support for the Spanish cause came from the French delegation. Louis XVIII's envoys were determined to do their utmost to prevent the former King of Rome from reigning one day over Parma and even—pending his mother's death—from playing the part of heir to the throne. "I must say that I consider this of the highest importance," Talleyrand wrote to Louis XVIII on January 19, "because by this means the name of Bonaparte could be struck off the list of sovereigns for the present and the future, since the Isle of Elba only belongs to the present occupant during his lifetime and the Archduchess's son would have no independent State of his own."

At the same time Fouché wrote to Metternich from Paris that the new government had stirred up so much discontent that if the Emperor's son were to appear at Strasbourg riding an ass, the first regiment he met would lead him straight to Paris without encountering the slightest opposition.

Metternich had to find a solution to the problem without delay. He saw Marie Louise fairly frequently and decided to try the effect of a hot-and-cold technique. One day he told her that she was certain to obtain Parma; the next day the Duchy was given to someone else. This alternation of hope and fear kept her in a state of constant anxiety; it also had the effect of preparing her for the sacrifices that were going to be demanded of her, and of increasing her desire to see her fate finally settled. Once the ground had been prepared for Neipperg's intervention, the Minister explained to the General that "among the various reasons for the delay in recognizing the Empress's rights, the Congress's reluctance to see her son accompany her to Italy" was the most serious.

Neipperg set to work and soon persuaded Marie Louise to "sacrifice herself for the good of her child." But if she refused the Duchy of Parma, what would become of her son? Neipperg advised her to state her terms, and she accordingly wrote to Francis:

> I cannot conceal the fact, my dear father, that it grieves me to agree to changes with regard to my son's future which I believed I had a right not to expect after all the immense sacrifices I had already made in the interests of European peace. Only the cession

of an equivalent territory in some other part of the Austrian monarchy and under the same conditions could persuade me to renounce the existing agreement, and I am fully determined not to accept from anyone any equivalent in the form of a pension. It is both my duty as a mother and my firm determination to see my son's future not only provided for but securely established in my lifetime. . . . If the conditions which I propose, and which are as moderate as they are just, were to prove unacceptable to the contracting parties of the Congress of Vienna, then I should prefer to risk leaving the question of the Parma open until such time as it should be raised again.

Had she gone too far? Might not her father take her at her word? She decided to add—and here Neipperg's influence can be distinguished: "It will grieve me deeply to go to Parma in accordance with your gracious decision to separate me from my son; but you know better than anyone else what is best for me and him, and in this, as in everything, I shall follow blindly your fatherly advice."

Francis promised to look after his grandson's interests: it might be possible to carve out a domain for him in Bohemia. As *liebe Mamma* wrote to her stepdaughter, without any ironical intent, she could now "gather the fruit of the sacrifices" which she "had borne with such nobility of soul."

In the interests of her love, her peace of mind, her bourgeois life, "Mme. Neipperg" chose to sacrifice her son. The ex-Prince of Parma was nothing now, nothing but a "little Monsieur," nothing but a carnival king. And indeed, at a Twelfth-night party at Schönbrunn, it was he who had found the royal bean. "The King!" they had shouted, and the child had puffed himself out with pride. . . .

"Shocked and grieved," Méneval tried to plead the boy's cause, but all in vain. Napoleon's old secretary spoke with heartfelt emotion about the fate reserved for this "child without a name."

"Because, Madame, we don't know what to call him now . . ."

Marie Louise replied by talking figures. In Parma she would set aside money for her son which, added to the promised revenue from Bohemia, would assure him of "an independent existence." Utterly disgusted, Mme. de Montesquiou gave up the fight, and when her husband urged her to return to Paris she replied:

My dear, do not make it my duty to return to France; as I have already explained, you would place me in the most embarrassing position, and my conscience would go on reproaching me for the rest of my life. If this child had a mother, well and good, I should leave him in her hands without the slightest hesitation; but she is anything but a mother; she cares less about his fate than the humblest girl in his service; what is more, the others would follow me if I left, for lack of any inducement to remain; as long as I am here, they have someone to console them, but if I went they would not know what to do and it would be the poor child who would suffer. . . . It is clear that if I considered nothing but my feelings, interests and inclinations, I should not stay here another week, but I do not think I can possibly take these things into account before coming to a decision. Our little company is often to be found weeping over this cradle.

It was already as if they were weeping over an orphan.

8

✤

Napoleon II

IT WAS SIX O'CLOCK in the morning of March 7, 1815. A courier bearing an urgent dispatch had just arrived at Prince Metternich's residence. The Minister had not gone to bed until three in the morning, after a meeting of the representatives of the Five Powers which had lasted far into the night. He had accordingly told his valet not to wake him, but the latter none the less decided to take the dispatch in to his master. On the envelope Metternich read the words: "From the Imperial and Royal Consulate at Genoa."

"I tried to go back to sleep," he wrote later, "but found it impossible to do so. About half-past seven I decided to open the envelope. It contained just the following six lines: 'The English Commissioner Campbell has just entered the port to ask if anyone had seen Napoleon at Genoa after his disappearance from the Isle of Elba. The reply being in the negative, the English frigate put to sea again without delay.'"

Metternich jumped out of bed, dressed as quickly as he could, and at eight o'clock sent his name in to the Emperor Francis.

"Napoleon appears to be looking for trouble," said the Emperor. "That is his affair. Ours is to give the world that peace which he disturbed for so many years. Go and find the Emperor of Russia and the King of Prussia; tell them that I am ready to order my armies to take the road to France again. I have no doubt my two brother sovereigns will follow my example."

"At a quarter past eight," writes Metternich, "I was with the Emperor Alexander, who spoke to me in the same terms as the Emperor Francis. At half-past eight King Frederick William III gave me an identical assurance. At nine o'clock I was back at my house. I had already sent for Field-Marshal Prince Schwarzenberg. At ten o'clock the Ministers of the Four Powers met at my request in my study."

Talleyrand limped in, stiff and arrogant, already planning the "outlawing of the brigand."

For the moment, wrapped in his customary imperturbability, he was almost the only one who was taking the news calmly. His colleague Alexis de Noailles started shouting: "Now he has escaped, we must hang him!"

To which the King of Prussia very sensibly replied: "We can't hang him until we've caught him, and that won't be so very easy."

The news was kept more or less secret all day, and only really started spreading in the evening, at a reception given by Maria Ludovica. Reactions varied, but the general mood was one of optimism. They would rush at the monster and destroy it. There was considerable comment when the King of Bavaria, one of Napoleon's former allies, elbowed his way through the crowd and shouted at Talleyrand: "You are on our side this time!"

He was indeed. But some people wondered. A feat of this sort could not have been carried out without assistance. What about the English squadron that was supposed to be cruising off the Isle of Elba? Those who were always ready to detect the hand of perfidious Albion in any shady enterprise were already hinting that Colonel Campbell, whose mission it had been to keep watch over the Ogre, had received orders from his government not to interfere if the Emperor tried to escape. There was talk of a journey the Austrian General Koller had just made in Italy. Had he paid a secret visit to Elba? "People remembered," writes Bausset, "the oracle who, as far back as the previous September, had indicated the rock of St. Helena as the hero's prison. Here at last was the explanation of all the vast military apparatus which contrasted so strangely with the assurances of friendly intelligence between the Powers, the strategic strangulation of the frontiers of France, the inexplicably slow progress made by the Congress, the oft-heard regrets that France had been left so powerful and rich in heroism and resources, etc. Napoleon's escape seemed such a bold and unexpected stroke that many people felt justified in believing that some mysterious guarantee had been given to him, unknown to the Emperor of Austria though in his name." A few more thoughtful commentators observed that by not paying the Emperor the two million he owed him in exchange for his fortune, Louis XVIII had practically forced him to escape or at least furnished him with a pretext. . . . Not to mention Louis XVIII's other mistakes and the general state of discontent in France.

There seemed to be only one haven of peace that evening, and that was Marie Louise's drawing room at Schönbrunn. "There was dinner, billiards and music as usual." The ex-Empress was as calm as M. de Talleyrand . . . but in both cases it was a feigned calm. The news of Napoleon's flight had been brought to her by Neipperg when she was out riding. When she dismounted on her return, her face betrayed no sign of emotion. Officially she knew nothing as yet. It was only the next morning that she received this letter from *liebe Mamma*:

My dearly beloved, it cannot unfortunately be unknown to you any longer, since it is common knowledge in all classes of society, that the Emperor Napoleon left his island with two thousand men on March 26 [February 26]. No one knows in which direction he is marching, but you will understand that hostile measures will have to be taken. I suffer for you with all my heart, and since last night you have occupied my thoughts to the exclusion of all else, for the rest does not alarm me in the slightest degree. I did so want to come to see you, to make sure that you did not hear the news from some indifferent person, but Papa would not allow me to go to Schönbrunn as he wants to see you himself. I beg you not to mention this note, and I implore you to burn it yourself immediately. . . .

Fortunately for the historian, Marie Louise did not comply with this request, and the note was found among her papers. We do not know what was said between Francis and his daughter, but we know the result of their conversation. On March 12, Marie Louise sent her father the following declaration, worked out with Neipperg's help:

On the occurrence of a new crisis which menaces the peace of Europe and threatens to bring down fresh misfortunes on my head, I cannot hope to find a surer shelter, a kindlier haven than that which I beg your fatherly tenderness to provide for myself and my son. It is in your arms, my dear father, that I seek refuge together with the person whom I hold dearest in this world. I place our fate in your hands and under your protection. I could not place it under a more sacred aegis. We shall know no other will but yours, and in your tenderness you will not fail to heed my entreaties in so difficult a moment. . . .

Without the slightest remorse she disowned the man whom she had claimed to adore a few months earlier, and snatched the son away from his father. It was Metternich's belief—possibly prompted by Talleyrand—that this appeal for help and protection would put an end to insinuations that the former Regent of the Empire and her son were being held captive in Vienna by Austria and her allies, an act of abduction and restraint which the outlaw might have taken as a pretext for coming to the rescue of his wife and son.

The same day, moreover, she wrote to Lannes's widow that she was "exceedingly vexed with *the person* who has thus placed the future of myself and my son in jeopardy." And the next day Napoleon's former Minister of Foreign Affairs and Grand Chamberlain, Prince de Bénévent by the Emperor's will, produced for his colleagues' approval an extraordinary document which one cannot read today without a feeling of disgust. Bonaparte's escape was described as "a crime against the social order." "By appearing again in France," stated the document, "with projects of confusion and disorder, he has deprived himself of the protection of the law and proved to the universe that there can be neither peace nor truce with him. The Powers consequently declare that Napoleon Bonaparte has placed himself outside the pale of civil and social relations, and that, as an enemy and disturber of the tranquillity of the world, he has rendered himself liable to public vengeance."

Tallyerand rubbed his hands with delight to see the Emperor Francis demean himself to the extent of calmly signing this document, a slap in the face administered to his daughter's husband, his grandson's father.

"He had to be persuaded to put his signature to a sentence of civil death," the Prince explained later, "and not a declaration of war. One can always deal with an enemy, but there is no remarrying a convict."

Meanwhile hope had not been abandoned that Louis XVIII might succeed in arresting the brigand. Maria Ludovica told her stepdaughter that Paris had been "intrigued" by the news, "but by no means alarmed." And she went on: "In a few days it will all be over. I hope to Heaven that it may end in the manner least likely to distress you, my beloved!"

"My poor Louise, how sorry I feel for you!" wrote the Archduke John. "For your sake and ours, I hope that he breaks his neck!"

But what if he didn't? What if the Eagle's flight took him safely to Paris and scattered the Bourbons to the four winds like a flock of sparrows? In that event, Napoleon would be sure to do everything in his power to have his wife and son beside him again. Baron Hager, President of the Police, began losing sleep over the possibility of an attempt to abduct "the Archduchess's child." The presence in Vienna of Colonel de Montesquiou, who had come to see his mother, worried him beyond belief.

On March 16 the guard was doubled at Schönbrunn and policemen disguised as servants were installed in the castle with orders to be extra vigilant. On March 18 they reported that the Frenchwomen on the staff had reproached Mme. de Montesquiou for "not taking the first opportunity to carry off the young Prince." It was rumored that Schulmeister, Napoleon's famous spy, had been seen at Elsberg in Upper Austria.

It was at this point that the wretched Hager persuaded the Emperor Francis to have the boy transferred from Schönbrunn to the Hofburg, where supervision would be far easier. Francis announced this decision the same day, March 18, when his daughter arrived with the child on her usual daily visit to her father.

"It is the Sovereigns' wish," he said.

Marie Louise bowed to his decision. After betraying the father, she now agreed without a murmur to deliver the son into captivity.

On her return to the castle she sent for Mme. de Montesquiou and told her that the next day—March 19—she was to leave for Vienna with the little Prince. The same morning a letter from Napoleon reached Vienna, written in Lyons on the 11th: "My advance guard is at Chalon-sur-Saône. I am leaving tonight to join it. The people run to greet me in great crowds; whole regiments have abandoned everything to join me. . . . By the time you receive this letter I shall be in Paris. . . . Come and join me with my son. I hope to embrace you before the end of the month."

This letter was not delivered to Marie Louise but taken to the Congress, where the allied ministers "tried to make out a scrawl that no one could read." Each in turn deciphered a word . . . and soon they had before their eyes the tragic certainty of seeing the Emperor installed in Paris. While he was being dislodged it seemed more than likely that secret emissaries would try to gain entrance to the Hofburg with the help of Mme. de Montesquiou, Bausset or Méneval. The guard would have to be doubled yet again, and there would have to be sentries "watching day and night inside the Palace and under the very windows of the young Napoleon; a permanent and active police force outside; a continuous though invisible inquisition, and countless lines of troops, not only in Austria, but also in the neighboring States."

The next day—March 20—was the birthday of Napoleon's son. Mme. de Montesquiou had spent the night in what she later described as "that state of agitation engendered by some vague anxiety." At dawn, wishing to be the first to greet the little prisoner of the Hofburg, she instructed Mme. Marchand to bring the child to her "as soon he opened his eyes." This was done.

"You are four years old today," she told him. "How long have you loved me?"

"For four years," he replied, "and I shall love you all my life."

At Maman Quiou's request, the child knelt down to say his "big prayers." He was only halfway through them when a valet announced the arrival of the Count of Urban, Grand Chamberlain of the Emperor of Austria. Thinking that this eminent individual had come to offer birthday greetings to his master's grandson, Maman Quiou enjoined "the greatest politeness" on the little Prince, took him by the hand, and led him up to the Grand Chamberlain. The latter seemed to be extremely ill at ease, and his embarrassment increased when, seeing his confusion, the governess announced that "His Highness the Prince of Parma" was celebrating his fourth birthday. It became clear to Maman Quiou that this was not the object of the Chamberlain's visit.

"Madame, I should like to speak to you in private."

Mme. de Montesquiou, somewhat alarmed by his solemn tone of voice, asked the child and her deputy governesses to leave.

"What do you wish to say to me, Monsieur?"

The Grand Chamberlain looked more and more uneasy. Finally he said: "The Emperor, my master, has asked me to inform you that political circumstances force him to make certain changes in his grandson's education. He thanks you for the services you have rendered him and begs you to leave immediately for Paris."

Utterly dumfounded, Mme. de Montesquiou felt her heart beating wildly. Making an effort to gather her wits together, she tried at first to plead her cause, but then changed her line of attack.

"Monsieur," she said, "pray tell the Emperor that, having been dependent on him alone for the past year, I wish to return into his own hands the charge which was confided to me."

The Grand Chamberlain went out; the child came back into the room and rushed into his governess's arms "as he was accustomed to doing when he had lost his Maman Quiou from sight a moment."

A few minutes later the Count of Urban returned bearing a letter from the Emperor:

> Madame la Comtesse de Montesquiou, the circumstances of the day leaving me no alternative but to effect certain changes in the personnel entrusted with the education of my grandson, I do not wish to miss this opportunity of expressing to you my gratitude for the services you have rendered him since he was born. Pray accept my expression of this sentiment and the token of remembrance which I have asked my Grand Chamberlain to give you on my behalf, Madame la Comtesse de Montesquiou.
>
>   Your affectionate: FRANCIS
>
> Vienna, March 20, 1815

"This token of remembrance," wrote Mme. de Montesquiou later, "was a beautiful sapphire necklace. My first reaction, on hearing a present mentioned, was that of the liveliest indignation. I said that I would accept nothing from the Emperor of Austria. The Chamberlain placed the packet on the table. I asked him once more to take it back to the Emperor and tell him that I had never expected anything in return for my services except kindness and courtesy. The Count of Urban replied that he could not deliver my message, that it was quite out of the question, that one could not refuse a present from the Emperor. He then went on to apologize for not giving me the necklace in a jewel case, explaining that it had been chosen in too much a hurry. This tactless observation was a new and supreme source of pain to me, for I saw that nothing I could say would be understood by this half-witted intermediary. This was a terrible thought, which completely discouraged me."

Suddenly the door opened. It was Marie Louise, looking "cold and embarrassed." She was visibly delighted at the dismissal of Mme. de Montesquiou, whom she had had to put up with for four long years. Now she would no longer have before her eyes the arch-enemy of her beloved Montebello, the woman whose every word and action for months past had been a condemnation of her behavior.

"Well, Madame," said the governess, "I suppose you will never stop believing what my enemies say to you about me?"

"What I hear is not very agreeable."

"Alas, I thought that my conduct was sufficient protection against spite."

Mme. de Montesquiou insisted on "a consultation of the Emperor's first physician, the child's physician in ordinary and the Empress's surgeon, so that my pupil could be thoroughly examined and I could be furnished with a certificate testifying to the perfect state of health in which I was leaving him." Marie Louise agreed. She also had to agree that the separation should not take place until that evening, when the little Prince would be fast asleep.

"I want him to have another twelve hours of peace and happiness."

"Do you intend to see the Emperor Napoleon?"

"Wherever he may be, I shall go and give him an account of my behavior."

Marie Louise retorted angrily under her breath: "That's all the same to me!"

She had gone red in the face, and paced up and down the room, waiting for the doctors to appear. They arrived with Neipperg. Mme. de Montesquiou undressed the child, "who understood nothing of what was happening," and the certificate was duly signed.

That evening the Eaglet was put to bed in his big room at the Hofburg. "I went up to the little bed where my pupil was sleeping," writes Mme. de Montesquiou. "I knelt down and commended him to Heaven's care. I prayed above all that his name should never be used to stir up trouble. I kissed him several times and only tore myself away after attaching to the bed curtains a little crucifix he had often asked me to give him."

The same day, March 20, Napoleon's lightning ride brought him back to Paris. Perhaps that evening, in the Tuileries, he went and stood for a few moments in the empty bedroom of his little King, the "poor little devil" as he called him.

Again on the 20th, Hager circulated the description of "the Arch-duchess's child" to all the police stations and customs houses in the vast Austrian mosaic. Thanks to this description we know that the child was tall for his age, that his cheeks were full, his eyes blue, his little nose "tip-tilted with wide nostrils," his mouth small with the lips pouting slightly and "divided by a dimple," and his hair golden-yellow and falling in great curls on to his shoulders. He was dressed either in a white jacket with gold buttons or "the blue tunic of the regiment of French hussars in which he holds an honorary command," with the grand cross of the Order of St. Stephen and a gold bar with four different crosses on the left side of his chest. On his head he wore either a beaver-fur bonnet or his plumed tricorn. He was very alert and talked vivaciously, "accompanying his words with sweeping gestures." We also learn that while he usually spoke French, the boy already knew a little German, thanks to his Austrian valet Unterschild.

Mme. de Montesquiou had not been able to leave Vienna and had to remain for another two months a virtual prisoner in a little two-room flat which she shared with her son. Méneval was luckier, in that he was given his passport for France almost immediately. Before leaving, he went to the Hofburg to say good-by to his master's son. He found that the boy was not called "little Napoleon" any more. but Francis, while his Austrian relations called him Franz, a name which the boy considered "ugly." Méneval was sorry to observe "his serious and even melancholy air. He had lost that playfulness and loquacity of his which had so much charm." He was forever asking Chanchan— Mme. Marchand—where his beloved Maman Quiou had gone. On this particular day he did not run to meet "Monsieur Méva" as he used to. On the contrary, he watched his father's secretary come in with apparent indifference, "giving no sign," wrote Méneval, "that he knew me." His suite was no longer exclusively French, and he seemed "to regard these new faces with suspicion." Méneval took his hand, told him of the imminent departure, and asked him if he had any message to send his father, whom he would be seeing very soon. The child gave him "a sad and meaningful look," withdrew his hand and went toward a window recess. "After exchanging a few words with the people in the drawing room," writes Méneval, "I went to where he was standing, watchful and alone; as I bent down to bid him farewell, struck by my obvious emotion, he drew me toward the window and, looking at me with a touching expression on his face, he whispered:

"'Monsieur Méva, you will tell him that I still love him very much.'"

On his arrival in Lyons on March 13, Napoleon had issued a decree summoning the electoral colleges to Paris in May, in order to alter the Constitution, but above all "to be present at the coronation of the Empress, our dearly beloved wife, and of our dearly beloved son." He had sent several pressing letters to Vienna, at least three of which had reached their destination. On April 1 he had written to his "dear brother and father-in-law," mentioning "that ardently desired reunion which must also be impatiently awaited by the virtuous princess"— and adding: "My efforts are simply designed to consolidate this throne which the love of my peoples has kept for me and restored to me, and to bequeath it one day, established on unshakable foundations, to the child on whom Your Majesty is lavishing his fatherly love."

Now, shortly before the middle of May, Méneval arrived at the Élysée, and in a lengthy interview with his master opened the Emperor's eyes to the true state of affairs, indicating the form which the "fatherly love" of the "dear brother and father-in-law" was taking.

In the Paris streets the people sang a cruel little song asking Napoleon what had become of his Marie Louise, but they were touched by the fate of the Prince Imperial—the new name given to the Emperor's heir. His popularity during the Hundred Days was all the greater in that the little four-year-old was in the enemy's hands. Because, as from Napoleon's return to the Tuileries, Europe considered herself as in a state of war with France. No reply would be made to the "escapee's" peace proposals, for in Europe's eyes M. de Buonaparte —without his wife and son—was nothing more than an escaped convict. And Napoleon knew it. As Frédéric Masson has observed, "one of his principal motives for risking the escape from Elba was to get back his wife and son. Once the miracle had been performed, it could only last if they returned."

Besides his letters to Vienna, the Emperor had sent several emissaries, one of whom—Montrond—was received, albeit coldly, by the Allied ministers.

"Read the declaration of March 13," Talleyrand told him: "There is not a single word in it that I do not endorse."

"No peace with Napoleon!" exclaimed Nesselrode.

Napoleon knew now that he would soon have the whole of Europe to fight. If the first attack did not lay him low, the second or third would. He was well aware of this, and wondered whether to try to save the dynasty at least by abdicating before the first shot was fired. Why should not Austria agree to a regency—the regency of Marie Louise during Napoleon II's minority? And might not England, Prussia and Russia accept this solution out of contempt for the Bourbons?

Why, one wonders, did Metternich, thinking on the same lines, send a secret—and officious—emissary to Basel at the beginning of May? Was it to "trip up" the Emperor, to "entangle" his enemy in a complex intrigue, as Louis Madelin believed? "To throw a new element of discord into the midst of a people who never stood so urgently in need of unity," as Frédéric Masson suggested? Or "to furnish the parliamentary delegates about to gather together the weapon with which, consciously or unconsciously, they would strike down the Emperor and deliver France to the enemy"?

Whatever the truth of the matter, Metternich's emissary, Baron Ottenfels, met Fleury de Chaboulon—whom he believed, incidentally, to be an envoy of Fouché's, since Napoleon's secretary introduced himself under an assumed name—and told him:

"I am authorized to give you a formal assurance that the Allied sovereigns have abandoned the idea of restoring the Bourbons to the throne, and that they agree to give you young Prince Napoleon. They are aware that the Regency was what France desired in 1814, and consider themselves fortunate to be able to fulfill that desire today."

But first of all, he added, the French would have to "depose" the Emperor.

"The Allies will then make what arrangements they think fit, in accordance with the circumstances; they are great, generous and human, and you may rest assured that they will treat Napoleon with the respect due to his rank, his marriage and his misfortune."

"They are weakening," exclaimed Napoleon on May 11, when he learned of these proposals, "since they offer me the Regency; my attitude has impressed them. If only they would give me another month, I should have no further fear of them!"

During the night of May 14-15, Baron du Stressard, whom the Emperor had sent to Vienna, returned to Paris with a message from Prince Eugene to the effect that "if Napoleon wishes to abdicate before the first shot is fired, his dynasty will be recognized by Austria, which country hopes to be able to persuade its allies to adopt the same course, but on condition that he delivers himself into the hands of his father-in-law, who offers him a place of residence in any city in his hereditary States. . . ."

The Emperor, whose eyes had just been opened by Méneval, waited three days before informing Stressard that he had no confidence in his father-in-law's word.

"After a victory, they will be forced to deal with me!"

After a victory! . . .

It was seven o'clock in the morning of Wednesday, June 21. Napoleon's post chaise, which had left Laon at eleven o'clock the night before, was rounding the outer walls of Paris and approaching the Barrière du Roule— the present Place des Ternes. The Emperor was in a hurry to get back to the Élysée. He had left the debris of his defeated army at Waterloo, clustered around their eagles, not one of which had fallen into the enemy's hands. As his carriage rattled down the Faubourg St.-Honoré, did the Emperor, one wonders, think of the little prisoner in the Hofburg? Perhaps he could go on fighting with the men who had got away from Waterloo, Grouchy's undepleted army corps and 160,000 men from the latest conscription levy? Or was the victory by which he hoped to impose his son on Europe going to slip through his fingers? If not, he would have to persuade the Deputies to help him. True, he could return to a dictatorship and dissolve that assembly of chatterboxes. . . . "Reign by the ax," as he said later to Gourgaud? That was repugnant to his nature.

It was an old man that Caulaincourt helped out of his carriage at the foot of the Élysée steps, an old man suffering from dysuria, an old man with a yellow complexion who found it hard to get his breath back. . . . He said later:

"I ought to have gone to the Chambers as soon as I arrived. I would have stirred them up and carried them away; my eloquence would have filled them with enthusiasm. I would have had Lanjuinais, Lafayette and a dozen or so others executed. . . ."

But he had neither the courage not the inclination to do anything of the sort. He was well aware that if he started shedding blood, there would be no end to the slaughter. He lacked the nerve to carry out a coup d'état, to violate the law: Brumaire was proof of that. He preferred to call for a hot bath and lie in it for an hour while Fouché and Lafayette plotted his downfall.

The same day, the Chamber of Deputies proclaimed itself in permanent session and declared that any attempt to dissolve it would be an act of high treason. The next day, the 22nd, seeing that their defiance of the master had gone unpunished, the Deputies decided to go a step further.

"I do not think," one of them said at the opening of the session, "that the Chamber can offer to enter into negotiations with the Allied powers, as they have declared that they would never negotiate as long as Napoleon remained on the throne. There is therefore only one course of action open to us, and that is to persuade the Emperor to abdicate."

There was loud applause, and even a few cries of "Depose him!"

"Tell your brother," Lafayette shouted at Lucien Bonaparte, "to send us his abdication, otherwise we shall send him his deposition."

From dawn that day, a large crowd outside the Élysée had been shouting: "Long live the Emperor!" As Louis Madelin rightly remarks, "this was to be the only time in the whole century that a crowd gathered outside a sovereign's palace, not to expel him from it but to maintain him in it." But what could it do in face of the ultimatum delivered to the Emperor by Regnault de Saint-Jean-d'Angély, the Minister of State? The Chamber gave Napoleon one hour to abdicate! One hour!

The wounded lion wanted at first to show his claws: he would turn those Jacobin hotheads out of their Chamber. But Regnault urged him to think again.

"By abdicating," he said, "Your Majesty would save his son's throne which deposition would bring down."

"My son! My son!" retorted Napoleon. "What a dream! If I abdicated, it would be in favor of the Bourbons, not my son. They at least are not prisoners in Vienna!"

It was half-past twelve when the Emperor dictated the following statement to Lucien:

"Frenchmen, when I began this war to maintain the independence of the nation, I counted on a combination of every effort and every will and the help of every national authority; I had reason to hope for success, and I defied the declarations which the Powers issued against me. Now, however, the circumstances seem to me to have altered. I therefore offer myself as a sacrifice to the hatred of France's enemies. May they be sincere in their declarations and have no animosity save for my person. . . ."

For the second time in a year, the dream of 1811 lay in ruins. Napoleon could think of nothing, not even his son. And Carnot and Lucien had to insist on his adding these two lines to his abdication:

"My political life is over and I proclaim my son Napoleon II Emperor of the French."

The Chamber showed a certain reluctance to proclaim Napoleon II Emperor, and his father had to tell a deputation which came to thank him for his abdication:

"I have abdicated only in favor of my son. If the Chambers will not proclaim him Emperor, then my abdication is null and void. The way things are shaping, you are going to have the Bourbons back. You will soon be shedding tears of blood."

In the Chamber of Peers it was nearly nine o'clock in the evening when Lucien went up to the tribune.

"What we have to do," he declared, "is to avoid civil war, to show that France is an independent nation, a free country. The Emperor is dead! Long live the Emperor! The Emperor has abdicated! Long live the Emperor! There cannot be an interval between an Emperor who dies or abdicates and his successor. That is the maxim on which constitutional monarchy is based. Any interruption is anarchy. I ask the Chamber of Peers, in conformity with the Constitutional Act and in a spontaneous and unanimous movement, to declare before the French people and the world that it recognizes Napoleon II as Emperor of the French. I hereby set the Chamber an example and swear loyalty to Napoleon II."

"If I have heard correctly," said Pontécoulant, "we are being asked to adopt a proposal without prior deliberation? . . . I firmly declare that I shall never recognize a child as my king, or someone living outside France as my sovereign. If we adopted this proposal, we should be told that the Emperor had to be considered a foreigner or a prisoner and that the Regent was a foreigner, and we should be given another Regent who would plunge us into civil war."

La Bédoyère, the general who had handed his regiment over to the Emperor at the gates of Grenoble, leapt up to the tribune and asked:

"Who are the people opposing this resolution? Who but individuals whose only loyalty is to power, who show as much skill in abandoning a monarch as they showed in flattering him? I have seen them at the sovereign's feet when he was at the height of his power, but they steal away as soon as he falls on evil days. They spurn Napoleon II as well, because they are eager to serve the foreigners whom they already consider as allies, and even as friends."

There was uproar in the Chamber—the peers went berserk just like ordinary deputies—and the young general was dragged from the tribune.

It was out of hatred for the Bourbons that the deputies were to agree to proclaim the "Prince of Parma" Emperor. A certain Dufermon had put the question in the clearest possible terms:

"Have we, or have we not, an Emperor of the French? We must conform to the Constitution. In that case Napoleon II is our sovereign. When they see that we have spoken in support of the leader designated by our Constitution, they won't be able to say that we are waiting for Louis XVIII!"

A great cry of "Long live the Emperor!" greeted the name of the King of Ghent. Anything rather than see the Bourbons return for a second time in the enemy's wagon train! Fouché decided that things were moving too fast. He pushed Manuel up to the tribune, and the latter proposed that the Chamber should "proceed with the business of the day on the understanding that Napoleon II had become Emperor of the French in consequence of the abdication of Napoleon I and by virtue of the Constitution of the Empire!"

To shouts of "Long live Napoleon II!" the appointment of a "government commission" was unanimously agreed to, and it was decided that a whole new series of coins—from five centimes to five francs—should be minted at once, bearing the inscription of "Napoleon II, Emperor of the French." However, Napoleon II had not really been proclaimed Emperor, but merely recognized as the *de facto* monarch. What is more, it was not a Regency which was to reign in the meantime, but a government commission.

Fouché's hour had nearly come. As early as the second day of the little Emperor's "reign," the Duke of Otrante, having become chairman of the government commission, ordered the release of the Baron de

Vitrolles, Louis XVIII's sometime Minister, and told him:

"You will go to the King and tell him that we are working in his interests, and though we may take a circuitous route we shall certainly end up by coming to him. At the moment we are having to go by way of Napoleon II, but we shall get to him in the end."

The Chamber, trembling at the idea of a return of the fleurs-de-lis, acclaimed the new Emperor more vociferously every day. Fouché asked it to prepare a new constitution, to keep it occupied.

Napoleon, who had withdrawn to Malmaison, presented another danger. Fouché sent the Minister for the Navy to inform him that "there was no longer any obstacle to his departure" for Rochefort, where two frigates were waiting for him before setting sail for America. It should be added that Fouché had just been advised that an English cruiser was also waiting off the coast, to pick up the sometime Emperor. . . . In order to rid himself of the liberal leaders, he sent them off, led by Lafayette, to negotiate an armistice and the recognition of Napoleon II with the Allies, knowing perfectly well that the plenipotentiaries would be passed on from one general to another. This would allow him to gain time and bring about the capitulation of the army, or at least its withdrawal toward the Loire.

Fishing in troubled waters, playing every trick he knew, and perpetrating the most remarkable betrayal in a career rich in recantations of every sort, he had no hesitation in asserting that the Allies were determined to restore Louis XVIII to the throne and that France had to yield to superior force—an act of high treason which Nesselrode described as criminal. The reign of Napoleon II took on the appearance of a myth. When it was learned that Louis XVIII had arrived at the gates of Paris, that Talleyrand had presented Fouché to the King—vice leaning on crime—and that His Majesty had given the chairman of the government commission the Ministry of Police, Carnot and Caulaincourt made no secret of their indignation. Fouché, to quote Chateaubriand's pitiless phrase, had "brought dishonor on the crime of '93." But the two other members of the commission held their peace. Quinette—another regicide—and Grenier, like the old revolutionaries who had returned to power during the Hundred Days, considered that after a precedent of that sort there was nothing to be feared from the new regime. On July 7, while Prussian bayonets were already appearing in the Place de la Concorde, the Chamber of the Hundred Days died "laboring to bring forth a constitution," leaving Napoleon II's throne to King Louis XVIII.

Marie Louise was taking the waters at Baden, near Vienna, when she received the news of Waterloo. The ex-Empress, it appears, was "beside herself with joy." So *liebe Mamma* told her husband, adding: "Our dear Louise thanks Heaven that he is in captivity, both for the general good and because she hopes to go to Parma soon."

The same morning the Baronne de Montet, who had also heard of the Emperor's "arrest," arrived at Baden. She was immediately received by her friend Élise, Marquise de Scarampi, who for the past three months had been occupying Mme. Montesquiou's place as governess to the little Prince, and who knew nothing of what had happened. As soon as the young woman heard the news, she began "jumping, singing and dancing all over the room. Napoleon's lackeys, who were serving us and who came and went with the saddest faces in the world, made no attempt to restrain her." Between two pirouettes Mme. de Montet asked: "Has the Empress Marie Louise been acquainted with this event? I must write to her at once, because the Empress never receives anybody before eleven o'clock."

The Marquise sat down at her desk, wrote a brief note, and sent it off to Marie Louise, who replied: "Thank you, I was already acquainted with the news you send me. I feel like going for a ride to Merkenstein; do you think it is fine enough to risk it?"

On July 21, at Schönbrunn, where the child had now returned, his French attendants talked about the news, taking no notice of "little Francis" lunching alone at his table. Suddenly the boy looked up. "My dear Papa is a wicked man," he said. "So will they kill him?"

One wonders what Mme. Scarampi or the Austrians who now surrounded him had said for him to talk like this. The few remaining members of his French household were heartbroken.

Marie Louise greeted the news of Louis XVIII's return to Paris with the same delight she had shown on hearing about Waterloo. She wrote to her father: "This has reassured me about a lot of stupid rumors which have been circulating here. . . ."

These "stupid rumors" concerned the proclamation of her son as Emperor of the French!

"My son," she went on, "kisses your hands and begs me to tell you that he is doing his best to become a very good boy; he reads French very well and Italian a little; I have promised him that when he knows that language fluently I shall ask you, on his behalf, for an Austrian regiment; that is his dearest wish, and if you graciously grant him this favor, I hope that my little Francis will prove himself worthy of it in time."

Thus, in the space of a few lines, Marie Louise rejoiced to see her son lose his throne, christened him Francis like her Austrian relations, and asked her father to give him—the ex-Emperor of the French—an Austrian regiment. In this way she paid her debt to the Congress of Vienna, which on June 10 had ratified the attribution of the Duchies of Parma, Piacenza and Guastalla to the ex-Empress, with a revenue of one million two hundred thousand francs. Did she feel a twinge of remorse when she received a letter dated August 6 from her father, telling her that Napoleon was going to be "transferred to St. Helena"? Did she remember her beloved "Nana" at Compiègne? Did she remember that only a year before she had written to him for his birthday on August 15: "No one loves you or ever will love you better than I do. I kiss you and love you with all my heart. Your true and loving Louise." No doubt she did, for on August 15, 1815—the Emperor's forty-sixth birthday—she replied to her father:

"Dearest Papa, I hope that we shall now have a lasting peace, seeing that the Emperor Napoleon will never again be able to disturb it. I hope that he will be treated with clemency and kindness, and I beg you, dearest Papa, to ensure that this is done. This is the only request I dare make to you, and it is the last time I shall trouble about his fate; but I owe him a debt of gratitude for allowing me to live in calm indifference instead of making me unhappy."

"Calm indifference"! Marie Louise's tender, loving letters to Napoleon, which have only been known to us since 1955, and those she wrote to her father, her stepmother and her sisters for four years—letters in which she proclaims her happiness on every page—condemn her out of hand today. If she had adopted Maria Caroline's advice to go to join her husband with her son—even if this had involved climbing out of the window—the greatest genius of all time would have been spared the martyrdom of St. Helena. For even supposing that the Emperor Francis had declared war on his "beloved son-in-law," how could the victors of Waterloo have sent their prisoner to die in the tropics if he had appeared before them on his wife's arm and holding the Emperor of Austria's grandson by the hand?

Meanwhile it seemed as if Marie Louise might be being a little premature in her delight at Louis XVIII's return to Paris and her son's definitive eviction. Imperial France, betrayed and hunted, might yet be able to derive sufficient strength from her martyrdom to destroy her oppressors. The White Terror had been in full force during the first two months since the return of the lilies, but the government was still finding it hard to get the situation under control.

"I have a letter from Papa," wrote Maria Ludovica to her step-daughter, "telling me that the *Rauferei* go on every day in Paris, that the French want neither the King nor his family, that the [an illegible word] wants a foreign prince, and that the army of the Loire has not yet made its submission to the King." The army in question was the old imperial army—the survivors of Waterloo, Grouchy's army corps, the defenders of Paris—which, under Davout's command, still constituted a far from negligible threat.

The situation was slow to clarify. Would it be necessary to have recourse to the Regency and Napoleon II? There were some who thought so. Marie Louise, thoroughly alarmed, had written to her father: "I beg you to remember in this connection, dear Papa, what I told you the day before you left, namely that never again, under any circumstances, would it be possible for me to return to France. I have just heard, from dear Mamma, that the King's party is very powerful, and that makes me very happy."

The "very powerful" party was none the less going through a difficult time, and on August 6 Francis, who was then in the French capital, replied:

You may rest assured that I will not make you come to Paris; I would not want even my worst enemy to rule or live here; in this I am doing my duty, although I am drawing upon myself—and this has been made clear to me—the hatred of the greater part of France. The people here and all over France have grown so much worse since the last year that they want to have you as regent, simply in order to obtain power for themselves; they have no thought for anything but their personal interests.

The King is sure to realize this and will be lost unless we help him.

In spite of this help and the machinations of the "very powerful party," the Restoration remained on a very insecure footing. Writing again to his daughter on August 11, Francis reported:

> The King is surrounded by rogues and very unsteady on his throne; if I declared that you and your son were going to occupy it, he would be instantly overthrown. But God forbid that I should do so, for behind this screen there are other people who would like to rule—something we could never accept—while you and your son might well suffer the most appalling fate. So I am happy to know that you are at home now, and will soon be in Parma. But you cannot imagine how much hatred and even threats this is earning me here; still, the future will justify my conduct, and in any event my conscience is always easy when I do my duty.

Marie Louise too made a point of doing her duty. Before returning to Vienna, the Duchess of Parma decided to go on a pilgrimage to Marigall, as she had sworn she would if she obtained her Duchy. On September 2, replying to Mme. de Montebello, who had asked her about "Francis's" education, she wrote:

> You ask me what I mean when I say that I intend to have him brought up according to the principles of my native land: I mean that I want to make a German prince out of him, as good and honest as the rest; and when he grows up I want him to serve his new country. . . . It is by means of his talents, his intelligence and his chivalry that he will have to make a name for himself, since the name he has by birth is an unfortunate one.

Marie Louise sometimes makes one feel rather sick.

She still hoped, in spite of everything, that her father might allow her to take her son with her, since no one could now point to Napoleon's dangerous proximity on the Isle of Elba as an objection. A letter from the Emperor Francis, written in Paris on September 6, undeceived her:

> You could not do better than to place your son in men's hands, some time before your departure for Italy, to see how it works out. You can leave a woman with them to begin with, if you like, but you will find if you do that it will not last long. If I want your son to stay in Vienna, it is because it is necessary for his own

safety, for until the storm now shaking the world has abated I cannot feel happy about him unless he is with people who, out of devotion to myself, will not allow anything untoward to happen to him. It must be remembered too that his father's wishes might prove a stumbling block, and that he has many enemies—you know what I mean. . . .

She knew. It was quite likely that the little ex-Emperor would be carried off one day. She was in complete agreement with her father. The Emperor Francis had left Paris by now, and on September 30 he wrote to his daughter from Melun:

> There is only one other thing I would ask you to see to if he is entrusted to the care of men, and that is to forbid his entourage ever to speak to him about his former situation, or to meet his unspoken wishes so well that he has no need to exert himself or even ask anybody for anything—this to prevent pride and selfishness from developing within him from early youth. God knows that I want to see him become a brave, upright and virtuous man; since he has the most promising of dispositions, may he grow up for the greater happiness of the men who will be entrusted to him, and not for the greater misery of the world.

The Emperor could set his mind at rest. On June 30, 1815—in the middle of his brief reign—the former Prince of Parma had been entrusted to the care of Count Maurice Dietrichstein, who furnished Marie Louise with the following outline of his plans for the education of Napoleon's son:

> It is necessary to banish everything that might remind him of the life he has led till now. People retain clear enough memories of their childhood years, that is to say of the age at which the Prince is now, to give us reason to fear, considering everything he is told, that he may one day hanker after the life he might have led. Above all, care must be taken not to instill into him exaggerated ideas about the qualities of a people to whom he can no longer belong, for fear that these ideas might follow him into his years of maturity. It seems to me that the Prince whose education I have been given the honor of directing must be considered as of Austrian descent and brought up in the German fashion. His education requires considerable attention. Many of

the tendencies of his precocious sensibility must be restrained, and many of the ideas which have been implanted in his mind must be gradually eradicated, without making him suffer and without hurting his pride more than is necessary.

They were all three agreed that the sometime King of Rome should be turned into a boy "of Austrian descent," "brought up in the German fashion," "a German prince" to whom no one would ever again speak of "his former situation."

But another will would pit itself against these merciless decrees: the will of a little boy of four and a half.

Part Two

THE DUKE OF REICHSTADT

I am nothing but an encumbrance. . . .

9

✣

Francis Charles

ON THE MORNING of Friday, June 30, 1815, Napoleon, wearing a brown dress coat and a round hat, left Rambouillet for Rochefort, on the first stage of his journey to St. Helena. His "warder," Becker, offered him a pinch of snuff now and then. Carved on the ivory lid of the snuffbox was Marie Louise's profile. Napoleon took the box in his hands, looked at it, then gave it back to his companion with a sigh, but without saying a word.

The same morning Dietrichstein arrived at Schönbrunn and was ushered into Marie Louise's presence. The Emperor Francis had appointed him tutor to the boy who—for another week to come—was still the Emperor Napoleon II.

Count Maurice Proskau-Leslie Dietrichstein, music attendant to the Austrian Court, was an extraordinary melomaniac. A patron of Beethoven and Schubert—who dedicated the *Erlkönig* to him—he would later, as Director of the Imperial Theater, introduce Weber's *Freischütz* to the Viennese. But these qualities scarcely fitted him for the difficult task of bringing up Napoleon's son. He was honest and straightforward, but cursed with a sickly sensibility and a persecution complex. Perpetually tormented by his responsibilities, and even terrified by them, he was so pusillanimous, according to Gentz, Metternich's advisor, that he would be afraid of "being compromised by his pupil's progress." He was also an insufferable pedant and—as we shall see—totally incapable of understanding or accepting the smallest caprice, the slightest breach

of his rigid code of behavior. Worse still, Count Maurice was more of
a bore than anyone has a right to be. A bitter mouth, curly hair, long
sideburns framing a broad forehead, and an imposing nose. This
solemn, anxious, humorless face rested on top of a high linen cravat.

"The Count does not suit me," Marie Louise had told her father
at first. But Neipperg, a great friend of Dietrichstein's, had got her to
change her mind. The Duchess of Parma admitted that there was
something to be said for the new tutor's "imperturbable English gravity." Neipperg even went so far as to urge his mistress to give his
friend a post in Parma and ask him to resign his tutorship. But when
the Emperor Francis was sounded on this point he replied:

"The appointment I have given him is intended solely to appease my
people; in any event he would not go to Parma, and you will have to
find someone else with the necessary qualifications. . . ."

His "people" had made no secret of their annoyance at seeing "little
Napoleon" still being looked after by Frenchwomen. The appointment
of Dietrichstein, followed soon afterward, on September 6, 1815, by
that of a second tutor, Captain Foresti, was therefore calculated to reassure them.

The first encounter between pupil and master, on June 30, 1815, was
a disaster. The boy would not even go into his mother's apartments,
where Dietrichstein was waiting for him, standing stiff as a ramrod in
the middle of the drawing room.

"I don't want to go into the drawing room," he said, "because the
Chamberlain is there."

That was doubtless what the French governesses called the new
tutor, who did in fact enjoy the privileges of a Grand Master, though
not the title. In the end, however, the child had to go into the room,
where the sight of the grim, stiff, solemn man whose piercing eyes
coldly sized him up did nothing to improve matters. As soon as he
could, he ran back to Fanny and Mme. Soufflot.

From the very first, Dietrichstein tells us, "the tears flowed abun-
dantly." "He is lazy in the extreme," complained the "Chamberlain."
And yet the child was often full of good intentions.

"I must learn properly," he would say, "because I have to become
very wise. You are pleased with me, aren't you, because you aren't sad
today?"

Dietrichstein was nearly always sad. Methodical soul that he was,
he made a list of the child's accomplishments soon after his appoint-

ment as tutor. Francis Charles already possessed the rudiments of the catechism, reading and French grammar.

"Just see how well the Prince reads," the governesses told Dietrichstein.

The boy then began mumbling to himself and the Count shook his head mournfully. At bedtime, before having his hair put in forty curl papers—Francis hated this operation and longed for the day when he would stop looking like a little girl—he would listen to a reading of the adventures of Robinson Crusoe. But alas, "just the narrative part," grumbled Dietrichstein, "and not the moral, technological and instructive parts." The son of Napoleon was then four years and three months old. . . .

Dietrichstein wrote the following description of the child at this time:

> The Prince possesses to a high degree what is called a natural and innate intelligence. This shows itself on countless occasions when he takes an idea, explains it and develops it, asks pertinent questions and makes sensible and witty observations. If he is reprimanded for some reason or other, or again if he is punished, he shows no resentment. A few minutes later he comes up to the person who has just been admonishing him, gives him a kiss, and then goes back to his toys. Although there is a great lack of seriousness in all this, one cannot doubt the goodness of his heart, which must be carefully fostered.

The child was endowed with an exquisite and delicate sensibility. Moved to tears at the sight of a dog being ill-treated, he wept again one day when he saw a lark eating a worm. Unlike most children of his age, he loved giving his toys away, and his tutor was obliged to set limits to his generosity.

He was always extremely polite. One day, at table, he said: "I want . . ."

He quickly corrected himself: "I mean I should like . . ."

"He thought it was disrespectful to the Virgin," Foresti tells us, "to say: 'Blessed art thou amongst women,' and seemed totally unconvinced when I assured him that the Virgin was quite happy to be addressed as a mere woman."

His natural politeness captivated everyone. One day he went to Hadendorf with Dietrichstein to see the Baronne de Montet—mother-in-law of the author of the *Mémoires*. She stood to one side to allow him to go into the garden, but he refused, saying: "I am too well aware of the respect I owe a lady."

Dietrichstein insisted that he should go first. Was he not the Emperor's grandson?

"But I can't behave here as if I were at home," he explained in a whisper.

All these attractive qualities did not prevent him from being as vain as a child of four can be. One day, on an outing in the forest, he saw his footman walking in front of him.

"What's this?" exclaimed the child. "Why are you walking in front of the Prince?"

After that the footman followed behind Mathieu de Collin, the new history tutor.

"Let's hope," said the boy, "that nobody thinks he's Monsieur de Collin's lackey!"

Francis kept constantly referring to his former life, and this infuriated Dietrichstein.

"That was when I was King," he used to say.

He would not wear anything that had not come from Paris.

"Can they make clothes like these in Vienna?" he asked.

Dietrichstein took the question as a personal affront. "Every day," he complained, "I saw how persistently all sorts of memories of his past life were kept alive in him. They talked to him of nothing but Paris, his Court, his bedroom as a child, and so on."

Something had to be done about it. In Dietrichstein's opinion the trouble was caused by the governesses, who had "fed the child's imagination with vain fancies, playing tricks on his memory and taking advantage of his innocence." Mme. Soufflot, her daughter Fanny and Mme. Petitjean were told they had to go. The day his little playmate left, the child, choking with sobs, gave Fanny his favorite toys—his bugle, the little gun with which he used to mount guard outside his grandfather's door, and the scimitar he used when he played at being a mameluke.

Once the three women had gone, Dietrichstein was free to put into practice the program he had worked out. This was a plan to change his pupil's personality by making a complete break with everything that still bound him to his past. He began by having the N's and the imperial arms removed from the child's clothes and linen, substituting the initial *F* of his new Christian name.

"What is your name?" he asked his pupil one day.

There was a moment's silence "which showed that he was thinking," then the boy replied: "My name is Francis."

Soon he was never called anything but Franz. The toys that had been sent from France were confiscated, especially those marked with *N*'s, eagles or bees. His decorations of the Legion of Honor and the Iron Crown of Italy were also taken away, though now and then he was allowed to wear the star of St. Stephen, which had been given to him shortly after he was born. Finally Dietrichstein removed "all those books and albums of prints which by their contents or their bindings recalled the past."

Meanwhile, pending the ex-Empress's departure for Parma, Émile, the son of Marie Louise's valet, was still at Schönbrunn, and the two boys kept reminding each other of the Paris they had known together. One day when they were walking along the Hutteldorf road with Captain Foresti, Émile asked: "Are we on the road to Paris?"

"No," answered the Captain, "we are coming to the castle gates."

The little Prince then began chanting: "Oh, I wish this were Paris, really and truly Paris! Oh, I wish this were Paris!"

"The Prince," writes Foresti, "went on repeating this ditty for such a long time and in such an unbecoming way that I found myself obliged to raise my voice and put a stop to it. The Prince pulled a face to show his displeasure."

All the boys' games revolved round the imperial life of the past.

"Let's play passwords!" suggested Émile one day. "I'll shout: 'Long live the King of Rome!' "

"No," said the little Prince. "Let's shout what they used to shout in the streets of Paris: 'Long live the Emperor and the Empress!' "

Toward the end of November a huge parcel arrived for him from France. It contained the little carriage which Queen Caroline of Naples had given him and which two sheep trained by Franconi used to pull along the terrace besides the Tuileries. Dietrichstein, reduced to utter despair, recounts that "this apparition revived, as if by magic, all those memories of Paris and the imperial splendor of the court which had been somewhat dimmed since October 25. The Prince's playmate, Émile, joined in, and from that day on the excessive and often frenzied gaiety of the two children, as well as their insufferable chatter, grew to such a pitch that it was quite impossible to keep them quiet."

Émile was in the habit of coming to see his little master before he went to bed, and gabbling: "Prince, I wish you good night. Will Your Imperial Highness permit me to kiss your hand?"

This was all so inappropriate in the circumstances that one day Francis himself explained with a laugh: "That's Émile saying his catechism. He can't help it—Fanny taught him to say it."

Émile would be going soon, and Dietrichstein told himself that once he had gone everything would return to normal. Chanchan could not be allowed to stay on much longer either. It appears that the boy saw his Chanchan go without showing much sorrow. Henceforth Foresti slept in his bedroom. It was not until a fortnight after his cradle-rocker's departure that Francis called out when he woke up: "Chanchan!"

He then corrected himself: "Monsieur Foresti, I should like to be dressed."

The tutor and his two assistants—Mathieu de Collin and Captain Foresti—thought that their pupil was heartless and unfeeling. "It is clear," writes Dietrichstein, "that there is no trace in him of filial tenderness and affection. The ladies themselves used to say so. He took the departure of the Comtesse de Montesquiou in the spring of 1815 as calmly as he did that of Mme. Soufflot and her daughter in October of the same year, that of little Émile in March, 1816, and—something which I find even harder to understand—that of Mme. Marchand, who had cared for him so devotedly."

The fact was that Dietrichstein's training—a method which consisted of repressing his pupil's every emotion—was beginning to bear fruit. Brought up from now on by men, without any feminine influence whatever, he had no alternative but to turn in upon himself.

Foresti asserts that the boy also saw his mother go without showing any emotion. True, two days before the Duchess's departure, the little Prince wept and sighed during his dinner, saying: "Oh, how unhappy I am! No, nothing can console me!"

But the Captain assures us that this was just affectation on his part. "It is my belief," he writes, "that Mme. Marchand had whispered something in his ear to awaken, in appearance at least, his affection for his mother."

Now Mme. Marchand had left Schönbrunn by this time. . . . With obvious bad faith, Foresti goes on trying to prove that the child had no heart, and asserts that just before setting off on her journey Marie

Louise brought some toys to her son, who was still in bed. "The child took them," he writes, "and parted from his mother without showing the slightest emotion." This assertion is refuted by Marie Louise herself, in a letter she wrote to Mme. de Montebello: "I went through some cruel moments when I had to leave my people and particularly my poor son, whose grief caused me considerable distress, but I had the courage to keep my departure a secret from them all, and I left without saying good-by, very glad to have made that sacrifice." How could the child have shown any emotion when his mother had not told him that she was leaving Vienna?

He was alone now with his tutors, alone with those grim, solemn, unfamiliar men, who, among themselves, did not speak the same language as he. For some time to come, the boy would not go to sleep without a scarf his mother had left behind clutched in his little hands.

When Marie Louise left Schönbrunn, on March 7, 1816, she was sobbing and "heartbroken." "I do believe," she later wrote to Dietrichstein, "that I should have died of grief if I had not the hope of seeing him again in a few months."

She was not to return for another twenty-seven months. . . .

The Empress Maria Ludovica, who was seriously ill at Verona—she was to die the following month—wrote in reply to a letter from Marie Louise describing her sorrow: "My dearly beloved, I have just received your sweet letter which touched me deeply, and I fully understand the different feelings you must be experiencing at the moment, leaving your child to begin a new life in which I hope you will find peace and tranquillity. . . ."

For *liebe Mamma*, that chapter was closed. Not all the members of the imperial family felt the same way, however. The Emperor's brother, the Archduke Louis, who was in England at the time with his brother John, was saddened by his niece's decision to go to Parma and abandon her son. On the other hand, the Archduke Rainer, another of the Emperor's brothers and Marie Louise's best friend, considered that his niece was perfectly right, but expressed the hope that her absence would not be "too lengthy."

Frederick Gentz, "the *enfant terrible* of the Vienna Cabinet," summed up the situation as follows:

What is particularly painful for her is having to part from her son. This child, to whom so many sad and glorious memories are attached, is nearly five years old and full of charm, but difficult to manage because he combines considerable native wit with a pronounced aversion for any kind of compulsion or coercion. Whereas if he were given a first-class education he might well become a man of remarkable distinction, he is doomed to languish in mediocrity. Because he still arouses chimerical hopes in the hearts of millions of Frenchmen who cannot believe that Austria has completely abandoned him, little Napoleon is an object of fear and terror for most of the Cabinets of Europe. . . . The Emperor, inspired less by his own anxiety than by scruples which, in my opinion, he pushes much too far in an attempt to remove every possible cause for alarm, wants there to be nothing that may remind the Prince one day of the state of grandeur into which he was born. He must see no more of the members of his suite or others who took a share in his early upbringing. They even want to detach him completely from the French tongue and leave him with no other language than German, to which the child, for all his intelligence, is finding it difficult to accustom himself. If the House of Austria had entered into a solemn engagement, not only to fight Napoleon's dynasty, but also to appease anyone in Europe who might take fright at his name or his shadow, it could not have adopted a more thoroughgoing system. . . .

The boy found it hard to understand why he should be left behind while his mother went off on Neipperg's arm. The questions he put to his tutors reveal his bewilderment in the face of this abnormal situation.

"If my Mamma comes back to Austria," he asked Foresti, "will Monsieur de Neipperg come with her?"

"Very probably."

"But why, Monsieur, why?"

"Because your Mamma is a princess of the highest birth and she must always be accompanied by some respectable subject."

"But she isn't Empress now, is she?"

Foresti tried to change the subject, but the boy went on:

"Will my Mamma marry again?"

"You will have to ask your grandfather about that, because I just don't know."

"Perhaps she'll marry one of my uncles? Perhaps . . . perhaps . . ."

Marie Louise's departure left Dietrichstein free to go ahead with his policy of "defrancization." "The Prince no longer having the good fortune to breakfast with his august mother," he wrote on March 26, "I began a fortnight ago—in collaboration with Dr. de Frank—to put forward his mealtimes by easy stages, so that now he dines at two o'clock and sups at half-past ten. His breakfast is at eight o'clock as before. His two tutors are at present both engaged on the same work, which consists simply of teaching French (something which is going badly, because the Prince is still too inattentive), teaching German (which he cannot succeed in doing for a long time to come) and reading to him for his amusement and instruction. M. de Collin is particularly concerned with teaching him religion and the Bible, a large part of which had already been read to him, but in an incoherent fashion."

These changes in Francis's life were not effected as easily as Dietrichstein had imagined they would be. The child behaved like a regular little rebel. His favorite amusement consisted of ringing for Foresti as soon as he had gone to bed, to tell him that "the prisoner Lolo" was in the bedroom. "To begin with," writes Dietrichstein, "we imagined that he was thinking of the Templar in chains in that Gothic castle of Laxenburg; but we soon realized that it was a new device he had found for tormenting us." Pretending that he had grown so much that his bed was too short for him left them unmoved; but he managed to throw his tutor into a panic by "taking a fancy to limp with the left leg." Remonstrances and punishments were administered, but all in vain: the child went on limping. People started talking about it at court, and Rainer was afraid that he had really hurt himself.

Baths were prescribed after which he was left to lie still for an hour. There was no improvement in his condition. "On his own confession" he could feel no pain—but went on limping! Why?

"Because I have got into the habit!" he explained.

One fine morning—May 16, 1816—he tired of the game and started walking normally. Furious at having been taken in, Dietrichstein wrote: "Patience is doubtless a necessary weapon, but strictness is too. . . ."

Two months later he started all over again. This time the tutors took no notice and, somewhat annoyed, Francis Charles asked: "But what will you do if it isn't a bad habit?"

Dietrichstein having declared that in that case he would not be able

to sit at the Emperor's table, the child said that his leg was "not hurting so much." And a few minutes later he ran happily up to Dietrichstein shouting: "It doesn't hurt any more!"

Dietrichstein gravely recorded these exchanges in his *Bemerkungen,*
failing to see to what extent his pupil was making fun of him. One
day when little Émile was still at Schönbrunn and sharing the Prince's
lessons, the valet's son suddenly rolled on to the floor.

"What do you mean by lying down like that," asked Dietrichstein,
"when I'm reading to you for your amusement?"

To which Francis quietly added: "And our instruction."

He loved annoying them by adding an *l* to the end of every French
word—calling Dietrichstein "Monsieur le Comtel"—or an *n* to the end
of German words. And when Collin and Foresti scolded him, he
would say ironically: "Now, don't lose your temper, whatever you do!"

If Collin tried calling him to order, he would gently admonish him:
"My dear Collin, bear your misfortunes patiently!"

For Dietrichstein, whom he particularly enjoyed annoying, he had
some real finds. One day when the tutor was heaping "the liveliest
reproaches" on him, he declared between two sobs: "But I assure you
that Aunt Leopoldine misunderstood me when she thought I said you
were an old crosspatch!"

"These words, which had no connection with what I had been saying," writes Dietrichstein, "convinced me that he had in fact said
something like that."

He told Foresti on June 23: "When I'm a man, I'll order my Grandpapa to put you in chains, and if he doesn't obey me I'll make war on
him with the Italians, and not with cardboard weapons either!"

The captain described this as "an instance of somewhat excessive
gaiety" and did not retaliate. He was not always so patient. Once, when
his pupil had been "naughty and lazy," Foresti shut him up in his
room.

"Aren't we going for a single walk all day?" he asked.

"Not one, Prince."

"Not one? In that case, I'll write to my dear Mamma as soon as I
can to get you into trouble."

"Prince, seeing that you don't know how to write yet, I'll take you
by the hand so that you can communicate your thoughts more easily
to your dear Mamma."

"No, I don't need your help. I'll write to her by myself and tell her

how beastly you are to me. And I'll do everything I can to annoy you."
But his anger went as quickly as it had come.

The Emperor Francis knew what an immense sacrifice he had ex-
acted from his daughter, and had promised the new sovereign of
Parma that he would act as a father to the child she had abandoned.
He kept his word, and as often as he could spare the time from his
multiple occupations—conferring with his cooks, modeling bits of wood
or making sealing wax—he came and bent his long, angular face over
his grandson and kissed him tenderly.

Archdukes and archduchesses now made up the boy's only family.
They regarded the "Corsican's son," this intruder imposed upon them
by politics who had become their nephew, rather as they would a
strange animal. They took him with them on their walks—the Court's
principal distraction in the summer. "Nothing is odder or more delightful," Dietrichstein told Marie Louise, "than to see him in the midst
of his aunts and uncles, either walking solemnly along or else darting
in between them to get up to some prank or other."

One of the "august relatives" was himself in the habit of getting up
to pranks. "Our brother Ferdinand," wrote Leopoldine to her sister
Marie Louise on August 30, "has been behaving dreadfully for some
time. . . . His great distraction after a meal is to wedge himself into a
wastepaper basket and roll over and over like a ball, without ever succeeding in getting his feet free of the basket. . . ." It should be mentioned that the heir to the throne—then twenty-three years old and
known as "the Court's problem child"—was mentally retarded. The
poor man was none the less extremely kind to his little nephew and
loved him "with all his heart." But it was his mother's younger brother,
the Archduke Francis, who was his favorite companion. Unfortunately,
according to Leopoldine, he taught little Francis Charles "to be not
only rude but indecent." "Francis is giving him frightful habits," added
Maria Theresa, Queen of Saxony, on March 29, 1816. "He has taught
him that when his tutors scold him and he does not like it, he should
say '*Scheissen*' to them. Dietrichstein scolded your son for putting his
tongue out and your son said '*Scheissen*' to him, for which he was
punished and did not dare dine with his Grandpapa. . . . But I would
have punished M. Francis too. . . . It is a good thing the little one
does not spend much time with him. . . ." "What a pity," wrote the
Archduke Rainer for his part, "that your brother Francis should keep

on teaching him improprieties. He ought to be strictly forbidden to do so and severely punished if he continued." Rainer had promised Marie Lousie to look after her son, whose heart he had won by giving him a little basset hound. "Your son, whom I see quite frequently," he wrote to Parma, "is in perfect health, he is making daily progress in wisdom and grace, he often thinks about you and often talks about you and is delighted to have been able to write to you, with Foresti holding his hand." The child had in fact written these three lines in this way: "Pray believe, dearest Mamma, that your departure makes me very unhappy, and that I shall love and respect you all my life. I shall not cease to pray to God for you and for your speedy return to the arms of your loving son."

The delightful and little-known Leopoldine, the future Empress of Brazil, had also promised her sister to watch over "Franz," whom she considered "too sweet for words," and to protect him "against the spiteful remarks which are already being made about him." Certain members of the Court chose in fact to regard him simply as "the Ogre's son." "I am always afraid," wrote Marie Louise, "that people will forget that it is not his fault that he has such a father. . . ." "I am entirely of your opinion," replied Leopoldine, "and it makes me choke with anger to hear certain self-important people being as spiteful as they can about him to dear Papa. Neipperg will be able to give you the details, because I have discussed the subject at length with him; as for myself, one of these days I shall certainly place the child officially under my protection." She was especially critical of the methods employed by Dietrichstein, whom she called "the abominable Count Moritz." She would have liked to see much more of her "adorable" nephew—"Papa's darling and mine too"—but unfortunately "there are people who will not always allow it, and whose eyes I should like to scratch out." When the boy, for some reason or other, was prevented from going to play in his little garden, Rainer, faithful to his promise, intervened; and the following month—May, 1816—Leopoldine could tell her sister that Francis was "blooming like a rose" and "taking the air a great deal, in accordance with Uncle Rainer's prescriptions."

The child was not lacking in wit. One day in the summer of 1816 he was explaining to Baroness Hohenegg how a fortress was built. She kept asking him in a teasing voice: "What next? What next?"

Finally, losing patience with her interruptions, he snapped: "Madame, this is not a subject for ladies, so I shall say no more."

Warlike games were the only ones that interested him. Did he remember that his great-grandmother Caroline of Naples had spoken in his presence of "making a monk of him"? Possibly, for in July, 1816, he declared:

"I would never want to become a priest. I shall be a soldier all my life, but I shall always make my regiment march in front of me to protect me, because I don't ever want to die. Must everybody die in a war?"

The constant visits by members of the imperial family greatly annoyed "the abominable Count Moritz" and Captain Foresti. The latter complained of the child "taking advantage in a way of his uncles' and aunts' protection, refusing to obey, and later insulting his tutors by turning his back on them with a great show of indifference and contempt." And to show how "unseemly" his pupil's behavior had become, the Captain declared in horror that Francis sometimes spoke "just like a common Republican."

He was another who would not need much encouragement to decide that Napoleon's son could not be expected to speak in any other way.

The imperial family was about to gain a new member. The Emperor Francis could not remain unmarried for long, since his temperament demanded a partner while his piety forbade him to take a mistress. On October 8, 1816, he had informed his daughter of his approaching marriage—his fourth—to Princess Charlotte of Bavaria. The future Empress Caroline Augusta was extremely ugly, if we are to believe the King of Saxony, but "agreeably ugly." She also appeared to be very healthy, and this pleased the Emperor enormously.

"At least this one should stand the strain," he told his aide-de-camp. "With her I don't risk having another corpse on my hands in a week or two."

During the wedding festivities—at the beginning of November, 1816 —the little Prince's "beauty and amiability" attracted considerable attention. The Empress thought he was adorable and soon fell in love with him. From then on she never called him anything but Fränzchen. The day before his new grandmother's birthday, at the beginning of December, Dietrichstein, who the month before had complained of his pupil's lack of "childish sensibility," asked him what he was going to say to the Empress.

"I shall say: 'Dear Grandmother, I wish you all possible happiness for your birthday.' "

"And do you think that's enough, Prince?"

"No. I shall add: 'And I beg you to give me your blessing.' "

It would be doing Dietrichstein an injustice to imagine that he would be satisfied with this answer.

"That is all very well," he said, according to his account of the conversation in a letter to Marie Louise, "but I think there ought to be another wish, in conformity with your age and the sentiments you must desire to arouse in Her Majesty, who has shown the most touching affection for you."

"Yes, that's true," admitted Fränzchen, "so I'll say to her: 'And I beg you to give me your blessing and your affection—*um Ihre Gnade und um Ihre Liebe.*' "

For it was in German that the child was to recite his little compliment. Dietrichstein had had considerable difficulty in persuading him to express himself in his new language. To begin with, Fränzchen had declared that "he would not learn it."

"You would have thought," says Foresti, "that he was afraid he would cease to be French if he spoke German. He persisted in his resistance for a very long time for a child of his age. But in the end he had to give in." He made extremely rapid progress. On June 21, 1816, he never left his grandfather's side during the Corpus Christi ceremony, and followed him on to the balcony, "hanging on to his coat, to everybody's admiration." Every eyeglass was fixed on him. At the end of the ceremony the Emperor asked him in German: "Well, how are you?"

"I am very well, dear Grandfather," the boy replied in the same language.

"Your son was as sweet as ever," Leopoldine informed her sister. "He spoke German to dear Papa, who was absolutely delighted and thought he was charming, well-behaved and terribly handsome."

A few days later, he was able to address a whole compliment to his *Grossvater.*

"At present," the Archduke Louis told his niece on October 18, 1816, "he speaks nothing but German, even when somebody addresses him in French. . . ." He expressed himself, so it appears, in a more "distinguished" and "noble" manner than his uncles and aunts. "Your Majesty would be delighted if you could hear him speaking German,"

Mme. Lazansky assured Marie Louise two months later. "He pro-
nounces it wonderfully well and with all his customary charm." On
September 5 Dietrichstein was able to inform Marie Louise: "I can
scarcely ever talk to these gentlemen in his presence without his joining in the conversation, and we are all delighted that this is the case."

In the course of a walk in the Tiergarten one day, Franz had a
long talk in German with the forester. Dietrichstein, pleased at having
achieved his purpose after only a year, congratulated him on his
fluency.

"But I don't want to be German!" exclaimed the boy. "I prefer being . . . I don't dare say it. . . ."

Collin was there, and he was so insistent that the boy should finish
what he was saying that Francis finally confessed in a frightened
whisper: "I want to be French!"

One can imagine Dietrichstein's despair. It cannot be denied that
he was obtuse, austere, overscrupulous and insufficiently perceptive,
but in all fairness it must be admitted that his duties as tutor to Napoleon's son often presented him with delicate problems. He himself
admits this when telling how the boy would put his father first in his
prayers: "However, it is no easy task when speaking to him about
filial sentiments, which ought to be consistently fostered in his mind,
to pass skillfully over his father without his noticing."

The child noticed every time. Neglected—not to say abandoned—by
his mother, and living among Austrians whose duty was to adapt him
to his new country, he clung secretly and tenaciously to his memories
of the Emperor. "It is a curious psychological phenomenon," the Archduke Rainer was to write to his niece, "that a child of that age should
know so much about the past and about his father, and that, far from
talking about it, he should keep that knowledge such a closely guarded
secret."

This "curious phenomenon," which Dietrichstein called "hidden dis-
obedience," consisted above all of a daily struggle that was both painful and moving.

Francis had not seen his father since the beginning of 1814, but
when, in the course of a French reading, he heard the word *pataud*,
he exclaimed: "*Pataud?* That's what my Papa used to call me when he
came to see me, and after that he used to go to sleep in an armchair."

On May 23, 1816—two years almost to the day after his arrival at

Schönbrunn—the little five-year-old was heard sighing: "Oh, if only I were in Paris!"

He was well aware that the French had beaten the Austrians and that later the Austrians had taken their revenge.

"Is that the Battle of Austerlitz?" he asked Dietrichstein, pointing to a little picture in his tutor's bedroom.

And once he stated coldly: "When the Austrians entered Paris, people shouted: 'Shut the shops!' "

Foresti was explaining to him one day the meaning of the words "cousin," "uncle" and "aunt," naturally taking all his examples from the Austrian imperial family. The child saw what he was doing, because when the lesson was over he said: "I've some more relatives, but they aren't here, they are in Paris."

"I know what I should like," he told the Captain another time. "I should like to be in a certain country where the people who looked after me so well are living."

One of the first observations that Captain Foresti made after taking up his duties was: "Knows a great deal about the past, but in this connection maintains a silence which is quite extraordinary in a child." Dietrichstein for his part was to write to Marie Louise: "I feel I must tell you again, Marie, that the Prince knows practically everything there is to know about his father. He has always concealed this from you." For Fränzchen knew perfectly well that he had no right to talk about France—or rather that if he did talk about France it embarrassed his tutors.

"I know something," he would say, "but I don't say it because it's a secret."

Not that this prevented him from seizing every opportunity to interrogate his teachers. How were they to answer all the questions that he fired at them? The Emperor Francis, who the previous year had advised them to conceal from his grandson "the state of grandeur into which he was born," decided, in view of the failure of this method, to abandon the policy of dissimulation. But honest answers addressed to a mind as lively as Fränzchen's were bound to lead to thorny complications.

"Grandpapa," the boy asked one day, "when I was in Paris, is it true that I had pages?"

"Yes, I believe you had pages."

"And isn't it true that I was called the King of Rome?"

"Yes."

"But Grandpapa, what does it mean to be King of Rome?"

"My child," replied the Emperor after a moment's thought, "when you are older it will be easier for me to answer that question properly. For the moment, all I shall say is that besides the title of Emperor of Austria I bear that of King of Jerusalem without having any sort of power over that city. Well, you were King of Rome as I am King of Jerusalem."

The questions increased in number, and on June 29, 1816, Dietrichstein wrote to Marie Louise:

> I have always noticed that people talk a great deal about his father in his presence while at the same time they are forbidden to mention the subject to him. This constant and very obvious restriction is a positive martyrdom for so precocious a mind. His Majesty the Emperor, weighing all the dangers of this situation and thinking that the silence or evasive answers we should oppose to the Prince's questions would soon end up by depriving us of his trust, has authorized us to reveal his father's situation to him little by little, and his own too of course, with such caution as prudence demands, in order to make these explanations as useful as possible. However, His Majesty the Emperor wishes this decision to be communicated to you, Madame, so that you also may give it your approval.

"I believe," replied Marie Louise, "that you should speak truthfully to him about his father and, while never saying that he was a bad man and mentioning only his brilliant qualities, persuade him that it was inordinate ambition which led him from the finest throne in the world to the prison where he is today, so that his son never conceives the idea of imitating him."

In any event Dietrichstein had not waited for this authorization to reply to the child's questions. "A change had to be made," he writes. "The embarrassment and silence of the old system had become utterly unbearable." But the new system did nothing to reduce the number of questions put by little Francis. As inquisitive as ever, the child tried to join together the scattered fragments of his past.

Foresti—on July 18, 1816—translated the word "page" for him in the sense of "page of a book."

"How would you translate a page at Court?" asked the child.

He had to repeat the question. Foresti, fearing that worse was to come, made no reply at first.

"*Edelknabe*," he said in the end.

Plucking up courage, the former "little King" went on: "I used to have several in France when I was in Paris; why haven't I any now?"

"Because it isn't the custom here," explained Foresti. "You know perfectly well that the Emperor, even when he goes out, doesn't like that sort of fuss and bother."

"Then who is the Emperor of France now?" asked the boy.

"France hasn't got an emperor; there's a king ruling there now."

"And who is that king?"

"Louis XVIII."

"Will his sons rule after him when he dies?"

"He hasn't any sons, only nephews."

Did Francis think that one day he would succeed the King of France? Perhaps he did, for he continued: "And who will rule when all his nephews are dead?"

"I don't know; only God can know that."

"But there used to be an emperor in France, I'm sure; who was that emperor?"

"Prince, it was your dear Papa, who lost his crown and his empire on account of his unfortunate propensity for war."

Foresti was rather pleased with the way he had answered his pupil. "The Prince," he writes, "was entirely of my opinion." The officer who had fought against Napoleon and been captured at Regensburg took advantage of the boy's good humor to "talk incidentally about the iniquitous war against Spain": "I told him how courageously and doggedly the Spaniards had fought, and the Prince said: 'I consider that perfectly natural seeing that they had their own king!'"

After a short silence, the boy returned to the subject of his father. "I know too," he said, "that he escaped from an island." And he added (one can almost hear his pathetic little voice): "If my dear Papa did so much harm, does that mean he is a criminal?"

How was it that Foresti never realized that it would have been human to show a little sympathy now and then for this five-year-old? "I answered that it was not for us to pass judgment on him; all that he could do was to go on loving him and praying for him."

It appears that the Captain decided that this was too good an opportunity to be missed, for he in his turn asked the child:

"Have you noticed, Prince, how the Emperor of Austria is received when he returns from a long journey? Isn't he received like a good father coming home to his children?"

"Yes."

"And why is that, Prince? Because your Grandpapa has fought great wars too, and sometimes he has lost them!"

"It's because he only fought when he was forced to do so in order to defend his country," came the dutiful reply.

Strange as it may seem, once his curiosity had been satisfied, the child was neither saddened nor impressed by these supplementary details which Foresti might have spared him. He seemed to be delighted to have added to his memories and talked about subjects which his masters usually avoided. And when Collin came into the room he gaily announced: "Monsieur Foresti and I have been talking about France."

A few days went by. . . . Then, "quite unexpectedly," Francis asked: "What was my father's name?"

"As I was convinced," writes Foresti, "that he knew all the time and I realized that he had no desire to be scolded, I answered that he, the son, ought to know his father's name better than I. The Prince dropped the subject and took on an air of indifference."

Another day he asked an even bolder question: "Surely Napoleon must have been a very great general to become King?"

Foresti thought he could wriggle out of it by saying: "Napoleon wasn't a king."

"Yet he was the same man who later married my mother a year before I was born. Why isn't he Emperor any more?"

Foresti made no reply.

Several times, still in July, 1816, Francis asked for a book "which he had found very interesting in the past."

"Which book is that?" asked Foresti.

"It's the story of the French people."

He was referring to *The Glorious History of the French Nation*, which had been removed from the library "after the governesses' departure." Foresti hypocritically opened the bookcase.

"You can choose whichever book you like best."

"I see," declared the child, after rummaging through the cupboard, "that somebody has been silly enough to take the book away."

Some time later, on August 12, Foresti heard him saying to himself: "Oh, if only I could remember something of *The Glorious History of the French Nation*. There were some splendid battles in that book!"

The "splendid battles" which his father had won . . .

Three days later, at St. Helena, Gourgaud made up a birthday bouquet to be taken to Napoleon "on behalf of the King of Rome." But at eight o'clock in the morning the Emperor came into his companion's room. Gourgaud showed him the bouquet and Napoleon sighed: "Bah! The King of Rome thinks no more of me than . . ."

If only he had known! If only he had realized what a fight his little five-year-old King was putting up! But it appears that he did not even know that his son had been abandoned by Marie Louise and parted from all the French members of his suite.

"What sort of education will they give him?" he asked Las Cases. "What kind of principles will they instill into him? And what if he should turn out to be weak in the head? What if he should take after his mother's family? What if they should inspire him with a hatred of his father?"

He seemed to be deeply affected.

"Let us talk about something else. . . ."

"But he did not talk about anything," writes Las Cases.

The memory of his son haunted him. One day he handed Marchand the snuffbox decorated with a picture of the "little King."

"Lock that away," he said. "I can't bear seeing it all the time."

On November 22 the outlaw went over his Russian and Spanish campaigns with Bertrand, trying his best to discover what mistakes he had made. He had been mad to stay more than a fortnight in Moscow. And as for the Spanish War, he should never have taken it on.

While Napoleon looked sadly back over the past, a little boy at Schönbrunn, even lonelier than his father on his island, played soldiers in his bedroom, equipped with a stick and a box that did service as a drum. All of a sudden, stopping his din, he planted himself in front of Foresti, drew himself up, and asked: "Have you ever seen the drum majors of Paris, those handsome drum majors with their beards and their curly mustaches, their big sticks and their colored shoulder straps? They are a wonderful sight and every regiment has a different uniform. I used to see them every day in Paris."

"I have never been to Paris," Foresti replied scornfully. "But I know the madmen you are talking about, because I have seen them in other places."

"Why do you call them madmen?"

"Because they make faces like madmen, and because everything about them, from the way they behave to the way they dress, suggests that they are mad. What I don't understand is how you, Prince, who have never seen them, can praise them like that."

"Why shouldn't I?" retorted the Prince. "I was born in Paris and I spent two years there. I can remember them perfectly well."

The contempt which Foresti displayed for the drum majors of Paris in no way diminished the child's enthusiasm.

"When I'm Emperor," he said, "I shall have drum majors like that."

"That doesn't worry me in the slightest, Prince," declared Foresti, "because you will never be Emperor."

At St. Helena, Las Cases remarked one day to his master that Austria might eventually wish to be useful to the King of Rome and also make use of him. Napoleon replied: "Yes, as an instrument of intimidation perhaps, but never as a means of doing good; they would be too much afraid of him. The King of Rome would be a man for the people; he will be the man for the Italian people; and so Austria will kill him."

No doubt at the beginning of his exile Napoleon the *commediante*, building up his legend with consummate art, play-acted to a certain extent. They had snatched his son away from him; he had no news of the boy; they refused to give him any! An Austrian commissioner was sent to the island but brought no message from the grandfather for the child's father! Combined with all the petty restrictions his jailers inflicted on him, this was splendid material to use to touch the public's heart. But soon he began to feel real suffering. The thought of never seeing his son again and the complete absence of news brought tears to his eyes. He spent hours looking at Isabey's drawing of the boy and at the child's little toy cannon in bronze which he had found in Paris and taken with him into exile. And he was deeply moved to receive the lock of hair which Chanchan had sent him through a young Austrian botanist who came to St. Helena to collect herbs. This young man was called Welle and had arrived on the island with the Austrian Commissioner Stürmer. The hair was enclosed in a letter which the King of Rome's sometime cradle-rocker had sent her son with the message: "I am sending you some of my hair. Your mother, Marchand." Since Mme. Marchand was dark and the lock was fair and silky, there could be no doubt that this was the "little King's" hair. Discovering what had happened, Hudson Lowe sent Welle back to Europe.

"I gather," the Emperor told O'Meara on February 28, 1817, "that the botanist is on the point of going without my having seen him. In the most barbarous of countries they would not refuse even a prisoner condemned to death the consolation of conversing with someone who had recently seen his wife and child. . . . The cannibals in the South Seas would not behave like that: before eating their victims, they at least allow them to see and talk to one another. . . ."

The same day, little Franz asked Foresti: "Did my Papa do a great deal of harm for everybody to become his enemy?"

Foresti could scarcely believe his good fortune. "I told him that it was simply his inordinate ambition and his insatiable love of war which had exasperated all the nations of the world and led them to defend themselves with all their might."

On March 10 the boy inquired "with stupid politeness": "Would you be so good as to tell me, Monsieur de Foresti, how much time has elapsed since the last war?"

"Do you remember when your grandfather came back to Vienna?"

"Yes, because I saw him arrive at Schönbrunn."

"Well, he had brought the war to a victorious conclusion a few months before his return."

"Was that war waged against French troops?"

"Yes."

That evening, in his little windswept house at Longwood, the captive Emperor read aloud Racine's *Andromaque*, "the play for unhappy fathers" as he called it. When he reached the point where Andromache speaks of going to kiss her imprisoned son, his voice faltered and he closed the book.

It was with immense pride and emotion that he received a bust of the future Duke of Reichstadt, which was nothing but a fake executed by a sculptor who had never even seen Fränzchen and had decorated him with the eagle of the Legion of Honor, which the child had not worn for a long time past. It was such an obvious fraud that

Reade, the Governor's adjutant, had proposed refusing the bust and even having it thrown in the sea, declaring that it was not worth the hundred louis the sculptor was asking for it.

"It is worth a million to me!" exclaimed the exile.

On June 11 he called O'Meara in to show him the bust on the drawing-room mantelpiece.

"Look at it, just look at that face. Don't you think a man who would want to destroy an image like that must be a barbarian, a monster? Why, that face would touch the heart of the fiercest of wild animals! The man who gave orders for the destruction of that image would plunge a dagger into the heart of the original, if it lay in his power to do so."

And he gazed silently at the bust for some time with tears in his eyes.

On June 15 little Francis Charles had lunch with the new Empress. We do not know what they talked about, but afterward the boy went around pretending to beat a drum and chanting: "I shall go to another country. . . . I know where, but I shan't say. . . . To a country where there was a war . . . in France, not so long ago . . . a war with the Austrians."

One evening, before going to bed, he seemed very thoughtful and was heard to sigh: "When I'm big I shall take a sword and go and free my Papa, whom *they* are keeping in prison."

The thought of his father never left him. Once when General Sommariva named the three greatest captains of his time in the little Prince's presence, the boy said "sharply": "I know a fourth whom you haven't named!"

"And who is that, Monseigneur?"

"My father!"

And he ran away, blushing and frightened at his own audacity. The general ran after him and brought him back.

"You were right, Monseigneur," he said, "to speak as you did about your father; but you were wrong to run away."

On August 15, 1817, he asked question after question about the war of 1813-14. How long did the final campaign last? Against whom were the powers fighting? Against whom? Foresti tried to satisfy his curiosity but avoided mentioning his father.

Similarly, at St. Helena, where the Emperor's birthday was being

celebrated that same day, people avoided talking about the little prisoner at Schönbrunn. They even hesitated to dress up little Tristan
Montholon in his lancer's uniform for fear of distressing Napoleon by
reminding him of the King of Rome.

On November 2, 1817, Foresti wrote in his diary: "Today I was at
Schönbrunn with the Prince. While we were walking down from the
Tyrolean garden toward the park, there were several young street Arabs
standing near the big ornamental lake. One of them recognized the
Prince from a distance and shouted to the others: 'There's young Napoleon!' The Prince heard what he said and became so thoughtful and
distrait that I was unable to obtain a single reply to all my questions,
either during the walk to the carriage or during the drive to the high-
street of Mariahilf."

On January 20, 1818, he asked the Captain: "Monsieur Fo, where
are those two precious portraits I used to have that were framed in
brilliants?"

"Which portraits do you mean?"

"They were portraits of my dear Mamma and . . . my dear Papa."

"I have never seen them."

"Perhaps the ladies took them away with them."

Dietrichstein was perhaps not entirely mistaken in asserting that
the French governesses had talked to the child so much about Paris and
his father that many of his memories were simply recollections of what
Mme. de Montesquiou, Mme. Soufflot or young Fanny had told him
in Austria. But this was only partially true and did not apply to more
than a few details. Francis had an amazing memory and, four years
after the governesses' departure, in 1819, he was still asking questions
which astounded his entourage, questions which Dietrichstein admitted
he generally answered with silence. One day in May, 1818, when the
tutor asked him to cite three European empires, the boy remarked:
"There used to be four, because France was an empire too!"

"Yes, but now it is a kingdom again."

There was a brief silence, then Francis added: "My father was an
emperor too as long as he was on the throne."

"I answered him in the affirmative," writes Dietrichstein, "without
saying anything more."

In the course of the summer of 1818 it was Mathieu de Collin's
turn to be interrogated:

"Why did they used to call me King of Rome?"

"That was at a time when your father's rule extended as far as that."

"So Rome belonged to my father?"

"Rome belonged to the Pope by a sacred deed of gift."

"And where is he now?"

"In Rome."

The child hesitated for a few seconds, then said: "I believe my father is in the West Indies?"

"Oh, no."

"Then perhaps he is in America?"

"Why should he be in America?"

"Then where is he?"

"That I can't tell you."

"The French ladies told me one day that he had been in England and that he had escaped."

"That is untrue. Besides, you know very well, Your Highness, that you often misunderstand French."

"Yes, I know."

"I can assure you on my honor that your father has never been in England."

"I think too that I heard that he was living in poverty."

"In poverty?"

"Yes."

"How could that be possible or even probable?"

"No, it isn't possible, is it?"

He seemed to have been relieved of a great anxiety. Someone had mentioned *Sainte-Helene* in his hearing, and he had confused the second part of the name with the German word for poverty—*Elend.*

On his rock in the tropics, Napoleon thought constantly about "Astyanax." His driving ambition now was to turn his own death into a slow murder and thus prepare the way for Napoleon II. He rejected the plans for his escape which were put forward from time to time. He had to stay on his rock . . . and die on it.

"It is better for my son that I should be here," he declared. "If he lives, my martyrdom will win him a crown. . . . If I die on the cross—and he is still alive—he will come to the throne."

After a year and a half of tutoring, Dietrichstein was still complaining in his *Observations* and his letters that his pupil was "stubborn, heartless, and full of a cold, calculating wickedness which reached its highest point when he used to give his tutors a sidelong look and burst out laughing, to show them that he was doing his best to annoy them and tire them out. . . . He also got into the habit of screaming at the top of his voice to make the servants in the anteroom feel sorry for him."

The boy was certainly something of an actor—taking after his father in this respect—but his irreverent attitude was in a way his only means of defense. It was not possible for him, as it is for most children, to seek refuge and consolation in his mother's arms. In a letter to Marie Louise dated November 21, 1816, the tutor spoke of "vices which have taken root in the Prince more deeply than one might imagine" and which, he said, "form the object of our anxiety." He went on to explain: "Nothing is more attractive than his face and his words when he wishes to please, but he is not sufficiently childlike, and he is clearly too intelligent for his years. It is not that he knows it too well, but that it harms his character and does not help it to gain in flexibility. An outrageous lie last week earned him a reprimand from H.M. the Emperor; when I spoke to him about it, he wept a great deal but there was no other result. . . ." In reality—but the pedagogue was quite incapable of seeing this—the child was not a liar but a storyteller. Leopoldine explained this very well in a letter which must have reached Marie Louise by the same courier:

> Your son is charming and very lively, but he has got into the dreadful habit of telling lies and that distresses me more than I can say, for people are attributing it to innate wickedness, when in fact it is simply the result of his vivid imagination; it is certainly not because he is ill-natured, and making fun of him or constantly scolding him will not rid him of the habit, for I know from my own experience that it was by showing me how contemptible my lies were that I was cured of lying; all the same, it would help if you came here soon to see him and also to take control of his education. . . .

Another major defect in Dietrichstein's eyes was the boy's lack of "childlike sensibility." "When I consider what the heart of a six-year-old ought to be like!" he sighed. "I am thinking of having a wooden rocking horse made for him. . . . I could use this horse as a touchstone by removing it as soon as the Prince deserved to be punished, and it would perhaps serve as a barometer for his sensibility. . . ."

The Prince was far from being incapable of showing affection—he was to prove this on many occasions—but one can understand his not being drawn to a tutor given to using a rocking horse as "a barometer for his sensibility." And how could he be expected to like Captain de Foresti, whose principal task it was to dirty the images engraved in the child's heart?

In Leopoldine's opinion, Fränzchen's apparent coldness was due to "the educational plan they have been following with him for some time and which as far as I can see is contributing to it." Marie Louise must have decided that her sister was right, for she asked Dietrichstein to show her son a little more indulgence.

"Your Majesty," replied the Count, "remarks that the Prince is still very young . . . but I on the contrary feel that every toy of his, everything that interests him, ought to remind him of what he owes his mother, and I am always telling him so and preaching filial affection to him."

Preaching filial affection to a child of six! There is the essential Dietrichstein, decorticating, analyzing and commenting on impulses, sighs and heartbeats. The only times his pupil could touch his heart were when he reflected credit on his tutor in public. "You have to see him in the Prater or somewhere else," he wrote, "to gain some idea of the interest he arouses in people and the spell he casts over them." On January 23, 1817, Fränzchen appeared at the *Kammerball* with his hair prettily dressed and wearing his little white suit. The previous year he had been too nervous to dance: this time he did not miss a single waltz, quadrille or gallopade. "He did not fall over," reports Dietrichstein, "except once when he was running to talk to H.H. the Archduke Anthony; then he picked himself up, blushing furiously, and when I tried to console him he repeated several times: 'That was disgraceful, absolutely disgraceful!'"

And the tutor, his heart softening a little at long last, concluded: "Everyone thought he was perfectly adorable."

In the spring of 1817 Leopoldine left Schönbrunn to become Empress of Brazil. "Nothing remains for me to do," she wrote to Marie Louise on April 4, "except weep with you and curse the word politics for causing me so much suffering. Prince Metternich is accompanying me as far as Leghorn as my official escort; you can imagine how delighted I am!?!? . . . We unfortunate princesses are like dice whose happiness or unhappiness depends on the throw."

Before taking the road to Leghorn, Leopoldine went and gave her beloved, curly-headed nephew a farewell kiss. She would often speak of her "treasure" in the letters—the unhappy letters of an exile—which she was to write from Brazil.

10

✤

"Sweet Reichstadt"

THE SIXTH BIRTHDAY of the little Prince without a name was "fittingly" celebrated, Dietrichstein informed Marie Louise. It could not have been otherwise since he had organized everything. "I made him go into another room, so as to get Your Majesty's presents ready, and when *the horse* had been brought in, I placed the Prince on the left of it with his eyes blindfolded, enjoying his surprise, which was very great. It is indeed a masterpiece which everyone admires—the Prince did not want to leave it. . . ."

At the same time that she had sent her son his birthday presents, the ex-Empress had asked Mme. de Montebello to dispatch some child's vests to Parma. "You may be surprised," she wrote, "that I should be taking an interest in baby clothes, but the fact is that Mme. de Scarampi has just given birth to a fat little heir. . . ."

The fact was that she herself was preparing for the birth of the child Neipperg had given her. Convinced that her marriage to Napoleon was no longer valid, had she contracted a secret union with her beloved one-eyed General? The Viennese gossips said that she had. So did the Emperor Francis's brother Anton. "He tells me," Leopoldine wrote to Marie Louise on March 16, 1817, "that he has received some letters from Parma saying that you are going to marry a General Nova Monte. Translate that into German. I nearly died laughing at such silliness, and in the end we had quite a quarrel, because he is convinced it is true. . . ."

True or not, on May 1 the Duchess of Parma gave birth to a little girl, Albertine Marie, who would later be granted the title of Countess of Montenuovo, the Italian translation of her father's name. Parma was highly amused, but the news did not travel as far as Vienna. Even Metternich, it seems, did not hear about the event for some considerable time. And meanwhile Marie Louise, who was to have come to see her son that year, decided that she could not leave her daughter so soon, and therefore stayed in her little Duchy.

Franz was badly upset by the news that he would not be seeing his mother.

"Do you know," he said to his tutor, "I think my dear Mamma is going to stay in Parma this winter to help the poor."

"I never lavished so many caresses on him as I did at that moment," writes Dietrichstein. "He assured me that he often thought about his dear mother and that he loved her very much. I clasped him in my arms, I mingled my tears with his, I begged him to confide all his thoughts to me, to talk to me at any time about the things he held dearest in the world, and to do his best to deserve his mother's affection. He started weeping again. Collin found him like that when he came in and was deeply moved, and since then we have been much better friends than before."

In the course of that summer of 1817 the child went on several occasions to the Baronne de Montet's house, where he played with young Rudolph de Merveldt, a boy of about the same age. Mme. de Montet records that at this time Francis always used to stand with his hands behind his back and one foot forward, "just like Napoleon." She discovered a certain resemblance to his father "in his mouth and general bearing."

One day Rudolph appeared in the garden holding a bundle of guns, sabers and spears. Francis, who was having a snack, stopped eating straight away. "He went red in the face and rushed to see the weapons; he seized hold of a musket and started drilling Rudolph, who promptly did as he was ordered. We were all astonished by the way Francis gave his orders and the promptitude with which Rudolph obeyed them. There was above all something in young Napoleon's expression when he pronounced the word *marschieren*—or rather *marrrrrrschieren*—which boded no good for the future. Mme. de Merveldt, annoyed at seeing Rudolph in a subordinate role, had him giving the orders in his turn. The little Prince did wonderfully well; nobody had ever taught him, but he remembered everything he had seen. . . . The child is certainly very intelligent. History is his great passion. He is shy and always glances at Count Dietrichstein, his tutor, before doing anything or accepting anything."

He had such a passion—an "innate ardor" Dietrichstein called it—for "military apparatus" that his grandfather gave him a complete Landwehr uniform. Visitors admired him mounting guard outside his grandfather's door and presenting arms to the officers who went in and out. Sometimes he would play in a corner of the Emperor's room. A few feet from where Francis I of Austria was working—that is to say, solemnly annotating his ministers' reports, "correcting their spelling mistakes and substituting others that were even worse"—he would take his lead soldiers out of their box and line them up in battle order. They were imperial infantrymen, dressed in the white uniform which he dreamed of wearing himself one day. . . .

In June, 1818, Marie Louise finally left Parma to go and see her son, from whom she had been separated for two years and three months. On July 1, with Neipperg beside her, she arrived at the little village of Theresienfeld, close to Wiener Neustadt, where she was to meet her son. "But if other people should have the same idea," she had told Dietrichstein, "be sure to dissuade them, for in the first tender moments after a long absence I would rather be alone with my son than with the whole of my family."

She had hoped to be able to clasp in her arms a child who had at last received a name, a title and lands, but the letters patent giving "Prince Francis Charles" civil status had not yet been signed. During the two years the matter had been under discussion, Marie Louise had given the Emperor "fresh proof of her filial affection" and had shown him "to what extent she subordinated her interests to those of the community at large": she had finally agreed—on November 24, 1816—to renounce on her son's behalf the succession to the States of Parma which the First Treaty of Paris had granted the son of Napoleon. It was the ex-Queen of Etruria who became the ex-Empress's heir. After that Marie Louise had to plead and argue for a whole year before the Emperor would agree to have a protocol drafted by which he was to renounce, in favor of his grandson "and his male heirs in lineal descent, possession of those lands in Bohemia known as the Bavarian Palatinate."

The Duc de Richelieu, speaking on behalf of Louis XVIII, expressed horror and surprise that anyone should seriously envisage a legitimate line of Napoleons and the creation of a Napoleonic duchy in Europe. Had there not been a suggestion, he asked, that the heir to the "French Empire" should be destined for the Church? As the journalist Hudelist observed to his friend Metternich: "I've had enough of your precious Prince of Parma. In your place I'd have made a priest of him and then a bishop!"

But the Emperor wanted to meet his daughter's wishes. The Austrian delegate succeeded in reassuring Louis XVIII's government with a declaration to the effect that "this stipulation in no way prejudiced the Prince's future career and condition." In other words, the possession of the Bavarian Palatinate did not debar him from taking holy orders.

Finally, after a great deal of grumbling and moaning on the part of the French and Spanish Bourbons, the protocol was signed on December 4, 1817. Marie Louise wrote to thank her father, who replied that only "modest" credit was due to him, since he loved his grandson "with all his heart." Now a name had to be found for "Prince Francis Charles." The Emperor Francis suggested the title of Duke of Mödling, but this name had already been borne by the Babenberg family, which had ruled in Austria before the Habsburgs. But why not choose the name of one of the domains in the Bavarian Palatinate, which could then be raised to the dignity of a duchy? It was not as simple as that: Prince Francis Charles was about to become the ruler of an appreciable number of domains whose names—including among others Tachlowitz, Chrustenitz, Kron-Porzitschen, Plosskowitz, Trnowan and Buschtierad —were difficult to pronounce, except of course for Bohemians.

"I must confess," wrote Marie Louise, "that I would rather go on hearing my son called Prince Francis Charles all his life than that he should become *einen ausgebackenen Herzog* (a half-baked duke) whose ridiculous name of *Bustierad* would make me blush for shame every time I opened the Court Almanach." Fortunately one of the domains—Zakupy in Slavonic—also had a German name, that of Reichstadt. And so it was that Prince Francis Charles, "son of our dearly beloved daughter Madame Marie Louise, Archduchess of Austria" (*and of a father unknown . . .*) became Duke of Reichstadt, after having borne successively for seven years the names of King of Rome, Prince of Parma, Prince Imperial and Prince Francis Charles.

The new Duke was to rank immediately after the Archdukes. He was to lose the title of Monseigneur—*Durchlaucht*—which was to be replaced by that of Serene Highness—*Hoheit*. While his mother had kept her title of "Her Majesty the Empress" to rule over her sometime department, Francis was no longer an "Imperial Highness," and later this would cause him annoyance and distress.

In Rome, when Madame Mère heard what was going to be done with Napoleon's son, she sighed. "My grandson will never bear a finer name than that of his father. The title of Duke of Reichstadt has a hollow sound. The name of Napoleon Bonaparte will ring round the world forever, and the echoes of France will not fail to pick it up."

Marie Louise, to do her justice, had done everything in her power to obtain something better. However, she felt obliged to thank her father, who replied: "I am glad that you are satisfied with the solution in so far as it concerns you and your son. I believe that as things stood this is the best we could do. I hope with all my heart that your son will prove himself a true gentleman."

A true gentleman! That was indeed all that was left for him to be! The son of Napoleon had been transformed into a sort of mediatized prince, a bastard even. . . . A child without a father, a child who had been deprived of his surname, a child who had been transplanted from one country to another and stripped of his decorations, titles and arms, a child whose spirit his tutors were patiently and doggedly trying to shape to their own ends. . . . But a child who, by the mere strength of his heart, by the mere power of his memories, eluded them. They would find it impossible to kill the little Napoleon in him.

Meanwhile, on this July 1, 1818, when Marie Louise was due to be reunited with the "Duke of Reichstadt," the letters patent beginning: "We, Francis the First, by the grace of God Emperor of Austria, King of Jerusalem, Hungary, Bohemia, Lombardy and Venice . . ." were still waiting to be signed.

When Francis Charles learned that his mother was coming to see him, he asked Collin with an innocent air: "Why isn't my father coming with my mother?"

Highly embarrassed, Collin replied: "You must ask your grandfather."

"That's what I'm going to do. Take me to him this very instant."

Collin warned the Emperor what his grandson wanted to know,

whereupon Francis exclaimed: "Well, he's only got to come and ask me—I'll answer him!"

As soon as the little seven-year-old came into the room he ran up to his grandfather and shouted: "My mother's coming! Why isn't my father coming too?"

"Why isn't your father coming? I'll tell you why! It's because your father was wicked, so he has been put in prison, and if you are wicked too, you'll be put in prison as well."

The boy hung his head and went out with his eyes full of tears.

At Theresienfeld on July 1, he had forgotten his chagrin and stood waiting for his "dear Mamma," stamping his feet with impatience. As there was no sign of the carriages, Fränzchen was taken into the house of a certain Bernhard Petri, the proprietor of a model merino farm. The crowd of onlookers gradually edged their way into the garden, among them King Jerome, who was living in the nearby castle of Schönau, and Queen Caroline of Naples, who under the name of the Countess of Lipona had bought the Frohsdorf estate where the Comte de Chambord—the new Duke of Reichstadt's second cousin—would live one day. It was what Marie Louise called "an unpleasant neighborhood." With Napoleon's brother and sister were Murat's children, the two exiles' modest suite, and some retired officers of the imperial army —a little Napoleonic colony in fact. "Young Napoleon's entry into the drawing room," writes an eye-witness, Charles Auguste Petri, "was the signal for a scene which was both unforgettable and indescribable. Men who, in various countries, had probably fought in more battles than there are days in a month, and from whom no variety of human suffering could easily draw tears, bowed low, then drew themselves up and cheered the son of their God of Battles. They spoke eloquently but without a word; every sound, every sob recounted a whole life filled with memories of France, Spain, Egypt, Russia, Germany, the entire world."

"Gentlemen," said Dietrichstein, terrified that Jerome and Caroline might speak to his pupil, "gentlemen, calm yourselves, the Prince speaks only German. . . ."

The arrival of Marie Louise cut short this dangerous scene and put an end to Dietrichstein's agony. The ex-Empress did not leave her carriage. Neipperg picked the boy up in his arms and carried him to the berlin, and a few minutes later the procession disappeared at a gallop.

Marie Louise had left a child. She found a little boy—a little boy who spoke nothing but German. They settled first of all at Baden, where at long last the ex-Empress received her son's letters patent. They then joined the imperial family at Persenbeug, a romantic castle on the left bank of the Danube, upstream from Melk, with a bulbous keep that was mirrored in the river.

The boy was wonderfully happy here. "My little companion does not leave me for a moment from nine in the morning until ten at night," Marie Louise told Mme. de Montebello. "What a sweet, handsome child he is, and what happy hours I have been spending with him!"

He "tormented" his mother "to have a *titus,*" that is to say to have his long, girlish hair cut short. Dietrichstein had thought of having this done a year before, and Pierre, the court hairdresser, had been called in; but at the last moment the tutor had changed his mind, so that Marie Louise should find "the Prince's hair in curls as it had been on her departure."

Now, delighted to look like a real little boy, he went shooting for the first time in his life. Standing close to Marie Louise and Neipperg, he shot a hare full in the breast. "It turned a somersault and dropped dead," he wrote in the account which Dietrichstein made him set down on his return to the castle. The holiday ended at Schönbrunn. A week before his mother was due to leave, the little Duke started crying. On September 19 Marie Louise embarked at Persenbeug in order to join the Parma road further up the Danube. "You had scarcely left the boat," the Empress Caroline Augusta wrote to her stepdaughter, "before your son installed himself at the little window, and long after you had been lost from sight, his eyes still seemed to be searching for you. He was in a pitiful state."

On his return to Vienna, the child remained lost in a dream. When he received a letter which Marie Louise had written to him from Lambach, he burst into tears. "I did nothing to calm him down," writes Dietrichstein. "He kept on sobbing as he read the letter, and when he had finished it he wept some more. This proof of his sensibility moved me deeply." His thoughts never left his mother, and he was always talking about her and "groaning" as he read and reread her letters. Every day Dietrichstein heard him say: "Oh, if only my mother could come back soon!"

However, he was still as mischievous as ever; witness this anecdote related by the Baronne de Montet: "The young Duke of Reichstadt went out for a walk to Hietzing the other day with his uncles the Archdukes and Prince Anthony of Saxony, who is the kindest of men but is said to be no genius. The conversation turned upon great men and each person named the individual who in his opinion was most deserving of that description. Little Napoleon, who was walking behind Prince Anthony, drew a huge nought on his back with a piece of chalk. The Archdukes saw what he had done and were hard put to it not to laugh. Denounced to the Emperor, he was kept in for three days; but the Emperor was much amused by his grandson's judgment."

The Tsar Alexander, who arrived in Vienna a month later, wanted to see Napoleon's son again. He kissed him, "said several kindly things to him and found him very handsome and charming." Francis was shy and embarrassed, especially as the Tsar spoke French to him. By this time—as we know from a letter written by Countess Lazansky—the boy had almost completely forgotten his mother tongue. He still wrote in it —though rather clumsily—but scarcely ever spoke it. In this respect Dietrichstein had succeeded beyond Metternich's wildest hopes.

Marie Louise had promised her son that she would see him again in 1819, but Neipperg, to use Chateaubriand's trenchant phrase, was still laying his eggs in the Eagle's nest. In the spring she was six months' pregnant and in no condition to travel to Austria. She let it be understood that she would come in September, and explained the postponement of her journey by saying that a visit the imperial court had recently made to Parma had ruined her. The Archduke Rainer, who, like everyone else, knew nothing of the truth, wrote to his niece: "Seeing the effect all this has on your son's heart, it is absolutely essential that he should see you every year, if he is not to die of unhappiness, in view of his extreme sensitivity."

On August 9, 1819, the Duchess gave birth to a son—William—who from the legal point of view was a son of Napoleon's and who, like his sister, would be called Montenuovo. To recover from her confinement, Marie Louise decided to go on a tour of North Italy, and asked Dietrichstein to tell her son. It was "in the course of a spelling lesson" that the tutor performed his mission. There followed, he wrote, "a fit of absent-mindedness which did him honor"; and inevitably the master had to point out to his pupil "the difference between this and his reprehensible absent-mindedness." The boy promptly wrote his mother one of his last letters in French:

My dear Mamma, I am going to be alone again, instead of enjoying the happiness of seeing you. Am I not right to say as I
used to as a child: That makes me very sad! You are going to
travel a long way; my eyes and my heart will follow you on the
map. Geography interests me much more now; I should like to
know Italy and all the cities you are going to see. My cold would
not prevent me from traveling any more, but I am too young. Oh,
if only I were twenty! At least I shall try to acquire enough learning quickly to appear older than I am. Do not worry about my
health or my behavior, dear Mamma, and think often, I beg of
you, of your most obedient son Francis.

The letter was dictated by Dietrichstein and was really little more
than a handwriting exercise. Henceforth he would write all his letters
in German—letters in which one can sense the watchful tutor leaning
over his shoulder, letters so commonplace that the historian is no more
tempted to reproduce them than Francis liked writing them. Little
Reichstadt obviously derived much more enjoyment from describing his
shooting expeditions. The first was near Hasendorf. "The Prince,"
writes Dietrichstein, "was given two guns loaded with powder and he
soon tired old Kurz out, for he fired sixty-nine times with remarkable
speed. From where I was I saw him striding across the plowed fields
and the covers for three-and-a-half hours, without falling once, raising
his gun and taking aim every few minutes. H.M. also had him fire
with small shot at some wounded hares, but he did not succeed in dis-
patching them. At least he has shown that he is not afraid of guns; that
does him honor and will be talked about—something which pleases me
very much when he deserves it." In October he was luckier and, if we
are to believe the Archduke Anton, killed thirty-six pheasants, hares
and partridges. "What is more," writes Dietrichstein, "he gave the
coup de grâce to a number of hares, ducks and pigeons not included
in the above total."

Winter brought with it the Carnival balls, and the whole imperial
family wrote to Marie Louise describing the success her "charming son"
was having on these occasions. His blue dress coat with the star of St.
Stephen sparkling on it set off his fair, curly hair. In his white waist-
coat and "fashionable" white trousers, "sweet, adorable Reichstadt"
was the darling of the Court. Even Dietrichstein was impressed by his

easy bearing, his graceful bows, his way of talking "to everyone he knows, especially generals, with wit and amiability." He danced with all the women and "they are already fighting over him."

Dietrichstein, however, soon began to think that his pupil was "forgetting his age" at these *Kammerbälle* and becoming more "difficult" as a result. What is more, although his health was reasonably good, the slightest chill produced a sore throat. The tutor therefore insisted that his pupil should not go to every *Kammerball* that was held in the Hofburg. On the other hand, there was no question of making Reichstadt lead a cloistered life. Dietrichstein was well aware how important it was for the boy to please his Austrian relatives, on whom his future depended. On this point he had nothing to fear, for everyone loved "sweet Reichstadt."

He was no longer obsessed by the past; his memories had grown dim with time. He no longer spoke of his father, no longer asked those questions which had caused his tutor so much embarrassment. He had even forgotten all his French. Marie Louise, the Emperor and Dietrichstein had attained their object; for the next seven years the boy would be what they wanted him to be—an Austrian prince. The tutor's triumph would have been complete if only Francis had not been so lazy. The nine-year-old preferred dancing to working, while writing to his mother became a fearsome chore which he put off from day to day, so that sometimes three months would go by without his sending a letter to Parma. Dietrichstein's hair, which was rebellious enough to begin with, began to stand on end.

It is interesting to compare Count Maurice's letters and those from the imperial family. Dietrichstein wrote only to complain, and sent Marie Louise continual jeremiads, while Maria Theresa of Saxony, to take only one example, was full of praise for Reichstadt: "It is astonishing how much he knows, and I admire his memory and the way he learns and expresses himself."

It was undeniable that when the boy was willing to take the trouble, he could be really brilliant. This says a great deal for him, since with the exception of history and geography, which appealed to his imagination, "all the rest was a chore for him." He was very willing, and put up a creditable performance in a two-hour examination which he sat on April 15, 1820, in the presence of his grandfather and the Empress. This examination was not only in his two favorite subjects but also in religion, arithmetic, German and French. "I must confess," wrote

Dietrichstein, "that I was very pleased with him today, and if it is possible I love him all the more. . . ." "If Maurice was satisfied with him," Mme. Lazansky commented ironically, "then he cannot have acquitted himself too badly!"

"I keep hearing that you are coming in April," Francis had written to his mother at the end of 1819; "if only we had already reached that moment, which I have been eagerly looking forward to for so long!"

But Marie Louise was happy in her Duchy and was in no hurry to take the road to Vienna. The banks of the Parma suited the indolent Archduchess, whose second marriage had failed to rouse her from her natural apathy. There she could recover "strength and plumpness," while in Vienna, so she maintained, life was "such a physical and moral frenzy" that she "felt ill after only a week." It was so much more pleasant botanizing in the Colorno garden and looking after her two children—her love-children—than listening to Dietrichstein's grumbles and trying to conceal the true nature of her feelings for Neipperg. However, she could not postpone her journey indefinitely. Every courier brought letters from members of the imperial family calling for what the Archduke Anton described as her "well-nigh indispensable presence."

Meanwhile, on Dietrichstein's advice, Marie Louise addressed some far from indulgent letters to her son, urging him to work harder. "The letter which Your Majesty wrote to the Prince is a masterpiece," enthused Dietrichstein on April 8, 1820; "he read it with me and appeared to be impressed. . . ." But the maternal exhortations had little effect. "His behavior calls for severe measures," declared Dietrichstein, after telling Marie Louise about her son's "impudence." He cut his pupil's Easter holidays and suggested giving him a taste of the whip. The Duchess of Parma admitted to "an aversion for its use," and would not agree to it except as a threat—a threat which in her case had proved "salutary at the age of ten."

She could not postpone her journey any longer and announced that she would be coming to Vienna in July. "I find it impossible," Francis wrote to her, "to tell you how much I look forward to seeing you again after such a long absence."

As in 1818, it was first at Persenbeug and then at Schönbrunn that Marie Louise spent nearly three months with her son. During this holiday Reichstadt lived what was almost a family life with his mother,

Neipperg, and the latter's son Gustave, who was only a little older than he. There were fishing parties not far from Pöggstall, and excursions such as the one on July 10 to the Valley of Hell near Gutenbrunn, with Marie Louise, the Emperor and the Archduke Francis on horseback and Reichstadt riding with the Empress Caroline Augusta in a carriage.

If this summer holiday delighted the boy, it also enabled Marie Louise to get to know her son better, and she realized that making a priest of him was out of the question. Yet the idea was still in the air, and word of it reached Leopoldine, who wrote from Rio de Janeiro that she was revolted by such a "cruel" project.

When he had to leave his mother, on September 16 at Mariazell, Franz—that was what Marie Louise called him now—was terribly distressed—so distressed, in fact, that Dietrichstein made him take a tonic. But the tears went on flowing, and flowed faster after the scolding which Dietrichstein thought fit to administer at this of all moments. To calm the boy down he took him into the church at Mariazell to pray. Then, after two days on the road, it was back to Vienna and the Hofburg. Dietrichstein suggested to Francis that he should describe his distress to "his dear Mamma" and tell her about his return journey. For the first time in his life, the little nine-year-old wrote without any help:

> Dear Mamma, I have arrived in Vienna safely and in good health. The Lasing waterfall, which I did not expect to see, was superb. I feel very sad to think that only the day before yesterday at this time you were with me, and that now it is all over. The road, yesterday and today, seemed gloomy to me, for I had traveled it with you. At least come back without fail in nine months' time, dear Mamma, as you promised me you would, and think often of your most obedient son Francis.

Dietrichstein attached this commentary to his pupil's note: "Here is the Prince's letter, which has cost him a certain amount of trouble and in which I have had no part whatever. He spoiled the first copy and the second is no better. The agitation of the journey is his excuse, but I think that Your Majesty might well speak to him about the style, handwriting and form of his letter. . . ."

Marie Louise thought that all considering her son did not write as badly as his tutor maintained, but she none the less obeyed Dietrichstein and sent a severe missive to her *"gehorsamster Sohn Franz,"* a reprimand which left the boy fairly indifferent but delighted Dietrichstein: "I have been waiting for some days now for the Prince to make up his mind to answer the charming and inimitable letter which Your Majesty was good enough to write to him and which I read and reread with him several times. . . ."

With that instinctive understanding children sometimes have, did Francis realize what a small place he occupied in his mother's life? Possibly, for it was only after three days of "meditation" and under pressure from his tutor that he sent her a few lines of the least spontaneous prose imaginable. One again Dietrichstein complained; once again Marie Louise wrote reprimanding her son. "Heavens," enthused the pedagogue, "but such perfect advice should electrify him and wake him up; his heart should melt, his eyes should fill with tears of emotion and joy. . . ."

This heart of which, as we have seen, Dietrichstein was fond of talking, was starved of affection. What a tutor too concerned about questions of good behavior failed to see, a mother, a real mother, ought to have felt. What was needed was a little less criticism and a little more love. The boy replied as follows:

> Dear Mamma, you complain in your last letter that my letters are far too stiff; if my letters betray certain constraint, pray do not attribute this to a lack of affection. I shall try to correct this defect, which is due to nothing but want of practice. I assuredly love you as much as a son can love so good a mother, and I want to prove this to you in every way I can.

The "Grand Master" derived some consolation from the next Court *Kammerball,* at which his pupil shone once again, touching the hearts of the imperial family. Dietrichstein was obliged to recognize Franz's success—"which is saying a good deal," observed Countess Lazansky. As had been the case the previous winter, colds and chills prevented the little Prince from dancing as much as he would have liked. Recovering from a "rheumatic affection" in January, 1821, he none the less put in an appearance at the *Kammerball* on the 16th, but it was so hot and crowded that he had to forgo the last waltz and the galoppade. "In spite of that he would not sit down but went on talking to the Archduchess Henrietta and the Ladies." Dancing was all the rage in Vienna that winter, and everyone was talking about the amazing *pas de deux* created at Princess Esterházy's house by Taglioni and little Eberl.

Francis was bitterly disappointed to learn that his mother would not be leaving her Duchy that summer. "Alas," he wrote to her on May 7, "this is sad news for me; however, I promise to bring you comfort and consolation and additional hope in the year to come. The death of that excellent Councilor of State Frank [the boy's doctor] has greatly distressed me; he liked me tremendously and the liking was mutual. Admittedly my new doctor is a capable fellow, but I hope that God will keep me in good health for a long time to come and spare me many medicaments. Schönbrunn, where I am going tomorrow, should help in that respect. But I shall not find there the joy I knew last summer."

Sure enough, the next day, May 8, Reichstadt installed himself at Schönbrunn, in new apartments whose windows opened, not onto the Gloriette, but onto the courtyard. Dietrichstein observed that "the sentry is something of a distraction, but there are ways of preventing this which will doubtless prove to be necessary." The boy was to make his first communion the following month, and religious instruction had been added to his other lessons.

Tuesday, May 8, . . .
That day, at St. Helena, the Abbé Vignali celebrated a Requiem Mass before the Emperor's coffin. . . .

11

*

"To My Son . . ."

AT ST. HELENA, on March 20, 1821—his son's tenth birthday—
Napoleon sighed: "The machine is worn out; it can't go on any more.
It's all over—I'm going to die here."

The Emperor no longer hoped for any help from Parma; he was
well aware that "dearest Louise" flinched at the very name of Napoleon.
In February, 1818, Gourgaud, convinced that he was being persecuted
—as indeed he was, by Napoleon's exactingness, selfishness and obtuse-
ness—had abandoned Longwood to the nauseating intrigues of the
Montholons and the mediocrity of the Bertrands. On his arrival in
Europe, he had written to Marie Louise—on August 25, 1818—begging
her to ask the power gathered together at the Congress of Aix-la-
Chapelle to improve the prisoner's lot. "What comfort it would afford
him to see you do this. . . . Oh, Madame, in the name of all that you
hold dearest in the world, do everything you can to help the Emperor. . . ."

She made no reply to her husband's former aide-de-camp, especially
as Gourgaud had thought fit to add: "The shade of Marie Theresa
orders you to take action."

The General had then addressed himself—on October 25—to the
Emperor Francis: "Sire, the Emperor Napoleon is dying in the most
horrible and fearful agony. He will succumb before long, that is
certain . . . !"

The "dear brother and father-in-law" had remained silent too. In

May, 1820, Napoleon sent a letter to Marie Louise through a Neapolitan called Tito Mansi, who had been in King Murat's service. Now —unknown in all probability to the Bonapartes living in exile in Rome —Tito Mansi had become a councilor of the imperial government. He thought it his duty to inform Metternich that he had been instructed to deliver a letter from St. Helena to the Duchess of Parma. Metternich promptly asked his master to sign the following lines:

> Dear sister and well-beloved daughter, advised that M. Tito Mansi has been charged to deliver a letter from St. Helena into Your Majesty's hands, and that he has been expressly instructed to ask for a receipt for it, I feel it all the more incumbent upon me to inform you of this in that I know your feelings well enough to be convinced that you would certainly refuse to receive the letter which has been entrusted to M. Tito Mansi, unless you were expressly authorized to do so by myself. Considering however that this letter may contain certain important information, I have no hesitation, in the general interest of the maintenance of peace in Europe, in asking you to receive the aforementioned letter and to give a receipt for it couched in the following terms: *I have received from M. Tito Mansi the letter from Rome which was entrusted to him for me.* When you are in possession of the letter which he has been charged to deliver to you, I beg you to forward it directly to me without opening it. . . .

Without opening it! In spite of all the pledges the ex-Empress had given the Austrian government, and in spite of all the sacrifices she had made, it was clear that Metternich had very little confidence in Marie Louise. The Duchess obeyed without a murmur, and the letter, whose contents remain unknown to us, arrived at the Hofburg with its seals unbroken.

Henceforth nothing remained for the prisoner of St. Helena to do except wait for death. In his narrow iron bed—the bed in which he had slept on the morning of Austerlitz—the green curtains closed upon his dreams . . . dreams in which Marie Louise sometimes came to haunt his nights.

"She was holding my son by the hand," he told the faithful Marchand one morning. "She was as fresh-looking as when I saw her at Compiègne, and I clasped her in my arms, but however much strength I exerted in order to hold her, I felt her slipping from my grasp, and when I tried to seize hold of her again everything disappeared and I woke up. . . ."

In April he sensed that death was prowling the plateau of Longwood around his wretched little wooden house. Between two fits of vomiting, his body covered with viscous sweat, he started making his will. At his bedside Montholon held an inkpot in his trembling hands—a quadrangular inkpot in English porcelain in which the Emperor dipped his little goose quill.

"Sire, there is no hurry!"

"It is time to make an end of it. . . . I can feel it in my bones."

And he wrote:

I have never had anything but praise for my beloved wife, Marie Louise; to the very last I retain the tenderest regard for her. . . .

He was perfectly well aware that Neipperg had succeeded him in her affections, but he was writing for history. The quill scratched as he went on:

I beg her to take care to protect my son from the dangers which still threaten him.

I recommend my son never to forget that he was born a French prince, and never to lend himself to being a tool in the hands of triumvirs now oppressing the peoples of Europe. He must never fight against France or harm her in any other way. He must adopt my motto: *Everything for the French people.*

He bequeathed to his son the relics of his glory, "retracing for his benefit the memory of a father of whom the world will inform him":

My arms; to wit: my sword, the one which I wore at Austerlitz, the saber of Sobieski, my dagger, my glaive, my hunting knife, my two pairs of pistols from Versailles.

My gold dressing case, the one I used on the mornings of Ulm, Austerlitz, Jena, Eylau, Friedland, the Isle of Lobau, the Moskva and Montmirail; for this reason I hope it will be precious to my son.

I charge Comte Bertrand to keep and care for these objects, and to deliver them to my son when he is sixteen.

Three small mahogany chests containing: the first, thirty-three snuffboxes or comfit-boxes; the second, twelve boxes bearing the imperial arms, two small spyglasses and four boxes found on Louis XVIII's table in the Tuileries on March 20, 1815; the third, three snuffboxes decorated with silver medallions. . . .

My camp beds, which I used in all my campaigns.

My field glass.

My toilet case, one of each of my uniforms, a dozen shirts, one complete set of each of my outfits, and of everything pertaining to my clothing.

My washstand.

My two watches and the chain made of the Empress's hair.

I charge Marchand, my first valet, to keep these objects, and to deliver them to my son when he is sixteen.

My collection of medals.

My silver plate and Sèvres porcelain which I have used at St. Helena.

I charge Comte Montholon to keep these objects, and to deliver them to my son when he is sixteen.

My three saddles and bridles and my spurs, which I have used at St. Helena.

My sporting guns, five in number.

I charge my groom Noverraz to keep these objects, and to deliver them to my son when he is sixteen.

Four hundred volumes from my library, selected from those which I have used most frequently.

I charge Saint-Denis to keep them, and to deliver them to my son when he is sixteen.

Dying on his lonely rock, fighting his last battle, struggling with all the energy of an old warrior against the disease which was to carry him off, he took pains to write legibly the seven words which came back again and again like a litany:

To my son when he is sixteen.

And the list went on, mingling epic souvenirs with humble objects used in his captivity: Frederick the Great's alarm clock which he had taken at Potsdam, the seals of France, his silver flasks, his collar of the Golden Fleece, his hats, the saber he had worn at Aboukir, his field glasses, his spurs, his watches, the blue cloak he had worn at

Marengo, his linen, his pillows, his handkerchiefs, his braces, his slippers, his silver-gilt cassolette, a "little box full of snuff," and finally the little gilt clock in his bedroom which he had consulted so often during his long sleepless nights, while the wind howled outside.

To his "beloved wife" Marie Louise he bequeathed a bracelet made of his hair, his lace . . . and his heart.

The 25th was the worst day of all. Bent double with pain, and vomiting without stopping, he copied out the codicils. Then, in a voice broken by hiccups, he dictated to Marchand his instructions to his executors:

As soon as my son has attained the age of reason, my mother, my brothers and my sisters must write to him and make contact with him, whatever obstacles the House of Austria may put in their way, impotent though that House will then be, my son having the power of understanding. They must urge my son to resume the name of Napoleon as soon as he has attained the age of reason and can conveniently do so. If there were to be a turn of fortune and my son mounted the throne, it would be the duty of my executors to make plain to him all that I owe my old soldiers and officers and my devoted servants.

The next day he read the codicils again and signed them, with Bertrand standing stolidly at his bedside.

"It is my wish that the Empress should not marry again . . . but they will probably marry her off to some little archduke among her cousins. She is to supervise my son's education, and she must be on her guard against the Bourbons, who are sure to try to rid themselves of him. There will probably be attempts to make my son a cardinal; the most important thing for him is never to become a priest. He must always take pride in having been born a Frenchman; no one can tell what his fate will be; perhaps one day he will rule over France. . . ."

He was calmer now and dictated to Montholon:

"My son must not think of avenging my death; he must profit by it. May the memory of what I have achieved never forsake him; may he, like myself, always remain a Frenchman to his fingertips. The aim of all his efforts should be to reign by peaceful means. I have implanted new ideas in France and in Europe; they cannot retrogress; let my son bring to blossom all that I have sown. . . ."

Often, during the last struggle, his eyes fell on the portrait of the little King and its inscription: "I am praying for my father and for France. . . ."

On the 29th, at nine o'clock in the evening, he asked Marchand: "Have you some writing paper?"

The valet was there, beside the bed, without any light. He picked up a playing card and a pencil.

"Write this: I leave my son my house in Ajaccio with its outbuildings, two houses close to the saltpits with their gardens, and all my property in the Ajaccio district. This will bring him in an income of fifty thousand francs. I leave my son . . ."

He stopped short.

"I am very tired, we will go on tomorrow."

During the night his mind started wandering. It was Montholon's turn to write in the dark on playing cards, at the Emperor's dictation:

"I leave him my iron crown and the Italian crown. In fact I leave him everything, though it is good that he should have an income of fifty thousand francs in Austria; after all, he's a Teuton!"

Was it the fever that led him to express all the rancor in his cankered, bruised, embittered heart?

On May 4, the eve of his death, he was twice heard to ask: "What is my son's name?"

"Napoleon," answered Marchand.

He did not open his eyes all night. About four o'clock the next afternoon he murmured:

"My son . . . The head of the army . . ."

The tropical night fell swiftly. Without a single movement to betray what was happening, the Emperor rendered up to God "the mightiest breath of life that ever animated human clay." The Grand Marshal stopped the hands of the mahogany clock, which ever since have stood at eleven minutes to six.

The news of Napoleon's death traveled for nearly two months before reaching England on July 4, 1821.

Metternich learned of the event nine days after London, thanks to a courier of the House of Rothschild who outdistanced the diplomatic services.

"This event," he calmly declared, "puts an end to a good many hopes and criminal conspiracies. It has no other interest for the world."

For the Austrian Minister the French Empire was now nothing more than a memory—an unpleasant memory. Marie Louise, sovereign of a former French department, had become blissfully quiescent in her Neipperg's arms; the King of Rome, transformed into a Bavarian duke, spoke only German now; and finally his old enemy, chained to his rock at two months' sailing distance, and already struck off the list of the living several years before, now lay in a quadruple coffin in the depths of little Geranium Valley.

On July 13 the Emperor Francis, in Dietrichstein's absence, entrusted Foresti with the task of informing his grandson of his father's death. The captain chose "the peaceful hour of evening" and the boy burst out sobbing. "I saw more tears shed than I would have expected," wrote the officer, who had never understood the child's character. Another fit of sobbing greeted Collin when the tutor came into the room.

It was a letter from Mme. Amelin de Sainte-Marie—lady-in-waiting at the Court of Parma—posted at Milan on the 16th, which told Marie Louise of her husband's death. The news did not prevent her from going to the Opéra on the 19th to hear *The Barber of Seville*. While she was at this performance, incidentally, she could have read the official announcement of Napoleon's death as printed in the *Piedmont Gazette*. The Hofburg had forgotten to inform her of the event, but their negligence was excusable: Marie Louise had done nothing to suggest that she thought about her husband any more.

This slight on the part of the Court of Vienna—so she told her Uncle Ferdinand—was "in the circumstances" her "greatest affliction." Napoleon's death only affected her "extremely." "I cannot forget," she wrote on July 19 to Victoire de Créneville, "that he was the father of my son, and that far from treating me badly, as the world imagines, he always showed me every consideration, which is all that one can hope for in a political marriage. I was therefore extremely upset by the news, and though one must rejoice that he should have ended his unhappy life in Christian fashion, I would have preferred him to enjoy many years of life and happiness, provided they were spent far away from me." She appeared to be just as "upset" by the mosquitoes which had stung her so badly in the face; she wrote in the same letter that "I look like a monster and I am glad that I have no need to show myself in public." All the gladder in that Marie Louise was at this time over eight months pregnant . . .

On the morning of Tuesday, July 24, the *Parma Gazette* published the following announcement, which was not even surrounded with a black border:

> In consequence of the death of the Most Serene spouse of our august sovereign, which occurred on the island of St. Helena on last May 5 Her Majesty, the knights and ladies of the Court, the staff of the ducal household and the livery will go into mourning as from tomorrow the 25th inst. until October 24 next inclusive. Mourning will be divided into three classes: from July 25 to September 4, first class mourning; from September 5 to October 2, second class mourning; and from October 3 to 24, third class mourning.

The "Most Serene spouse" was a find of Neipperg's. He wrote about it to Metternich, who is said to have been highly amused on reading these lines: "The most difficult problem, in view of the absolute necessity of sparing Her Majesty's delicate feelings while at the same time respecting the principles generally adopted with regard to the deceased, was how to announce his death in the *Gazette* and motivate the adoption of mourning by Her Majesty and her Household. I hope that the expedient which I thought fit to employ, avoiding as it does all mention of the titles of Emperor and ex-Emperor or the names of Bonaparte or Napoleon, which were inadmissible in any event and would have offended Her Majesty's heart or the political principles now in force, will find favor with Your Highness. The word *Serenissimo* is even more generic in the Italian tongue than any other. . . ."

Intent upon protecting Marie Louise's "heart" against any further possibility of "offense," Neipperg hit upon another "expedient" for the Requiem Mass: the *Serenissimo* became the *consorte ducis nostrae*. Napoleon in death became Prince Consort of Parma.

On July 19 Victoire de Créneville had sent a letter of sympathy to Marie Louise. She remained convinced that the ex-Empress would "bestow her tears" upon the deceased and that she would "make her august son sensible of the feelings he owes a father." Marie Louise was also informed—doubtless by the same post—of her little Reichstadt's grief, and on the 24th she finally wrote to him:

> I hear, my dear son, that you have been deeply affected by the misfortune which has befallen us both, and I feel that writing

to you and talking to you on this subject will comfort my heart more than anything else. I am sure that your grief was no less profound than mine, for you would be an ungrateful wretch if you could forget the kindness he showed you in your infancy. You must endeavor to imitate his virtues, while avoiding the reefs upon which he came to grief.

Dietrichstein went into raptures over this missive. "The Prince," he wrote on August 1, "received Your Majesty's letter yesterday and read it in my presence and that of these Gentlemen. Oh, how adorable Your Majesty is! . . . Your Majesty always anticipates my most secret thoughts, because nothing can equal either her genius or her affection. I repeat that this admirable letter leaves nothing to be desired, and the Prince should read it again and again, the better to appreciate his good fortune in having so perfect a mother and to remember the duties she has prescribed him. . . ."

"I am delighted that my son showed so much feeling on the occasion of his father's death," replied Marie Louise on August 10. "Death wipes out all one's unpleasant memories, as I found on this occasion."

What unpleasant memories could she have retained of Napoleon, for whom she had felt a deep and passionate love? People had pitied and comforted her so much, and had congratulated her so often on having escaped from the clutches of the Corsican Ogre, that she had ended up by believing that she had suffered martyrdom. Marie Louise, who had deserted him in the most cowardly fashion when fortune had turned against him; was now playing the generous woman with the forgiving nature. "For I thought only of the good he had done me," she went on, "of his cruel death agony and of his last unhappy years, and I wept bitter tears for him."

Alone in Vienna, the Duke of Reichstadt's household went into deep mourning for Napoleon. No ceremony, of course, was held at Court in memory of the Emperor's son-in-law. "The day after the arrival of the courier who brought the important news of Napoleon's death," writes the Baronne de Montet, "I was awakened early in the morning by the noise of horses and carriages; it was a magnificent hunting party—the Emperor, the Empress and the entire Court."

A few days later the Baronne met the Duke of Reichstadt walking "with his head down and a mournful expression in his eyes." Feeling lonelier than ever, and isolated in his suffering, he kept his grief hidden away in the depths of his being, together with the now very indistinct memories of his infancy. The idea of confiding in his mother seemed to embarrass him and it took a fortnight of violent reproaches by his tutor before he would resign himself to doing so.

Dear Mamma, I thank you for your letter, so full of maternal affection, in which you tried to console me for my father's death, which has plunged you too into such profound grief. Overwhelmed by the unexpected news, and suffering the greatest unhappiness I have ever known, I did not dare to write to you about this sad event, which would have caused you even greater pain had you learned of it from your son. Looking to your maternal love for my happiness, I shall try, for my part, to pay the greatest attention to the exhortations which you addressed to me on this sad occasion, and I join with you in your prayers for the repose of the soul of my late father. Whatever reasons I may have to be grateful to my grandfather and grandmother, I am well aware, and this occasion has afforded me further proof of the fact, that they love me and care for me like a son. It is a comfort to me to know that in spite of the sadness which has afflicted you your health has remained unaffected; that is my only consolation in these days of mourning. Permit me to offer you, on the occasion of your birthday, my sincerest good wishes, and to commend myself to your kindness, assuring you that I remain your most obedient son,

FRANCIS

We know from Dietrichstein that the boy wrote this letter with the help of Foresti and Collin. "I am not at all pleased with it," sighed the tutor, "because these are not his own ideas, which we should wait for in vain, and because his handwriting is getting worse every day, as a result of faults which he makes no attempt to correct."

Reichstadt's letter and Dietrichstein's complaint were both dated August 15. The same August 15—Napoleon's birthday—Marie Louise brought forth a little girl who incidentally was to die before the year was out.

At the beginning of the following month, the ex-Empress of the French became Neipperg's wife. The Emperor Francis, after asking Metternich's opinion, had given his consent to the match. Marie Louise was in no way moved when she learned of Napoleon's last words to Antommarchi:

"I want you to take my heart, put in spirit of wine, and take it to Parma to my dear Marie Louise. You will tell her that I loved her tenderly, and that I never ceased to love her."

More horrified than touched by this unwelcome gift, "dearest Louise" refused to accept the heart which had beaten for her.

"My only desire is that his heart should remain in his grave," she wrote to her father. "Ill-disposed persons would take it as a pretext for making a pilgrimage to Parma, and that would be exceedingly painful to me, since there is nothing more I wish for on earth but peace and quiet. . . ."

Hudson Lowe seemed to have foreseen what her reply would be, for he had not granted Napoleon's last doctor permission to take the relic to Europe. Antommarchi arrived in Parma in October. Mme. Neipperg refused to receive him and asked her new husband to show him gently to the door. Some time later, a doctor—one Hermann Rollet—saw the children of Marie Louise's steward "playing with a plaster object which they had attached to a piece of string and which they were pulling along the floor as if it were a carriage." The doctor picked the object up and recognized Napoleon's death mask, which, failing the Emperor's heart, Antommarchi had presented to Marie Louise.

In France, the Emperor's death had the effect of crystalizing Napoleonic enthusiasm around the Duke of Reichstadt and furthering the imperial cause. During the early years of the Restoration the memory of the "little King" held prisoner in Vienna had served Bonapartist propaganda well. The theme of the Eagle at St. Helena and the Eaglet in Vienna was calculated to rekindle—if the need arose—the courage of "Bonaparte's Vultures," the "Knights of the Dagger" and the members of the "Black Pin," supporters of Napoleon II who at Bordeaux and Lyons in 1817 and in Paris in 1820—a more serious affair, this—tried to dethrone Louis XVIII and proclaim Napoleon II Emperor of the French. For more peaceable opponents of the monarchy the street hawkers offered for sale pictures of the Duke of Reichstadt dressed as a French sergeant and snuffboxes or neckerchiefs depicting the "little prisoner of Schönbrunn," and handed out bills announcing that Napoleon had escaped from St. Helena to come and place his son on the throne.

At the 1817 Salon a sensation was caused by a portrait of the son of a counselor at the Bavarian Embassy. The child was fair-haired and was holding a bunch of blue flowers in his little hands. Everyone promptly decided that the fair-haired child could only be the King of Rome and the flowers forget-me-nots, the symbol of remembrance. Crowds of Bonapartist pilgrims came to see the picture, and the police finally had to remove it.

Once the death agony of St. Helena was over, the captive Eaglet took the place of the chained Eagle in the popular imagination. The year 1821 saw the creation in Paris of a vast range of Bonapartist bric-a-brac, from patriotic liqueur bottles with labels depicting the little exile, and tricolor suspenders bearing the portrait of the Duke of Reichstadt, to prints representing the Emperor being welcomed to the underworld while Napoleon II was receiving his scepter and crown from the hands of Glory and Fame.

A certain Cellier put on sale a pentagonal trinket showing on its various faces a tomb in the shape of a pyramid, a child enveloped in a tricolor flag, a pansy intertwined with an immortelle, and two inscriptions: "Weep, People of France, the great man is no more" and "Diogenes would rekindle his lantern in vain." Cellier solemnly asserted that "all this referred to the Duc de Berry," whom Louvel had assassinated the year before. According to him, the King's nephew was a victim worthy of everlasting regret—hence the need to erect an impressive tomb in his memory. He declared that it was useless for Diogenes to light his lantern again, since he would never find a prince to compare with the murdered Duke. And finally he swore that the child in the tricolor was not the Duke of Reichstadt but the little Duc de Bordeaux.

He was none the less convicted.

From now on it was in the interests of Napoleon II, the "prisoner of Vienna," that the conspirators plotted and planned. At the beginning of 1822 General Berton set off from Thouars with fifty men and a tricolor flag, and made for Saumur to shouts of "Long live the Emperor! Long live Napoleon II!" Sold to the police by one of his accomplices, Berton was arrested, but his failure did not deter one Colonel Caron from organizing another conspiracy at Colmar. Nine hundred men marched out of the city shouting: "We aren't the soldiers of the King any more, we are the soldiers of Napoleon II!"

The troop was riddled with informers, and—once their leader had been arrested—it was to shouts of "Long live the King!" that the soldiers returned to Colmar.

The intervention of Louis XVIII's army in Spain in order to restore King Ferdinand VII to the throne began in the most unexpected way. Arriving at the frontier on April 7, 1823, the soldiers of the Duc d'-Agoulème found themselves face to face, not with Spanish *Exaltados* but with a handful of French Bonapartists. Grouped in front of Behobia, on the left bank of the Bidassoa, they were waving a huge tricolor, singing the "Marseillaise," and acclaiming Napoleon II. The Eaglet's soldiers thought that they had before them the advance guard of the French army which had been skillfully won over to the imperial cause. But the plot had been discovered and the advance guard transferred to the rear. The Royalist General Vallin gave a stentorian bellow of "Long live the King!" and opened fire on the tricolor, which collapsed. The Bonapartists fled, leaving eight dead and four wounded. And Vallin, promoted to lieutenant-general, was assured in all seriousness that "his cannon shot had saved Europe."

Louis XVIII's government would doubtless have felt even happier if they had known that the Duke of Reichstadt now appeared to have been completely "Austrianized." Strangely enough, since the announcement of his father's death he had asked none of those questions which Foresti used to dread so much. This puzzled his tutors, but it was natural enough. Since his father—so he was constantly informed with unctuous and respectful sighs—had been a bloody despot, it was better for him to remain silent and keep to himself the shame of being the son of "a wicked man who had been put in prison." Keeping silent presented no difficulty, for the education that had been inflicted on him had turned the frank, outspoken child into a reserved, suspicious, uncommunicative boy. Dietrichstein was astonished: "He does not ask me a single question, and the same is true of these gentlemen." He considered this silence "somewhat unnatural," never imagining that it was he himself who was largely responsible for it.

The rule which Reichstadt had imposed on himself—this apparent "indifference" of his—had led him to forget for a while that he had been "born a French prince." If not a bishop *in partibus,* as Metternich would have wished, he was going to become an Austrian archduke who might one day be destined to mount the throne of France and thus fulfill Dietrichstein's hopes.

"Our principal aim," the tutor explained to Marie Louise, "is to form his mind, his heart, and his taste for all that is noble and great and suited to the education of a prince destined to take his place in history."

In order to "form his mind," Dietrichstein had devised a scheme of study so vast that one can understand why sometimes—only too often, said his grandfather—the boy showed a certain weariness and made "deliberate mistakes" in the hope of discouraging his masters. Collin taught him Latin and Greek, Foresti mathematics, history and—already—the elements of tactics and strategy; Msgr. Wagner and the chaplain to the Court were responsible for his religious instruction; Podevin and Barthélemy—two French masters living in Vienna—taught him French; the Abbé Fina and Foresti, Italian; and Professor Baumgartner, physics, chemistry and the natural sciences. Franz still showed no taste for music. "No one could have less talent in this direction," declared Foresti. He had "no ear for rhythm" and his voice was "excruciating." He sang as badly as his father—which was saying a great deal. And he took no pleasure at all in listening to music—a matter for regret at a time when the highly critical Viennese saluted Beethoven after the first performance of his Ninth Symphony with five rounds of applause—two more than the number laid down by Court etiquette for the imperial family.

Conversation at the Emperor Francis's Court—as Dietrichstein and Foresti later complained to Prokesch—tended to be coarse and vulgar. "In this respect," Marie Louise remarked, "my family is a bad influence on my son. I have never known less attention to be paid to what is said in front of young people, and have never understood how people so upright and devout can allow themselves to say things which have often made me blush." The Archduke Francis was perhaps the chief offender. As the Queen of Saxony told her niece on January 31, 1822, Reichstadt was fond of imitating his uncle's bad manners and "his crude and smutty jokes." The passing of the years had done nothing to improve the Archduke.

There were few surprises in the boy's life. Summer was spent at Schönbrunn, which he loved for its long façade with the green shutters and for the Gloriette silhouetted on the horizon. Every year, too, he joined his grandfather in one of his so-called "country" residences—at Baden, a little watering place just outside Vienna, at romantic Persenbeug, or at the castle of Laxenburg, where he would go for a walk every day with his grandfather and in the evening, yawning a little, listen to the Emperor "making music." In July, Countess Lazansky would have liked him to stay with her, but "Dietrichstein's fury" put an end to that particular project.

At the end of the hunting season Francis returned to the Hofburg— a cheerless setting, heavily if comfortably furnished, and yet one which he loved because the windows of his apartments—on the second floor above the great doorway flanked by the labors of Hercules—looked out over the courtyard with its crowds of visitors, couriers and aides-de-camp. The boy could also see the carriages of the Court driving in and out, the sentries presenting arms, and the occupants of each carriage acknowledging the salute in the time-honored fashion, by raising or lowering the window several times. It was with a connoisseur's eye that he looked at the horses, for he was already a good horseman and could drive a carriage and four with more than average skill. When the gay music of the changing of the guard started in the courtyard, Dietrichstein himself could not prevent his pupil from running to the window to watch the soldiers marching up and down, obeying the raucous commands of their officers with puppetlike movements. And the boy would begin dreaming of the white uniform he would wear one day.

Before having lessons in strategy and fortification from Major Weiss, he would sometimes inspect the terrain with Foresti—at Wagram, for instance—and draw a map for his grandfather to see. Dietrichstein was able to write to Marie Louise on January 23, 1822: "His knowledge of matters military is truly astonishing; he does not treat this subject superficially, but wants to make a thorough study of it, and there can be no doubt that if he continues like this he will know more about it at sixteen or seventeen than many high-ranking officers." His admiration for anyone who wore uniform led him one day to refuse to take his usual place in the imperial dining room and go and sit instead at the foot of the table.

"There are some generals here," he explained, "and they must take precedence of me."

This taste for "matters military," as Dietrichstein put it, grew steadily more pronounced. At the end of 1822 a Feldwebel's uniform was made for him. He appeared in it at the imperial table one day in January, 1823, and presented a report to his grandfather, who put him through a few drill movements. He acquitted himself "wonderfully well." The King of Naples, old Nasone, Reichstadt's great-grandfather, was just as impressed as the Emperor. The Empress was "radiant with joy" and afterward declared that the boy had never before made such a *ganze conquête* of Emperor and King.

"There is no doubt that with his martial air he is quite irresistible," admitted Dietrichstein. Franz seized the opportunity to ask his mother to come to Vienna: "You will find in me a Feldwebel of the imperial infantry who will endeavor to display to you all his military lore and who, moreover, having mastered the art of driving his carriage, will be able to offer you his services with absolute confidence. . . ."

12

❀

Dietrichstein's Pupil

MARIE LOUISE, who was again pregnant, had not been to see her son in 1822. She continued to lead a quiet, carefree life at Parma. "I rise at nine o'clock," she wrote. "I then deal with affairs of state and correspondence until eleven, when I get dressed; lunch is at midday. At one o'clock, everyone retires to his apartments; I do some embroidery or some painting in water colors or oils. About three o'clock I go out riding, driving or walking, and return about five or six. I work for another hour, and then play some music, sing, read some English or have some French read to me. At nine o'clock we have dinner or supper, and then we play billiards or chess, backgammon, etc. After a little conversation we retire about midnight."

Sometimes an importunate visitor would disturb this bourgeois routine. Such a one was Marchand, who after trying in vain to bring her a bracelet made of Napoleon's hair in accordance with his master's last wishes, wrote to her: "I had retained until the present day the hope of expressing personally to Her Majesty my sympathy with her in her loss, and of delivering into her hands the hair with which the Emperor deigned to entrust me, but all the efforts I have made to obtain a passport have proved unsuccessful and a few days ago I received a positive refusal from the Prefecture of Police. This refusal is all the more painful to me in that it deprives me of the honor of making known to Your Majesty the sentiments of love and esteem which the Emperor retained for her, as well as the courage with which he

243

constantly confronted his misfortunes."

As may be imagined, she never wore the bracelet Marchand sent her; and at the Congress of Verona, which she attended at the end of the year, she preferred to wear a bracelet made out of a piece of Juliet's tomb, a whim which caused Chateaubriand considerable surprise. The early League of Nations had been called together to settle the affairs of Spain. It was a picturesque medley of Emperors, ministers, aulic counselors, officials and secretaries. In order to remind the assembled sovereigns that ten years before they had been at France's mercy, Louis XVIII had sent an imposing delegation to Verona, headed by the Minister of Foreign Affairs, Mathieu de Montmorency. Chateaubriand, then French ambassador in London, had begged to be allowed to join it, and imagined that he was going to be treated as a great statesman. He had even engaged a duke as his secretary. But the members of the Congress were not impressed. The *coup de grâce* was administered to the author of the *Martyrs* by the Queen of Sardinia, who asked him "if he was related to the M. de Chateaubriand who wrote *pamphlets.*" Marie Louise was kinder and invited the writer to her table. He refused at first. "She insisted, so we went. We found her extremely gay. . . . She made some insignificant reference, almost in passing, to the King of Rome. She was pregnant. Her suite had a somewhat decrepit, old-fashioned look about it, with the exception of M. de Neipperg, a man of good breeding. . . ."

She returned to Parma to have a miscarriage and resumed her correspondence with her Parisian and Viennese friends, asking them to buy her a hundred and one things—trinkets, shawls, hats, music . . . and medicaments. Dietrichstein himself was not spared and had to turn errand boy. In his replies he referred—respectfully but insistently—to the bad impression produced on Viennese opinion and on her son's character by Marie Louise's overlong absence. The Duchess yielded and spent the summer of 1823 with Reichstadt. He was happy once more, even very happy, and seven years later he would still remember these days as the happiest of his childhood. Mother and son stayed first at Baden and Laxenburg, then once again at Persenbeug, and finally at Weinzierl. Dietrichstein inevitably took the opportunity to make his pupil keep a diary of his travels, a document written in a stilted style worthy of Count Maurice himself and virtually unreadable today. If Dietrichstein had not constantly curbed and criticized his pupil, the result would certainly have been far better; witness this letter which the boy wrote during the same holidays to Collin, with whom he felt more at ease:

I added a couple of lines in Italian to the Count's letter to Foresti. They were somewhat laconic in style, but then I am a young Spartan. "Oh, yes, a fine Spartan," I can hear you saying, "who will not take black broth unless they have put eggs in it!" But here I really am leading a Spartan life. I rise at half-past six, get dressed, say my prayers, have breakfast, and jump all over my bedroom with a long branch doing service as a whip. Then the hard work begins, under the Count's direction. After that I am summoned to see my mother and often go for a walk before dinner. Then comes dinner, followed by a pause for digestion. In the afternoon there are walks and excursions, though not on the lake; afterward, supper and bed. I write you these lines feeling fortified and refreshed. . . .

A few days later, employing the same easy style, of which solemn Dietrichstein would almost certainly have disapproved, he wrote once more to Collin: "I am at Persenbeug now, in a very big room, at least for this place, and I am writing to you at the window, not in order to look outside, but simply in order to see properly. However, my eyes keep leaving the paper, even though I have made a resolution not to look around me."

What was the little Duke of Reichstadt dreaming about? Possibly—as he admitted in one of his exercises—about Parma, where he would have dearly loved to spend his holidays. But he was aware that he was more or less a prisoner, and that it was out of the question for him to leave Austria or even the neighborhood of Vienna. Everyone knew that the mere mention of the name of Napoleon's son might rouse the greater part of Italy to action.

During these few weeks he was indescribably happy to have his mother with him, to feel a woman's presence at his side. He was full of tender affection for her. How could he have guessed that when her china-blue eyes lit up as she spoke of her approaching return to Parma it was because she was thinking of the children whose existence she had to conceal from him, those children born of a love which she could not acknowledge? It was natural that she should feel sorrier for Alber-

tine—the "poor darling"—and William—"fat little Patapouf"—than for
her son Reichstadt, who was titled, richly provided for, surrounded with
tutors, and treated as a favorite grandson by the Emperor.

She certainly felt no remorse as she set off on the return journey to
Parma, on September 4, 1823, leaving the orphan of Schönbrunn sobbing bitterly behind her. All the way home—so Dietrichstein tell us—
tears poured down his cheeks. He had been told that he would not
be seeing his mother for another two years, and two years is a long time
when one is twelve. If only he had known that Marie Louise was going
to allow herself even more time and not come back to Vienna before
1826. A "fit of choking" overcame him as he showed Dietrichstein
a little flower his mother had given him at the moment of parting, and
the tears flowed faster than ever when they caught sight of Persenbeug
and he pointed out the windows of the apartments Marie Louise had
been occupying. They had scarcely got back to Weinzierl and greeted
the Emperor and Empress before he was writing to Parma: "Oh, how
difficult I am already finding it to wait for the moment when I shall
see you again! Yet when I consider the difference between two years and
twelve hours—for that is how long I have to wait to be reunited with
you, and we were together only a little while ago—I feel even un-
happier. All the scenery from Wels to here seemed sad and dreary to
me, because I was not looking at it with you, as I was yesterday. . . ."

Henceforth Francis was to write to his mother more often than he
had been accustomed to doing in the past. Dietrichstein no longer
dictated his letters, confining himself, so he explained, to "offering his
criticism once the terrible chore—for that is what it is for him every
time—is over." However, the master's influence can still be distinguished
in these letters, which may strike us today as commonplace but which
certainly do not deserve the harsh judgment Dietrichstein made on one
of them in 1824: "The Prince wrote his letter last night alone and un-
aided; this is obvious. The trouble is that he thinks it is well planned
and well written. His laziness and obstinacy are as calamitous as ever.
I have altered nothing, to show the truth of what I am saying, but I
feel ashamed of it, even though Collin and I have never spared ourselves in his service. If only he would write as he talks, but as soon as
he picks up his pen his repugnance shows itself. . . ."

The missive in question undoubtedly lacks the freshness and spon-
taneity of the amusing letters to Collin, but then Dietrichstein inhibited
his pupil and the boy did not dare to display his skill before him. And

the tutor for his part took this timidity for "self-consciousness" which prevented the Prince from "showing all he knows."

Collin's death, which occurred on November 23, 1824, caused the Duke considerable distress, for he was the only person of whom the boy was genuinely fond.

> Dear Mamma [he wrote to Marie Louise], I received the day before yesterday from Count Alfred Neipperg, who greatly resembles his father, your letter of November 7; it acted as a soothing balm on me in my grief at M. de Collin's death. The more I think of the deceased, the greater and more grievous the loss I have sustained appears to me. Collin was certainly one of the men I most loved and respected, and it will be difficult to replace him. I have reason to believe that he is now happy in Heaven, and it is therefore I for whom I feel sorry rather than he. Yes, dear Mamma, I am deeply affected by his death, for I have lost more than I can say in that excellent man. How perfect he was in so many respects! How dearly he loved me, and how grateful I must be to him for the little I know! And how unexpectedly all this happened! I was far from imagining that anything of the sort might occur. And you too, dear Mamma, have lost in him a man who was full of loyalty and respect for you. My greatest consolation lies in the conviction that you will be as generous to his widow and his orphans as to those whom you succor daily in their distress. . . .

However, Reichstadt rapidly recovered from his grief—too rapidly, indeed, for Dietrichstein's liking. "His heart is cold," complained the tutor, "and that is a calamity." The fact was that the Court just then was a whirl of gaiety, and the boy, as Countess Lazansky observed, was too fully occupied to remain inconsolable. For November, 1824, witnessed the marriage of the Emperor's son Francis to his wife's half-sister, Princess Sophia of Bavaria, the future mother of the Emperors Francis Joseph and Maximilian. During the wedding festivities Reichstadt enjoyed what the Empress described to her stepdaughter as "a prodigious success." This caused some concern to the Marquis de Caraman, Charles X's ambassador in Vienna, who reported that Napoleon's son "amuses the entire Court with his lively wit, which offers a singular contrast to the habitual gravity of the imperial family." According to the French diplomat, no one could resist "the charm of his manners."

Fortunately Europe's prisoner was well guarded. M. de Caraman had ascertained that "all the officials in the Duke of Reichstadt's service have been placed in their present positions by the police and are directly responsible to that part of the administration." The ambassador even assured his Court that the Minister of Police, one Sedlinsky, had the former King of Rome watched and protected "with religious conscientiousness." Yet he was justified in wondering what would happen when the charming and highly intelligent young man "comes to know all that has happened and the part which he was expected to play in the future." "It is difficult to foresee," he went on, "what effect the development of such novel ideas will have on a lively mind which personal interest may excite even further and which an already too exalted situation will have prepared to receive germs of ambition which it will be only too easy to bring to fruition. . . . I fear there will come a time when the position of this young man will become extremely embarrassing." All the more "embarrassing" for the Bourbons in that the sentimental conspiracy of seditious neckerchiefs, prints, comfit-boxes and snuffboxes was gaining strength in Paris. One police officer complained in his report that selling portraits of Reichstadt "depicted on horseback in a hussar's uniform, and putting at the bottom of the print an N surmounted by a crown and surrounded by a halo, is going too far, since the Duke of Reichstadt himself has renounced the name of Napoleon and recalling this name by applying it to his son is an improper procedure."

It was true that as far back as the end of 1814 the boy had been obliged to abandon that terrible four-syllable name which set kings trembling on their thrones. Europe's little prisoner had not been consulted on the subject, and there was a time when "Franz, Herzog von Reichstadt" would also perhaps have found it "improper" not to be called after his grandfather any more. In 1821, in his letters to the Emperor, he signed himself *ein so kleiner unbedeutender Mensch*. But in 1824, when he was nearly thirteen, Reichstadt no longer considered himself *such an insignificant little man*. His personality was hardening.

On December 21, 1824, Reichstadt thanked his mother for "approving Count D.'s choice of M. von Obenaus as my new preceptor." Baron Joseph von Obenaus, who was Collin's successor, was a man of taste and culture. From the moment he took up his duties, Reichstadt confided in him, as the new tutor's diary shows. The boy no longer talked about France and his father, but about his future as "a half-baked duke":

> January 18: During our midday walk, conversation with the Prince about his position with regard to the imperial family and the rest of the world from the political point of view.

And just before his fourteenth birthday:

> February 26: Conversation about his destiny.

Was Reichstadt's confidence well placed? Prokesch, who often had occasion to meet Obenaus, describes him to us as an unpleasant, bad-tempered individual. His face always wore a shifty expression, and he thought that his pupil had a character similar to his own. He considered the boy to be sly and cunning, and treated him rather harshly. Like Dietrichstein, he was always on his guard with Francis, and in the evening he would solemnly enter his observations into his diary:

> January 13. The Prince has been wetting his bed since the departure of the Bavarian Court and trying to conceal it with his blankets. As a punishment, he was not allowed to dine with Their Majesties. . . . Impatience and deliberate clumsiness while dressing.

> January 16: During the night of the 15th-16th, the bed was not wet, as a result of my exhortations. . . .

> January 26-27: Serious reprimand on account of his habit of bed-wetting and lies. Tears showed that the Prince was sorry. All day, quiet, conciliatory, full of good will.

> January 28–February 2: Bed not wet, but then I have been waking the Prince every night at two o'clock and five o'clock; he sleeps so soundly that he does not hear the alarm clock next to his bed. Disobedience while dressing, buttoning his shirt collar, putting his jacket on, etc., for which he was severely reprimanded. February 1 was uneventful. On January 30 the Prince refused to put on his new hat for fear of damaging it in his carriage, and as a result he caught cold. In the evening he put on an old hat to go to the theater.

> February 8: No desire to work because it was H.M. the Empress's birthday.

Baffled by their pupil's rebellious attitude, Obenaus and Foresti would often turn for help to Dietrichstein, who on one occasion replied: "We must tame the insolent boy, otherwise we are done for."

His principal recourse was still to complain to Marie Louise. Thus on January 15, 1825, a fortnight after Baron von Obenaus's arrival, he wrote to the ex-Empress: "He only tries to shine in society in order to appear emancipated, and as soon as opportunities to satisfy his vanity cease to present themselves he relapses into his customary apathy and naughtiness. Nothing interests him then except his personal appearance, about which he is insufferably vain. . . ."

"To appear emancipated." That was to be his ambition in the years to come.

"You cannot imagine, dear Mamma," he explained on February 27, 1825, "how happy I am that I shall soon have finished with my childhood and be able to feel that I am a young man. The idea excites me so much that I should like to anticipate Nature in order to attain that happy moment, on the eve of which I once again resolve to rid myself of all my bad habits and childish inclinations. . . ."

Every "well-bred" young Viennese was expected to speak impeccable French, but despite all the efforts of his masters—Podevin and Baron Barthélemy de Saint-Hilaire—Francis showed an evident reluctance to learn his mother tongue all over again. Since November, 1819, he had never written to his mother in anything but German. On his fourteenth birthday—March 20, 1825—and again at the beginning of June, Dietrichstein made him write to her in French, but the result was so pitiable that for another two years Reichstadt would be allowed to continue his correspondence in German.

The tutor's despotism was severely criticized by the entire Court. This can be seen from certain letters written by Mme. Lazansky—even though she was a friend of Dietrichstein's—or by the new Archduchess Sophia, who, in 1826, expressed a desire to take her nephew to the theater, but "without his tutor." The King of Bavaria's daughter was already bored with her incurably vulgar husband, and soon—to use the Viennese expression—it was Sophia who "wore the suspenders." But there is no documentary support for Octave Aubry's belief that the young Archduchess bestowed her favors on the Eaglet, and certain letters which will be quoted later would appear to prove the contrary. Whatever the truth may be, in this spring of 1825, a few months after her wedding, she enjoyed laughing and joking with her nephew, who was only six years younger than she was, perhaps a little disturbed, even though she did not realize it, by this boy who was already eager to play the young man. He had "grown prodigiously," his voice was beginning to break, and he had taken to addressing such "extravagant" compliments to the young bride that Sophia had to call him to order: "You know that I do not like them at all, and I prefer you to write very simply to me." She showed great affection for her nephew, closing this particular letter with the words: "Adieu, my dear Francis. I kiss you with all my heart. Adieu. She who loves you deeply." There was a brief postscript: "My regards to your wife."

This was a reference to Dietrichstein. They made fun of the tutor in this harmless way, possibly because, faced with Francis's ardent declarations and Sophia's obvious affection for her nephew, Dietrichstein had so to speak assumed the role of the watchful wife. He must have known what they called him, because one can scarcely imagine Reichstadt conducting a clandestine correspondence at this time. The Archduchess was then in Italy, where—at Mantua—she had made the acquaintance of her sister-in-law Marie Louise.

Mme. Neipperg was to disappoint her son yet again this year. A fifth pregnancy—ending once more in a miscarriage—prevented her from going to Vienna, where her presence might have helped to settle the state of conflict which now existed between master and pupil. Commenting on a letter to the ex-Empress which had had to be rewritten six times, Dietrichstein complained: "Nothing can compare with my anguish at seeing, day after day, how mistaken I was in my expectations, and I tremble to think of the consequences, as sad as they are alarming. . . . Indolence, falsehood, obstinacy and the ideas of freedom which he has conceived are the source of all his vices."

In spite of the somewhat extravagant nature of these comments on the failings of a boy of fourteen, Dietrichstein was genuinely upset. His disillusionment was sincere, his distress immense.

In the tutor's opinion all his pupil's "charm" was just "varnish." In private, "his rebellious character and his policy of perpetual contradiction paralyze every effort." But whose fault was this but Dietrichstein's? Obenaus—and surely he was right—considered that bringing the boy up without a companion had been a grave error. Moreover—again in the Baron's opinion—Francis's "boundless" confidence in himself and his immense pride did him considerable harm. He imagined that he could do anything, but he gave up at the first difficulty he encountered.

On the other hand, his letters, in spite of what Dietrichstein said, showed a marked improvement. When the Empress Caroline was crowned Queen of Hungary, Francis went to Bratislava for the ceremony. At Malmaison one can still read the boy's description of the dress worn by *liebe Mamma's* successor, and his careful assessment of the feelings of those present and the happiness of the Emperor's fourth wife. "However," he adds, "the pleasure she derived from the ceremony and the affection everyone showed for her were spoiled by a violent headache produced by the weight of her heavy crown and the eight hours of fatigue she had to undergo. As she said herself, she would be glad if the acquisition of a crown brought with it no greater hardship. My grandfather, wearing St. Stephen's cloak and crown, suffered a great deal too, but he soon got over it. The streets echoed with the sound of cheering, and the skies themselves seemed to wish to favor such a happy day with their brightest sunshine. I shall abstain from any further details; the gazettes which Count D. is sending you will give you more than I ever could. But I would add that I am still dazed by it all, and that the memory of this day will never leave me."

Dietrichstein was not always there. He had—especially at this time when music reigned supreme in Vienna—other occupations which often took him far away from his pupil. Reichstadt would then spend all day with Obenaus and Foresti, with whom he felt much more at ease. Dietrichstein, as he admitted to his mother, made him tremble, and the boy only became himself again when he was left with his two deputy tutors. He was capable of great affection and felt happy when he could spread joy around him. But the presence of Count Maurice, standing over him, watching his every gesture, criticizing his words and checking his actions, froze his heart.

I recognize only too well [he wrote to his mother on December 20, 1825] the justice of your discreet allusion to the labored style of my letters. All I can say in excuse is that when I write to you I am no longer master of my feelings, and hence the expression which I give to them is not as well ordered as I would wish it to be. I none the less wish to learn how to express my thoughts and feelings, and it would help me greatly if you, dear Mamma, for your part, would from time to time, through your own letters,

offer me models and incentives in the epistolary art. You hope,
next year, to find me changed for the better. . . . How happy I
shall be if you are pleased with me!

It is difficult to understand why Dietrichstein should have "blushed"
over this letter and asserted that it showed his pupil's "negligence" and
"lack of sensibility." To cite another example, here is a letter written
by the Eaglet on April 18, 1826, on the occasion of the Emperor's
recovery from a serious illness. The Duke of Reichstadt's grandfather
had come close to dying during the night of March 13-14. For several
days the people of Vienna, who worshiped their ruler, had waited in
silence around the ancient palace. Then, little by little, the news spread
across the city: the Emperor's life was safe and he would soon be con-
valescent. And on April 6, fully recovered, he was able to go out for
the first time.

The streets [wrote Francis] were packed with cheering crowds
giving voice to their feelings; chairs, café benches and windows
were filled with people whose happiness consisted in seeing the
Emperor, even if it was only for a moment; the crowds ran beside
the carriage, following it as far as the pools in the Prater and back
again. All these demonstrations of affection and respect, the warm
sympathy which the people displayed during his illness and then
the delirious joy they showed on his recovery, seem to have acted
as a tonic on the Emperor. . . . The day my grandfather went out
the capital was illuminated; we went to see it with my grandmother, first of all driving haphazardly all over the city, then
going out through the Stubentor, then coming back through the
Burgtor. I thought of you a great deal, especially when the street
arabs, using the name "Marie Louise," gave me an ovation. A
few days later the *Te Deum* was given by the garrison, which
was lined up along the Neues Tor with the orchestra's tent on the
gate. Unfortunately a heavy downpour spoiled this magnificent
occasion. . . . The whole thing appealed to me tremendously; tears
came to my eyes as I looked at all those brave fellows thanking
Heaven, like myself, for their father's recovery, and as I thought
that, through my own fault, I would not be one of them for a
long time to come. Count D. was only a year older than I am
when he became an officer! If the Count could do that, why
should not I do it too?

Reichstadt regretted his laziness and with touching willingness promised his mother yet again to do "the maximum" to make up for lost time. "The Emperor keeps asking me when you are coming, and I always say the end of June; show that I am a liar by setting off at the beginning of May! But above all, dear Mamma, please tell me exactly when you expect to arrive here, so that I can inform the Emperor; perhaps the impatience with which he awaits your arrival will encourage you to put forward the date of your departure, but without cutting short your stay in consequence."

This time Marie Louise yielded to her son's wishes and those of a father who was growing impatient of seeing *sein geliebtes Kind* so rarely. She gave the date of her arrival as the 30th. Reichstadt grew positively feverish with excitement.

"My heart is even more agitated than usual," he told Dietrichstein.

On the 28th, two days before his mother was due, he sent a courier to meet her with this message: "You cannot imagine how much I am looking forward to the day after tomorrow; my most heartfelt desire is going to be fulfilled, and I have become so accustomed, these last three years, to seeing your arrival postponed that, if I did not know that you were on your way, I should still have my doubts. You will find me much bigger. . . ."

It was indeed a young man who greeted Marie Louise on her arrival. He was only fifteen, but he was as tall as his mother. The holidays began at Persenbeug.

The castle there was illuminated for Marie Louise's birthday. Reichstadt, accompanied by his uncle the Archduke Louis, was admiring the sight from his carriage when a smartly dressed man succeeded in drawing near. A packet fell at the Archduke's feet, and he picked it up; Reichstadt had not noticed anything. The packet contained a tricolor cockade enclosed in a piece of paper bearing these words: "Sire, thirty million of your subjects await your return. Come back to France. I bring Your Majesty the morning star." The Archduke promptly took the "infernal machine" to the Emperor, who gave orders to search the neighborhood and arrest the conspirator. He was not to be found, having set off immediately for the frontier, but his identity was discovered: he was a Parisian housepainter called Joseph Romain Doudeuil. The French authorities having been informed, he was arrested as soon as he reached home and imprisoned in the fortress of Ham.

If Reichstadt had been told about the incident, he would have been utterly dumfounded. His thoughts at this time were very far from France, and his only ambition was to become an officer in the Austrian army as soon as possible. As it happened, this same month Marie Louise had asked the Emperor to give the young man a rank in the army, as was the custom with archdukes. Dietrichstein had raised his voice in protest. The "rebellious" prince did not deserve such a signal honor!

There was no longer any attempt to keep Francis in ignorance of the details of his father's life—after all, how could Napoleon be expunged from world history? However, Reichstadt learned his history from books written by Austrians whom the French had beaten several times, whose land they had occupied, and who could not be impartial—with the result that he saw contemporary events through Austrian eyes. In his written exercises he called the French *the enemy*. . . . It seems that it was Foresti who, in this same year of 1826, conceived the idea of making him write an essay on Schwarzenberg. "At first sight," writes the Baron de Bourgoing, "it may appear cruel of them to have made Reichstadt write a study of the man who had beaten his father. But if they did this, it was not in order to belittle Napoleon in his son's eyes but to enable the Duke to understand the Emperor's defeat." Which amounts to the same thing. If they did not want to belittle Napoleon, why did they allow his son, describing Schwarzenberg's noble attitude when the Austrian Embassy in Paris was burned down at the time of Marie Louise's wedding, to write these words: "On this occasion the Prince's grandeur of soul filled the Emperor with admiration and touched *his inaccessible heart*"? And why did they let him spell his father's name *Buonaparte*?

But the Austrian Duke within him would soon begin to disappear, giving place to the French Prince.

An important change occurred, in fact, during the autumn of 1826, and it appears that Marie Louise had something to do with it. Writing to his mother on October 14, 1826, a few days after a new and painful parting, Reichstadt declared: "I am determined to keep my promises and I wish to prove myself a man under all circumstances. During your stay in Vienna, other young men eclipsed me and you yourself had to call me to my senses so often that I have made a firm resolution to draw level with everyone else, to attain all the skill I see in others, if possible to surpass them, but above all to become steady and upright as you want me to be." He repeated that his aim was to become an officer, but admitted that "as I possess as yet few of these qualities, it would have been disagreeable for me to be given a commission; being unworthy of it, I should have lagged behind my comrades—something I should have found most painful."

Dietrichstein took some time to discover that his pupil had changed, and his complaints continued. One wonders how he could criticize—as he did on January 16, 1827—this letter, written by Francis three months before his sixteenth birthday:

> There is talk of a ball which the Crown Prince is to give on Thursday and which will be my first this year, unless the news of the Duke of York's death, which is expected any day now, plunges the Court into another period of mourning which would probably not finish as quickly as that for the Duchess of Nassau; and even if it lasted only a fortnight, there are so many old princes and kings that one can never be certain one day, during this mortality season, that one will be able to dance the next. For my part, the fate of the Carnival is a matter of indifference to me, since I do not like dancing and am really quite pleased when mourning puts a stop to the balls at Court, which are unpleasantly hot on account of the number of people invited. These balls spoil my sleep and always make the next day most disagreeable, preventing me from devoting myself to my studies with the ardor I have applied to them for a couple of months and which has won your approval.

He did not like dancing any more and he was working with "ardor"! Dietrichstein himself was impressed. At the beginning of February, Francis put up a brilliant performance in an examination he sat, winning high praise from Colonel Schindler, an officer in the engineers who was one of his examiners. But then Reichstadt went down with a cold. At first he paid no attention to it and even went to several balls which, he admitted, "have made my cold worse." Dr. Goelis, who usually attended the Prince, had just died, and a Dr. Staudenheim was called in. "He ordered me to stay in my room, gave me some medicine, and made me spend the last days of the Carnival in the saddest way possible, shut in between four walls."

At the beginning of March he was able to resume his studies. "However," wrote Dietrichstein, "we shall have to limit the work he does for some time, partly because he is still growing and partly on account of his chest, which is not as strong or as broad as it might be, because out of laziness he always stands with his shoulders hunched instead of throwing them back."

Announcing his convalescence to his mother, the Duke wrote on March 3, 1827:

> On Saturday I sat my last examination in psychology and hasten to give you this news and talk at greater length with you, having more spare time now than in the last few weeks, which have been taken up with the revision which usually precedes an examination of this sort. I am glad to have done with psychology, which gave me a great deal of trouble as an introduction to philosophy, a subject whose very name used to make me tremble and which, together with my classical studies, filled all my morning hours during the summer and autumn. I spent all last year translating Julius Caesar's commentaries on the Gauls, and this enabled me to finish a complete work, which is always preferable to reading scattered extracts, not only for the beauties of the style but also for the historical content; I was examined in this subject too on Saturday, but rather briefly. This week I made a start on logic, which strikes me as more abstract but also easier than psychology. . . .

At Malmaison one can still see his exercise books, which were presented to the French nation by Obenaus's descendants. Francis was now a model pupil who appeared to be passionately interested in his work. He had translated Tacitus's description of Germany, "so beautiful in its clarity and the elegance of its style," and had also studied the history of the Holy Roman Empire down to the Hohenstaufens.

"Your education must be as complete as possible," Dietrichstein told him, "for you are destined to play a leading role in Austrian affairs and to attract everyone's attention."

He declaimed long tirades from Corneille, whom he preferred to Racine, read Chateaubriand's *Journey from Paris to Jerusalem,* liked La Bruyère, and admired Schiller, learning by heart the speech from *Don Carlos* ending with the words: "I do not know what it is like to have a father . . . and I am the son of a king!"

It had now become impossible to deny him access to the imperial library, and he soon immersed himself in the eight volumes of the *Memoirs of St. Helena,* which Las Cases had published in 1823, Montholon's *Memoirs,* which had also appeared in 1823, *Napoleon in Exile,* published in 1822, and Antommarchi's *Memoirs,* which the doctor had brought out in 1825 and which contained the text of the Emperor's will. He also read the memoirs of Bourrienne and Rovigo, translating and copying out many passages, which are likewise preserved at Malmaison. One can imagine his feelings as he copied out this observation which his father made one day to his secretary, long before the King of Rome was born:

"The hereditary principle is an absurdity, irreconcilable with the sovereignty of the people and impossible in France. . . ."

Little by little the amazing past from which he had sprung opened up before his eyes. He became acquainted with the words his father had addressed to him from his distant rock before dying. Napoleon became for him "the greatest man of all time," and he waxed indignant over such attacks on his father's memory as that made by Baron Hormayr. Soon he was drunk with glory. Rostand, with all the prescience of a poet, guessed this when he came to write *L'Aiglon,* but the change in Reichstadt did not take place in 1830, as has hitherto been thought. Already, on November 21, 1826, in a letter to Parma, he wrote to Marie Louise about Napoleon in terms which, said Dietrichstein, "will surprise Your Majesty." No doubt Reichstadt's ambitions were still centered on the "white uniform" of an Austrian officer, but the tutor was none the less rather concerned about the ex-Empress's possible reactions on reading these lines written by a son whom she wanted to turn into "a German prince," a son who had received at birth a name which, she said, was "an unfortunate one":

> I am indeed convinced of the need for study and, putting as I do the prospect of the white uniform above everything else, I know that I can only attain it by making good progress. I am therefore trying, as best I can, to make up for lost time, in order to offer you, dear Mamma, on your return, the sight of a morally superior and nobler being and thus show you the foundations of a character which will remind you of my father's; for a soldier on the threshold of his career, can there be a finer and more admirable model of constancy, endurance, manly gravity, valiance and courage?

He had already come a long way—in only a few months—from the *Buonaparte with the inaccessible heart.*

In Paris, Napoleon's companions got ready to fulfill their obligations as the Emperor's executors, since Napoleon's son was now sixteen years old. The faithful little group entrusted with the relics from St. Helena wanted to set off for Vienna and applied to the Austrian ambassador Apponyi, who passed on their request to his government. Metternich replied that Marchand, Bertrand, Montholon "and persons in the service of the ex-Emperor" were at liberty to leave "the objects entrusted to their care" at the Austrian embassy in Paris, but "it is not His Majesty's intention to authorize the coming here of M. Marchand or any other executors."

Did the latter fear that the rags and tatters of a glorious past "entrusted to their care" would never reach the Emperor's son—in spite of the promise of a receipt signed by "Msgr. the Duke of Reichstadt"? *
Whatever the truth of the matter, they found it impossible to obey the last instructions of Prometheus bound:

"To deliver them to my son when he is sixteen."

One cannot but admire the astonishing prescience of the father who had guessed that at sixteen his son would be ready to come into his glorious inheritance.

* On the Eaglet's death, they delivered the relics to Madame Mère, who left them to her children; they now belong to Prince Napoleon.

13

❦

"Not a Prisoner, But . . ."

FRANCIS WAS GROWING extremely fast, so fast that he was now as tall as Dietrichstein. His face had perhaps lost its childish beauty, and he was excessively thin, but his charm of manner and bearing drew every eye and won the hearts of the girls of Vienna. He dressed with careful distinction, hoping to become the arbiter of taste. He had started a collection of walking sticks of which he was not a little proud. "He can converse with anybody," noted the Archduke Louis, "adapting himself to his interlocutor"—an indispensable quality in princes. Marie Louise would be able to see for herself how much he had developed, for in June, 1827, she announced that she would soon be arriving in Vienna. But on July 27 a letter arrived at Schönbrunn from Parma cancelling the journey for reasons of health. Once again, Francis's summer holidays were divided between one country residence and another, between the "monotonous" walks of Schönbrunn—the description is Reichstadt's—and the colorful gardens of Laxenburg. The whole imperial family were gathered together, but the only person who counted for Reichstadt was Sophia, to whom he was still "paying court."

His health left much to be desired. One evening at Baden, at the imperial table, he had a fit of dizziness which was put down to puberty. But Staudenheim, who was promptly called in, diagnosed "a tendency to scrofula and to phthisis of the trachea."

However, Francis refused to take the precautions recommended by the Faculty. Once at Laxenburg, when Dietrichstein was away, he spent part of the night driving at breakneck speed with his Uncle Francis in an open carriage. The Emperor had expressed his displeasure to the tutor, who defended himself in a letter to Parma by attributing the escapade to the "obstinacy" of a pupil who refused to obey his masters.

He had begun coughing a great deal—a "dry" cough—and was always falling a victim to colds and chills. His doctors accordingly prescribed a remedy very much in vogue at the time: cold baths. He was taught the rudiments of swimming, and threw himself into the water for the first time in the Prater with amazing intrepidity, watched by a crowd of people. He later confessed that he thought he was going to drown, but that "he would have rather died than shown any signs of fear in the presence of so many spectators."

The same courage can also be seen in the *Abhärtungs-System*, a "toughening method" which he adopted principally in view of his military career, on which he hoped to embark the following year. Strangely enough, hydrotherapy appeared to have made him much better. He was working hard, especially on his French, in order to have done with his program of studies as soon as possible. In this he was following the advice of Neipperg, to whom he wrote a letter of thanks on September 22, 1827, incidentally praising Napoleon to the man who had taken his father's place in Marie Louise's heart:

I thank you most sincerely, General, for your advice concerning the French language. You have not sown it on barren or ungrateful ground. I have every imaginable reason for wishing to perfect my knowledge and master the difficulties of a tongue which has now become for me the most essential of my studies, because it is that which my father used to give his orders in all the battles in which he won glory for his name, because it is that in which he had left us his instructive observations in his incomparable memoirs on the art of war, and because it was his wish, expressed up to the very end of his life, that I should not remain in ignorance of the country in which I was born; hence I have made the firm resolution, which I have already begun putting in practice, to apply myself with all possible assiduity to this branch of study. Next week I hope to sit my examinations in metaphysics, Latin, statistics and history—in which I have got as far as Charles the Fifth . . .

He signed the letter: "Your most obedient and affectionate Franz von Reichstadt," assuring the General of his "deep affection."

Two months later—on November 17—he gave further details, but this time to his mother: "I have acquired a physics master, and find this subject most interesting. It is generally necessary, and as I wish to obtain a thorough knowledge of every branch of the army, a course of physics and chemistry—which I hope to finish within seven months—will be extremely useful to me with regard to the artillery and the engineers, if taken in conjunction with mathematics. I am in good health; I am not coughing any more, but my colds in the head come back now and then. The medicine I am taking, and the precautions to which I must submit, and which in spite of myself I recognize to be prudent and wise, will soon make me feel stronger. . . ."

When the winter came, Dr. Staudenheim once again insisted that he should go to no balls. His shooting expeditions would also be less frequent than the year before. Reichstadt used his extra leisure to prepare a surprise for his mother, a surprise which must have caused Marie Louise considerable astonishment and perhaps some annoyance. "I crave your indulgence, dear Mamma," he wrote on December 22, "for a little drawing which I am sending off to you on Tuesday in a packing case. It depicts my father's warhorse. The accessories and the greater part of the subject itself are my own work, and it was only at my request that my master touched up the clouds, which were darkening the picture too much and spoiling the effect."

In spite of a quieter life and all the precautions Staudenheim had insisted on, colds, throat ailments and chills reappeared, alternating with painful toothaches which, in February, necessitated even more painful extractions. That same month, Francis's grandfather noticed that he was looking out of sorts and told Marie Louise, attributing his grandson's ill health to the fact he was outgrowing his strength.

Shortly before his seventeenth birthday, the Duke had to submit to an examination in the Emperor's presence. "I find that he has made real progress in certain essential subjects," noted the Empress. In June, Dietrichstein drew a pen portrait of the young man for Marie Louise. He noted with satisfaction that he had stopped telling lies, but expressed regret at Reichstadt's "maliciousness," which led him to poke fun at the failings or stupidity of others "in order to show himself in a more favorable light." True, he indulged at times in "insignificant arguments in a bombastic style" which most people—but not, of course,

Dietrichstein—would forgive in a seventeen-year-old. True, he occasionally made a rather vulgar joke in which the influence of the Archduke Francis could be discerned. But he none the less remained by far the most intelligent of all the princes in the Hofburg.

This year, Marie Louise found it impossible to postpone her visit to Vienna. Indeed, the Emperor Francis told his grandson that "he would send a firing squad" to his mother if she refused to leave Parma. When, at Mölk, on July 1, 1828, she saw her son coming toward her, she could not conceal her astonishment. The young Prince had become "an absolute giant," about six feet tall. Marie Louise decided that it was impossible for an archduke, even a "half-baked" one, to remain a sergeant, and spoke to her father. On August 17, after the Emperor's game of billiards, Reichstadt was about to retire when his grandfather asked him: "There's something you have been wanting for a long time, isn't there?"

"I, Sire?" replied an embarrassed Francis.

"Yes, you. As a mark of my satisfaction and of the services I expect from you, I appoint you a captain in my regiment of Tyrolean cavalry."

"Drunk with joy and scarcely able to stammer out a reply," the young man told Foresti, "I left the Emperor's presence. In the great drawing room the Empress was waiting for me, together with the archduchesses and all those gentlemen; they all offered me their congratulations. Then I went to find my mother, to whom I really owe my appointment." He also owed it to Dietrichstein, who, this time, while regretting the commonplace fate in store for the "poor boy," had decided that his pupil could not decently attend the forthcoming army maneuvers at Münchendorf in mufti or in the uniform of a noncommissioned officer.

His mother gave him the curved saber which General Bonaparte had used in Egypt—one of the few souvenirs of the Napoleonic epic which Mme. Neipperg had kept. The young officer was speechless with gratitude, and would often wear the saber during his periods of active service.

The three stars which his grandfather had given him marked the beginning of his emancipation. But talk of this emancipation evoked only a scornful shrug of the shoulders from Dietrichstein. "I have sworn that it would not take place until he had learned how to write," he declared in November, 1828. Reichstadt himself knew that he was not ready yet to undertake the formidable task which his tutor had outlined to him—"reconciling the world with his father by glorious acts." This did not, of course, imply the conquest of Europe: the acts in question were to be performed "within the limits of Austrian law" and "for the good of Austria." As the tutor constantly pointed out, people still regarded his pupil as "an ordinary youth," forgetting his origins and all the other factors which made him "an absolutely exceptional case." "The memory of the grandeur he has lost," remarked Dietrichstein, "his father's glory, the latter's fate and the loyalty of his supporters, all occupy his mind greatly and will naturally occupy it more as time goes by. Many things which he hears about, as well as the military events of that period, arouse emotions in him with which one cannot but sympathize, while treating them calmly and frankly."

What is more, Francis's sense of values was as yet somewhat deficient, so that in that same year of 1828 we find him writing Neipperg letters of appalling banality, in which he claims to discover "a certain analogy" between the fates of Napoleon and General Mack, since both, so he declares, were "honored in their abasement" because they had "won respect in their glory."

It was not without some anxiety that Dietrichstein looked forward to the time when Obenaus would make a start on the history of the French Revolution. He expected "a hard fight" between master and pupil, but felt sure that Obenaus would "be able to repress the Prince's ardor with the necessary sang-froid." Often remarks made in the imperial drawing room would set Francis's imagination on fire. He could already see himself called upon to play a part in European affairs—on the French throne or elsewhere—and he confided his hopes to his tutor. As he listened to his pupil, Dietrichstein maintained a pretense of indifference . . . but he was well aware that the Austrian army was convinced that Reichstadt had "inherited his father's genius." At the mere mention of his name, "officers and men thrilled with enthusiasm." But what was most important was to protect the Duke from the plots and intrigues of those who, in Paris, looked hopefully to Napoleon II —to protect him, in fact, from "the loyalty of his supporters."

It was a poet—the Bonapartist Barthélemy—who was to reveal the Emperor's son to the French people. He had arrived in Vienna on January 1, 1829, in the hope of presenting the Duke of Reichstadt with his poem "Napoleon in Egypt," which he had already given to the other members of the Bonaparte family. After being questioned by the police, the writer was given permission to spend a month in the Austrian capital. He then applied to Count Czernin, the venerable Grand Master of the Court, who received him "kindly" and sent him on to Count Dietrichstein.

On January 3 the tutor gave Barthélemy a cordial welcome when he arrived with two copies of his poem under his arm. After presenting Dietrichstein with one of the volumes, suitably dedicated, the poet—if we are to believe his account of the interview—decided to make "a decisive overture" and held out the second copy to the tutor.

"Monsieur le Comte," he said, "I have come to Vienna with the sole object of presenting this book to the Duke of Reichstadt; no one can help me in this purpose better than his Grand Master; I hope you will be so kind as to grant my request."

According to Barthélemy, Dietrichstein's face "took on an expression, I will not say of annoyance, but of uneasiness and constraint." This is not at all surprising to us today. Considering the instructions which we know Dietrichstein had been given, he could scarcely have been expected to bring his pupil into contact with an ardent Bonapartist whose poems were fired with a spirit which he was bound to consider dangerous.

"You have really come to Vienna to see the Prince?" he asked after a short silence. "But who asked you to undertake this mission? What you ask is quite impossible."

"I have come to Austria of my own accord," replied the poet. "In France it is generally imagined that it is not difficult to be introduced to the Duke of Reichstadt. I am not asking to speak to the Prince without witnesses, but in front of you, in front of ten people if need be— and if a single word escapes me which might alarm the most suspicious of politicians, I am ready to finish my days in an Austrian prison."

Dietrichstein, understandably embarrassed, said that he was afraid that the Prince could not grant an audience to a foreign visitor and that this was a general rule, adding as a final excuse that they had to be constantly on their guard against a possible attempt at assassination.

Barthélemy remained unconvinced.

"Perhaps," he said, coming back to the subject, "you are afraid that too free a conversation with strangers might reveal certain secrets to him or inspire him with the desire to make certain dangerous experiments; but with all your power you surely cannot prevent someone from openly or secretly handing him a letter, a petition or a note, when he is out walking, or at the theater, or somewhere else?"

"Listen, Monsieur," replied Dietrichstein, "you must understand this —that the Prince hears, sees and reads only what we want him to hear, see and read."

A chill came over Barthélemy and he answered:

"From what you say, Monsieur le Comte, it appears that Napoleon's son is very far from being as free as we in France imagine him to be?"

Dietrichstein then made the reply which Rostand was later to make famous in his *L'Aiglon:*

"The Prince is not a prisoner, *but* . . . he is in a very special position."

And the first conversation came to an end.

A fortnight later, Barthélemy, seeing the end of his permitted period of residence approaching, returned to the attack.

"I really don't understand you," said Dietrichstein, obviously lying. "You attribute too much importance to seeing the Prince. Try and be content with my assurance that he is happy and entirely lacking in ambition; his career has been worked out for him; he will never go to France and the idea of doing so will not even occur to him."

The Baron de Bourgoing, in his anxiety to defend the Court of Vienna, declares that all this is a complete invention. However, Dietrichstein's attitude as described by Barthélemy fits in very well with what we know about the network of precautions with which Austria's ward was surrounded. There was every reason for these precautions: in this same month of January, 1829, we find Apponyi, the Austrian ambassador in Paris, writing to Metternich that "Msgr. the Duke of Reichstadt" was an "object of interest and fear for the various parties in France." And we know from a letter from Metternich to Marie Louise that all Bonapartist emissaries without exception were shown to the door.

"I don't ask you to treat what I have told you as confidential," Dietrichstein had said to Barthélemy. "On the contrary, I beg you to make it public on your return to France."

Barthélemy obeyed. In Paris, the tutor's words had all the more of an inflammatory effect in that they were used as a preface to the poem "Le Fils de l'Homme," in which Barthélemy depicted Napoleon's son as an unhappy prisoner. "Le Fils de l'Homme—which in French signifies not

only "the Son of the Man" but also, and primarily, "the Son of Man"
—was a phrase which had never been applied to anyone but Christ and
which, applied to the Duke of Reichstadt, evoked the idea of a victim
crucified by Austria. After the martyrdom of the Eagle, chained to his
rock by England and dying as a result of the hardships inflicted on
him by his jailer, Barthélemy now engraved in French minds the picture of a sick and suffering Eaglet held prisoner by Austria. Describing the young man he had seen one evening at the Hoftheater, he
wrote that "in his pale face, life and death seemed to mingle." He was
exaggerating a little, but Reichstadt had in fact been suffering for two
years from fits of coughing and chronic colds and chills. People who
saw him every day thought he looked pale, and he regarded himself
as something of an invalid. On February 7, a week after Barthélemy
had left Vienna, he wrote to Parma: "I am taking care of myself in the
present cold weather, partly because I am forced to and partly out of
conviction. However, I am defying Staudenheim's wrath and dancing
French country dances which do not make me too hot."

This young Prince, already lymphatic and soon consumptive, was
not very different from the romantic vision evoked by Barthélemy, a
picture which would serve the Napoleonic legend just as well as the
image of "the terrifying meteor" coined by the same poet. For that was
what Barthélemy called his "Fils de l'Homme," when inviting him to
"repeat the history of an exiled father" and "enter like a king into his
city."

Charles X's government took this invitation badly, and on July 29,
1829, the author was taken to court. He conducted his own defense—in
verse—but in spite of a brilliant display of histrionic and poetic talent
he was sentenced to three months' imprisonment, while an indignant
crowd left the courtroom protesting against royal justice.

Dietrichstein was also fiercely criticized by the readers of "Le Fils
de l'Homme." On August 6 he proudly declared to Marie Louise: "The
honor of enjoying Your Majesty's confidence, and the glory which
awaits me if the Prince succeeds in life, are my great pride and enable
me to scorn the insults which the revolutionary party in France have
been heaping upon me for some time past. It is for the Prince to reply
to them and to defend me one day by his brilliant conduct."

Neipperg—or *il signore*, as Marie Louise and their children called
him—had suffered from heart trouble for many years and was now

dying of dropsy. Reichstadt had watched the progress of the disease with infinite concern and anxiously awaited the arrival of every courier from Parma. "You are to be envied, dear Mamma," he wrote to Marie Louise, "in that you can see him and look after him, while we are condemned to wait five days, from Thursday to Tuesday, before receiving old news about the state of his health."

Dietrichstein, who regarded Neipperg as his best friend, was even more anxious and hoped for the impossible. At Parma, Marie Louise, to whom the doctors had revealed the truth, stayed constantly at the sick man's bedside. "I feel as if I were dying little by little from this death," she told her father. "Day after day passes in grief and desolation."

The ex-Empress's morganatic husband died on February 22, 1829. "I shall never have a sincerer friend," wrote Francis on the 28th, declaring that he considered Neipperg a model of chivalry.

Neipperg had left behind a will which was to spark off a dramatic conflict between Reichstadt and his mother. The dead man declared himself to be the Duchess of Parma's husband and the father of the two Montenuovos whose existence Marie Louise had revealed to her father only the previous autumn. Although Marie Louise could not go into mourning, Metternich decided that it was impossible, "in view of certain considerations affecting the Empress," to conceal any longer the morganatic marriage the Archduchess had contracted. The Chancellor wrote asking her to accord him "the confidence she would place in her confessor." "I do not know," he went on, "the ages of the children or the exact date of Your Majesty's marriage." In reality Metternich suspected the truth and simply wanted to humiliate Marie Louise. He continued with a certain cruelty: "Napoleon died on May 5, 1821, Three months went by before the news reached Parma, so that August, 1821, constitutes the earliest possible date for a second marriage. Supposing, even though it would be in contradiction with the proprieties, that Your Majesty's second marriage took place in that same month of August, the first child could not be born before May, 1822, and would then be seven years old in May, 1829. I venture to submit these calculations to Your Majesty since it is most important for me to know whether they are accurate."

Poor Marie Louise had to own up. "It is time for me to confess," she replied on March 17, 1829, "that when the Emperor questioned me on this subject, I answered him in such a way as to lead him to suppose that the children were born after the Emperor Napoleon's death, whereas in fact the elder, who is called Albertine, was born on May 1, 1817, and the younger, who is called William, on August 8, 1819. As regards my marriage to the General, it was not consecrated until September, 1821."

The next day, March 18, she summoned up all her courage and wrote a letter to her father revealing the true state of affairs. "I cannot hide from you," he replied, "the profound sorrow which this situation causes me—a situation about which nothing can now be done but which should never have existed before God and man."

This intrusion in the Habsburg family weighed "like a burden" on his heart. But, he went on, "in the hearts of parents there is always more indulgence for their children's failings than children show of their parents' failings. Never forget that truism. In conclusion I must say that you have hurt me deeply. But I am your father, and my love for you absolves you of everything it can forgive you."

Marie Louise turned for comfort to Caroline Augusta, to whom she had apparently confided the truth on taking leave of her at the end of September, 1828. Her stepmother assured her that she was still the Emperor's "favorite child," and went on:

> Do not hesitate therefore to come here this summer. I know that the first few moments will be terribly painful for you, but you will be comforted by the certain knowledge that V. will not be long in showing you that he is as fond of you as ever. . . . He has not forgotten either the immense sacrifice you made in the interests of the State in 1810. He is as anxious as you are that your son should never find out the ages of the two children of whose existence he is still or was recently ignorant. Your father for his part will do all he can to this end, but you yourself must take care not to introduce them into society until you can do so without giving rise to embarrassing calculations, that is to say as many years later as you are subtracting from their actual ages. . . . Oh, that wretched will! If illness had not impaired the mind of the deceased, he would have seen how much embarrassment that will would cause you, and he would have spared you all this trouble. . . .

There remained, however, the most delicate and difficult problem of all: that of revealing to the Duke of Reichstadt that his mother had forgotten his father and had married again as soon as she had become

a widow. Informing him of the existence of the two children, Francis
I naturally took care to say nothing of their ages. "He did not ask me
any questions about the children," the Emperor told his daughter on
April 5; "if he does so, I shall talk about them without mentioning
their ages. Unfortunately this particular detail cannot remain hidden
from him for long, and in this respect there is of course risk that his
most sacred feelings toward you may be unfavorably affected."

Reichstadt, deeply wounded by his grandfather's disclosures, was
careful to conceal his thoughts. "He was profoundly affected," reported Dietrichstein, "but it will be some time before I can discover
what his feelings are. Yesterday he was much calmer and one thing
he said struck me forcibly: he thought that Your Majesty most be
suffering *doubly* in so far as you envisaged your sad loss from the
point of view of grateful friendship and also a more intimate relationship." At the very most he displayed a certain "displeasure," mentioned
the matter three or four times to Dietrichstein, then said no more about
it. He asked no questions about the dates of birth of the Montenuovo
children and affected an apparent indifference. His silence worried
Marie Louise.

"I am glad that the Emperor has spoken to my son," she wrote, "but
believe me, I am sure that this will have had anything but a good
effect. I have had many conversations with him which have convinced
me that he would never understand or forgive anyone who forgot his
father, and I cannot blame him and quite understand, for he knows
only the good side of his father's character and must never know any
other."

However, a letter arrived from Francis which must have reassured
her. On April 11 her "most obedient son" wrote to Marie Louise: "I
feel doubly sad when I think of your sorrow, which I share to the
full. The memory of the deceased, of his friendship for me and of his
distinguished qualities will always remain engraved in my heart and
will always keep him alive in my mind. I shall try to copy him and
perhaps I may succeed one day in reminding you of your most devoted
friend. . . ."

Such was his love for his mother that, filled with pity, he forgave her
her weakness, feeling reluctant to add to her grief. But he did not
know the worst: the adulterous birth of the two bastards brought into
the world during his father's lifetime.

Marie Louise still could not bring herself to face her son, and preferred to travel to Switzerland, where, at the Grand Saconnez near Geneva, she would go unnoticed. The Prefect of the Rhône noticed her, but dismissed her in a single brutal phrase: "I cannot imagine that any harmful agitation could result from the presence on the frontier of a person so utterly devoid of political importance or personal standing as the Duchess of Parma." What had become of the freshness which had so attracted Napoleon at Compiègne? Marie Louise now displayed a blotchy complexion and the thin, flaccid figure of a woman who has once been plump. She apparently looked a "badly preserved" fifty and dressed in a very slovenly manner. People poked fun at her, made jokes about her old-fashioned carriages, and practically laughed in her face.

She sent her son a whole parcel of Parisian cravats and walking sticks for his collection, in the hope of diverting his attention from the fact she was holidaying in Switzerland when she could so easily have come to Austria. Francis was none the less surprised, and wrote with gentle irony: "I hope that you may find in the air and waters of Switzerland all that you expect from them, although I cannot help thinking that the company of your father and so many other persons dear to you would have had a more advantageous effect on your health than the sight of the icy peaks of Mont Blanc."

The somewhat offhand tone of this letter gives a good idea of Francis's state of mind at this time. He continued to refrain from asking his grandfather and his tutor any questions, which greatly puzzled them both. But it was not from them that Reichstadt expected to get the truth which everyone was carefully concealing from him. He had changed his method of approach, and entered into his notebook an aphorism which revealed his intentions: "Nature has given us two ears and one mouth so that we can hear a great deal and say very little." It was not hard to "hear a great deal." There were too many contacts between Parmesans and Viennese for rumors not to reach the Austrian Court. Quite a few people now knew when the two little Montenuovos had first appeared on the Parmesan scene. And the Emperor's entourage was full of gossips and scandalmongers who enjoyed nothing better than discussing the sex lives of father and daughter. "You can have no idea," Dietrichstein wrote to Marie Louise, "what the Prince picks up at table, after dinner and at the theater in his conversations with the family and now with Prince Leopold of Salerno, or how skillfully he questions the latter and gets everything he wants to know out of him."

In the end it was Gustav Neipperg who fell into the trap. Dietrichstein had told him one day "not to talk too much and to be on his guard," but Francis, with consummate cunning, pretended to know more than people imagined and claimed that the Emperor and Dietrichstein had told him everything. The General's son promptly told him all that he knew. Francis was utterly dumfounded. While he was languishing in Vienna, far from his mother; while his father, a modern Prometheus, was dying on his windswept rock in the tropics and writing for all the world to read: "I have never had anything but praise for my beloved wife, Marie Louise; to the very last I retain the tenderest regard for her," his mother was forgetting the prisoner, repudiating him, bringing bastards into the world!

Francis concealed his resentment and went on writing his mother letters full of tender affection. He could not stop loving her. But neither could he refrain, a year later—and who can blame him?—from passing this harsh judgment on her:

"If Josephine had been my mother, my father would not be buried at St. Helena and I would not be languishing here in Vienna. Oh, she is kindhearted but weak; she was not the wife my father deserved."

Obenaus's diary, which the deputy tutor filled in day by day, gives us some precious indications as to Francis's state of mind during this spring and summer of 1829:

May 7, 1829: During his lesson in civil law, the Prince declared that he would never be content with life. As soon as he had attained some object, he would, like his father, immediately aim at something higher. There followed a discussion of Napoleon's conduct in the course of which the Prince expressed the opinion that one could not judge great men in the same way as ordinary mortals.

May 21, 1829: A very bad day for the Prince. Nothing went right for him—work, riding or driving. One of the reins broke and the coachman had to turn the horses suddenly to one side in order to stop them. Remarks by the Prince on his habit of not praising others. On military life: that it was necessary to sacrifice honor to discipline; that in the presence of military men he felt a different man; that he would never feel cold or hunger.

July 16, 1829: Referring to the execution of Louis XVI, he said: "It was right and proper; why was he so weak?"—which earned him a reprimand.

August 13: Conversation about "Le Fils de l'Homme."

Obenaus and Foresti took it in turns to accompany their pupil four times a week to Mauer, where the young Captain learned his job drilling a company from Prince Wasa's battalion of grenadiers. He would get up at four o'clock in the morning, arriving on the parade ground an hour later. At half-past seven he returned to Schönbrunn, where he immediately went out riding. "All this," observed Dietrichstein, "together with his studies, taxes his strength, and he must learn to husband it."

On July 14, 1829, Francis wrote to his mother: "On Saturday at Baden I was examined in law, statistics and history—subjects to which Their Majesties kindly sacrificed a couple of hours. In studies which absorb the faculties to such an extent and in which the dangerous reefs had been so carefully pointed out to me, shipwreck would have been shameful. But if the approval which I won was due simply to indulgence, I am none the less conscious of having striven to deserve it. Today I am making a start on the penal code and modern history. . . ."

The study of contemporary history had the effect of making him sad. On the evening of October 29, Obenaus heard him say with a sigh: "What tremendous changes have taken place in such a short space of time! Napoleon, who once had the whole of Europe in his power, was afterward reduced to showing delight when he was given a new coat!"

And what of his own case? He who had found a king's crown in his cradle was now nothing more than a captain *in partibus*. What was to become of Franz von Reichstadt? There had been talk of giving him the Polish throne, but Metternich had quashed the idea. For, as Apponyi wrote to the Chancellor, Austria would be committing political suicide if she helped the Duke of Reichstadt to power. As for Dietrichstein, he hoped to see his pupil ruling in France one day, but when Francis spoke to him of his hopes he replied by pointing out his spelling mistakes. There seemed to be no point of contact between master and pupil. "He listens to me without replying," complained Count Maurice, "and will not take the trouble to correct his mistakes. I have so many reasons to be dissatisfied with him! And after all the trouble and care that have been lavished on him, all that he wants is to be free to do nothing at all and forget everything he has learned. . . ."

What he wanted was not "to do nothing at all." Obenaus was nearer the mark when he wrote that "his love of honor might have degenerated into inordinate ambition." He thought indeed of nothing but his career in the army: "Military glory seemed to him to be the highest goal in life. Everything else was desirable only in so far as it helped him to achieve that object. . . ." The only subjects he enjoyed were those which "could lead him to military glory": mathematics, history, mapmaking, riding and fencing. He treated the rest "with indifference." What did spelling matter? He went so far as to say to Dietrichstein that his father "wrote very badly."

"That is no excuse," replied the tutor. "Failings of that kind are not inherited."

In this respect, however, Francis carried "indifference" rather too far. That was the Duchess of Parma's opinion when she saw her name spelt *Luoise* on the envelope of a letter posted on November 20 by her son. "I must confess," she wrote, "that I was absolutely dumfounded. He might at least make his spelling mistakes in his letters, and not on the envelope where everybody can read them."

Francis was unmoved. He only flared up—and his anger was terrible to see—when he was publicly humiliated. On one occasion Obenaus reprimanded him in front of Marshal de Bellegarde for speaking to a colonel and a chamberlain in preference to a marshal. Francis, "his eyes flashing angrily," snapped: "That finishes it! Our relations are at an end! I shall never forgive you for what you have just said, and I shall make you suffer for it!"

Thoroughly alarmed, Obenaus warned his son that the Duke of Reichstadt had sworn to ruin his career. But as soon as his anger had subsided—and, like his melancholy moods, it never lasted long—he told his tutor: "When I am in command of a regiment, send me your son, I shall make a good soldier of him."

He wanted to do everything by himself and nothing but what he wanted.

"Not even a god could divert me from my purpose," he would sometimes say.

If he was asked what his reasons were for making certain decisions, he would reply: "Because I want to!" or else: "Because I don't want to, dammit!"

However, other people's opinions—except Dietrichstein's—mattered to him, and at the end of a conversation he would often ask what had been said about him. Reading an account of the Archduke Charles's campaigns, on October 6, 1829, he was surprised to learn that his great-uncle admitted his own mistakes.

"In similar circumstances," he declared, "I would never have admitted that I had made a blunder."

He was growing increasingly impatient to obtain his freedom, and the subject of his approaching emancipation was a constant source of friction between himself and his tutor. At the end of 1829 Dietrichstein was still of the opinion that, "physically, morally and intellectually," the Prince was not mature enough to stand on his own feet. Once Francis was emancipated, Dietrichstein, Foresti and Obenaus were to be replaced by a military household: three officers who were to instruct Napoleon's son in "the superior art of warfare" and at the same time "accompany him, watch him and guide him." Dietrichstein's influence would be greatly reduced during the five months when the household would be both civil and military; after that, he would have no choice but to retire, especially as the Emperor Francis was planning to send his grandson to join the garrison in Prague. One can understand why the tutor was in no hurry to see his pupil emancipated. Yet although the Emperor recognized that *der Dietrichstein* was "partial"—he even said so to his grandson—he left it to him to decide when his pupil no longer had any need of his services. The result was that a series of somewhat complicated intrigues was set in motion. While the Count insisted that his pupil was a dunce who needed to remain in his tutelage, Count Feodor Karaczay, who hoped to become Reichstadt's intendant in Prague, wrote to Marie Louise that her son's thoughts were "already those of a grown man." Together with that "masterpiece of mediocrity," Kutschera, the Emperor's favorite, he began plotting, so Dietrichstein maintained, to "hasten the Prince's emancipation." The tutor was horrified to learn that the Emperor himself was encouraging his grandson's hopes, even telling him that his private life in Prague would be "his own affair."

In fact Dietrichstein had no reason to be alarmed. Metternich was determined that Francis should be subjected to supervision as strict as the tutor could possibly desire—supervision so strict that young Gustav

Neipperg refused to consider going to Prague with Reichstadt "to be watched by a lot of spies."

On one point the Chancellor was in entire agreement with his master: ordinary regimental officers would be adequate for this jailer's job. He had no intention of giving Napoleon's son a "suite" of "distinguished officers," as Dietrichstein hoped he might. Francis, as Gentz remarked, "was an open sore in Metternich's system." He reminded him of his old enemy and the Chancellor's only desire was to hear no more about him. Sending the former King of Rome to Prague, not as a prince but as an ordinary officer, gratified his spite.

The Eaglet was naïvely convinced that he would be able to take wing in September, 1830. He "could scarcely contain himself for impatience" and fondly hoped that "some misfortune would overtake the Tsar and bring about a war which he longed for in order to escape from the Count's tutelage." He dreamed of taking part in a battle. "What a day that will be; my ambitions go no further at present, for the happiness of a war would be too much to hope for, especially at a time when the return of our regiments to their quarters suggests that our Cabinet's intentions are anything but bellicose. Indeed, I have a melancholy presentiment that I shall die without receiving my baptism of fire. I have already decided what to do if that dreadful eventuality should occur. I shall leave instructions in my will that my coffin is to be carried into the first battle that offers itself, so that my soul, wherever it may be, may have the consolation of hearing the bullets it has so often dreamed about whistling around its bones."

He did not show his letter to Dietrichstein, but the tutor knew what his pupil had in mind and appealed to Metternich and Marie Louise to do what they could to calm him down. Werklein was asked to send Parma a list of officers chosen by Count Maurice. Dietrichstein would have liked to spin the matter out, but the Emperor on the other hand told his grandson: "This autumn you must and shall be free!"

Everything seemed to be conspiring against the unfortunate tutor. At the end of April, General Prince Alfred von Windischgrätz met Reichstadt at a "lunch-dance" and said to him: "I am delighted at the prospect of having Monseigneur in my brigade. Only one battalion from your regiment is coming to Prague, and that is yours; the others are to be transferred to the country. You will be accompanied by two officers whose names I know but cannot divulge."

A few days later, early in May, the Emperor told Francis: "Jacobi

has found a house for you in the new part of Prague. . . . I shall pick
two officers for you, either from the Salins regiment or from another
regiment in the Prague garrison."

The choice of these watchdogs was still a source of concern for
Dietrichstein, who was anxious to avoid at all costs the nomination of
two junior officers. The only person who could influence the Emperor
on this question was Marie Louise, but Mme. Neipperg had not
seen her father since her confession about the birth of the two bastards and trembled at the very thought of facing him. "If Your Majesty
is firm," wrote Count Maurice, "you will have no trouble at all."
Since everything now depended on his mother, Francis begged her to
let him take up his military duties in the autumn:

"There is something of the warrior in my blood; and nothing but
military service can make me happy. I assure you, dear Mamma, that
you can help me to make a start. I am no Socrates, it is true, but I have
thought deeply about my position, I believe I can see it in its true
perspective and I am firmly resolved to do everything in my power to
become a great man. The same inventory which I have made of my
character has shown me what is lacking in me, and I am convinced of
the need to provide myself during the first years of my emancipation
with sources of wisdom and knowledge."

Here Francis shared Dietrichstein's views:

"The officer destined to introduce me to the world must be a friend
as well as a guide. I beg you, dear Mamma, to use all your maternal
authority to make sure that the choice falls on someone who is
superior to me in every respect, and not on a mere *Kommis-Kerl*."

Reichstadt's delicate health was another pretext which Dietrichstein
used to curb Francis's aspirations and his longing for freedom: "His
physique is a major factor which Your Majesty can stress and which
calls for careful attention." At the beginning of April, 1830, Francis
had begun coughing again as soon as he awoke every morning. He had
no fever but his voice remained hoarse all day. Dietrichstein would have
preferred him to have "a proper cold like everybody else" rather than
that hoarse voice and dry cough. Staudenheim called in his colleagues
Herpex and Goelis, and all three diagnosed "a weakness of the chest."
They prescribed "white powders," but Francis was a difficult patient and
paid no attention to their advice, imagining that they were exaggerating
the poor state of his health in order to postpone his emancipation. He

concealed the symptoms of his illness, asserted that he was "invulnerable," and "defied the seasons as he did his doctors."

Marie Louise grew anxious and wrote to her son, who on May 26 reassured her with this letter:

> The whole trouble was really nothing but a stubborn cold which I neglected to begin with. I coughed a little and that scared the poor old Count. But the fine weather has cured me. Staudenheim, a hard worker and an excellent wit, has died of a violent attack of colic. They have given me the doctor for pregnant women, Mons. Malfatti, whose diagnosis strikes me as eminently reasonable. He has stopped looking for the source of my illness in the throat, and says that it is caused by an irritation of the skin; this will have to be gradually toughened. I have begun taking baths using soap, for which we shall later substitute salt. Milk and salep, a disgusting drink, has purified my liver; and the forty bottles of soda water mixed with milk, which I am to start drinking in June, will strengthen my throat. I hope, dear Mamma, that all these changes in my constitution will be over by the time I find myself once again in your arms . . . when your presence will be sure to produce a change for the better in the heart of your devoted and most obedient son,
>
> FRANCIS

The "violent attack of colic" which had killed Staudenheim was going to prove no less fatal to Napoleon's son. Henceforth *Mons.* Malfatti of Montereggio, obsessed by the disease of the prisoner of St. Helena, would go on treating his new patient for an affection of the liver. As for the "weakness of the chest," that was a mere "irritation of the skin" and a few soap or salt baths would soon take care of it.

The fact that Marie Louise, among innumerable more or less imaginary ailments, showed genuine signs of pulmonary weakness did not strike Malfatti as at all significant, any more than the number of members of the imperial family who were afflicted with the same disease. He declared that Napoleon's son had a liver complaint which required active attention. He did not deny that Francis's chest was weak—he would have had to be blind to do that—but he regarded this as a secondary ill. "However, growing as he is at a rate out of all proportion to his organic development, any *accessory illness* may become dangerous," he admitted, "either at present or in the future. The Prince must take care to avoid too much exertion, especially of the voice, and also changes of temperature. . . ."

That was all in the way of medical attention that Mons. Malfatti gave his patient, when the only remedy which might have saved the Duke of Reichstadt was to send him to Italy or the Alps. But in the interests of European peace, Napoleon's son could not be allowed to leave Vienna.

"They consider him far too dangerous to let him go to Italy," admitted Marie Louise.

At the beginning of May, in spite of "constant colds," there was a noticeable improvement in the Prince's health, which must have delighted Malfatti and convinced him that his *salep* had succeeded in "purifying his patient's liver." On May 30 Reichstadt wrote to his mother:

> I am writing to you from Schönbrunn, where I arrived yesterday in a heavy downpour. I am on the third floor, with a view of the Gloriette, and very comfortable, thanks to the Archduchess Sophia's kind attentions. We shall be dining here most days with all the ladies and gentlemen, and I supped here yesterday with your sister and the Archduke Louis. The afternoons are free, thank Heaven, for I intend to spend them riding; after all, what can people say to one another if they spend all day together with nothing to do? I shall be making a start soon on the theory of economics, so that I can do practical economics before long, and I shall be going into Vienna three times a week for lessons with Messrs. Weiss and Nobili. At present I am reading Chambray's history of the Russian campaign, a very praiseworthy work. His ideas on that war are extremely clear, and the disastrous circumstances of the retreat are depicted in a masterly manner. I should like to see the Russians invade Austria one day, to make them go through a similar retreat, only with the difference that it would be our courage and not the bitter cold that would send them back to their snow. Forgive me for such a short letter, dear Mamma, but I must close it despite myself; Mons. Malfatti came to see me when I was beginning it and kept me a whole hour; and at present I have to go into Vienna to offer my best wishes to the Crown Prince, whose mouth always reminds me of a funnel. . . .

The way in which Francis describes the mouth of the future Emperor Ferdinand, Marie Louise's brother, shows that Dietrichstein no longer had any check on his correspondence. . . .

Due to see his mother again at the beginning of the summer of 1830, Francis was determined to make no mention of his half-brother and half-sister. Marie Louise was worried, however, and it may have been to reassure her that Francis became increasingly affectionate in his letters. Remembering his Mme. de Sévigné, he wrote to her: "If I cannot produce many variations on the one theme: 'I love you,' that does not mean that I feel it any the less sincerely. But my heart is fallow land; my feelings have not come up yet. You, dear Mamma, are the sun which will make them grow."

The meeting was due to take place at Grätz, where Marie Louise was to arrive after crossing the Adriatic on a steamboat—a great novelty at the time. During the entire journey from Schönbrunn to Grätz—on June 17 and 18, 1830—Francis and Dietrichstein talked of nothing but the future that was in store for Napoleon's son.

The appointment of Prince Albert, the Archduke Charles's thirteen-year-old son, as *Obers-Inhaber,* or proprietary Colonel, of the 44th Infantry Regiment had infuriated Dietrichstein but left Francis unmoved. Nor had he shown any indignation when, at eighteen, he had not been given the Golden Fleece like the other archdukes. To his tutor's despair, Captain von Reichstadt, the Little Corporal's son, was convinced that it was best to begin one's military service in the lower ranks and become friendly with officers of the same rank. What is more, he was forever shaking hands with them—a new habit which Dietrichstein described as "ridiculous and unseemly."

Now, as he told Dietrichstein, Francis had high hopes of his interview with his mother. The Emperor would also be at Grätz and his fate could therefore be decided there and then. The Duke was confident that he would be allowed to set off soon for Prague, where he would lead his own life without taking any notice of the three officers on his staff. . . . As soon as they arrived at Grätz, he rushed to Baron Mandl's castle, where his mother was staying. After the first effusions, he went straight to the point: when would he be free and when would he be leaving for his garrison? There was a great deal of discussion, but soon Reichstadt was forced to bow to the facts, and in his diary he wrote with wry humor:

"The Congress of Grätz has so far failed to arrive at any decision as to my emancipation. This particular bill will not go through Parliament until our return to Vienna, for Mons. Malfatti's vote has to be recorded. The Parmesan Court's contribution to the debate consisted of insisting on the choice of two of the officers it had itself proposed and refusing to the appointment of anyone else."

After countless walks, maneuvers, calls, visits to the theater and illuminations—at the latter there were shouts of "Long live Napoleon!"—Francis noted in his diary on June 22: "We dined with the retired General Natzel, Colonel Firet, Major Jordis and Major Prokesch, who comes from the East . . ."

14

❦

Napoleon's Son

THE LAST ROCKETS in the firework display fizzled out. As darkness gradually closed in on Grätz, a few voices in the crowd shouted: "Long live young Napoleon!"

We do not know what Marie Louise's reactions were; she probably hurried back to Baron Mandl's castle muttering: "What a disgusting mob!" as she had done at Bologna when Italian patriots had called out to her: *"Viva Napoleone il grande et la sua infelice sposa, l'Imperatrice, nostra sovrana!"*

As for Francis, he merely wrote in his diary: "The money spent on festivities of this sort is completely wasted. It would be better to use it for some act of charity or present it to some useful institution."

Two days later—on June 20, 1830—a gray-haired general stood before Napoleon's son with tears in his eyes. His name was Count Alois Mazzuchelli and he was in command of the army corps at Grätz. Before entering the service of Austria, he had fought in the Napoleonic armies. A veteran of Marengo, and Berthier's aide-de-camp in the Prussian campaign, he had fought and worked with the Emperor every day, and when he saw Francis before him, the old soldier of the Grand Army could not hold back his tears. At the earnest request of the Eaglet, who for the first time in his life found himself face to face with one of his father's comrades-in-arms, he recalled his memories of the Emperor, ending with the words:

"You have a great name, Monseigneur. It lies within your power to become the guardian angel of your poor country, threatened as it is on all sides, and to serve our beloved ruler with distinction."

Deeply moved, Reichstadt replied: "General, I should be glad if God had given me the twentieth part of my father's talent, but what talent I have I dedicate entirely to Austria, which I am happy to serve with you."

On his return, Francis made a note of his own words in his diary. Two days later—on June 22—he called on Countess Mazzuchelli. That evening, at dinner, he found himself sitting next to an officer of thirty-four whose gentle, intelligent face was framed in curly side-whiskers. As a young ensign in the Austrian army—"the handsome ensign," he had been called—Antoine de Prokesch-Osten had taken part in the final campaigns against what he described as "Napoleonic despotism." "I felt within me," he wrote later, "both a growing hatred of that régime and a growing astonishment at the redoubtable Emperor's energy and personality." However, "when, the following year, we had to wear the white cockade with our own national colors, I did so only with reluctance, and it was a joy to me to throw it into the Rhine when, in the early days of 1814, we left France to cross the bridge at Mannheim and tread German soil once more. The entire regiment in which I was serving did the same. The restoration of the Bourbons struck me as an anachronism and a step on the way to further revolutions; the despotism of Napoleon as a grave error and a sign of a totally unjustified lack of confidence on the part of the Powers."

Once Napoleon had been shipped off to the tropics, the young officer had been disgusted to see "mediocrity and arrogance attacking the prisoner of St. Helena." The victors even went so far as to dispute the military competence of the fallen genius; so in 1818, when he was just twenty-two, Prokesch had published a study of the Battles of Ligny, Quatre-Bras and Waterloo in the *Österreichische Militärische Zeitschrift*. This essay, in which he paid tribute to the Emperor where tribute was due, did not compromise the author's career as might have been expected. He had become one of Marshal Schwarzenberg's aides-de-camp and a welcome guest in the houses of the Viennese intelligentsia.

But on this particular evening the conversation turned neither on Vienna in Schubert's day nor on Napoleon. The Empress and the Archduke John persuaded Prokesch to talk about his travels.

The General Staff had thought of turning him into a naval officer and had sent him off to sail the seas of the Middle East for six years. In this way he had spent long periods in Greece. That country, helped by France, England and Russia, had just shaken off the Turkish yoke, was about to become a kingdom, and was looking for a king. While he was talking, Prokesch could not help looking at Francis. All of a sudden he felt himself gripped by a violent emotion. "I had a presentiment such as takes hold of an adolescent when he happens for the first time to meet the girl to whom he is going to lose his heart."

Taking advantage of a moment when Reichstadt was talking to another guest, Prokesch put forward "the idea that the throne of Greece, lacking candidates since the refusal of the Prince of Coburg, could not be given to any worthier person than the son of Napoleon." Much to his surprise, this suggestion won general approval. Even the Empress expressed her agreement.

That evening Francis and Prokesch exchanged only a few commonplace remarks. But when the time came for the guests to take their leave, and Prokesch was bowing to the nineteen-year-old Prince, Reichstadt clasped him by the hand and murmured: "I have known you for a long time."

"That handshake," Prokesch wrote later, "was really a pledge for the future. It could only have been given in that sense and I placed no other interpretation upon it."

The very next day, Dietrichstein brought Prokesch to see the Prince. As soon as he came in, Reichstadt ran up to him "with all the enthusiasm of youth" and said: "I have held you in affection for a long time. You defended my father's honor at a time when all and sundry were villifying him. I have read your study of the Battle of Waterloo, and in order to obtain a thorough grasp of every line, I have translated it twice over, first into French and then into Italian."

Prokesch expressed his appreciation of the compliment, and the two young men immediately began talking about Greece. Reichstadt soon saw what his new friend was driving at and "took fire" at his words. Ruling over Greece, he could render immense services to Austria, which had to import Greek provisions while Greece stood in need of Austrian products.

The conversation was interrupted by the arrival of General Prince von Hohenlohe. Prokesch got up to go.

"No, stay!" said Reichstadt. "The General is only passing by and I should be sorry to see you go just now."

The old General soon saw that he was *de trop* and went off. Dietrich-stein, who was present at the conversation, seemed to have changed: he in no way disapproved of Prokesch's suggestion that Reichstadt should offer himself as candidate for the Greek throne. In the tutor's opinion, however, there was only one crown which was suitable for Napoleon's son, and that was the crown of France . . . on condition that Metternich was kind enough to give his consent!

As soon as his father's name was mentioned, Reichstadt grew excited. "One could sense the warmest admiration in his words." The Emperor was his model in life, and his only ambition was to become a great soldier like his father. When the conversation turned to questions of strategy, Prokesch was amazed at the Duke of Reichstadt's knowledge. "I would stake my life on it," he wrote to Gentz, "that he knows more about the art of war than the cleverest of our generals!"

Francis went on to complain of his isolation. He had been alone since childhood. . . .

"Remain with me," he said, "sacrifice your future to me, remain with me! We were made to understand each other! . . . If I am destined to serve Austria as another Prince Eugene, the question I ask myself is this: how can I best prepare myself for that task? I have doubts about the choice of a man capable of initiating me in the exacting requirements and the noble duties of a military career. I can see no one of sufficient caliber in my entourage."

Prokesch, drawn by a feeling of sympathy which was all the stronger in that he sensed it was mutual, came back the next day to see the Prince. Francis was just about to go out riding, but readily gave up the idea to return to the subject closest to his heart: Greece. The pros-pect still appealed to him, but he considered that he was too young and "appeared to be afraid that he would not be allowed to rule by him-self." These were just excuses, and Prokesch soon saw that "his hopes and aspirations aimed higher still." Taking advantage of Dietrichstein's absence for a few moments, Francis seized his new friend by both hands and said to him:

"Tell me frankly, is there some good in me and am I capable of a great future, or am I no use at all? What is to become of the great Emperor's son? Will Europe allow him to occupy an independent posi-tion? How am I to reconcile my duties to France with my duties to Austria? Oh, yes, if France called me—not the France of the anarchists but the France which has faith in the imperial principle—then I should hurry to answer her call, and if Europe tried to turn me off my father's throne, then I should draw my sword against the entire continent. But is there an imperial France today? I don't know. A few isolated voices without any influence don't count. Resolutions of such importance deserve and require more solid bases than that. If it is my fate never to return to France, then I earnestly desire to become another Prince Eugene for Austria. I love my grandfather; I feel that I am a member of his family, and for Austria I would gladly draw my sword against the whole world, save only France."

For the first time in his life, Reichstadt was talking freely and opening his heart:

"No one has ever understood my father; it is a shameful calumny to attribute no other motive to his actions but ambition; his life and conduct were entirely dictated by the grand and beneficent plans which he had conceived for the happiness of Europe. Austria in particular misjudged him and misjudged her own interests; she played the Russian game. I should like nothing better than to win my spurs fighting the Russians."

On his return home Prokesch wrote to Gentz: "After two conversations lasting several hours with the Duke of Reichstadt, I am astonished by the liveliness of his mind and judgment, the clarity of his thought and practical intelligence. There is no doubt whatever that we have in him a potential supporter of the social order and our ideas on government and the State."

Dietrichstein viewed the growing friendship between the two young men with a favorable eye, and took the opportunity to complain to Prokesch of his pupil's dislike for any subject other than war and mathematics. He was fundamentally good-natured, it was true, but he could be proud and difficult. Above all—and this was the tutor's principal grievance—"his spelling was fanciful and individualistic"! In other words, Dietrichstein continued to treat as a recalcitrant schoolboy a prince whom others considered ready to mount a throne. Prokesch passed on some of his complaints to Reichstadt, who "paid tribute to the Count, especially to his excellent heart, but in fact did not praise him for anything else. . . ."

The person he most admired was undoubtedly his grandfather. "He is the fairest man in the world," he told Prokesch. His comments on the other members of the imperial family were more critical. The Empress? Intelligent but insensitive. The Crown Prince? A feeble-minded creature worthy of pity. The Archduke Francis, his beloved Sophia's husband? "Spiteful, deceitful and vulgar," he was no friend of Reichstadt's now. Apart from the Archduke John, whom he knew and liked better than the rest, the archdukes and archduchesses and their suites struck him as insufferably vulgar, and the conversation at the imperial table made him feel positively ill.

Prokesch was all the more prepared to believe this in that the Prince seemed to him to "spring from a nobler stock." "His bearing, his manners, his look were all impressive and inspiring . . . he reminded one of the young god Mars." The affection and gratitude which he felt for his grandfather did not prevent him—as he hastened to assure his friend—from "remembering at all times who had given him life" and where his father's body "lay rotting."

"I am convinced that the Bourbons are doomed," he told Prokesch. And he listed his chances of mounting the throne Napoleon had once occupied.

"I am very far from feeling ungrateful to Austria," he declared, "but it seems to me that once I was established on the throne of France I could render greater service to my adoptive country than if I confined myself to following in Prince Eugene's footsteps. . . . I am no adventurer and I refuse to become the plaything of political parties. The situation in France would have to become clearer before I would agree to set foot in that country. For the moment, my task in life is to render myself capable of commanding an army. I shall neglect nothing which might help me to attain that object."

It was at Baden that Reichstadt, on July 7 or 9, received his appointment as battalion commander in the 54th Lamezan-Salins regiment. This news, which should have filled him with joy, did not succeed in rousing him from the reveries in which his conversations with Prokesch and the news from France had plunged him. The French electors had just sent to the Chamber 274 opposition deputies—Bonapartists, Republicans and Liberals—as compared with 143 deputies belonging to the government party. What is more, of the 221 deputies of the old Chamber who had voted for the famous Address which had revealed the gulf between the monarch and his people, 202 had been re-elected. Charles X considered the result of the elections a positive provocation, while the Dauphin—the well-meaning but unintelligent Duc d'Angoulême—asserted that the electors were guilty of "impertinence" toward his father.

It seemed certain that the old monarchy was about to collapse once again. Returning to Schönbrunn at the beginning of August, Francis learned that on July 25 Charles X had put his name to three royal decrees suppressing the freedom of the press, dissolving the Chamber, altering the electoral law and fixing new elections for the following month. Signing these ordinances, Charles X had signed the monarchy's death warrant. For on the 26th, while indignant Parisians were reading the ordinances in the *Moniteur,* Thiers and forty-three journalist colleagues had issued a declaration that smelled of gunpowder: "The rule of law is interrupted; the rule of force has begun. . . . Obedience ceases to be a duty!"

The next day, the 27th, saw the barricades go up all over Paris. It was the first of the Three Glorious Days of the July Revolution. . . .

At the house of General Gourgaud, Napoleon's companion in captivity, a number of former officers of the Empire met together. Was this the moment they had been waiting for? And were the revolutionaries prepared to fight for the Emperor's son? The answer seemed to be that the people of Paris were more interested in getting rid of Charles X, who was hanging on to Saint-Cloud. The 28th found the capital covered with barricades draped with tricolor flags. Among the cries of "Long live liberty!" and "Down with the Bourbons!" there could be heard a few timid shouts of "Long live Napoleon II!"

Why did not Gourgaud follow the example of the unknown General Dubourg, who had been carried to the Hôtel de Ville that morning by the mob, simply because he was wearing a general's uniform, and had come close to forming a government as a result? After all, one of the insurgents was the son of another of Napoleon's companions at St. Helena—Las Cases. But it was felt that he was too young and obscure to lead a movement, and the Bonapartists had accordingly allowed themselves to be swept along by events.

On the 29th, Marmont's troops had abandoned the Louvre, retreated through the Tuileries, and fled in disorder toward Saint-Cloud. The future Louis Philippe's star began to rise in the sky. Gourgaud tried to gather together a few Bonapartist officers, but all in vain, and on the 31st the first step was taken toward the establishment of the bourgeois monarchy: Louis Philippe, preceded by a street arab banging a damaged drum, left the Palais-Royal to go and meet Lafayette at the Hôtel de Ville. The scene enacted there is well known; the Duc d'Orléans tried at first to speak up for Charles X, then gradually allowed himself to be won over, and finally embraced Lafayette at one of the windows of the Hôtel de Ville, enveloped in a tricolor flag. This "republican kiss" of Lafayette's made a king . . . and robbed Napoleon's son of his throne.

Without either a program or a leader, Napoleon II's supporters had missed their chance. In their defense, it should perhaps be pointed out that they knew nothing of Napoleon's son except the pale, romantic face described by Barthélemy. They did not know that the former King of Rome was now a young man of exceptional intelligence whose every thought was centered on his father; they did not know that this Austrian major in his white uniform who had been given a German education had none the less remained a true "French prince," in accordance with Napoleon's dying recommendation—perhaps indeed more of a French prince than if he had stayed at the Tuileries; they did not know that he was fired with that passionate ardor which only imprisonment or exile can engender. They did not know. . . .

The first steps taken by the July Monarchy were faltering and uncertain. Many officers who, for want of anything better, had rallied to the new régime were convinced that if the Eaglet presented himself at Strasbourg with a tricolor in his hand, he would be escorted by his father's soldiers all the way to Paris and it would be the end of Philippe Egalité's son.

On the other hand, the day before Louis Philippe picked up the crown Charles X had dropped, Apponyi, the Austrian ambassador in Paris, wrote to Metternich that the Bonapartist party no longer had any chance of success. He none the less advised the Chancellor of the departure for Vienna of a certain Colonel Deschamps, a former officer of the Imperial Guard, who in the cafés of the Palais-Royal had advertised his intention of going to Austria to ask for the Eaglet's cage to be opened. The Duc d'Orléans "did not deny the fact," said Apponyi, "but held it to be of no importance."

Three weeks later, the ambassador paid rather more serious attention to the plans of certain conspirators who had tried to sound him "as to the intentions of the Court of Vienna." The Emperor Francis's representative had told them: "I know no son of Napoleon, only the son of Marie Louise."

He then hastened to warn Vienna that the Bonapartist party would become "extremely formidable" and "most embarrassing" to the new government if the Duke of Reichstadt returned to France. "The whole army would go over to him, and all the malcontents, whose number is growing day by day, would rally to his cause."

At the same time General Belliard arrived in Vienna to inform Francis I officially of the accession to the throne of the King of the French. The Chancellor was all the more surprised by the new government's choice of ambassador in that he had in his desk a secret document which had apparently been sent him by Athanase Fouché, the Duke of Otrante's son, who was now one of Bernadotte's aides-de-camp. This document had been signed by Belliard, Marshal Maison and the colonels of all the regiments quartered between Strasbourg and Paris.

"They all undertook," Metternich later told Prokesch, "to bring the Duke of Reichstadt back to Paris in triumph."

If we are to believe Metternich's subsequent account of their conversation, the conspirator-turned-ambassador actually mentioned the possibility of the Duke's return to France.

"What guarantees can you offer him? What security would he find there?" the Chancellor asked the strange envoy.

"The love and enthusiasm of the French people would be like a wall around him."

"In my opinion," retorted Metternich, "within six months' time the Duke of Reichstadt would be driven to the edge of an abyss by the forces of ambition, greed, resentment and hatred. The Emperor Francis has too great a regard for his principles and his duties toward his peoples, as well as for his grandson's happiness, ever to lend himself to a scheme of that nature. . . ."

According to Prokesch, Louis Philippe's envoy also asked the Emperor to allow Reichstadt to return to France. Francis I replied that "as the Duke's second father, he loved him too much to expose him to the hazards of political life." However, the rule of the bourgeois monarch appeared to be so unstable that the Emperor spoke to his grandson "of a possible change which might bring him to the throne of France."

"Such as you see me today," Reichstadt asked Prokesch when the latter next came to see him at Schönbrunn, "am I worthy of my father's throne? Am I capable of repulsing flattery, intrigue and falsehood? Am I capable of taking action when necessary? Might I not allow myself to be caught unawares when the decisive moment arrived?"

Prokesch reassured him. The fall of the July Monarchy seemed to him to be inevitable, but it would not necessarily occur immediately. By the time it did, "Napoleon II" would have attained the requisite maturity.

Far less comforting was a conversation Francis had with Prince Dietrichstein, his tutor's brother, who had stayed in France the previous year and met Montholon, one of the last surviving companions of the prisoner of St. Helena and also his executor.

"France," the Prince told Reichstadt, "does not want glory any more, but only liberty and equality. Does anyone expect Napoleon's son, brought up at the Court of Vienna, to fulfill that desire? Surely not. If, during the recent events in Paris, the name of Napoleon was often mentioned, it was simply in memory of his military genius. But how many voices really called for Napoleon II? It is said that if you came to France at the end of the year you would be given an enthusiastic reception. That is probably true, but no one is seriously thinking of restoring the Empire. During the reign of the last two Bourbons, you were Napoleon II for a great many Frenchmen, but since the July Revolution you have just been the Duke of Reichstadt."

Had Prince Dietrichstein judged the situation correctly? Possibly not! Fifteen years after the fall of Napoleon, in this month of September, 1830, the government born of the Three Glorious Days was so insecure that every kind of hope was permissible.

The Napoleonic legend had taken on a new lease of life. All over France pictures of the two Napoleons were being sold, inscribed with the words: "Past, Present and Future." A contemporary records that for one portrait of Louis Philippe you could find twenty of Napoleon and his son. There was a stage version of *Le Fils de l'Homme*, with Virginie Déjazet playing an Eaglet whose tutor, one van der Bruten, was as hard and cruel as his name would suggest. "However," wrote the *Journal des Débats*, "when the Duke of Reichstadt declares that the ward of Austria can never rule over France, the cheers of the whole audience showed that the public was entirely of his opinion." The reporter of the government newspaper had chosen to hear only the cheers of the "Philippist" minority. The public as a whole could not have its fill of imperial glory, after being starved of it for so long, and every theater had its Napoleonic production. In August, 1830, the Cirque Olympique had put on *The Crossing of Mount St. Bernard,* and in October the Nouveautés staged *Bonaparte at the Brienne Academy, or The Little Corporal.* And pending the première of Alexandre Dumas's *Napoleon Bonaparte,* the Porte-Saint-Martin presented the public with *Napoleon, or Schönbrunn and St. Helena.* A hundred and fifty old soldiers had been hired for the scene showing the Guard at Schönbrunn. Before the curtain went up, Gobert, who was playing the Emperor, went up to one of the veterans.

"Well, my man," he said, "do you recognize your Emperor?"

"Oh, yes, Sire, it's you, all right!" exclaimed the old man, with tears in his eyes.

"That's good enough for me," said Gobert. "Curtain up!"

The sight of the Guard being inspected by Napoleon-Gobert, while the drums beat the general salute, sent the audience into a frenzy of enthusiasm. A great shout of "Long live the Emperor!" set the chandeliers trembling. And Mlle. George wept unashamedly in her box.

"Sire," King Joseph wrote to the Emperor Francis about this time, "if you will entrust my brother's son to me, that son whom he instructed in his will to return to France, I guarantee the success of the enterprise."

The idea of entrusting his grandson to the good-for-nothing Joseph was so laughable that the Emperor did not even trouble to reply. The letter from the sometime King of Spain had been brought to Vienna by Athanase Fouché, who, on behalf of the *Napoleonides,* explained to Metternich that "Napoleon II would prevent republicanism from developing in France, Italy, Spain and Germany. As Emperor of the French he would be attached by sentiment and political interest to Austria, his only ally on the Continent. . . ." Metternich—following his master's example—did not reply either . . . and took care not to let Reichstadt know about all these transactions.

Francis's heart continued to beat wildly every time anyone spoke to him of Paris. The Belgians had just shaken off the Dutch yoke and a provisional government had been set up in Brussels. On November 10 the country was to become a kingdom, which meant that there was another throne waiting for an occupant. Once again, the Duke of Reichstadt's name was mentioned. "The idea," Dietrichstein wrote to Marie Louise, "makes the Prince laugh, but everything that happens, what people say and what he thinks of himself, all goes to excite his imagination."

If he was to obey his father's last instructions, Francis could not become King of the Belgians. On November 9 Prokesch found him with the second volume of Antommarchi's memoirs in his hands. He was rereading the paragraph in Napoleon's will in which his father urged him never to forget that he had been born "a French prince." Prokesch heard him sigh: "That sentence is the rule of conduct for my whole life."

One evening—probably November 11—Francis called at Obenau's house in the Ballplatz. As he was about to go upstairs, a woman dressed in a voluminous tartan cloak appeared out of the shadows and seized his hand. "The staircase lamp," Francis later told Prokesch, "scarcely enabled me to make out her features, but these were already familiar to me."

The woman was Countess Camerata, a daughter of Prince Bacciocchi and Elisa Bonaparte. Married to Count Camerata, she had left her husband on the grounds that he had "stifled her noblest aspirations" and since then had been leading a somewhat unconventional life. At the end of the previous month she had had a brief conversation at the Spinnerin-am-Kreuz crossroads with Marie Louise and her son, which presumably justified the latter's statement that her features were familiar to him. The Duke of Reichstadt's first cousin looked very like her uncle and carried with distinction a name that was not easy to bear: Napoleone. She even left off the final "e" when signing her letters. Nearly always dressed as a man, she spent most of her time fencing, riding, or occupying the coachman's seat on her carriage. Her reputation suffered from these mannish tastes, and since her arrival in Vienna she had tried in vain to approach her cousin, whether at the theater, on the bastions or in the Prater. She was under constant police supervision; on this particular evening she had succeeded in giving her guardians the slip and attaining her object, but while she was kissing her cousin's hand, a voice called out from the top of the stairs: "What are you doing, Madame?"

It was Obenaus.

"Who would prevent me from kissing my sovereign's hand?"

Francis bowed, and moved on . . . and neither he nor Obenaus said a word about the incident.

"I have seen the Duke of Reichstadt here," Napoleone wrote on November 14 to her cousin Felix Bacciocchi, who was then in Paris. "I saw him from a distance on the threshold of his palace, without treading its flagstones. Sadly I shook the dust off my sandals. He is tall and handsome, reminding one of the Emperor N. in face and gestures, and he has a sad, unhappy look which makes him even more interesting."

Her ambition was to abduct the Duke of Reichstadt and take him to France—to stage a return from Schönbrunn on the model of the return from Elba. Not a single one of the *Napoleonides* had thought of the idea: it was a woman who taught them this lesson.

A few days later, Francis received this letter through Obenaus's servant:

Vienna, November 17, 1830

To the Duke of Reichstadt.

Prince, I am writing to you for the third time. Please let me know whether you have received my letters and whether you wish to behave like an Austrian archduke or like a French prince. If the former, then hand over my letters. By bringing about my ruin, you will probably attain a more exalted position and your public-spirited action will be counted to your credit. But if, on the contrary, you are willing to take my advice and act like a man, then, Prince, you will see how quickly obstacles give way in the face of strong, calm determination. You can find a thousand ways of speaking to me that I, by myself, cannot employ. You cannot trust anyone but yourself. Do not let the idea of confiding in someone so much as enter your mind. Let me assure you that if I asked to see you, even in front of a hundred witnesses, my request would be refused—that you are dead in so far as anyone who is French or related to you is concerned. In the name of the fearful torments to which the Kings of Europe condemned your father, the exile's agony by which they made him expiate the crime of having treated them too generously, remember that you are his son, that his dying gaze rested on your portrait; show your awareness of so great an honor, and inflict no other punishment on them than that of seeing you seated on the throne of France. Seize your opportunity, Prince. Perhaps I have said too much; my fate lies in your hands, and I can assure you that if you use my letters to bring about my ruin, the thought of your cowardice will make me suffer more than anything they could do to me. The man who gives you this letter will bring me your reply. If you have any sense of honor, you will not refuse me an answer.

NAPOLEONE (COUNTESS) CAMERATA

The servant stood waiting for the reply.

"I shall reply tomorrow," said Francis.

"Where are the first two letters?" asked Prokesch, to whom Francis had lost no time in communicating Napoleone's appeal.

"I haven't received them."

"This letter is dated the 17th and it is now the 24th. There can be no doubt whatever that the police know about these letters."

"That is my opinion too."

Obenaus's servant was in no one else's pay but Countess Camerata. However, the first two letters which he had given to one of Reichstadt's footmen had been delivered, not to the Duke, but to Dietrichstein, who, as a loyal servant of the State, had immediately passed them on to Sedlinsky, the Chief of Police.

Francis and his friend were highly perplexed. Was Napoleone Camerata really acting on behalf of Napoleon's family? If so—this was Prokesch's opinion—nothing could be done. For the Emperor's brothers and sisters had no political standing whatever, and it would be folly to trust those mediocrities, some of whom had shamelessly betrayed the man to whom they owed everything. Even supposing that Elisa's daughter had been sent to Vienna by a group of Bonapartist conspirators, Prokesch still thought it would be unwise to have anything to do with her.

"What can you expect from party leaders," he asked, "who pick such a dubious means of making contact with you?"

Fearing that his letter might fall into the hands of the police, Prokesch recommended the greatest prudence to his friend, and persuaded him to send Napoleone a somewhat brutal reply:

I have just received this morning a letter dated the 17th, whose, contents and delayed delivery I cannot understand and whose signature I can scarcely decipher. It seems to be in a lady's hand, and courtesy requires me to reply. You will readily understand that I cannot treat it either as an Austrian archduke or as a French prince, to use the terms employed in the letter; but honor impels me to inform you, Madame, that I have not received the first two letters of which you speak, that the one to which I am replying will be consigned to the fire, and that the contents, in so far as I can guess at their meaning, will remain forever buried in my breast. Although deeply touched by and appreciative of the sentiments which you express, I beg you, Madame, to send me no further communication.

THE DUKE OF REICHSTADT

Vienna, November 25

This letter, which is not exactly remarkable for its courtesy, crossed a fourth note in which Napoleone begged her cousin to receive her: "I will go anywhere you wish to speak to you."

Francis took fright and decided to tell the whole story to Obenaus, who was unaware of anything but the staircase scene. He immediately alerted Dietrichstein. Count Maurice, who had read the first two letters from Napoleone, was thus acquainted with the entire affair. His dearest wish was to see his pupil mount the throne of France, but he was not unreasonably alarmed at the presence in the plot of this fanatical Amazon. Should he perhaps inform Metternich? Together with Francis, he asked his brother's advice first. The Prince, Prokesch tells us, "promptly took the Duke's side and thus averted the most pressing danger, which was his brother's alarm."

"At your age," he told Francis, "I should have acted as you have done; at mine, I should have read the letter, made a copy of it, then burnt it and said nothing about it to anyone."

Reichstadt felt somewhat ashamed of having sent his cousin such a harsh letter and asked Prokesch to go and present his apologies to her. She gave the messenger a chilly reception. "I spoke enthusiastically to her about the Duke's person and character," writes Prokesch, "about the complete freedom he enjoyed to study his father's life, about the passion which he brought to this study, about his views and ambitions, and about the books which we used to read together, among which I mentioned O'Meara, Las Cases, Antommarchi, Montholon, and generally speaking everything which had come out of St. Helena. She listened with surprise and visible satisfaction. I expressed certain doubts as to the strength of the party which was offering to support the Emperor's son. She was unable to say anything on this subject except a few generalities which bore witness to her aspirations but not to her resources." The Austrian major's words were a source of comfort and joy to the young woman, and they parted on the best of terms.

Sedlintsky and Dietrichstein did not dare expel Napoleon's niece immediately. Countess Camerata might be generally regarded as "mad" —that was certainly Metternich's opinion—but the effect of expelling her would be to provide disastrous confirmation of Dietrichstein's reply to Barthélemy:

"The Prince is not a prisoner, but . . ."

The authorities waited three weeks before intimating to Napoleone that she was to leave Vienna before December 22. She obeyed and settled in Prague. In spite of all that Prokesch had told her, she was disappointed, but she did not lose faith in her cousin's destiny. "One day," she wrote to her cousin Clary, "he may recover from his temporary abasement and prove himself worthy of his lofty origins. . . ."

"What strange and fascinating times we live in!" Francis wrote to his mother. "Events which would normally fill whole centuries have taken place within six months. They call for the participation of real men, and I shall try to become one. . . ."

The wind of freedom which had started in Paris was blowing across Europe. Would it, people wondered, lift Napoleon II onto a throne? Pending the time when he would rule over France, would the great Emperor's son accept a lesser crown? After Belgium, which had been an independent kingdom since early November—and was still looking for a sovereign—Poland rose in rebellion during the night of November 29-30, and General Chlopicki, a veteran of the Grand Army, became dictator. The Russian forces left the country, and a French officer was seen galloping through the streets of Warsaw shouting: "Long live Napoleon, King of Poland!"

This time Francis was deeply moved. The Belgian revolution had merely stirred his imagination, but the Warsaw insurrection made a profound impression on him. "He loved the Polish people," Prokesch tells us, "for their military qualities and also for the devotion they had shown toward his father. He thought them capable of greater heroism and enthusiasm than the French. The idea of putting himself at the head of the Polish nation obsessed him to the exclusion of every other thought, and there is no doubt whatever that he would have agreed to flee to Poland gladly and without hesitation if someone had impelled him in that direction." By becoming King of Poland, he thought that he might be able to avenge his father for the harm the Russians had done him.

Before sweeping on to Parma, the wind of freedom roused little Corsica, which "desired and proclaimed" Napoleon II, as Dietrichstein informed Marie Louise. But he added disdainfully: "It would be a contemptible kingdom."

These different candidatures were the subject of eager discussion in Viennese society. Princess Grassalkowich, *née* Esterházy, conducted a campaign—a drawing-room campaign—in favor of the Polish project, which she claimed could prove of great benefit to Austria. On December 26, in Metternich's drawing room, Countess Molly Zichy, who regarded Reichstadt as a bastard, uttered genuine cries of horror at the mere idea of seeing the son of the Corsican Ogre occupying the throne of Poland. Metternich reassured her with a smile and a shrug of the shoulders, saying simply: "Once for all, excluded from every throne."

But the Emperor was of a different opinion.

On January 4, 1831, Francis learned from the Paris newspapers, which were already a fortnight old, that in the course of the Polignac trial, Louis Philippe's government had succeeded in maintaining order with the help of the army and the National Guard. The July Monarchy was clearly becoming more stable and secure. "The young Prince is wrapped in profound obscurity," wrote Méneval, "which does much to injure his cause." And the future Napoleon III asked: "What true Frenchman would want as his sovereign the Emperor Francis's grandson and Metternich's pupil, thereby submitting to Austrian domination? No! No! Austrian influence has always been baneful to us!"

More and more Bonapartists joined the Republicans and made common cause with them in their hatred for "Philippe." Francis grew increasingly worried and consulted his grandfather, who told him: "If the French people asked for you, and if the Allies gave their consent, I should do nothing to prevent your mounting the throne of France."

Francis saw at once that this was a promise which his grandfather would find it easy to keep, since the Allies would never give their "consent." He complained to Prokesch and the Archduke John that he was being treated like a child. The Emperor Francis's brother was "sincerely indignant" and wrote: "They have been discussing the matter of his emancipation for over eighteen months and are still spinning it out. The truth is that they do not want to emancipate him. In intelligence he far surpasses his entourage, which is neither up to his level nor capable of securing his affection."

The Eaglet would have to wait many more months before being allowed to spread his wings, and even then they would carry him no farther than the Alslergasse, a little street in Vienna where his future battalion was quartered. . . .

By that time the mantle of oblivion would have been cast over Napoleon II.

15

✦

The Eaglet

WHEN THERE WERE so many countries hoping to have Napoleon's son at their head, the Emperor Francis could not do less than give his grandson the rank of lieutenant-colonel in the Duke of Nassau's 29th Infantry Regiment, garrisoned at Brünn. Reichstadt wrote his grandfather a letter brimming over with gratitude, but even so his promotion did not cause him the delirious joy which his appointment as captain had provoked.

To his mother he simply wrote, on November 11, that he had been "agreeably surprised" and that the Emperor's "gracious act" would be "a new spur to my zeal."

The composition of Francis's household had finally been established. Francis would have liked to have Prokesch beside him, but Metternich had objected, saying that he needed him himself. The Chancellor intended him for a diplomatic post, but that was not his real reason, which he expounded to the Emperor as follows:

"Prokesch is a strange character who would fill the Prince's head with a lot of madcap plans. Between them they would turn the world upside down!"

Three officers had been chosen to form Francis's household, and while waiting to take up their duties they called on him every day. The senior officer, General Count Hartmann, aged forty-three, had obtained every promotion at the point of the sword. Prokesch describes him as a good soldier without any education and "extremely submissive and obsequious in manner." At their first interview, he trembled with fear in front of Francis and did not dare to look him in the eyes. The poor man had also been unnerved by the instructions which General Kutschera had drawn up for him and which the Emperor had amended and signed in his own hand:

"I hope that the Prince will allow you to guide him without offering any resistance, but if the vivacity of his character should make it necessary to apply stricter and more energetic treatment, I give you full authority to that end and ask you only to furnish me with information from time to time, so that I may expect frank and sincere reports from you, without having to ask for them."

Hartmann's duties as Chief of Staff were more like those of a jailer. He was even expected to prevent Reichstadt from reading foreign newspapers and to do everything in his power to see that the only people he met at Brünn had been carefully hand-picked.

"I think," added the Emperor, "that relations with persons of the opposite sex may be useful to him, but such relations must be even more strictly supervised." In order to do this, all that Hartmann had to do was to get in touch with the Chief of Police at Brünn. Reichstadt was of course always to be accompanied by one of the officers dogging his footsteps. Another duty fell on the unfortunate Hartmann: "It is possible that some of the passions and inclinations of the Prince's late father—most of which are *extremely* culpable [the Emperor had added the word "extremely"]—may have been handed down to his son. That is what you must combat with all the strength at your command, by reasoning and by example, in order to guide his feelings in the right direction, so that he may become an upright, honest and virtuous person, incapable of malice or deceit."

The second officer appointed to Francis's staff was Captain Baron de Moll. This "good fellow of excellent appearance," as Dietrichstein described him, had been trained at the Pavia military academy, which Napoleon had founded, and had spent part of his career in Italy. Prokesch thought he was "a gay, likable officer, capable of feeling real affection for the Duke."

To begin with, Francis treated Moll airily and Hartmann contemptuously. Feeling in need of moral support, Hartmann had one of his protégés, thirty-eight-year-old Captain Joseph Standeisky, appointed as the third member of the household. Francis judged him at a glance: he was completely uneducated. Indeed, Francis's household as a whole was mediocre in character and, as Dietrichstein observed, "in no way consistent with the Prince's good sense, character and rank, or with the part which he is going to play one day in world affairs." Napoleon's son created the impression of "a thoroughbred"—the image is Prokesch's—"between two Bohemian cart horses and an Italian cab horse."

Pending his departure for Brünn—his entry into active service had been postponed to the following spring—Francis spent his time planning his future establishment. "Every morning," he wrote to his mother on December 4, 1830, "I try a good many horses that people keep bringing me from all over the place; I have not bought any yet, but I shall have to make up my mind to do so soon. I am just like a little wife arranging her house; I also feel as innocent as a virtuous maiden among all these shady horse-copers. Count Dietrichstein is busy most of the time drawing up lists in the kitchen, and is wearing himself out making arrangements. At the moment we have not got enough houses in Brünn, but that is going to be seen to. Hartmann and Moll are here, and I am gradually getting to know them. A third comrade in arms is due to arrive shortly: a certain Standeiski. He is endowed, so I am told, with every imaginable quality save one whose importance I am only just beginning to appreciate—and that is money. He lives on his pay, and as in my service he will be obliged to dress well and incur other expenses, I venture to ask you, dear Mamma, if in your kindness you could give him some little help. . . ."

This was an amusing, spontaneous, lively letter, but the "little wife arranging her house" and "the innocence of a virtuous maiden" horrified Marie Louise. "I nearly fainted reading his letter," she exclaimed. "What a style!"

Dietrichstein considered that his pupil's departure for Moravia was premature. "It is prudent, proper and necessary that the Prince should spend the winter in Vienna," he wrote to Marie Louise. "It would be most improper to send him to join a garrison in the middle of winter without the slightest justification. There really would be reason then for saying that he was being degraded and neglected. . . . No, this will not happen if I can help it!"

Far from Vienna—and far from Dietrichstein—how would it be possible to avoid "regrettable" encounters wtih hotheaded fanatics such as Napoleone Camerata or the poet Barthélemy?

The Prince was not a prisoner, but . . .

Dietrichstein eventually calmed down. In view of the fact that Francis's state of health was always precarious in winter, the decision was postponed until the spring of 1831. On the other hand, it was impossible to put off any longer the entry into society of the Emperor's grandson, who so far had attended only the Hofburg balls. Metternich asked General Hartmann to draw up *himself* the social program "which he wished to be assigned" to the Duke of Reichstadt. The General did not feel adequate to the task . . . and asked Reichstadt to work out the program for him!

"These are the men I am given!" exclaimed Reichstadt. "It is from them that I am supposed to learn, and it is their example I am supposed to follow!"

On January 25, 1832, Francis, "radiant with youth and beauty," made his social début in the drawing rooms of the British ambassador, Lord Cowley. His arrival caused a tremendous stir. He smiled, that smile which no one who saw it could resist. The guests did not know what to admire most in him—the fair hair which was the envy of every woman, the delicate skin, or the "beautiful hands with the nails trimmed in the Chinese fashion." Every eye remained fixed upon him. Dietrichstein was "in the seventh heaven of delight," but kept spoiling the Eaglet's pleasure by "fluttering" around him and whispering in his ear: "You aren't talking enough," "You aren't standing properly" or "You are being too familiar."

Francis eventually became annoyed and also a little anxious.

"What am I to make of Dietrichstein's reproaches?" he asked Prokesch in a whisper.

"Never forget that you are Napoleon's son; that thought will always stand you in good stead."

His behavior was studied all the more closely by the guests in that among their number were Marshals Marmont and Maison. The latter, General and Count of the Empire by the grace of Napoleon, and Marshal, Marquis and Peer of France by the grace of Louis XVIII and Charles X, had finally been appointed Minister of War and Ambassador of France by Louis Philippe and represented the new July Monarchy in Vienna. His "coarse and vulgar" manners were found offensive in Viennese society. He studied his former master's son with curiosity and also "considerable embarrassment." "I had been told," he later wrote to Mme. Godard-Duvivier, "that the young Prince would be sure to speak to me, that he was very talkative. I was on my guard all the time, determined to avoid an encounter of that sort. I succeeded in that object without giving offense, although once I was very nearly caught."

The ambassador expressed his surprise that Marie Louise's son should appear so un-Austrian. "Seeing him on his own in the midst of the young men of Vienna, without knowing who he was, one would say straight away: That is a Frenchman. And yet he has mixed in no other society." Like all who met Francis, he fell willy-nilly under the young man's charm, attracted by the "meditative look" he noticed on the Eaglet's face and by "something dogmatic in his bearing."

"In any case," he concluded, "he is a handsome young man of good address. He will have considerable success with the more lovable half of humankind with memories of his name and the advantages of a pleasing exterior."

He had noticed Napoleon's look in his eyes, and that was also the first reaction of Marmont, who, defeated in the Three Glorious Days, had followed Charles X into exile. His gaze never left the young man whom he had dethroned in 1814. The look in Francis's eyes made his heart beat wildly. "It is in that," he wrote later, "that he resembles *him* most. His eyes, smaller than Napoleon's and deeper set, had the same expression, the same fire, the same energy. They were big blue eyes, sharp and piercing and perpetually on the move. His forehead too recalled that of his father, and there was another point of resemblance in the lower part of the face and the chin. Finally his complexion was that of the young Napoleon: the same pallor and the same color of the skin."

Marmont anxiously wondered how Francis would behave if they met. Would he remember his father's cutting reference to the Duke of Ragusa in his will: "The two unhappy issues of the invasions of France, when the country had such powerful resources, were due to the treachery of Marmont, Augereau, Talleyrand and Lafayette. I forgive them. May the posterity of France forgive them as I do!"?

Suddenly the fascinated guests saw Napoleon's son, with Dietrichstein at his side, go up to Marmont and hold out his hand.

"Marshal," he said, "I am delighted to see one of my father's first brothers-in-arms."

Marmont, "moved to tears," bowed. The "brother-in-arms of Toulon" and Napoleon's son, leaning against a console table, began talking quietly to each other so that no one could hear what they were saying. "However, the room never emptied completely," Dietrichstein tells us, "for all the inquisitive onlookers stood on tiptoe in the next room, in order to watch this tête-à-tête, which particularly interested the English and the people from the French Embassy."

In another drawing room Marshal Maison was holding forth in disapproval of his old comrade: "Ragusa . . . has embarked on a conversation which, with what I consider to be typical thoughtlessness and imprudence, he is prolonging far too long. . . . He is showing off, without realizing that in his position he is committing a grave error."

It seemed to him that the conversation lasted "a good hour." Marmont's emotion was clearly visible. The onlookers decided that the Marshal was weeping because the Duke of Reichstadt was reproaching him with ingratitude toward Napoleon.

Nothing could have been further from the truth.

In their conversation Marmont recalled the first hours of their friendship, at a time when Francis's father was an artillery lieutenant and Marmont a noncommissioned officer. Then he talked about the Siege of Toulon, Egypt, Brumaire, the last campaigns. He even ventured to explain—if we are to believe his account of the conversation—how "that noble genius, so clear-sighted in the early years of his great career, was obscured by proud illusions which distorted his judgment." Francis responded by talking enthusiastically about his profession, adding that he would be happy to learn how to fight under the Marshal's orders— at least, so Ragusa maintained.

"France and Austria may one day be allies and their armies fight side by side. For I cannot and must not fight against France. An order left by my father forbids me to do so, and I shall never disobey it. My heart too forbids me to do so."

Before taking leave of the Marshal, Francis asked him if he would agree to give him a sort of course in Napoleonic history two or three times a week. Marmont prudently refrained from giving any undertaking without obtaining Metternich's approval. Since the Chancellor was present at the ball, it was a simple matter to ask his permission, once Reichstadt had left.

Did Metternich consider it piquant to allow the son to gain insight into his father's character through the very man who, by going over to the Austrians, had hastened the fall of the Empire?

"I can see no reason why you should not see the Duke of Reichstadt

and talk to him about his father; he could not be left in better hands
than yours," replied the Chancellor, with an irony which was lost on
Marmont, since he proudly reproduced the Minister's words in his
Memoirs. "I should regard it as wrong," the Chancellor went on, "not to
allow him to see Napoleon as he really was, with all his eminent
superiority; but it is also good that he should know about his illusions,
his pride and his ambition—passions which brought about his ruin and
led him to destroy his own strength. You more than anyone else are
capable of helping him to see the truth."

Metternich was no fool, and he had understood the motives prompt-
ing Francis's behavior—behavior which Viennese society found so surprising.

"The Duke is a play actor," he had once remarked.

Reichstadt certainly had no intention of confiding in Marmont.
What is more, according to Prokesch, he had greeted the Marshal with
the words: "In you I wish to see *only* the oldest of my father's comrades-in-arms!"

The Duke of Ragusa, who had provided the French language with
the new verb *raguser*—to betray—was nothing to him but an instrument
enabling him to learn about Napoleonic history from one of the actors
of the epic. This understandable curiosity relieved him of all his
scruples.

Three days after the ball at the British Embassy—on Friday, January 28—the Duke of Ragusa gave Francis his first "lesson." There were
to be seventeen in all, in the course of which Marmont, harried with
questions by the Emperor's son, revealed all that he could remember.
Before a table littered with maps and plans, the whole amazing story
was re-created. To begin with, there were the days spent at the
Hôtel de la Liberté in the Rue des Fossés-Montmartre where the young
Bonaparte waited for a command—days when, if there was anything to
eat, the future Emperor shared it with his future Marshal. Then came
the glorious Italian campaign, "with no clothes, no shoes, no guns,
often no cartridges, twelve days with no bread, but never any lack of
courage."

Arcola . . . The Commander-in-Chief fell into a swamp and Marmont, with Lucien Bonaparte's help, pulled him out under heavy fire
from the Austrians.

Francis listened in fascination to what his father had said to the man who was before him now:

"My dear fellow, they have seen nothing yet. . . . Fortune smiled at me today, and I'm not the man to spurn her favors. She's a woman, and the more she does for me the more I shall ask of her. . . . No one in our time has conceived anything that bears the stamp of greatness: it is up to me to create an example."

The Pyramids . . . The miraculous return to France . . . Brumaire . . . The crossing of the St. Bernard . . . The famous names echoed through the gilded rooms of the Hofburg . . . Marengo . . . no longer a defeat, as it had been on Obenaus's lips, but a victory—a victory due in part to Marmont and his guns.

Francis lived through the epic days. With Marmont and the French troops he marched into Vienna in December, 1805. He was with the Marshal in July, 1809, at Wagram, and pursued "the enemy"—who for once was not French—as far as Znaim, twenty-five miles from Brünn. But the pursuit had been slow and clumsy, and the Duke of Ragusa did not tell the Duke of Reichstadt of Napoleon's exclamation:

"Marmont, you maneuvered like a fool!"

Not that that had prevented the Emperor from giving him the Marshal's baton that same evening. . . .

The epic continued, and now Francis shuddered as one reverse followed another: the Arapiles, Salamanca, Leipzig, the Battle of the Nations. . . . Marmont evoked a picture of Napoleon at Mainz at the end of 1813, when he had just lost nearly half a million men: a "grim and silent" Napoleon who admitted that he was in "a difficult position."

When Marmont came to describe the state of mind then obtaining in France and "King Joseph's weakness," Francis remarked "with great emotion": "My father and mother ought never to have left Paris, the one for the sake of war and the other for the sake of peace!"

Finally Marmont reached the chapter which caused him most concern: that of his "treachery" and the "patriotic intentions" which, so he maintained, had been the only ones to guide him. Reichstadt considered the man of conscience superior to the man of honor, and perhaps, judging Ragusa less severely than his father, he decided that there were extenuating circumstances which excused the Marshal's conduct on that April day at Essones. . . .

At the end of the final "lesson," Francis presented his "master" with a portrait of himself by Daffinger. The painter had represented him gazing at a bust of Napoleon. Prokesch considered that this gift "would create an unfortunate impression in the Marshal's hands." But all that mattered to Francis was the fact that thanks to Marmont his father had come to life before his eyes: he was no longer just a character in his history books but a creature of flesh and blood. What is more, the ill luck dogging Marmont's footsteps had aroused his sympathy for the Marshal. As he later remarked to Moll:

"Marmont is not a wicked man, just an unlucky one. Everything he has undertaken apart from war has gone wrong. His first political act damned him, perhaps unjustly, in the eyes of the world, and cost me the first crown in Europe."

These long conversations with Marmont had made Francis more impatient than ever to get out of his jail. His only ambition and aim in life was to distinguish himself from other men. In the meantime he champed the bit and cursed the poor state of his health. It was a bad winter for him. "He has been ill for the past month," Marshal Maison reported to Paris. "He drags himself around, looking alarmingly thin. I would not be surprised if there were something seriously wrong with his chest. The ladies are doubtless helping to develop the disease, if he already has it, or to give it to him if he is still free of it, for they are all after him."

Maison was exaggerating, though it seems that love—still only platonic perhaps—had made its appearance in Francis's life. This was, of course, another argument for not sending him away from the capital. "The idea that Vienna is dangerous for the Prince is just too ridiculous," Dietrichstein had told Marie Louise. "He will have love affairs everywhere, but they will have a nobler character here than anywhere else."

Reichstadt had in fact fallen in love with the pretty Countess Nandine Károlyi, *née* Princess Kaunitz, whom he had met through Maurice Esterházy. The two young men, who had now been on friendly terms for some months, called Nandine "the Chinaman" for some unknown reason. Prokesch disapproved of his friend's infatuation, probably because he felt that Francis needed the love of an intelligent, warmhearted woman, whereas in his opinion Nandine was "frivolous, vapid and superficial." Instead of strengthening his character, this liaison would cover it with "the rust of banality":

"In your position, the slightest gesture is important, because the attention of the whole world is fixed upon you. . . . You belong too much to history to permit yourself the luxury of taking part in a love story."

Francis refused to take his advice and went on seeing Nandine in secret. In May he wrote to Esterházy, who was acting as his postman: "I am still convinced that she is the only person who can suit me." How far did their relations go? We cannot tell. We know only that Francis enjoyed supping and dancing with the young woman. Schubert's *Lieder* were forgotten, and Vienna was frenziedly dancing the waltzes of sentimental Joseph Lanner and dynamic Johann Strauss. The city was divided into "Straussians" and "Lannerians." Strauss— they called him the Austrian Napoleon—"black as a Moor" and armed with his magic baton, conducted the amazing Sperl orchestra night after night, and it was often to the swirling rhythm of his haunting compositions that Francis and Nandine abandoned themselves.

In the evening of February 15, however, it was to the Salle de la Redoute that Reichstadt, Countess Károlyi and Esterházy, all wearing masks, went to waltz to the music of Lanner's orchestra. Afterward the Countess took her two friends to her house, where they found a crowd of people intoxicated by the music to which they were dancing. Recounting his escapade later to Prokesch, Francis, delighted at having escaped from his warders, claimed that "the two masks, whose identity was known only to the mistress of the house, had remained an inscrutable enigma for all the guests." If we are to believe the beautiful Countess Lulu Thurheim, however, Francis took his mask off and came up to her, "quite out of breath." "His hair, falling untidily over his forehead, made him look more than usually handsome." While the other guests went on dancing around them "in a frenzy which could only be described as bacchanalian," Lulu Thurheim apparently had a conversation with the Eaglet "which was far removed from the usual ballroom gossip," and which she recorded as follows in her diary:

"You must take me for a madman tonight," the Duke said with a smile.

"No, Your Highness, only for a very young man. But then, like myself, you have two ages."

"One which already belongs to the past, and the other?"

"One is indeed the age we both are, and the other the age of a man of mature years and experience."

"Then I must try to be serious."

"All the same, you are going to go out sometimes, aren't you?"

"Sometimes, yes, although the stupidity of drawing-room society bores me. I prefer a good book."

"Your Highness, you seem to want to turn serious straight away?"

"You may think I am not telling the truth, but I assure you that I am so used to solitude that I am not afraid of it. I am always alone, and my position is so peculiar, like . . . like . . ."

Francis hesitated, "searching for a comparison," and the young woman smilingly suggested:

"Perhaps like an eaglet on a perch?"

"No, rather like a chicken shut up in the poultry yard. All around me, everyone is free, but all I can do is flutter my wings in captivity."

"Your Highness, I can't say that I like that comparison with a chicken."

"Perhaps you would rather I compared myself to the cock waiting for the sunrise?"

In more serious mood he added:

"For the moment my ambitions go no further than Brünn and later the rank of General in the Austrian army; that is my destiny and my career."

And Countess Lulu Thurheim concluded: "There is no other destiny to compare with his. Born to rule over France, Poland, Belgium and Italy, he can now scarcely hope to wear a colonel's epaulets."

It was indeed doubtful whether he would ever "wear a colonel's epaulets" in these troubled times when he could not be allowed to take command of a regiment leaving for Italy. For the peninsula had been caught up in the wave of revolutionary fervor which had started in Paris and already swept over Belgium and Poland.

It had all begun on February 3 in Modena, where the revolutionaries had issued a manifesto proclaiming Napoleon II King of Italy and put Duke Francis IV to flight. Bologna, Ferrara, Ravenna, Forli and eventually the whole of Romagna had followed suit, in an endeavor to shake off the Austrian yoke and remind "the now sovereign people" of the existence of a "king of Italy, sprung from the blood of the immortal Napoleon." The movement was supported by the Bonapartists—the future Napoleon III and his brother would soon be fighting beside the carbonari. The news of the collapse of the little dynasty of Modena rejoiced the hearts of all those, in England and France, who preached the right of every people to decide its own fate. "The world is very sick," Metternich wrote to Marie Louise. "This is a dreadful crisis. . . . The source of the evil is to be found on both sides of the Channel; I would be hard put to it to decide whether it was in Paris or in London that the Revolution had the more zealous support. . . ." And to his ambassador in Paris he declared: "This is a Bonapartist revolution, supported by the French anarchists."

Metternich hoped to see these "anarchists" brought to heel by the July Government. Impatient to intervene as quickly as possible in Italy, he saw Marshal Maison on February 12 and explained to him what Austria's position was with regard to the Bonaparte family:

"We will have nothing to do with any plan which would favor that party which is trying to tie us to the Duke of Reichstadt. Here in Austria we are 'Philippists' from head to foot and nothing can divert us from the policy we have adopted."

The next day—February 13—Maison, completely reassured, wrote to Mme. Godard-Duvivier: "You may be certain that the Austrians sincerely want peace and the present state of affairs in France with Louis Philippe, and do not imagine that I say that because I have been taken in by M. de Metternich."

The Marshal had however been "taken in" to some extent, for on the 15th the Chancellor sent rather more precise dispatches to his ambassador in Paris. If France did anything to prevent Austria from suppressing the insurrection and restoring order in Italy, Austria might allow the Duke of Reichstadt to find his way to the peninsula and—as Rostand later put it—"let the little Colonel out of his box."

"Has it never occurred to anyone in Paris," asked Metternich, "to show a little gratitude for the way we have treated Napoleon II? We deserve something in return for what we have done. . . ."

In other words, if France did not want to be co-operative, Austria would find the means to compel her.

"And we hold the means in our hands!" declared Metternich.

Had not the Bolognese envoys asked Austria to let them have Napoleon II? Would the July Monarchy prefer that solution? In that case, the Emperor Francis would place his grandson on the tottering throne of his brother-in-law Francis IV of Modena—Marie Louise's *Jugendliebe*.

But events moved faster than diplomacy.

On Thursday, February 10, 1831, the insurrectionary movement reached Parma. A terrified Marie Louise tried to take flight but was held captive by the mob. In the night of the 14th, however, she succeeded in leaving her palace and took refuge at Casalmaggiore, then at Cremona, and finally, on the 18th, at Piacenza. The internment of the ex-Empress at Parma was transformed in Vienna into a magnificent act of resistance, and her escape into an epic adventure. "The joy I felt at your deliverance from the hands of the rebels," Francis told his mother on February 20, "your journey to Piacenza and the loyalty of your troops can only be compared to the pride I felt at the manly and courageous way in which you have behaved. Your conduct shines forth in unique splendor in our storm-swept times. . . ."

It was no longer a matter of asking France through diplomatic channels to shut her eyes to Austrian intervention in Italy. The Emperor's daughter was in danger! An army corps was promptly dispatched to Parma, with instructions to restore Austrian authority in Modena at the same time. "The spirit of those insane trouble-makers will be broken by our troops," Francis told his mother. Sure enough, Austrian bayonets soon restored order to the whole Duchy. Reichstadt wanted to go to his mother's assistance at the head of his battalion—and in fact fight his own supporters. He begged the Emperor to let him go, but his grandfather refused.

"Never," writes Prokesch, "have I seen him so agitated. Tears filled his eyes. He was impatient to take up arms, and one would have thought he was in the grip of a perpetual fever; he could not settle down to any kind of work."

He even went so far as to hope that the revolution would spread to Austria. "The people of Vienna are still asleep," he wrote to Marie Louise, "but if they ever decided to wake up, then we should have enough guns here, not to mention fifteen thousand swords and bayonets, to plunge them back into a deep sleep."

He was in a fever of excitement, all the more so as the Emperor, in a private conversation, had said something very strange to him, perhaps in order to convince his grandson that a better future awaited him one day in France than in Italy.

"Franz," he said, "you will no sooner have appeared on the Pont de Strasbourg in Paris than it will be all over with the Orléans family."

"I shall only set foot in France," replied Francis, "if I am called back by the French army. I shall never return behind foreign bayonets!"

The Emperor had looked at him sadly, and Reichstadt had heard him sigh: "Franz, why aren't you a few years older?"

But he was reckoning without Metternich. As Marshal Maison wrote to his usual correspondent: "If he had any chance in France—this is going to surprise you—it is here that he would meet with the strongest opposition."

His grandfather's words had increased Reichstadt's agitation. His spirit, Prokesch tells us, "bent under the pressure of all these emotions as under a burden which grows heavier day by day." The two friends began wondering whether to try and escape. "We often thought about that possibility and considered it from every angle. We should have succeeded. . . . He thought of everything, and had entered into relations with Marmont and Delarue [Marmont's former aide-de-camp] simply in the hope of receiving some proposal or at least learning something about the strength of his party." He also saw Delarue to hear talk of France. When Delarue told him that some French grenadiers had presented woollen epaulets to the Prince de Carignan in honor of his brave conduct in the attack on the Trocadero, Francis exclaimed with tears in his eyes:

"In Russia, when they want to punish a general, they reduce him to the ranks. In France, when they want to honor a prince, they make him a grenadier. Oh, beloved France!"

These moments of enthusiasm and hope were followed—such was his nature—by periods of profound depression. He was afraid that his hour might come too soon, "not," explains Prokesch, "because he was a few years too young, as his grandfather believed, but because he felt that he lacked experience of the world, he did not know enough, and his judgment was still immature. These ideas sapped his confidence, and I could do nothing to restore it." These periods of depression, during which he sank into a state of torpor, recalled the sixteen-year-old Duke of Reichstadt who would sometimes abandon a task he had begun, complaining that it was "too difficult."

The two young men were disappointed in their hopes. "We scoured the horizon as if we were in a desert, but all in vain." Nothing came into sight, either supporter or plan. Francis accordingly confined his ambitions to obtaining his long-delayed independence. He was now so hungry for freedom that he was only happy in high places where he could enjoy a vast perspective, and found Vienna with its narrow streets insufferably stifling. The return to the Hofburg at the end of the summer became more of an ordeal every year.

Failing a wide horizon, he longed for action. But alas, he was now provided with no less than six warders, three soldiers and three civilians. "Nothing has been decided about the Prince," complained Dietrichstein on April 9. "I wear myself out telling them that he ought to be given a grenadier battalion permanently garrisoned in Vienna, at least until peace is restored to Europe; for any other destination would compromise the Prince in the eyes of France . . . and the future is so uncertain and so important!"

Metternich detested Francis more and more, the stronger his personality became.

As Gentz explained to Prokesch on March 24, 1831, the Chancellor "hates in him all that he has done to Napoleon's son. The very fact that he has to occupy himself with his affairs makes him more odious in his sight."

At the end of March, 1831, Metternich managed to carry out a plan he had had in mind for a long time: a plan to get rid of Prokesch. He sent him to represent the Austrian government in Bologna. "This is the first time since our friendship began," wrote Reichstadt on the day they parted, "that we have been separated for such a long time. Great events will no doubt take place before we meet again. For me, the hourglass will perhaps mark nothing but a succession of futile and wearisome tasks; perhaps honor and the voice of destiny will require me to sacrifice the dearest ambition of my youth at the very moment when its fulfillment offers itself to my eyes in such seductive colors."

Dietrichstein too was sorry to see Prokesch go. "That is the man he needed," he wrote to Marie Louise, "and the criticisms that have been made about that officer are absolutely scandalous. The Prince has vowed eternal friendship for him."

Doubt has often been cast on the quality of this friendship, but Prokesch's memoirs in no way exaggerate the immense affection Francis felt for him. We know this now from a delightful letter to Marie Louise in which Reichstadt wrote:

I was delighted to hear, dear Mamma, that my best friend, Major Prokesch, has recently been in Parma and that this time he did not have the misfortune of displeasing you; yes, dear Mamma, believe me when I say that that remarkable man is the only one who, by entering into my spirit and character, could have

guided them toward the objective which my name and my love
for Austria prescribe for them. Prokesch combines an ardent, judi-
cious spirit capable of the greatest sacrifices with rare perspicacity,
great breadth of vision, wide knowledge and incredible energy and
activity. I know that his great eyes which give him a childlike
look and the elegance of his speech create an unfavorable impression upon those who have often been taken in by appearances;
his physiognomy suggests a fanatic, whereas in fact he is forever
preaching prudence and moderation. I miss him as one misses a
beloved mistress, and I am always hoping to see him arrive unexpectedly one day.

What was Francis's life like at this time?

Almost every day he went for a drive in the Prater in his carriage
drawn by white, long-tailed Russian horses; or he galloped across the
Viennese countryside as far as Weidling, Salmannsdorf or the Tiergarten on his horse Mustapha; jumped gates and ditches on his white
stallion Harry or his bay mare Rouler, leaving his suite far behind him
—on April 30 he took thirty-seven minutes to cover the ten miles between Laxenburg and Vienna; lunched and dined with his grandfather,
the Prince of Salerno or some archduke or other—he ate very little, disliked exotic dishes and rarely drank wine; went to see the steamboat at
the Lusthaus; went to the ballet at the Opéra or the Burgtheater—he
loved staying up late and hated rising early; supervised the building of
the carriages he had ordered from Koller's; inspected his horses; avoided
Francis and Sophia in the Prater out of a spirit of independence;
wished the Crown Prince, now the King of Hungary, a happy birthday; went to his fencing school; had a "very animated" discussion with
Hartmann on the situation in France and the Battle of Austerlitz, or
else discussed Bernadotte's conduct with him "in a grandiloquent tone";
admired the Archduke Anthony's poppies at Schönbrunn or Bred-
mayer's tulips; drove in a cab to Daffinger's studio to pose for one of
his countless portraits; talked about "the way the Marshals behaved in
1814" with Obenaus, and gave them his approval; went through his
father's old comrades, making a note of those on whom he could count
if he returned to Paris; bought a new walking stick; matched a cravat
or a handkerchief with the color of one of his waistcoats; lost his temper
if he thought he had been snubbed—but soon calmed down, thanks to
his natural kindliness and compassion; devoured a book on the Napo-

leonic epic; expressed his indifference toward the long line of ancestors on his mother's side and pride in his father's glory; sharpened his quill with immense care—a task he entrusted to no one else; chose a high-spirited horse of the kind he liked best; grew angry because he read a book attacking his father's memory; told Obenaus that "if God gave him permission to address a prayer to him which He promised to grant, he would ask Him to come down to earth and give him His place"; disliked mixing with the crowds in the Prater; went to social gatherings where his exquisite kindness and courtesy were commented on by all and sundry; paid court to "the Chinaman" or Sophia; spent hours gazing at Gérard's portrait of Napoleon; kept worrying about what people thought of him; listened to readings of the *Allgemeine Zeitung*; played billiards; expressed his admiration for Alexander the Great "because he held the hand of his doctor Philippe while showing him a letter asserting that he intended to poison his master"; listened to Dietrichstein's perpetual complaints; pleased his tutor by leading to the altar—in his capacity as groomsman—Julie Dietrichstein, when she married Prince Ottingen-Wallenstein; called Hartmann "narrow-minded"; ran through the streets like a madman to see a march-past at the Graben; earned a severe reprimand for not taking part in the Corpus Christi procession; skimmed through the books he read; admired his fingernails; sat smoking by his window in the Hofburg; worried about his mother's health and wrote her delightful, spontaneous letters. . . .

And when night fell, he gave himself up to his dreams.

When he awoke, it was to a sad awareness of the realities of his life —the life of a twenty-year-old lieutenant-colonel without a battalion. It was a life which seemed all the emptier in that his friend Maurice Esterházy had also left Vienna. He had even greater affection for Esterházy than for Prokesch. The latter was the confidant of his political hopes; the former of his idle thoughts, his military aspirations and his amours.

"I never feel more at ease," he told Esterházy, "than when I write to you; I can then abandon myself entirely to the verve of my imagination or the feelings of my heart; reflection strikes me as an offense against friendship."

He wrote just as freely now to his mother, as he declared in this letter of May 25, 1831:

It is only to you, dear Mamma, that I can, must and wish to give my entire confidence; you to whom I owe everything since the day I was born, and who have always shown me so much love, even at times when my coldness and insensibility were bound to wound a heart as sensitive as yours; please believe that I deeply regret those occasions. I repeat all these statements which I have already made to you many times because, once my emancipation has taken place in a few days' time, I shall find myself among people I do not know and I shall be glad to find a few minutes every day in which to write to you in the language of the heart. But may I please beg you, dear Mamma, to write to me yourself from time to time, sending me your instructions, your advice and whatever requests you may wish to address to me. I swear to be absolutely trustful and frank with you. I am convinced that you will grant my request, for a mother such as yourself cannot know greater joy than that of being her son's guardian angel.

The terrible wound inflicted on him by the discovery that his mother had borne another man's children during his father's lifetime had now healed. He was touched by his mother's thoughtlessness and weakness. And he spoke to her now as he might have done to an elder sister for whom he had unlimited resources of indulgence and understanding.

16

❦

The Colonel

ON JUNE 14, 1831, the anniversary of Marengo and Friedland, Baron von Obenaus wrote in his diary:

"The military gentlemen have taken up their duties. General Hartmann came as early as eight o'clock in the morning and complimented the Prince on his uniform. Count Dietrichstein arrived next and said that our work was finished and that we were going to withdraw without any fuss."

The poor tutor was so upset and so unhappy that his hand shook when he wrote to Marie Louise. Yet he had got his way: Francis would not be leaving for Brünn or Prague, but staying at the Hofburg or at Schönbrunn. His grandfather had posted him to the 60th Regiment of the Hungarian Infantry, whose colonel was Count Ignatius Gyulaï, the Minister of War, soon to be replaced by Prince Gustave Wasa. To Dietrichstein's great and understandable disappointment, Francis was not given the colonelcy of a regiment but merely put in charge of a battalion. He had blushed with pleasure for all that. Dietrichstein was more ambitious. Though he was sincerely upset at losing his pupil, up to the very last moment he went on heaping reproaches upon him on the slightest pretext: Francis's "dissimulation," his "boastfulness," his "insistence on trying everything" and his "refusal to take advice" formed the substance of his litanies. As late as June 11 we find him writing that "the Prince likes living expensively and ringing the changes, simply to copy the young men he hears about. The way he

has of continually forgetting himself and what he owes his name causes
me some painful moments. We shall see if and when reason conquers
these penchants and this spirit of opposition. . . ."

On the 15th, a few hours before he went on active service, there
was a dramatic scene in Francis's room which he later recounted as
follows:

On the eve of my taking up my regimental duties, Count Die-
trichstein searched every drawer in my cupboard; finding a drawer
that was locked, he pressed me so hard that I opened it immediately.
Inside was my correspondence with Maurice Esterházy while he
was in Vienna, and the words "the Chinaman," as we called the
lady in question, occurring in the first lines of one letter, revealed
the nature of their contents. Furious, as usual, he snapped:
"What's this? An amorous correspondence?"
I answered coldly:
"You can guess with whom."
"You write to her?"
"No!"
"Then you use an intermediary who is known to me?"
And he guessed straightaway who it was.
"For the love of Heaven," I said, "keep calm!"—for we were not
alone in the room and everyone was looking at us—"You will have
all the letters by tomorrow."
The good man was satisfied with that, and an hour later every-
thing had been burned. He was rather put out when he was told,
but the whole affair was soon forgotten.

The next day Dietrichstein had not forgotten—especially as he had
discovered that with Esterházy Francis called him, not just "my wife"
as with Sophia, but "my old woman." He wrote again to Parma complaining about his pupil's independent spirit and what he called his
"follies." "I have given him the benefit of my advice, but once I have
handed over to Moll, who is to be in charge of the household, I shall
stand aloof, for there is nothing I can do and if I knew what was happening I should die of grief and anger. . . . I fear for his health, if he
fails to look after it and those gentlemen lack the courage to oppose his
follies."

The unfortunate tutor hoped that he might receive "some public token of gratitude" for having educated Napoleon's son. But nothing of the sort happened and he considered that he had been turned out "like a lackey": "What an outrageous way to behave after years of hard work and devoted service!"

For his part, Francis was beside himself with joy. At six o'clock on the morning of the 16th, dressed in a white tunic with steel-green braid and blue breeches trimmed with silver, he had gone to collect his battalion at the Alslergasse barracks and had taken them out to drill on the glacis. At eleven o'clock he had made a point of taking personal command of a "function" at the Hôtel des Invalides. He could have got out of this, "but," sighed Dietrichstein out of force of habit, "he is already beginning to do as he pleases." Dietrichstein had furnished a few rooms for him at the Alsler-Kaserne, and it was from there that Francis wrote to his mother the same day: "I am very happy, very pleased with the battalion which the Emperor has been kind enough to give me. Over half the men are new recruits and there are a good many young officers, but officers and men are actuated by the best will in the world; we shall do our training together and that will be another bond between us. I beg you to believe, dearest Mamma, that I should have liked to be able to write you a very long letter, but I am prevented from doing so by more service matters of which my aide-de-camp has just informed me. . . . Pray be content, dearest Mamma, with these few lines; I could not refrain from telling you of this initial joy of mine. . . ."

The letter was only sixteen lines long. Dietrichstein found it on his ex-pupil's desk and exclaimed: "What a way to write a letter! And it is badly folded too! His obstinacy and his nonchalance are shown in the smallest things. I would never have dared to send my mother a letter like that! And although I have provided him with paper and envelopes, he scorns to use them. . . ."

The next day Francis wrote again from the barracks, after taking his first parade:

> I have come back bathed in perspiration, for the heat is stifling and our uniforms are not designed for summer. On the whole they are pleased with my battalion, which is showing quite astonishing enthusiasm for such young soldiers, who usually see nothing but the unpleasant side of army life. I am in good health; I have changed my habits slightly, having to get up at four in the morn-

ing every day and having to do more riding than I was accustomed to. You will be justly annoyed at the laconicism and brevity of my letters, but I write them only to make you the repository of my first feelings; pray believe, dearest Mamma, that this habit is necessary to my heart. . . . I kiss your hand, assure you of my liveliest gratitude and sincerest love, and remain for life your very obedient son,

FRANCIS

He became an excellent battalion commander, "strict but just toward his subordinates." His "fiery temperament" soon captivated his chief, the Prince of Wasa. His "young soldiers" worshiped him. One day when he rode slowly by on his white horse, he looked so handsome, so serious, so soldierly that they could not refrain from giving him a cheer, in defiance of their machinelike discipline.

Why though did Kutschera and Hartmann force Francis to perform duties more consistent with the rank of sergeant-major than that of lieutenant-colonel? Marmont, who was disgusted by this "pedantic interpretation of the military profession," has given us the explanation: for the Austria of that time "being a general" consisted of "knowing how to drill troops." These maneuvers on the glacis, these endless hours spent on horseback in front of his two hundred men tired the young lieutenant-colonel. After shouting orders intended to be heard above the noise of carriages rattling over the cobblestones a few yards away, his voice would suddenly give out. "Often," Prokesch tells us, "he would grow angry with his physical constitution and try to force his body to obey him as if he were breaking in a horse. . . ." Malfatti did what he could to restrain this excessive zeal. In his opinion the loss of voice from which Francis suffered had nothing to do with his bronchial trouble but was simply due to the strain imposed by his command. However, Francis merely shrugged his shoulders at the doctor's prudent recommendations. To make matters worse, he had started smoking in the barracks, either, as Marie Louise maintained, "out of Anglomania or the desire to imitate his late father" or "out of bravado and the desire to imitate others," as Dietrichstein believed. The latter "remonstrated" with him, pointing out that his voice and throat were bound to suffer if he went on smoking, but all in vain.

Francis was like a young colt that had broken loose and wanted to enjoy his comparative freedom to the full. He lived beyond his means, got into debt to buy a gig, and insisted on costly changes both in his stables and in his domestic staff, whose livery he wanted to have altered. In everything he did there was the same feverish ardor with which he galloped through the Vienna Woods, riding his horses to death, the same disturbing tendency to burn the candle at both ends. His health became worse every day as a result. "The Prince," wrote Dietrichstein on July 16, "is going to cause me serious anxiety, especially as he refuses to listen to any advice and our doctors can think of nothing but cruel and drastic remedies which are more likely to kill than cure."

Francis was deeply touched by his old tutor's concern for him, and decided to give him a surprise. One evening Dietrichstein came home to find a portrait of Reichstadt standing beside his bed. "This was the most gracious and thoughtful idea imaginable, and Daffinger has done a masterly portrait which is also a perfect likeness. The Prince is shown full-face, informally dressed in a frock coat, sitting with his left arm resting on the armchair and his right on the table. In his left hand he is holding a glove and a colored handkerchief, and in his right hand he has a pencil with which he is writing on a sheet of paper these words: 'Eternal gratitude' [which he actually wrote himself, in a fine and delicate hand]. Beside him there are two books, one of which has *The Story of Napoleon* in gilt lettering on the spine! An ingenious thought, which gives some idea of my relationship with the Prince and the frankness and sincerity that I have always shown him. I was completely overwhelmed and wept for all of an hour, recalling the whole of my career and thinking of the comfort the Prince was now bringing me by his conduct toward me."

On July 29, Francis led General Salin's funeral procession through the streets of Vienna. He was wearing the grand cordon of St. Stephen across his white uniform, as well as the star of that Order and the Parmesan Order of St. George. The crowds lining the route looked at Napoleon's son with a certain tenderness mingled with curiosity. All the girls, so it was said, were in love with this Prince Charming. "I have often noticed," says an eye-witness, "that when he looked at them, roses blossomed in their cheeks and their eyes sparkled like stars, sending out flashes of fire."

His voice was still muffled. He had grown much thinner and perspired a great deal. Five days later, he took a parade in front of the Hofburg. Watching him from one of the palace windows were the

Archduchess Sophia, little Francis Joseph—the future Emperor—and his governess, Baroness Sturmfeder. The latter expressed disquiet over Francis's yellow complexion which seemed to her to bode no good. As for Sophia, she gazed tenderly at the handsome young Colonel—her "dear old friend" she called him. But Reichstadt had eyes only for his troops and did not look up at the balcony. He made every effort to resemble his father, trying to sit his horse like Napoleon and even wearing his hat the same way. And the curved saber he raised so proudly had once flashed in the sunlight of the Pyramids.

He was a prey to considerable anxiety at this time. Metternich had just signed the Carlsbad Convention with Russia and Prussia, an agreement clearly directed against France. There was talk of another war. This time Reichstadt—so he wrote to his mother on August 2—feared that a conflict might start in which he would have no right to take part: "Mind and heart, duty and honor forbid me ever to act against the interests of France." Keeping faith with his father's last orders, he would be condemned to see his comrades coming home "crowned with victory" while he had nothing to show but "a sword doomed to go rusty in time of war and to shine only on the parade ground."

Summer, 1831.

Cholera had fallen upon Europe and was exacting a fearful toll. When it first appeared in Poland it was decided to cut Europe into two parts with a triple line of troops stretching from the North Sea to the Adriatic. This ancestor of the twentieth-century Iron Curtain had no perceptible effect. "If the disease is really contagious," wrote Francis very sensibly, "then birds can carry the germ to us just as well as men." Sure enough, taking no notice of the sanitary cordon, the cholera soon reached Vienna and the imperial family took refuge at Schönbrunn.

"Never," Francis told his mother, "has Schönbrunn been so crowded as it is now, with fear driving all and sundry to discover some business connection with the Court, which is shutting itself up in the castle as if it were a huge monastery. The Emperor, the Empress, the King and Queen of Hungary, the Archduke Francis and the Archduchess, Prince Leopold and his wife, the Archdukes Louis and Anthony, the whole Metternich family, Count Kollavrath and Revitski and all the ambassadors hope to find a place of refuge from the cholera in the precincts of Schönbrunn, which is being surrounded with quarantine posts."

Reichstadt for his part refused to leave Vienna and his beloved Alsler-Kaserne. However, Dietrichstein tells us that "he has done no drilling now for four or five days, in an attempt to save his voice, but it is no better for all that. I gather that Malfatti has prescribed a remedy for him, but alas, the great doctor no longer inspires any confidence in me. The trachea is the Prince's weak point; it is causing me the liveliest anxiety, as does everything that concerns him."

But it is an ill wind that blows nobody good. Francis was ordered to go to the "monastery" at Schönbrunn. Dietrichstein had won his case.

The Emperor [Francis informed Marie Louise] has finally given in to the entreaties of those who put my future health before my present honor, so that I too must enter that privileged abode. Imagine my delight, dearest Mamma, at being parted from my battalion; an officer should share every danger with his men, and being forced to leave one's post at a time when one's hand should be on one's sword to protect the State against possible perils is just as shameful as deserting in the face of the enemy, since fighting the latter is not a more vital duty than maintaining law and order. The fact that it is the Emperor's wish that I should go to Schönbrunn saves my honor but cannot ease my conscience, and I am disgusted at the idea of running away from any kind of danger when duty calls. . . .

The Eaglet arrived at Schönbrunn pale, drawn and out of breath, and settled into his apartments in the west wing. Malfatti had prescribed—and with some difficulty obtained—a fortnight's rest. "No one," lamented Dietrichstein on September 3, "suffers more than I do on seeing how thin and ill the Prince is looking; I do believe he has actually grown taller since March 20 and I want to make sure. The state of his health is worrying the Court. Why have they never taken my advice? I keep harping on the same string because the advice I tendered was inspired by my innermost feelings. The colonel of a regiment, that is what the Prince ought to be, and that is what would save him. . . ."

Dietrichstein was thinking of an honorary command which would relieve his former pupil of the thankless tasks which he was performing with as much passionate energy as if he were fighting a battle. In point of fact, of course, he *was* fighting a battle—a struggle to conquer his disease and go on living.

"I am angry," he told Malfatti one day when the latter found him stretched out on a sofa, "I am angry with this wretched body of mine which can't obey the dictates of my spirit!"

"It is indeed a pity," replied the doctor, "that Your Highness cannot change bodies as he changes horses when he has tired them out; but I do beg you to remember, Monseigneur, that you possess an iron spirit in a body of crystal, and the continued abuse of your will power can only do you harm."

This time he felt so ill that he could no longer conceal his illness from his mother:

"A rather severe catarrhal chill prevented me from writing to you on your name-day as I would have wished. My health had suffered somewhat from the strain of this summer and my chest especially had been affected by the efforts I had made as a battalion commander. I had already been coughing for three weeks when a violent chill, which lasted only one evening, put me in the hands of Malfatti, who is treating me wonderfully well."

For his part, Malfatti informed Marie Louise of her son's illness on September 3, in a letter written in Italian. In his opinion "the catarrhal infection accompanied by a passing fever, a cough, slight expectoration and rheumatic pains in the right shoulder" was the result of "the indescribable zeal and passion with which H.H. has thrown himself into his new career." The doctor's blindness and incompetence are self-evident.

"Thanks be to God," he added, "H.H.'s condition has greatly improved and his complete recovery is within sight. The principal difficulty which I still have to overcome is how to gain time, hold him in check, and restrain a very determined and enterprising spirit."

Forced to rest, Francis took up reading.

I am taking care of my physique [he told his friend Esterházy on September 2] and furnishing my mind with vast quantities of instructive literature—the only pastime left to me. When I look back over the past fortnight, I am astonished at the amount of reading I have done. Among other things I have read some extremely interesting observations on Italy in which the poet of *Le Génie du Christianisme* [Chateaubriand] has skillfully woven an elegant tissue around a treasury of ancient inscriptions. This work interested me greatly, but as a compilation and not an original study, for every line bore the stamp of a bored and sated spirit, an aimless wanderer with no knowledge of the realities of life. I have also read a work on the first principles of astronomy. This is a field of study which must surely increase our admiration of the universe, remind us of our insignificance, and inspire us with a philosophy which, based on positive, palpable and incontestable laws, makes the soul aware only of what is in conformity with the purpose of the universe; it should fulfill the same service for me as a bath does for the body, by ridding my mind of all the futile ideas which have become attached to it. I am looking in vain for a real man: so far I have not found one. . . .

Prokesch had not come back from Boulogne, and Francis felt lonely and abandoned. He was therefore delighted to be able to wring from Malfatti permission to resume his military duties. On September 14 he was once again drilling his battalion. It was a cold day, and the lieutenant-colonel's voice was so weak that it "startled" Dietrichstein. He addressed certain "observations" to his former pupil, but Francis took them very badly. A big parade was going to be held on the Schmelz on the 27th, and he wanted to get ready for it. "I can understand how he feels," sighed the tutor, "but like this he is going to injure his health, perhaps permanently, and all for two hours of futile pomp. It bodes no good for him in my opinion." Francis was out drilling again the next day, and his voice struck onlookers as "alarmingly weak." Then some cases of cholera were reported at the Alsler-Kaserne, and Francis returned to Schönbrunn. The epidemic was assuming terrifying proportions. "It is not just the lower classes it is attacking here," observed Dietrichstein, "but the well-to-do. This is all the more disturbing in that it shows that the air is polluted with this miasma, which spares no one and appears in the unlikeliest places. I have lost count of those who have already fallen victims to it."

Francis dragged himself about from one room to another. At the parade on the Schmelz, which was attended by the entire Court, he was in the front rank at the head of his battalion. He managed to make himself heard by his troops, but when the march-past was over Malfatti told the Emperor that the Prince's condition called for two months of complete rest. Turning to his grandson, the Emperor said: "You heard what Dr. Malfatti has just said; you will go to Schönbrunn immediately."

The young colonel bowed in acquiescence, but as he straightened up he shot an indignant look at the doctor and snapped: "So you're the one who's putting me under arrest."

To please Sophia, who wanted to give the Emperor a portrait of his three grandchildren for his birthday on October 4, he agreed to turn his inactivity to good use by posing for Johan Elder with little Francis Charles on his lap and by his side Maria Caroline of Salerno, the future Duchesse d'Aumale, holding Francis I's canary in one hand.

On October 1, to his complete surprise and "indescribable joy," Prokesch arrived at Schönbrunn. "He seemed to come to life again when he saw him," reports Dietrichstein. "Conversation with him is extremely useful to the Prince, who can discuss anything he likes with him and so acquires a mass of news and information which would otherwise remain unknown to him. . . ." And Francis for his part wrote the next day to his friend:

> My heart filled with joy at the sight of you, and I myself was surprised to see what power you have over it. Countless thoughts keep crossing my mind in connection with my situation, politics, history, this military science of ours which can consolidate or destroy the power of States, and many other things which badly need your intelligence, your knowledge, your advice and your judgment to come to fruition. I have so many ideas—and as it is almost a crime here to entertain ideas of this nature, I thrust them back into the recesses of my soul, whence they emerge only very occasionally. . . . And now you have come back. You will not reprove me when my thoughts fly rather too high . . . and you will not hasten to bring them down.

Prokesch however had found his friend less hotheaded than of old. "His ambitions had not altered," he tells us, "but his hopes had diminished. During the lengthy period in which we had been living far apart from one another he had seen no indication on the political horizon that his return was seriously desired in France; in Poland the insurrection was now nothing more than a seditious movement on the point of being suppressed; in Italy only the secret societies were still active and the country itself offered no political arena worthy of his name. Here and elsewhere he could see this name of his, which he regarded as a sacred heritage, being profaned by the Revolution."

Yet the name of Napoleon II had been put back on the European chessboard. It is true that on September 29 Sébastiani had accepted a general disarmament plan which obliged all the powers to reduce their armed forces to peacetime proportions, and it is true that this had produced a marked improvement in Franco-Austrian relations—more especially as Belgium had ceased to be another subject of discord since a Saxe-Coburg had become King of the Belgians—but even so Metternich still had nothing but contempt for Louis Philippe's government.

"Louis Philippe will go under," he prophesied, "and Henri V will succeed him."

Henri V or Napoleon II?

During the riot in the Place Vendôme on May 9, 1831, the crowds —in what Apponyi called "a queer hotch-potch"—had sung the "Carmagnole" and the "Marseillaise," and had shouted "Long live Napoleon II!" and "Long live the Republic!" After all, for Napoleon II's supporters, an alliance with the Republicans was one way of advancing the Bonapartist cause. . . .

On September 6, 1831, Victor Hugo wrote to King Joseph:

> Providence usually moves slowly. She can be encouraged to move faster. It is because I am devoted to both France and liberty that I have faith in your royal nephew's future. He can give notable service to his country. If he were to offer, as I have no doubt he would, all the necessary guarantees to honor the ideas of emancipation, progress and liberty, no one would rally to the new order of things more eagerly than I; and with me, Sire, I think I may safely say all the young people of France, who reverence the name of the Emperor and over whom, obscure though I am, I may have certain influence. It is to the young people that we should turn now, Sire. The old men of the Empire have either shown base ingratitude or else are completely worn out. The young people are everything in France today. They carry within themselves the future of this country, and they are well aware of it. Count on me, Sire; what little I can do, I shall do for the heir to the greatest name in the world. I believe that he can save France. This I shall say; this I shall write; this, God willing, I shall publish. . . .

At the same time the Chamber of Deputies was debating at great length the ban on the Bonaparte family which had already been decided on by the previous Chamber and applied also to Charles X's family. This time the question was whether to abrogate the death

penalty provided for in the event of the Duc de Bordeaux or the Duke
of Reichstadt ever returning to France. After interminable discussion
it was decided that the pretenders should remain under sentence of
exile, but that their appearance on French soil should not involve them
with an execution squad.

In the same month of October, 1831, Chateaubriand's mighty voice
was heard on this question. Francis eagerly devoured his pamphlet
On the Banishment of Charles X in which he himself was frequently
mentioned. According to the poet, France's only hope lay with Henri
V, but he nonetheless gave due weight to Napoleon II's chances after
the "Three Glorious Days" of the 1830 Revolution:

> What antiquity bestowed on the Duc de Bordeaux, the Duke
> of Reichstadt derived from his father's glory. Napoleon had moved
> faster than a royal line: taking giant strides, in ten years he had
> put ten centuries behind him. What is more, the Duke of Reich-
> stadt offered men of religion and men swayed by the prejudices of
> blood what was most likely to appeal to their ideas: a crown con-
> ferred by the Sovereign Pontiff; nobility conferred by a daughter
> of the Caesars. As I have observed elsewhere, his mother gave him
> the past, his father the future. There were still whole generations
> all over France who, in recognizing Napoleon II, would only have
> been returning to the allegiance they had sworn to Napoleon I.
> The Army would have been proud to accept the offspring of their
> victories.

Francis himself had said to Prokesch: "The son of the Archduchess
Marie Louise and the Emperor whom the whole of Europe had
acknowledged as its master could surely offer the Powers more solid
guarantees than the son of Philippe Égalité. . . ."

Yet Reichstadt must have felt disheartened as he read the rest of
Chateaubriand's pamphlet, for he knew that the objections raised in
August, 1830, still held good in 1831: "But the Duke of Reichstadt's
foreign upbringing and the principles of absolutism which he was
bound to have imbibed in Vienna raised a barrier between himself and
the French nation. The people would always have seen a German on
the French throne; they would always have suspected the existence
of an Austrian cabinet at the Tuileries; the son would have appeared
to have inherited his father's despotism rather than his father's glory."

There was not the slightest suggestion of despotism, however, in the aim of those who were plotting to put the King of Rome on his father's throne: what they had in mind was a democratic empire. First of all there was Napoleon's brother Jerome, who had married one of the Emperor Francis's nieces, and after him Lucien and Joseph. Then there was General de Montholon, agitating as fanatically as ever, this time with the support of the Republican deputy Mauguin. In the early summer of 1831 Napoleon's companion on St. Helena had gone to see the Comte de Bombelles, the Austrian Minister at Berne, armed with the draft of the most liberal of all imperial constitutions.

M. Mauguin [the diplomat wrote to Metternich] asks for no written engagement from Austria which might look like a preliminary secret treaty, but would be content with a verbal promise made to General de Montholon by Your Highness that Austria would not declare war but would ally herself with Napoleon II. In return for this promise, M. de Montholon, who is in M. Mauguin's confidence, undertakes that the latter will give our Cabinet the key to all the secret conspiracies which have brought about the troubles in Germany, Belgium, Poland, Italy and even Russia. He also undertakes to turn against Jacobinism all the forces employed in its development since the fall of Napoleon.

Metternich had made no reply, but Montholon, in no way discouraged, had put forward further proposals:

"If the Vienna Cabinet were to allow the Duke of Reichstadt to go to the French frontier, a hundred thousand National Guards would go to meet him and escort him to Paris, where the Chamber of Deputies would invest him with dictatorial powers for a period of five years."

This time Metternich expressed a certain surprise:

"It is astonishing to say the least," he wrote to Bombelles, "that a man who wants to deal with us as one Power with another, who pretends to regard our silence as a declaration of war, who talks of moving a hundred thousand men hither and thither, and who has the Chamber of Deputies at his beck and call, has not thought it necessary to furnish any proof in support of his assertions—assertions so far-reaching as to presuppose the possession of great power and unlimited resources."

Metternich was right, but the fact that he did not show Montholon the door proves that the Austrian Chancellor wanted to keep the Napoleon II card in his hand.

The conspirators' plans became clearer when Montholon expounded them to Prince von Dietrichstein in the middle of September, 1831, when the latter was passing through Berne. Count Maurice's brother shrugged his shoulders but nonetheless passed Mauguin's proposals on to Metternich. The Deputy offered Austria a choice of three different arrangements designed to replace Louis Philippe. This is the text of Prince Dietrichstein's report:

Either: Napoleon II replacing the present régime with Europe's consent, leaving their compatriots to decide between him and Henri V.

Or: Napoleon II supported by Austria alone, with some assistance from Italy; French assistance to be provided at Lyons on the route taken by his father in 1815.

Or again: Napoleon II by himself, escaping from Germany and provided with money.

Thus far—provided that Louis Philippe kindly agreed to take himself off—there was some sense in these proposals. What followed, however, falls within the domain of psychiatry. Marie Louise was to surrender Parma and go to reign over Belgium, but the country was to revert to her son on her death. If Austria did not want to have anything to do with it, the restoration could be carried out with the help of "relatives on the father's side," though this solution would only be adopted "in the last extremity." And finally, if Metternich refused to open the Eaglet's cage, these odd conspirators—who were not so much Bonapartists as enemies of the bourgeois monarchy—had a spare monarch to put forward: Henri V, with the Duchesse de Berry as Regent. Marshal Soult would be made Constable of France, Lafayette a marshal and Chateaubriand a minister.

In other words, Mauguin did not care whom he joined forces with against Louis Philippe, provided the pickings were good.

Metternich had no liking for Louis Philippe—a king of the barricades—but he nonetheless preferred him to a change of régime which would lead France, not toward an imperial restoration, but toward a state of anarchy which would spread like the cholera all over Europe. In his opinion, a country was not governed by memories of vanished glory. The Duke of Reichstadt might be the last spark from the Napoleonic fire, but he himself was going to take care that that spark did not set Europe aflame. He therefore responded to Montholon's offers by denouncing Mauguin to Casimir Périer; he had the decency, how-ever, not to mention the name of the Emperor's companion in captivity.

One can imagine how furious Casimir Périer must have been. The measures taken against the Bonapartists were made harsher than ever, but at the same time Louis Philippe cunningly appropriated the glory of the Empire for himself. The bourgeois monarch slipped into the lion's skin. He surrounded himself with the Emperor's old servants and gave instructions for the decree of April 3 restoring the statue of Napo-leon to its place on the Vendôme Column to be put into effect. Alas, the imperial effigy would not return to the square designed by Louis XIV until a year, almost to the day, after the Eaglet's death. In the meantime, pending the moment when he himself would be turned out of the Tuileries and replaced by the third Napoleon, the bourgeois monarch could sleep in peace. In the course of the coming months, France's thoughts would be constantly with the son of Napoleon. But now she would think of him, not as the King of Rome, but only as the Duke of Reichstadt.

Francis had remained in ignorance of most of these plots to restore him to the throne, but what little had filtered through to him had con-vinced him that his supporters were to be counted among those hot-heads whose only achievement was to turn him into an adventurer.

The thought that his chances of returning to Paris were diminish-ing "burned him up," to use Prokesch's words. In an attempt to re-store his confidence, his friend tried to convince him that Louis Phi-lippe would be bound to fall in time, that a period of anarchy would follow, and that finally both France and Europe would summon the son of Napoleon to the throne.

He might perhaps be able to obtain his grandfather's support.

"If my father were alive, I should fight to the last gasp to bring about his return to France," he had said to the Emperor one day.

And the latter, after a moment's silence, had murmured: "You would have been right to do so, Franz, and I would probably have helped you, if not openly then at least by giving you money."

Surely the Emperor would stand up to Metternich in the event of an imperial restoration in his grandson's favor? Why, the two young men asked themselves, should they not force his hand by putting into operation the plan they had worked out the year before? Why should they not slip away secretly and "appear suddenly in France"?

However, they soon saw that this project was something of a pipe dream. After all, what kind of welcome could they expect? And would Francis's state of health allow him to undertake a journey of this sort? For the time being, they obviously had no alternative but to shelve their plan and think no more about it.

On October 15 Francis wrote a long letter to his mother describing the precautions being taken at Schönbrunn against the cholera and adding:

> In this colony of ours, composed of all those persons who have the most reason to be afraid since they have the most to lose, I have been pleased to discover none of that faintheartedness I had expected. We have only the Emperor's personal courage to thank for the high standard of behavior, if I may so describe it, which we have so far maintained; it has frequently been suggested that he should shut himself up, but he has always refused; he goes into Vienna three times a week to inspect public works, always dressed in his little brown frock coat and never imagining that he is doing something admirable—something indeed beyond the comprehension of heartless, calculating folk. The ladies of the Court hold a *conversazione* every evening, which I have attended twice for my sins, for it is as boring as can be. How can a social gathering be anything else without either some sentimental interest or superabundant wit? I go riding in the morning, I dine with the Emperor; I do some reading; I sup with the Emperor and I start reading again. I am well content with this kind of life, and if only I did not miss my troops I should be perfectly happy to spend the whole winter in this way, for I feel so sad and lethargic that it sometimes drives me to despair; I am too fond of action, perhaps because I know it so little, to find this state of mind natural.

He often discussed what he was reading with Malfatti, whom he had forgiven for putting him "under arrest" for two months. One of his favorite authors was Byron.

"There is in this great poet," he said, "a profound and melancholy sense of mystery which corresponds with my own innermost feelings; my mind takes pleasure in identifying itself with his."

"During your absence," he had written to Prokesch, "my imagination has busied itself with two subjects in particular: first of all, political relations in Europe today, and secondly religion; but this latter subject is too lofty and calls for too much time and attention for me even to broach it in this letter."

He had greeted his friend with the words: "You have always been perfectly frank with me. Do you believe in Jesus Christ? Do you believe in what the Church teaches?"

He had begun to lose his faith, but his grandfather's piety was helping him to overcome this crisis. He spoke admiringly to Prokesch of the Emperor of Austria:

> In the heat of this conversation, which revealed to me a side of his soul with which I was unfamiliar, the Prince jumped up, ran to a cupboard, took out a book, and with touching eagerness tore out a page which he handed to me with the words:
>
> "May this souvenir which I beg you to accept show you how precious this moment is to me!"
>
> I took the sheet of paper: it was the title page of Albach's *Heilige Anklänge,* on which the Emperor had written:
>
> "May God give you light and strength in every struggle and in every circumstance in your life: such is the sincere wish of your loving grandparents. Francis, Caroline Augusta."

On November 16, the specter of the cholera having receded, Schönbrunn emptied and Francis returned to the Hofburg. We know from Dietrichstein that Reichstadt continued to lead a solitary life for another two or three weeks and did not dare go back to the Alslergasse. He felt sullen, crabbed, morose. He wandered aimlessly about wishing that he could do some writing—that would allow him, he said, to "ransack his imagination"—but recognizing that that wish was "like mustard after dinner." The romantic Prince's life was uneventful. "Sadness delights me," he told his mother on December 2, 1831. "If one can succeed in creating a world of one's own within oneself by meditating and studying the sciences, then one can be sure of always sailing untroubled seas; and I can quite understand a philosopher who, from his lofty garret, looks down with contempt at the palaces of the great, and despises their rich dinners as he eats his morsel of bread. I see very few people, but the difference in their characters greatly enlivens my day. . . ."

Resting as Malfatti insisted that he should was a sore trial for Reichstadt, who found nothing harder than deferring to someone else's will. He had a genuine horror of obedience, except when it was required by military discipline. As Obenaus once observed, he "neglected the duties allotted to him in order to expend all his energy on unimportant tasks which he had undertaken of his own free will."

However, early this winter, he recognized that his doctor was right. He was leading a quieter life and feeling momentarily better for it. True, his voice had not come back, but the optimistic—not to say blind—Malfatti was nonetheless quite satisfied with his patient's condition. "He has even given the Prince permission to smoke from time to time," grumbled Dietrichstein, "and I keep seeing that dreadful box on his table with two enormous pipes, although he assures me that he does not smoke."

He spent the month of December in a semilethargic condition. He dozed and daydreamed, looking at the Gérard portrait of Napoleon which Marie Louise, at Dietrichstein's request, had asked her son to hang in his bedroom.

Finding him too morose for his liking, Malfatti urged him to go out in the evenings once more, and soon Francis could be seen again at balls and receptions. As had been the case a year before, on his entry into society, there was a "general stir of interest" as soon as his slim white silhouette appeared. He no longer took part in the dancing, preferring the pleasures of conversation, in which he indulged with "astonishing penetration." All who talked to him were impressed by the extraordinary maturity of his mind, the irresistible charm and fascination of his personality. He was only twenty years old, but he already seemed to possess the art of using other men, his father's greatest quality.

"In my opinion," said Malfatti, "his most striking and typical characteristic was the ability to penetrate to the very depths of a man's heart, the intelligence with which he obtained the truth by means of skillful questions which he put forward like so many traps."

Feeling decidedly better, Reichstadt went hunting four times with the Emperor and spent most of his evenings with Gustav Neipperg. They were seen together at the theater, and Vienna started talking again about the love affairs of Napoleon's son, to whom they attributed a whole series of liaisons. Nandine, who had been well and truly forgotten, seemed to have been replaced by the charming Countess Almassy. Francis had also been greatly attracted by a beautiful Circassian whom Count Pisani had bought as a child from some gypsies and later married. It was said that Francis wrote to her, but as with the Countesses Károlyi and Almassy, the "rest" will always remain their secret.

If Marshal Maison and many others doubtless exaggerate Francis's sensual excesses, Prokesch for his part is a little too naïve in his belief in his friend's "noble ingenuousness" and "innocent purity." "He went to the grave," he tells us, "without ever touching a woman." That is not impossible, of course, but it seems a little strange that Count Maurice Esterházy and Gustav Neipperg, who both belonged to Vienna's gilded youth, should never have taken their friend with them on one of their escapades, especially since Francis was extremely susceptible to feminine charm. His heredity, after all, was scarcely likely to encourage continence. . . . Nor should we forget that, according to Mme. de Montet, Austrian high society at this time was "the most dissolute" imaginable.

On the other hand we must accept Prokesch's assurance that Francis never spoke to Fanny Essler, of whom Théophile Gautier once remarked that men's eyes "traveled like caresses up and down her plump and pretty body, which one might imagine to have been copied from some divine statue of the time of Pericles." The loveliest dancer of her age probably never aroused the love of Napoleon's son, and this is a matter for regret. The young woman who held "the golden scepter of beauty" belonged at this time to Gentz, a bent old man of sixty-seven who wore pince-nez and a reddish wig. The body of Diana the Huntress which so delighted Théophile Gautier, whose voluptuously rounded legs and that delightfully full bosom—"a rare sight in the land of the entrechat"—would undoubtedly have been better matched with the twenty summers of the handsomest prince in Vienna.

So much the worse for the legend . . .

In the same month of December, 1831, Prokesch, Dietrichstein and Gustav Neipperg thought up a plot to rouse Francis from his apathy and depression. From his box at the Court theater he had noticed the singer Thérèse Pêche. Prokesch considered that a liaison with this young woman "endowed with wit and feeling" would have had a salutary effect on him. "I think that it would have saved his life by turning his thoughts away from the past and the future and giving new strength to his soul."

Mlle. Pêche was promptly told what was expected of her, and waited for Francis in her dressing room. He arrived with Gustav Neipperg. The young woman gave him to understand that she would be delighted to become the principal character in the plot.

"This assurance displeased me," Francis told Prokesch later.

And his liaison with the singer ended before it had ever begun.

As often as he could, he went off with Gustav, telling his "warders" nothing of what they planned to do. Dietrichstein was in despair at being unable to watch over him any more. "It is essential," he wrote to Marie Louise on December 13, "that you should urge the Prince to observe that *decorum* which he is so fond of ignoring, to give up those deplorable *incognitos* of his which are breaking my heart, and to remember *his station in life!*"

A few days later the poor man was reprimanding Francis for scamping his letters to his mother, "for to judge by the last one, that is to say by the address (written at the top, where no one ever puts it, and penned with a badly cut quill), I imagine that the letter itself was dashed off in morning, before you went hunting, instead of being thought out two days before. . . ."

One can scarcely blame Francis for paying no attention to the never-ending complaints of a sometime tutor who criticized a lieutenant-colonel for the way he cut his quills.

At the very beginning of 1832—his last year of life—Francis declared that he was cured, and Malfatti allowed him to resume his military duties. On January 16 he appeared in public at the head of his battalion at General von Siegenthal's funeral. It was bitterly cold—the thermometer, it is said, was at zero. Francis felt the cold air enveloping his thin body and freezing him to the marrow. When he reached the Josephplatz he lifted his curved saber to order a salute to be fired, but his voice broke and he could not make himself heard. With tears in his eyes he handed over to one of his officers and went back to the Hofburg shaking with fever.

He had caught pneumonia.

He could not hide his fury at having failed to conceal his illness any longer. Dietrichstein put the blame on tobacco for "drying up his throat and chest." But he added that "he does everything he can to injure his health, even though his sickly appearance and people's outspoken speculations and suppositions about it ought to make him behave more reasonably. I am curious to know how many days Malfatti is going to confine him to his room, for 'up there' [in the Emperor's entourage], while commenting sympathetically on his appearance, they seem to doubt whether he is really ill, regarding his indisposition as insignificant and imagining that my successors are just coddling him to back up my opinions. . . . They forget that the Prince has outgrown his strength, that he was given his freedom before he had attained his full development, that his constitution is still very weak, that he has overexerted himself in the last nine months . . . and that he wants to do just as he pleases without ever listening to reason."

Two days after the Josephplatz incident, he went to see Francis and poured out his usual remonstrances all in one breath: the Duke of Reichstadt, he said, was "held in low regard by the public." This time the Eaglet was touched on the raw, wounded in his pride. He attached considerable importance to the opinion others had of him. Was Dietrichstein telling the truth? How was he to find out? He wrote to Prokesch:

"Send me a few lines to assure me that I am not utterly despised, and perhaps you might discover through Count Dietrichstein, without giving me away, what people are saying about me: that would be a fresh proof of your friendship for me."

"Let Dietrichstein go on heaping reproaches on you," replied Prokesch, "in his affectionate but childish anxiety. He means well, but it cannot be denied that he sometimes attributes an exaggerated importance to certain things."

But it was anything but "childish anxiety" that Francis's former tutor showed on January 31, when he wrote: "Alas, why have they always rejected my advice, why have they always scoffed at my fears? Do they expect a boy of twenty to be a Hercules or an Achilles? The folly of giving him exhausting, purely physical work to do, instead of forcing him to look after his health while he is still growing, and instead of giving him a distinguished staff to make a general of him as quickly as possible and show what is expected of the heir to a great name who is fully capable of making a name for himself! But I have been talking to deaf ears. . . ."

Francis was getting thinner every day and constantly coughing and shivering. Dietrichstein blamed the feverish tremors that shook his body on his digestion, while Hartmann asserted that the Prince was suffering from "a slight chill of a catarrhal-rheumatic nature, probably caused by a change of temperature" and begged Marie Louise to "set her mind at rest."

The same day, January 31, Malfatti, who was still more concerned about his patient's liver than his bronchia, decided that Francis was cured and wrote to Marie Louise:

The report which I humbly submit to Your Majesty describes at once the beginning and the end of the indisposition from which H.H. the Duke your son has been suffering. As a result of overheating of the body, followed by a change of temperature, combined with excessive activity, H.H. caught a rheumatic chill, which particularly affected the head, the liver and the stomach. The fever, varying in intensity, lasted a whole week. The habitual vigor of youth and a certain reluctance to admit to being ill made it impossible to forestall this illness, but we have fortunately been able to check its progress. Yesterday for the first time H.H. spent the day out of bed, complaining of nothing but extreme weakness, which was only natural. Today, after a good night, he felt a little stronger when he got up, and in better spirits. His appetite is coming back, and his thirst is no longer morbific. H.H. has been docile and obedient during his illness; I hope that he will be no less docile and obedient during his convalescence, for it will be some little time before he has completely recovered.

On February 1 Dietrichstein went to see the invalid. He was still very thin and weak, but the fever seemed to have subsided, he had stopped coughing, and he was going to go for a drive with General Hartmann the next day. Everyone thought that he was cured. But immediately after the drive he started shivering and coughing all over again. Confined to his room once more, he took the opportunity to write on February 4 to his mother:

Pray forgive this short letter and trembling hand, but I am still rather weak. I have spent six days in bed and am now having a week's convalescence. The somewhat violent fever has completely abated, but the shivering fits which tire me more than any fatigue I can remember return without fail every evening. However, I hope they will stop one day. I have summoned up all my patience and am seeking glory in stoic endurance. My mind is quite alert, though it does not allow me to indulge in any serious occupation. Every day I devour a big bundle of newspapers, pamphlets and novels; I have just finished one which is worthy of your attention;

as usual you will find a lot of idle chatter in it, but also some rather piquant situations; it is Spindler's *Invalid.* I am sleeping a great deal, but very fitfully. The night before last I dreamed about you; you had arrived at Schönbrunn in a white petticoat; you shook me by the hand and I wept; you kissed me and I wept again; finally I awoke with a start in a perfect torrent of tears, and since then I cannot rid myself of the idea that some misfortune has overtaken you. I can scarcely wait to have news of you that will show that I am being ridiculously superstitious.

But what need have I to talk to you about my illness, dearest Mamma, when all the Counts in the world, and Monsieur Malfatti to boot, are sending you regular reports on it by every post?

The Vienna Carnival is full of life this year. . . . I only danced three times before my illness. The balls the King is giving are quite amusing; the Queen dances well, although the dresses she wears are still three hundred years out of date.

I mention dancing to you and not only do I feel my weakness returning but Malfatti is ushered in. . . .

Poor Malfatti! Three days after his visit, he wrote that "it was most important for me to discover whether the recurrent variations in temperature (rather than in pulse) were due to some hidden affection of the chest or to an intermittent daily fever. Everything I have done so far to establish the condition of the chest has been quite reassuring."

"It is as yet impossible," Dietrichstein told Marie Louise, "to determine the seat of the trouble, because the shivering fits are unaccompanied by any rise in temperature and the pulse has not altered very much." In his opinion it was simply "a case of intermittent fever which it should be easy to cure."

As for Francis himself, he seems to have guessed the gravity of his condition. This, he realized, was no "intermittent fever": he was seriously ill. When he discussed the state of his health with Dietrichstein at the beginning of February, the latter thought that he was pulling his leg and refused to take him seriously. Because the Duke had concealed his "indisposition" for three weeks, because he had gone "hunting, dancing and drilling," and because he had "exposed himself to the wind and the cold, on horseback and on foot," everyone imagined that Reichstadt was just pretending to be ill. "At the moment," wrote Dietrichstein in this same letter of February 4, "he is doing all he can to amuse himself at our expense *by exaggerating the seriousness of his condition. . . ." ***

Thus not only was Napoleon's son being treated for a disease with which he was not afflicted—as the autopsy was to show; not only was he in the last stages of tuberculosis and dying before his doctor's eyes without their having "determined the seat of the trouble"; not only did they consider the condition of his chest to be "quite reassuring"; but they accused their patient of joking when he told them he had not much longer to live.

* The words in italics were omitted from the catalogue of the Karl and Faber sale.

17

"The Terrifying Meteor"

THE FEVER HAD once more subsided. Francis was coughing and shivering less, and eating well. It was yet again thought that he was on the road to recovery. His thinness and pallor were still put down to the fact he had not finished growing. Meanwhile, in his Hofburg apartments lit by the aquarium light that filtered through the little greenish window panes, Francis pursued his daydreams. He spent long hours drowsing in the scorching heat from the porcelain stove that stood in one corner of his bedroom. Facing the bed and the Gérard portrait there was a big bookcase filled with books on the Napoleonic epic—and surmounted by a bust of Francis's grandfather. Now and then he would go and rest on the sofa in his drawing room. This room was hung with Gobelin tapestries which Louis XV had given to Maria Theresa and which depicted mythological subjects and the arms of France framed in interlaced L's and fleurs-de-lis. On the clock, two eagles guarded the sacred fire. The famous golden cradle presented long ago by the City of Paris gleamed in the shadows. Victory held her crown of laurels and stars over a void. At her son's request, Marie Louise had sent him Prud'hon's masterpiece, which she had taken with her to Parma. When Metternich had expressed surprise that he should want it, Francis reassured him with the smiling comment: "No one returns to his cradle once he has left it. So far it is the only monument to my personal history, and I am anxious to keep it."

On February 11 he went for a drive in a closed carriage. He had missed the ball the night before, but hoped to be able to attend the next. His pallor and his sickly complexion worried no one but Dietrichstein, who, in his letters to Marie Louise, inveighed against Malfatti's weakness and optimism.

"The Prince's convalescence progresses satisfactorily," announced Hartmann on February 25. "Only a little of the catarrhal affection now remains, and that does not prevent him from going to the theater, taking walks, and even, as from yesterday and with due circumspection, going riding." In the General's opinion, Francis was well and truly cured, and he informed H.M. the Archduchess that in the future he would stop "annoying" her with his reports. As for Malfatti, he attributed his patient's "catarrhal affection and occasional coughing" to the spring equinox. Until this cape had been rounded, he was allowing Francis "everything that was consistent with his duty to avoid extremes." He was aware that Dietrichstein and Hartmann were openly criticizing him. "I hope," he wrote on February 28, "that I do not deserve to be called either a timid or a foolhardy physician. In the midst of all the contradictory comments made on this subject, Your Majesty may be sure that I shall never allow myself to be put out of countenance."

Malfatti the timid informed his patient that not until the end of summer at the earliest would he be able to resume his military duties, "the source of all these ills," according to Dietrichstein. Francis accepted this decision, knowing better than anyone else that for a long time to come he would be incapable of shouting a command. He concealed his "expectorations" as best he could, and tried not to show the fatigue that took hold of him and left him helpless the day after any outing. He felt utterly exhausted, kept shivering and sweating, and to Dietrichstein's dismay took to staying in his warm bed instead of getting up. Yet the Count did not lose heart, and on March 17 declared that "however much they may oppress him or ignore him, he is destined to occupy a throne—I do not know which, but it may well be Bernadotte's!" On the same day Francis wrote his mother the last letter of his which we possess:

Your two letters, dearest Mamma, gave me indescribable pleasure; I promptly sat down to reply to you, but I was in such a morose and irritable mood that I was afraid of spreading sadness and distrust in a quarter from which only happiness and contentment come to me. This melancholy, which had been with me for three months, and which had rendered me incapable of work and insensible to the pleasures of life, was due to a stoppage of the liver. Malfatti has just cured me of this trouble by means of mixtures so acid and bitter that rhubarb is sugary in comparison. My health has suffered, I am extremely weak, and—you may be sure that this is true since I am telling you myself—a season's bathing is absolutely essential for me. My chief trouble is over-rapid growth, and I must try to broaden out; there is nothing better for this than salt baths, vapors and the pure air of Ischl. If I go on drilling a battalion of two hundred men abreast with carriages rattling past thirty paces behind me, I shall completely ruin my trachea, which has been giving trouble for the past five years and was subjected to considerable strain last year. Complete rest, a mild climate, and a course of whey and soda water may, on the other hand, give it back its original strength. When I think of the future which may lie before me, I feel that I have a sacred duty to humanity to get better, and that is the only reason why I am bothering you with details of my health.

I am leading a queer sort of life. I wake up at seven o'clock, stay in the bed till ten, then get up. At one o'clock I go riding, and I dine at five o'clock without very much appetite. I go regularly to the theater; this is the only time I pay court to the Emperor, who, believe it or not, has just had two more teeth out. At the Burgtheatre they have just presented a new tragedy by Raupach, *King Enzio.* The style is sublime and the subject touching: you would weep a great deal if you saw it; I myself shed one or two tears. . . .

Francis's talk of a "sacred duty to humanity to get better" worried Marie Louise: this resolution, she declared, was "so out of character that I tell myself he must feel very ill to make it." One would have thought that the Duchess of Parma would jump into her berlin and travel post-haste to Vienna, but she was prevented from doing so by a fresh pregnancy. Who was responsible for this troublesome state of affairs? Her Chamberlain, the Count of Sanvitale, who, having acquired a taste for the family, would later marry Albertine de Montenuovo? It is possible. But then, did she herself know for certain? Her sex life had become more dissolute than ever, if we are to believe Baron Marschall, who had taken over Neipperg's duties but drew the line at the Duchess's bedroom door—the door at which a sentry had to be stationed to bar the way to her overnumerous lovers. That is, until the morning when, as in *The Matron of Ephesus*, the sentry was discovered in the former Empress's bed. The guard was then doubled, according to the Prince de Faucigny-Lucinge, but that did not improve matters, and it was rumored that the two men were kept fully occupied attending to their sovereign's wants. . . .

On the 18th or 19th Francis went riding in cold, damp weather. As usual, he rode as fast as his horse could go, without bothering to see whether poor Hartmann was managing to keep up with him. In the evening, as if he were intent on punishing his poor body, he decided to go out again, and drove round the Prater till sunset in an open carriage. One of the wheels came off and he was obliged to walk some considerable distance. An icy mist was rising from the Danube. That night he had a fresh attack of fever and complained that he could no longer hear anything with his left ear.

On the morning of his twenty-first birthday—March 20, 1832—the Empress, the Crown Prince and his wife—now the King and Queen of Hungary—and the Archdukes Anthony, Charles and Louis came to his bedroom to wish him a happy birthday. Sophia was holding little Francis Joseph by the hand; the future Emperor gave the Duke two camellias with a shout of "Ava!"—his name for Reichstadt. "What comfort could they bring him," asked Prokesch, "these brief visits from members of the imperial family, all accompanied by their chamberlains and their ladies-in-waiting, when he had his cradle and his tomb before his eyes?" The same day, Dietrichstein too came and sat by his bed. Francis struck him as sadder than the day before. All the spirit seemed to have gone out of him.

"I shall certainly not get better," he said, "until I have taken some salt baths and moved to a warmer climate."

According to the mistaken medical ideas of the time, it was not to Ischl but to Naples that he should have gone. But alas, Napoleon's son could not leave Austria: political considerations—another name for Metternich—forbade it. His mere presence in Italy, even stretched out on a chaise-longue, might well set the whole peninsula on fire. By the time the Chancellor agreed to open the cage, Francis would be dying. . . .

Malfatti was surprised that the spring equinox had brought about no improvement in his patient's condition. "On the contrary," he wrote on March 24, "fresh disorders have appeared to which H.H. has clearly contributed by exposing himself, against my express wishes, to the dampest, coldest air we have had all winter." Malfatti forgot to mention that his prohibitions had been far from firm; indeed, on several occasions he had urged his patient to go on living a normal life, forbidding nothing but the resumption of his military duties. "For the past five days," he went on, "he has been suffering from fits of coughing and daily attacks of fever, as in the late autumn. It remains to be seen whether the attacks of fever are connected with an affection of the chest, or whether they belong to that type of intermittent fever which often recurs in the spring. I am inclined to favor the latter hypothesis in view of the nature of the paroxysms and the disappearance of the fever today after the fibrifuge. I must however confess that this deliberate relapse distresses me greatly and causes me some anxiety, especially on account of the chest and the liver, which is still congested. But his present treatment will prepare him for his stay at Ischl, which I earnestly look forward to as the only way of mastering the young patient and hence his illness."

Obsessed by Napoleon's medical history, the Eaglet's entourage were still most concerned about his liver. Thus on April 3 Dietrichstein wrote with unconscious irony: "It seems certain that the Prince's liver is seriously affected (let us hope that the same is not true of the chest!)" And the Count added: "He coughs from time to time, especially in the evening, but he does not expectorate very often; his face is pale and yellow, and I think he must have moments of sadness, for he prefers to be left alone. . . ."

However, once the crisis was over, Francis was to be seen again at the theater, looking like the pale ghost Barthélemy had described three years before. "His face fills me with indescribable sadness," wrote Dietrichstein on April 7. "Every movement he makes getting up or going upstairs or down makes him cough and last night he went on coughing until two in the morning."

The exhausting hollow cough persisted; so did the daily attacks of fever and the now "permanent" shivering fits which Francis went on concealing so successfully from Hartmann and Malfatti that the General begged Marie Louise on the 12th "not to give way to anxiety," while the doctor continued to send comparatively optimistic reports to Parma.

Then Malfatti himself fell ill—laid low by an attack of gout. However, he managed to drag himself along to Francis's bedside to join in a consultation with Dr. Wiehrer and Dr. Reiman, who, he proudly reported to Marie Louise, "agreed with my estimate of the condition of the liver and the chest." His colleagues, so he claimed, had warmly congratulated him on effecting a "palpable" improvement in the state of his patient's liver—a liver that had nothing wrong with it. . . . He had to admit that the two consultants had not found the lungs in the best of condition, but he went on to state explicitly that the fits of coughing had been put down to nothing more serious than "changes in body temperature and the patient's excessive activity."

In reality, Wiehrer and Reiman had been far less optimistic than Malfatti asserted. Thus on April 20 we find Princess Melanie von Metternich, the Chancellor's pretty wife, writing in her diary: "The Emperor told Clemens [Metternich] that he had called in some doctors to report on the Duke of Reichstadt's health, and that they had all declared that in their opinion the patient's condition was hopeless. He is already spitting pieces of lung and has only a few months to live. May God's will be done!"

Yet this did not prevent "Clemens" from writing a fortnight later to Marie Louise: "I know that Your Majesty is kept fully informed of the state of the Duke of Reichstadt's health. This, as you are aware, is causing us some anxiety. The doctors are still looking for the seat of the trouble in the liver, but I know only too well the ease with which disorders can change position at the Prince's age. Let us hope for the best, and rest assured that everything possible is being done for the Prince." He had no desire to see the ex-Empress insisting that her son should leave for Naples, as the two consultants had recommended in their report. "Everyone in Vienna is talking about the Duke of Reichstadt," wrote Victoire de Créneville to her childhood friend. "They say that he needs a mild climate and ought to go to Italy, but that Politics would not allow of it. . . ."

Metternich—Politics in person—had no need to poison his old enemy's son, as some writers have claimed he did: all he had to do was to let him die. For at the beginning of this spring of 1832, it seemed possible that Francis might still be saved. . . .

Meanwhile Marie Louise was growing anxious "in spite of the fact that all Malfatti's bulletins say that he guarantees a cure." She showed them to her own doctor, a certain Ferrari, who reassured her. "If it should happen," she wrote to Dietrichstein, "that he got worse and the cholera were here, I should be unable to go to Vienna, for I feel that it is a sovereign's duty to sacrifice her dearest affections in order to share the dangers facing her subjects."

In Vienna the real reason for her absence was well known, and Marshal Maison wrote unequivocally to his usual correspondent: "It is said that his mother, who has been as it were invited to come here, is too far advanced in the task of replacing her dying son and cannot decently put in an appearance. . . ."

On the other hand, in distant Parma, Marie Louise could be forgiven for not panicking, since she went on receiving reassuring letters from Hartmann. On April 26 he complacently reported that hemorrhoidal and bilious attacks had brought the patient "some relief." No doubt his appetite left something to be desired, but that was "not unusual" and he was sleeping "perfectly." He added that Francis went out every day "unless it is too cold, and part of the way on foot, and he seems to be approaching the state of health he was in before his relapse; it is with the doctors' approval that I have the pleasure of telling you this good news."

Metternich's wife, the Court, the Viennese gazettes and the French newspapers were now all talking about the tuberculosis from which the Duke of Reichstadt was dying. The Paris papers were so explicit—they were already burying the Duke—that everything was done to prevent Francis from reading them. Only Hartmann and the doctors went on avoiding the word *phthisis* and shutting their eyes to the symptoms of tuberculosis cachexy. Indeed, stung by the criticism to which he was being subjected, Malfatti wrote to Marie Louise on May 3 denying the presence of any tubercles or abscesses in the lungs, while on May 8 Hartmann went even further and asserted that Reichstadt's health had "not only not deteriorated" but seemed "on the contrary to have improved as a result of his doctors' attentions."

Dietrichstein, austere, rigid, exasperating Dietrichstein, with his never-ending grumbles, was perhaps the only person in Francis's entourage—since Prokesch was away—who felt a genuine affection for him. At long last the truth dawned on the ex-tutor, and he wrote to Marie Louise on May 17 to tell her how serious her son's illness was and how little trust was to be placed in his doctors; at the same time he asked her not to report his pessimistic remarks to Malfatti and Hartmann. Writing to her again on the 19th, he repeated his plea: "I must again *beg Your Majesty not to give me away* but to compare my observations with the observations of those two Gentlemen; I know that there will always be a great divergence between them, because I write this with *absolute* frankness, and the disease is too obvious to permit of any exaggeration." The Duchess, he went on, "would do well *first of all* to send a reliable man to Vienna on some pretext or other, to discover *through him* the state of the Prince's health, and then to make her own arrangements on the basis of his report."

But Marie Louise did nothing.

Francis was still sunk in melancholy. He could not even write to Prokesch, since Dietrichstein had forbidden him to do so, for fear that he would start riding his old hobbyhorses again now that he was just a ghost of his former self. On May 13 the Emperor had appointed him honorary colonel of the Prince of Wasa's regiment. This was putting an epaulet on a tomb, and he knew it. Failing a miracle—that miracle which Metternich refused to grant him—his life was over.

On May 17, giving a sad smile, he said to Dietrichstein: "Write and tell my mother that I am in a very bad way and she will come."

Dietrichstein repeated these words in his letter of the 19th . . . but the ex-Empress merely replied:

If only you knew, my dear Count, how much I long to go to Vienna, you would pity me, but I *cannot* unless it is *absolutely necessary,* and that because public feeling is still so bad and the political situation in Italy is so uncertain and critical that my departure would *cause offense,* something that *must be avoided at all costs.* What is more, we have the cholera on our doorstep, and if I left now it would create a deplorable impression. This is what *the world does not think or see;* it sees nothing but my son lying ill in Vienna, it does not see what is happening here and how impossible it is to leave. The situation in Italy is so precarious that even if I decided to follow the promptings of my heart and go to Vienna I could not stay longer than eight or ten days, and I do not know whether that would not create an even worse impression, setting aside all considerations of my health, which at the moment is in no condition to stand two long journeys at so short an interval. . . .

Nor did she arrive at any decision five days later when she received an even more alarming letter from Dietrichstein begging her to come at once. "I cannot conceal from Your Majesty," the Count had written on May 23, "the fact that the Prince is in the greatest danger and the disease is making rapid progress."

The day before—the 22nd—Francis had been taken to Schönbrunn in a closed carriage. Sophia—"that angel of loving kindness"—had had an armchair made for him which he found waiting for him in his bedroom. This room had been prepared for Sophia, but she had given it up to him. It was one of the high, white-ceilinged rooms on the first floor of the left-hand wing, and the windows looked across the flower beds and arbors to the Gloriette silhouetted against the bright spring sky. Napoleon had slept in it after Austerlitz and had come back to it after Wagram. Like his father, Francis had spurned the huge rococo bed with its carved figures, and had had an ordinary camp bed installed. The adjoining room—the famous Salon des Laques—which the Emperor had used as a study, was also at Francis's disposal.

The people of Vienna had watched him leave the Hofburg convinced that he would never come back.

I regard him as a shadow [wrote Marshal Maison the same day], a shadow with a little life left in him but whose melancholy sojourn on this earth is almost over. For a moment I believed that a miracle might happen, but today I have returned to my natural state of incredulity. I know that this will make you weep, but— you see how generous I can be—I am prepared not to take offense at such a display of grief over the fate of this embryonic emperor of the Republicans and the various sorts of clubmen. You would certainly shed more tears over his tomb than they are going to shed here. I have reason to believe that they are not excessively depressed by the prospect of his death. They would find his continued existence somewhat troublesome. . . .

"They" signified Metternich . . . and the Eaglet knew it.
"I am nothing but an encumbrance," he murmured sadly.

The day after his arrival at Schönbrunn, at ten o'clock in the morning, Francis performed his Easter duty in Sophia's oratory above the chapel. The ceremony tired him, and when he got back to his room he had another attack of fever. In spite of this he went to the Kaninchenberg to drink alternate glasses of cow's milk and ass's milk diluted with soda water, a course of treatment he was to follow every day. As soon as a little sunshine gilded the long, green-shuttered façade, he would install himself on the balcony of the Salon des Laques or else go down to the garden. But he was too weak to walk very far and had to come in again. It was already beginning to turn very hot and the heat upset him, but he never complained.

On June 1 he had a long—and last—visit from Marshal Marmont. The fever never left him now, and the heat brought "red streaks" to his face which alarmed Dietrichstein. The latter saw in them a symptom of a disease of the chest and lungs. "I have felt certain of the existence of this disease for some months, in spite of the so-called dominant disease of the liver, which undoubtedly also exists. . . . Malfatti will be writing to Your Majesty, and so will General Hartmann; but all their rose-colored or rose-tinted letters, all their fancy phrases, serve no purpose except to arouse doubt and distrust or else to send the recipient to sleep. In a case like this one must tell the truth, and that is why I repeat that the Prince is in danger and the disease is making rapid progress, while none of the remedies being tried can give him any relief because his vital force is visibly diminishing." He concluded by once more begging Marie Louise to have horses put to her traveling berlin if she wanted to see her son alive. "Your Majesty's presence is necessary, although no one can say how much time Providence will grant our beloved Prince."

Marie Louise was now at Venice, and in rather poor health: "They say it is my nerves, but I am convinced it is my stomach." The Emperor Francis was due to arrive at Trieste on June 4, and she would ask him whether she should really go to Vienna. "He will tell me what I must do."

On June 3 Count Maurice found Francis lying on his divan, wrapped in a cloak up to his shoulders, and with his teeth chattering in spite of the stifling heat.

"How do you feel tonight?" asked the ex-tutor, raising his voice on account of Francis's increasing deafness.

"Very well. I have had three days without any fever."

"Alas!" lamented Dietrichstein. "Why does he keep up this pretense, when it is obvious that the fever is there and that it is a slow fever which is burning him up? Naturally I took care not to show that I did not believe him, but his face, his hands hidden under the cloak, and his deafness all showed that he was not telling the truth."

On June 6 Malfatti and Wiehrer decided to substitute three glasses of Marienbad water for their patient's dinner. Francis grudgingly accepted their decision and said that he was going out. Just as he was getting into his carriage with Captain Moll, the two doctors changed their minds and gave him permission to have some soup. Reichstadt refused.

"They don't even know what they want themselves," he said as the carriage moved off at walking pace. "Far from curing me, they are making me so weak that I can't move."

The next day, after a bad night's sleep broken by fits of insomnia and coughing, Francis went with Captain Moll to the Staehl-Rouge, a fashionable inn. The barouche which took him there was new—"a real cradle" he called it. At the inn he drank a couple of glasses of Marienbad, took a few paces and sat down to drink an egg-flip. Moll placed himself to his right—he was now completely deaf in his left ear—and started reading. His droning voice sent Francis to sleep. Baron de Moll was now his only real companion. Dietrichstein no longer meant anything to him. Hartmann's stupidity, obsequiousness and "insinuating ways" irritated him in the highest degree; he even hated the general, according to Moll, because Hartmann "could give him orders on Metternich's authority." "He can't be trusted," said Francis. As for Standeisky, he was just a pale shadow of the General.

At three o'clock the carriage set off on the return journey to Schönbrunn. These few hours spent in the open air had exhausted Francis, and he was glad to be able to stretch himself out in the barouche. He lay motionless, buried under his blankets. "He made me read aloud to him," writes Moll, "but he kept dropping off to sleep, waking up when a violent fit of coughing shook his body." The officer lowered his voice every time the sick man fell asleep and raised it again when he awoke. Francis never noticed that he was missing whole passages.

Malfatti, who had now recovered from his attack of gout, arrived at Schönbrunn about eight o'clock with the news that a fresh consultation was to take place the next day. This was the culmination of a drama which had been played out in the wings. Dietrichstein had insisted that another doctor besides Wiehrer should be called in to collaborate with Malfatti. The latter had put on a great show of righteous indignation.

"His Highness is getting better," he declared. "If another doctor is called in, then I shall go!"

Sophia, who was another of Malfatti's patients, had intervened and the Italian had given in on condition that two doctors, the leading Viennese physicians Vivanot and Türkheim, were called in.

The next day, after a night in which Francis had spent scarcely a quarter of an hour without coughing, the doctors came and examined him. Retiring afterward to an adjoining room, they agreed—in spite of Malfatti's denials—that the patient's condition was hopeless.

"If he holds out till autumn, he will have to go to Italy."

On Saturday, June 9, after a bad night and a sleepy morning, Francis clambered painfully into his carriage, helped by Moll.

"To Haimlach!"

On the way to the Vienna Woods, Reichstadt came to life and started talking about the consultation the day before.

"So I'm going to spend the autumn and winter in Naples?"

But he began to worry in case Metternich should withdraw his permission. Moll reassured him. It was, after all, quite safe to lie to him now!

Then, like all who suffer from tuberculosis, he went from anxiety to hope. To Moll's delight he gave himself up to his dreams and talked about his coming journey, the route he was going to take and the towns he intended to visit.

"Carry out a thorough examination of the traveling berlin," he said. "Make sure it is in a fit condition to make such a long journey."

When they arrived at Haimlach he stopped the carriage and got out. It was here that Beethoven had composed his Pastoral Symphony while listening to the song of the yellowhammer. . . . But after scarcely twenty paces, Francis felt exhausted and had to go back to the barouche.

"Haimlach reminds me of my early childhood," he said. "I often came here with my French ladies. My mother would go riding and the equerry, Monsieur Charles, would take me on the saddle in front of him."

He had come back here many times since 1816, but accompanied by his tutors. . . . The best days were over.

"I had to pretend to be different from what I really was."

Talking excitedly, he confided to the young officer, his elder by ten years or so, that to win the approval of Dietrichstein, Foresti, Collin and Obenaus, and even of his chaplain Dom Wagner and his tutor Commander Weiss, he had had to conceal his true nature. Collin had wanted to awaken in him the spirit of an ascetic, a poet, a patron of the arts.

"And he succeeded in doing the exact opposite!"

Foresti too had failed to achieve his object. Why, Francis wondered, had they never thought of using ambition to encourage him, competition to stimulate him? Since little Émile—the son of his mother's valet —had left, he had never had a companion of his own age.

"I shall have my own children brought up with others, in a school I shall found myself."

"He is just copying his father's ideas on Meudon," thought the Baron. But he let the Prince continue his monologue "eagerly and earnestly, as if he were assured of having children of his own."

"My education was a complete failure, but at least it taught me what mistakes to avoid in the education of my own sons."

Back at Schönbrunn, dinner was served soon after three o'clock. The Eaglet's excitement had sent his temperature up, but as soon as Hartmann came into the room he expressed a desire to go out again—according to Moll "simply to rid himself of a presence which he found more odious every day." A bitter smile twisted his lips when he saw the General, whom he regarded as Metternich's familiar spirit. When he came out a panic-stricken Hartmann told the others that Reichstadt had spoken to him of going to Italy. Moll calmed him down, explaining that they had to encourage him in this hope to keep him happy.

"The doctors say he can't even go to Ischl, so how could he possibly go to Naples?"

Hartmann's alarm shows that by June 9 Metternich had not yet informed him of the reply which he later claimed to have given Francis:

"Tell the Duke of Reichstadt that except for France, a country to which it is not in my power to secure his admittance, he is free to go to whatever country he pleases. The Emperor's consideration is his grandson's recovery."

While the General was regaining his composure, Francis came through the anteroom, gave Hartmann a curt nod, and took Moll with him to his carriage. He seemed highly indignant.

"You know that Councilor Gentz died this morning?" he said. "Well, the General told me the news with a smile on his lips! Gentz was one of the most intelligent men who ever served the monarchy; the general isn't worthy to tie his shoelaces, and he smiles as he tells me of his death!"

He became angrier and angrier, and the blood rose to his head. Moll tried to calm him down, but Francis made no reply and went on brooding over the incident. Suddenly Moll noticed that the Duke was shivering. He persuaded him that there was no point in going any farther, and the carriage turned round. Back at the castle, Reichstadt sank on to his chaise-longue with a sigh of relief and soon dropped off into a doze. When Marmont sent in his name he refused to receive him.

"Tell the Marshal I am asleep," he said. "I don't want him to see me in this pitiful condition."

During the night of June 10-11 the Eaglet found it impossible to go to sleep. He rang for Kolb, his valet, and asked for some cold water to freshen himself up. He felt as if a fire were raging inside him. In the morning he called for a thick blanket and then fell into a heavy sleep. When he awoke he said that he was going out. His voice was feebler and hoarser than ever. This time his barouche did not remind him of a cradle; he complained that it was jolting terribly.

The people of Vienna watched "little Napoleon" pass by. Everyone knew that he was going to die, and there was not a single portrait of him left in the shops. In the streets people asked each other anxiously for the latest news of the Duke. The sight of his carriage reassured them a little.

When he got back Francis could not face the effort of climbing the stairs to the Salon des Laques. Moll advised him to take the lift, and he agreed, with a sigh of regret for the days when he used to enjoy running upstairs. Letting the servants see how feeble he had become struck him as utterly deplorable.

Only now, rather late in the day, did Malfatti begin to show some anxiety. The inner fire consuming his patient had at last opened his eyes to the truth. The symptoms were undoubtedly the symptoms of approaching death—and death due to tuberculosis! The doctor who had sent Marie Louise so many complacent reports—of which Dietrichstein had still been complaining on May 8—now feared the worst. If a crisis occurred, the end would come in a matter of hours. It was time Marie Louise arrived!

The Duchess was still in Trieste. The Emperor, who was also there, gave her to understand that she should leave for Vienna immediately, but she put off her departure from one day to the next. She had decided to leave Trieste on the 11th, but it was the 20th before she took her departure, claiming that she had been delayed by "an attack of fever" which in reality—at least so rumor had it—was nothing more or less than a miscarriage.

On the 12th Francis's pains had started again, and he kept asking for iced water and sorbets. He none the less set off for Laxenburg in an open carriage. On the way he was caught by a storm, and he came back to Schönbrunn shivering with cold and complaining of a pain in the right side. The night was appalling. In the morning Francis spat pus and blood. He found breathing increasingly difficult, and with every breath he took, a sound like bellows came from his chest. Blisters were applied and a frightened Malfatti urged him to take to his bed. He had scarcely gone before Francis was trying to get up. Moll attempted to reason with him, talking about medical advice.

"I don't care a damn about their advice!"

The captain refused to order the carriage. Francis reached for the bell rope, saying: "Well then, I'll order it!"

Moll grasped his hand.

"Monseigneur, don't make things difficult for me with the servants. I should be obliged to forbid them to put horses to the carriage, and since you are ill they will obey me rather than you. Everybody thinks we are mad to let you go out with a temperature. Reproaches are heaped on us from all sides on that account; so far I have kept silent, but today, Monseigneur, I should like to have those people here to witness the scenes we have to go through on these occasions."

That was enough for Francis, who stayed where he was. He had extra covers put on his bed and got Moll to read him accounts of the Republican and Bonapartist demonstrations which had occurred in Paris on the 5th and 6th on the occasion of the funeral of General Lamarque, an ardent champion of liberty. When Moll had finished reading, Francis said that he felt much better.

"My head is clear, my stomach is all right; all that is left now is this wretched cough."

About one o'clock he fell asleep. Moll, who had stayed by his bed, looked at him in consternation, imagining that Francis was going to die at any moment.

"His breath whistled; his eyes were half-open and the pupils slightly contracted; now and then a nervous spasm would shake the whole of his body and at odd moments there would be sudden contractions of his arms and legs when he stretched them as he was turning over. It was a heartrending sight. Most of the time he kept his eyes half-shut, but when he opened them he opened them extremely wide." It occurred to Moll that it would fall to him to perform the painful duty of preparing Francis to receive the Last Sacraments.

Suddenly Reichstadt became aware that the Baron was looking at him, and he turned over angrily. Later he complained of feeling feverish.

"It's just the cold, Monseigneur."

"No, it isn't the cold; it's a raging fever."

In the evening Moll came back to see him; he had finally calmed down.

"Good night!"

This was his way of dismissing Moll. The Baron asked if he might stay a little longer, so that the Duke did not fall asleep too soon. Francis did not answer, but a quarter of an hour later he said once more: "Good night!"

And Moll left the Eaglet alone with his illness, alone with his thoughts, alone as he had been for so many years, ever since Maman Quiou had kissed him good-by.

It had been stiflingly hot all day. A leaden pall hung over the castle. The night brought no relief. A storm was brewing. There was not a breath of wind. What was Francis thinking as he lay there on his little camp bed? About this life of his which was about to end before it had even begun?

"My birth and my death—that's the whole of my story," he said during these last months.

He was also heard to sigh: "Between my cradle and my tomb there is a great nought."

Suddenly the storm broke and there was a long roll of thunder, a sound like that of silk being torn. Lightning had struck the castle and it was raining heavily. The weight that had been pressing on Francis's chest had lifted. While the storm moved on, he fell asleep. The crisis had passed.

The 14th was a better day, and when the chaplain Wagner asked Francis when he could see him, the latter answered with a smile:

"About midday, because then I am never at home. I usually go out about eleven or half-past."

The next day—the 15th—the improvement continued.

"Can I go to the theater?" he asked Malfatti.

All the same, he stayed in bed, fell asleep, and awoke about six o'clock in the best of spirits and without any sign of fever. For the first time in days, he asked for some supper.

"Have you already had supper?" he asked Moll.

"Yes, Monseigneur. Does that question mean that Your Highness wishes me to go?"

"No, I should like you to stay."

When he had finished eating, he shot out: "Good night!"

"Does Your Highness wish to go to sleep already?"

"No, I shan't sleep."

"Then will you allow me to read to you until you fall asleep?"

"I shall be happy if you just stay here."

He gave him such a kindly look that the Baron forgot the far from amiable reception he had been accorded the previous year when he had arrived to take up his duties; he helped the sick man to take a few paces up and down the bedroom.

The last effort utterly exhausted Francis. During the night of June 15-16 he complained of a pain in the right lung, but this did not prevent him from telling Malfatti in the morning that he felt perfectly well. Nor did the doctor forbid him to go out.

In the anteroom he passed the chaplain, who had come from Vienna to see him, and greeted him coldly.

"What's the fellow doing here every day?" he asked Standeisky as they went downstairs.

On the 17th the bad weather prevented him from going out. He was "silent and apathetic." He received visits from the Archduke Francis and Prince Leopold and his wife, Marie Louise's sister. Ten minutes later Sophia arrived. They were left alone together. Francis's young aunt had been entrusted with the difficult mission of preparing her nephew to receive the Last Sacraments. Court etiquette called for an impressive display of ceremony. All the archdukes present in Vienna, together with their chamberlains and advisors, were required to accompany the Blessed Sacrament. Every effort would be made to conceal this crowd from him, and only Communion would be given to the sick man. If signs of a fresh crisis appeared, there would still be time to give him Extreme Unction then. Sophia told him that she intended to take Communion in the course of the week before her child was due, in the hope of obtaining a safe delivery. Would he keep her company and take Communion for her sake—and also for his own recovery? That day Francis said "neither yes nor no."

"It's hard to gain his confidence. He doesn't trust anybody."

But Francis had not been taken in. When Moll came back into the room he found Reichstadt in a very bad temper.

After dinner he lay down on the divan and groaned: "Now I'm starting to shiver again. What can I do to get well? Oh, what a long time I'm taking to recover!"

Moll covered him with his cape and a couple of blankets. For an hour and a half he was shaken by shivering fits and nervous spasms until a rise in temperature made him throw off his blankets and call for an iced drink.

For three hours Moll read aloud to him. Did he listen? Apparently, because as soon as Moll paused for a moment he expressed surprise. When Malfatti came in he told him that he was feeling very well.

"He has been like this all his life," complained Moll, "and now simple souls are going to come and tell us that we have not done everything we could to cure him."

On June 18, after a sleepless night and several violent attacks of fever which seemed to foreshadow a fresh crisis, the question of the Last Sacraments was raised once more. The chaplain Wagner spent some time alone with Francis and persuaded him to agree to what Sophia had suggested. Reichstadt gave in more readily than had been expected, and promised to take Communion two days later. However, the priest had scarcely gone out before he exclaimed, in a fury at being taken in so easily: "What a fool that chaplain is!"

The next day several people came to see him. After each person had gone he asked excitedly: "What did they say? How did they find me?"

In the evening he tried to take a turn round his bedroom, but he felt giddy and had to lie down on his chaise-longue. Moll heard him complaining: "Do you realize that tomorrow I've got to make my devotions?"

The next day—June 20—the Abbé Wagner heard his confession.

"I realize the gravity of my condition," he told the priest, "but I hope to get better."

A few minutes before, he had said with a sigh: "I am ready to die."

And while Francis waited, reading the Bible, the Habsburg ceremonial took its ostentatious course. A long procession left the chapel and slowly climbed the blue staircase between two lines of grenadiers. The Duke of Reichstadt's liveried footmen, the civil and military officers of his household, the Schönbrunn servants and finally the clergy preceded the members of the imperial family and their suites. Each person held a taper in his hand. The Archdukes Louis, Charles and Anthony walked in front of the Abbé Wagner, who was carrying the Blessed Sacrament underneath a canopy. Then came the Crown Princess—the Queen of Hungary—and the Archduchesses Sophia and Clementine. The female staff of the castle brought up the rear. After crossing the gallery, the procession reached the entry to Reichstadt's apartments, where Hartmann and Moll were waiting. The whole Court stayed outside, praying quietly so that Francis should not guess what was happening, while Wagner, wearing his ordinary vestments and accompanied only by the two officers, took the Host in to the sick man.

That evening Metternich wrote to his embassy in Paris: "In my opinion the Duke is done for: his illness is a pulmonary phthisis in its final stages. This disease, which can attack human beings at any time of life, kills them quickly at twenty-one."

The next day—June 21—the sick man was no better. On the contrary: he had not slept at all, he was still breaking out into cold sweats and suffering from fits of coughing, and his appearance was frightening. In a face which "looked like a dead man's," fever had brought an alarming brilliance to his eyes.

"I suffered martyrdom last night," he said.

Malfatti tried to magnetize Francis, "lifting him up and infusing new strength into him." "This is a secret between ourselves," wrote Moll. By now this treatment was no longer a matter of producing convulsions in the patient by means of magnetic passes, but of sending him to sleep. Somnambulism had taken the place of mesmerism.

The crisis reached its peak toward evening. Francis had sudden wild spasms and cried out: "I wouldn't wish this illness on my worst enemy. . . . What have I done to suffer like this?"

Moll tried to calm him down with a little magnetism.

"Your mother is on her way," he said. "She will be here soon."

"I shan't believe that until I see her."

The 22nd was a somewhat better day, although he never stopped coughing. The expectoration of blood and pus which was to continue until he died robbed him of all his strength.

That evening, Marie Louise, who had left Trieste on the 20th, was at Grätz. It was there she had spent happy days with her son two years before. "And now," she wrote to Sanvitale, "I know that he has one foot in the grave. . . ."

Meanwhile Francis had gone over the latest crisis, but it had left him utterly exhausted. He found breathing difficult and sleep eluded him. The future Emperor Ferdinand and his wife, Queen Maria Anna, came to see him on June 23. The call tired him.

"I am so hoarse today that I can scarcely say a word. Nobody can help me now and I shan't find peace again until I am in the grave."

"You must have patience, Monseigneur . . . just wait."

"What for? I have already waited too long."

His voice was full of despair.

The King of Hungary called again in the evening, but Francis refused to see him. He asked when he could come again to see his nephew.

"When he likes," answered Francis in a whisper. "I would rather it were never. . . . I beg you, in the name of all you hold dearest in the world, not to admit anybody. I don't want to see anybody at all!"

He was so hoarse that it was only with the utmost difficulty that he managed to say his usual: "Good night!"

On Sunday, June 24, he did not fall asleep until six in the morning and was still asleep when a landau drawn by four horses drew up in front of the castle. Marie Louise got out, helped by Dietrichstein, who had gone to Guntersdorf to meet her. In accordance with etiquette, the King and Queen of Hungary were waiting halfway up the stairs and they accompanied the Duchess of Parma to her apartments. There Sophia, the Archduke Francis and the Prince of Salerno came to see her. They found her weeping. When she was told that Francis had just awakened, she began trembling like a frightened child. She went into Francis's bedroom with Hartmann and stood there dumfounded, scarcely able to recognize her son in this skeletal figure, this dying man with the yellow complexion and hollow, staring eyes, who stretched out his thin arms toward her and tried—but in vain—to lift himself up in his bed.

They kissed and were left alone. Marie Louise knew now that Malfatti had been cruelly mistaken and that the end was near. In spite of her blindness and her selfishness, did she, one wonders, feel any remorse? Did she realize that if she had listened to Dietrichstein's pleas and come to Vienna before the end of the winter, she might have been able, with her father's assistance, to force Metternich to open the doors of the gilded prison? The hot sun of Italy and the company of friends such as Prokesch or Esterházy would have helped to counter her son's sufferings and melancholy. And perhaps Prokesch was right when he wrote: "I cannot help thinking that an active and happy early life would have benefited his physical formation, and that his development was arrested by mental depression. I knew him well enough to realize that his health was profoundly affected by his melancholia. But I did not expect the decisive crisis in his life to occur as early as it did, and I hoped for a change for the better. . . ."

If during the previous winter he had left the bleak Hofburg and the damp air of the Danube for the warm climate of Naples, the radical change in his habits might have reconciled him to life. True, the bitterness that springs from a thwarted destiny and the anguish that comes from seeing one's hopes blighted are not enough in themselves to produce tuberculosis, but in this case they may well have aggravated Francis's condition, lowered his resistance and prevented his recovery, by preying on a constitution which had been worn out as far back as 1827, the year when Staudenheim had diagnosed "a tendency to scrofula and to phthisis of the trachea."

Naturally Francis's foolhardy behavior, his insistence on performing the humblest military duties, his lies and pretenses, his love of pleasure and his determination to conceal the symptoms of his illness all enabled Hartmann to assure Marie Louise "in all conscience" that her son was responsible for his present condition. But he was certainly not alone in that responsibility.

The days dragged wearily by. Francis spent long hours dozing gently while Moll read the Prince de Ligne's *Military Miscellany* to him. Like his father, he asked for a second bed and was soon moving from one to the other. He did not want to see anybody. Even his mother made him tired.

"She annoys me," he told Moll.

She did not talk loudly enough, and on the 27th, after she had gone, Francis confided to Moll that he had not understood a single word the Duchess had said to him. That evening he seemed happy to be told that Marie Louise wished him good night "from afar."

"Then she isn't coming back?" he said.

While he was having a nap on the 29th, his suite discussed the inheritance. Would the officers receive pensions? Since Francis had no fortune of his own, could they inherit anything from him—his arms, for instance? And what would happen to the famous silver-gilt cradle?

"It can't be sold," said Hartmann regretfully. "That would create too much of a scandal."

"Why shouldn't it be sold?" asked Moll. "What harm would it do, seeing that the Prince would be dead?"

On July 1 Moll coldly submitted to Marie Louise an inventory of her son's effects, "so that she might make the necessary arrangements." For H.M. had let it be known that she would be returning to Parma as soon as her son was dead. . . .

On July 3 Francis awoke from the long torpor during which he had seemed to be drifting imperceptibly toward the other world, and declared that he felt better. But he could not stay still, changed beds, and complained of a burning sensation inside.

"I should like to drink a whole ocean!" he exclaimed. "Oh, if only I could soak my body in water!"

The improvement in his condition worried everybody. Hartmann declared that if Reichstadt recovered and went to Naples, he would resign.

"For a job like this you need somebody who can play the tyrant now and then, and that is something repugnant to my nature."

Moll too said that he would leave the Prince's service, but added: "I feel certain that he won't recover and that we shan't have to resort to extreme measures."

He had persuaded Hartmann to present a "memorandum" to Marie Louise regarding pensions for the staff and—naturally enough—for the three officers.

On the 4th Francis got up with some difficulty and, for the first time in thirteen days, remained for several hours on the balcony. The heat was stifling and the sun was gilding the Gloriette. He felt very weak, having taken nothing all day apart from three spoonfuls of soup and a dozen cherries. In any case he disliked Austrian cooking and regretted giving his mother his French cook Verlaine. But he did not dare ask Marie Louise in so many words to return him, and confined himself to telling her that the food at Court gave him stomach-ache.

Meanwhile Hartmann, Moll and Standeisky were sharing out the stables among them. They had already picked out three or four "high-spirited saddle horses," which, they decided, "would be unsuitable for H.M. the Archduchess's stables."

Marie Louise, for her part, was fulminating against her son's doctor. "Malfatti," she wrote to her daughter, "talks to everybody like the Delphic oracle; he does not want to commit himself by saying he is getting better, but on the other hand he does not want to say there is no hope for him, for fear that God might be given the credit if he were miraculously cured. He makes me so angry that I do not listen to him any more and prefer to rely on what my eyes and my experience of sick people tell me."

On the 5th Moll found Francis walking toward the balcony, leaning on a servant's shoulder. The Baron was moved to pity. "He looked quite frightening, white as a sheet, cadaverous, trembling with rage, his eyes starting from their sockets, his hands stretched out toward me."

"Monseigneur, the weather is unsuitable for going out on the balcony."

He answered in a choking voice: "Air! I need air! I want air!"

"It was horrible to see him so convulsed with anger, furious to the point of frenzy," wrote Moll. Suddenly Reichstadt noticed Prince Colloredo on another balcony, putting up an awning with the help of some carpenters. Ashamed at the idea that he might have been overheard, he went in again and lay down on his divan.

"They are trying to kill me," he complained. "I need more air—that's the only thing that might give me my strength back."

Two minutes later a torrential downpour showed Moll to have been in the right. Francis seemed upset at having lost his temper, and in his remorse he was particularly kind and amiable to Moll. The officer read to him for over three hours. Francis lay motionless with his eyes fixed on one point, his cheeks flushed, his breath coming quickly. He was thinking about Naples—"the gateway to Paradise." . . . The fact that Dietrichstein had gone off to Würzburg to attend his daughter's delivery put new heart into him. If Dietrichstein could leave him like that, then he could not be so very low. . . .

On July 6, while in another wing of the palace the Archduchess Sophia was bringing into the world little Maximilian—the future Emperor of Mexico with the tragic destiny—Francis, dressed in a red-and-white striped dressing gown, white trousers and a Grecian bonnet, spent the day on the balcony, protected by screens from the curiosity of passers-by. The heat made him suffer cruelly and he kept repeating: "Air, more air!" The wind rose and soon a fresh storm blew up. He had to go in again. He began fretting over the memory of a hunting party at Holitz, near the Moravian frontier, where he had accidentally fired his gun in the direction of the King of Hungary. Nobody had been injured, but this evening he started reproaching himself with this accident and talking "like a madman" about the "crime" he had committed. Moll tried to calm him down, but all in vain.

He felt lonelier than ever.

"My heart is empty," he said, "and I don't know what love is: not only love for a woman, but love for my fellow men too."

"That is the inevitable consequence of your cold, reserved nature, Monseigneur; of your mistrust too, which alienates all who approach you and whom you regard as treacherous and disloyal."

Moll cited himself as an example. Francis had never taken him into his confidence.

"I deluded myself in hoping that I might become a friend of yours."

"But aren't you a friend of mine?"

"Friendship must be mutual; have you given me yours?"

Francis did not dare to reply.

"I feel a sincere and cordial liking for you," the captain went on, "and I admire your intelligence, but I have always felt sorry that you haven't any heart. That is why you have had so little happiness in your life, and you won't have much more in the future as long as you go on mistrusting those around you and as long as you remain cold and selfish."

Moll's outspoken criticism went home. It was true that he had never confided in anyone except Prokesch and, to a certain extent, Esterházy. But that was not due to selfishness. The education which had been inflicted on him since early childhood had forced him to turn in upon himself. He mistrusted people? But of course he did! How could he be expected to do anything else? So many things had been concealed from him, and he had been told so many lies! He had not had a childhood like other children's. "They" had tried to repress his feelings. "They" had done their best to curb his emotions. "They" had endeavored to eradicate from his memory the picture he had kept of the legendary soldier who had clasped him in a rough embrace against his green uniform decorated with a diamond star. And now, in a pitifully broken voice, he asked this stranger, this captain who was waiting for him to die to take one of his horses: "Tell me, what must I do to have a heart?"

And he listened to the reply of this man who had not understood the drama of his life any better than the others:

"Be sincere, frank, loyal, trustful. No one on earth has the slightest reason to mistrust you: everything about you arouses interest and everyone would like to be on good terms with you; all that is necessary is that you should not repulse offers of sympathy and affection. So far your cold, reserved nature is familiar only to those of us who know you well, and there is no likelihood of our describing it to all and sundry; but once you enter into close relations with other people, they will have no reason to keep quiet about the unpleasant impression your cold, mistrustful character will have made on them. . . ."

Francis's only reply to this harangue was a murmured: "You know me very well."

On Sunday the 8th the Archbishop of Erlau—Ladislas von Purker—who had come to Schönbrunn to baptize Sophia's son, paid a call on Francis. He later wrote in his memoirs:

> To set the conversation going, I reminded him that the last time I had come to see him, when he was seventeen and growing very fast and the doctors had recommended cold baths to build up his strength, I had urged him not to indulge too freely in them, and I suggested that he might have contracted his pulmonary affection in this way. But he sharply retorted that there was nothing wrong with the chest, as the doctors mistakenly maintained, and that he was suffering from a liver complaint like his father; he hoped to be cured of it soon and was looking forward to leaving for Ischl. A violent fit of coughing interrupted him. I took his hand and told him that it was said that he was losing patience with his illness, but that he should be calm and patient and the medicaments would allay his sufferings. At the word "patience" he smiled and said:
>
> "So I should have patience, should I? That would be difficult now."
>
> And he began laughing quietly to himself, something which I understand was a characteristic of the Emperor Napoleon's. When another fit of coughing started I got up to go. . . .

Two days later—on July 9—Malfatti decided to move Francis into the little Schönbrunn garden known by the French name of the Poulaingraine. There, surrounded by tall fir trees, there was a summer house whose ceiling was decorated with an eagle with outstretched wings. Resting there, Francis would be able to look out over "a lawn of quite remarkable freshness, dotted with clusters of flowers."

Reichstadt agreed, but he was too weak to walk, so a sedan chair was sent from Vienna. The sick man was willing to use it, but only on condition that the curtains were drawn. The thought of being seen in an invalid chair struck him as profoundly humiliating. When he arrived at the Poulaingraine, he found a crowd of people gossiping with Marie Louise and the Archduke Leopold.

"That makes everything perfect!" he muttered.

Just at that moment the King and Queen of Hungary arrived. Francis took refuge in a surly silence. In the evening, after his mother had gone, and he was alone with Moll, he gave a sigh of relief and said: "Thank Heavens for a little peace: I like it best when there are just the two of us."

On the 11th he found the heat exhausting and agreed to go to the Poulaingraine.

"I don't want my mother to see me getting in," he said when the sedan chair was brought for him.

And then he asked: "Don't people laugh at me for letting myself be carried around?"

The fresh air did him good and he went back to the garden in the afternoon, but he had scarcely settled down to watch little Francis Joseph at play than he decided to go in again.

"There is no strength left in me," he complained. "I am completely worn out. My body is decomposing and I am dying."

On the 13th he found it impossible to remain in a sitting position in the Poulaingraine; he was laid out on a chaise-longue, but even then he could not keep his head upright: it nodded like an old man's.

Moll tried to cheer him up but he replied: "How can I get strong again? You can't imagine how exhausted I feel."

Malfatti finally admitted his inability to do anything for the Prince.

"We are no longer making any progress," he said. "On the contrary, we are losing ground. The heat has upset all my calculations."

That night, Francis was alarmingly weak and racked by fits of coughing. Twice he had to be lifted up in bed to allow him to get his breath back.

"You are the only person," he told Moll, "whose sympathy I really appreciate."

On July 14 he was still finding it difficult to breathe, but he was too weak to go down to the garden. Moll, Marschall and Hartmann used the spare time at their disposal to go and make an inventory of the stables.

"The Archduchess Mother," Moll was heard to say, "could have this provision carriage for her personal use."

Marie Louise had no thought for anyone but herself. As soon as the Emperor returned to Vienna, she meant to entrust Francis to his care if he was still alive and go back to Parma. In her latest letter to her daughter she had devoted seventy-six lines to news of herself and only thirteen to her son.

On Sunday the 15th Francis went down to the garden for the last time; he found breathing so difficult that he only stayed for a few minutes. Another storm was in the offing. Back in his bedroom, he complained of the stifling heat. He was dripping with sweat, but his forehead was cold as ice. He dropped off into a doze from which he was roused only by fits of coughing which left him pale and exhausted. In the evening he spat a great deal and this brought him some relief. The night was appalling. Marie Louise came three times to ask how he was, thinking that this was the end. The Eaglet had the windows thrown wide open and wanted to go into the garden, but he was so weak—he had stopped eating—that he was easily dissuaded.

The next day—Monday the 16th—he lost his voice and could only make himself understood by means of gestures. In his fury he threw himself about on the settee like a madman, striking his forehead with his fists. The application of leeches gave him no relief.

On the 17th his throat was sore and swollen. Pus appeared in his mouth and Moll removed it with a handkerchief. Francis was again completely speechless. On his face was written the question: "Am I dying?"

There was a dreadful smell in the bedroom. No one dared to move the sick man. His thoughts seemed far away, but he had still not given up the struggle. Moll opened a book and read for a while. When he had finished and asked if he might stay a little longer by the bed, Francis shook his head.

For the next two days he remained completely prostrate and had to be lifted up whenever he had a fit of coughing. His voice had come back a little, however. Marie Louise came to see him, but he did not notice, and after she had gone he asked: "Has my mother been yet?"

He became as meek as a lamb, and several times took Moll's hand and murmured softly: "I am very fond of you. . . . I never thought I could be as fond of anyone as I am of you. . . ."

On the 19th he started talking again about the journey he was going to make. Were the carriages ready? In a voice which already seemed to be coming from another world, he sighed: "Oh, just to be able to get away from Vienna! As soon as I am in my carriage I shall start getting better."

Wrapped in hot compresses, he fell asleep.

On Friday the 20th, Hartmann, Moll and Standeisky shared out "Monseigneur's" personal effects, with Marschall presiding over the operation. All the servants were to be dismissed, except for the groom who was to take the horses to Parma. Each of the officers was to have a horse and a saddle. "The timeliness of the proposed measures," wrote the shameless Moll, "does honor to General Marschall's tact." The three officers also hoped to be given Parmesan honors—Hartmann to be made a commander and the two captains to be knighted. But according to Marschall, Marie Louise thought of no one but her favorite of the day, Sanvitale. Marschall had insisted on her leaving him at Trieste, "to the Duchess's immense indignation." While her son lay dying she spent her time combing the shops of Vienna for presents "for her lovers and favorites." There were already three packing cases full of gifts in her apartments. But she had enough decency left to give orders that they should not be sent off to Parma until a month after her son's death.

In the anteroom charlatans and quacks followed hard on each other's heels. One had a potion to be taken every two minutes, night and day, for twelve days. Another recommended the consumption of sixty-four living snails.

On Saturday, July 21, there were signs that a fresh crisis was imminent. Francis could scarcely breathe, and murmured to Moll: "I want to die. . . . all I want is to die!"

Suddenly his breathing became easier, and with a sad smile on his lips he listened to Moll talking about his coming journey to Italy. The Captain read him a few pages of Spindler's *Wandering Jew* and Arlincourt's *Rebel*. The morning went by. At four o'clock there was a fresh attack in which the sick man came near to choking. The end seemed to be approaching rapidly. The Abbé Wagner came into the room with Marie Louise. She wanted to leave her son with the priest, but every time she got up to go, Francis rang for Moll. He had no desire to be left alone with the chaplain.

Toward evening he managed to get down a few spoonfuls of orgeat and egg-flip. He moaned softly like a child. . . . Malfatti gave instructions that packs and blisters were to be applied if his breath failed. After a few "magnetic passes" the doctor left the room. Francis asked in a whisper: "Is the carriage ready for the journey?"

"Koller hasn't quite finished with it."

He lost his temper and complained that "when he was in fit condition to travel, they would go on keeping him waiting because the carriage *would not be ready.*"

The same day—July 21—Prokesch called on Madame Letizia. He brought her news—the first she had received—of her grandson.

"You will tell him," she said, "that above all else he must respect his father's wishes. His hour will come. He will mount the throne of France."

Prokesch broke down and wept.

That night—the last night of his life—Francis was alone with his valet Lambert. His breathing had become increasingly noisy and painful. It already sounded like a death-rattle.

It was a torrid, sultry night. Thunder could be heard rumbling in the distance. Then there was a tremendous thunderclap followed by the same sound of tearing silk that had been heard during the previous storm. . . . Suddenly Francis's breathing quickened. The dying man was suffocating. Lambert rushed into the next door to fetch Moll. The two men lifted Francis into a sitting position. . . . It was in German that the Eaglet was to pronounce his last words:

"I am going under. . . . I am going under. . . ." *

The doctor came into the room. The dying man has started choking again.

"Call my mother! . . . my mother . . . Take the table away—I don't need anything any more. . . ."

* *"Ich gehe unter!"*

Moll hesitated. Should he send for Marie Louise? Just as the valet got to the door, Francis clutched the officer's arm like a drowning man and gasped: "Packs! . . . Blisters!"

He had scarcely uttered these two words before his eyes set in a glassy stare. But his heart went on beating, his breathing became easier, and he entered into a peaceful decline. The room began filling with people: Marie Louise, the Archduke Francis, Hartmann, Marschall, Standeisky, Moll, Malfatti, Dr. Nickert, Lambert and the footman Titz. The staff gathered in the doorway. Outside the castle a rainy day—Sunday, July 22—was dawning, but the shutters remained closed; the scene was lit only by candles which brought out the touches of gold in the room. A young priest came in, visibly trembling—it was the first time he had ever administered Extreme Unction—and went over to the bed to apply the holy oil. Francis came out of his lethargy and followed all the priest's gestures closely.

"Do you want to read the prayers now?"

Reichstadt shook his head.

"Do you want me to recite them?"

He nodded.

The priest's voice droned on in a gentle monotone. Marie Louise, kneeling beside the bed, gazed at the dying man's waxlike face, a gaunt face with the nose and cheekbones jutting out and the mat skin covered with beads of sweat, a face which, on the threshold of death, bore a striking resemblance to that of the first Consul.

An hour went by. . . .

A few minutes after five, the Eaglet shook his head twice . . . and then his breathing stopped.

The son of Napoleon was dead.

The fragments of one of the eagles on the roof, shattered by lightning during the night, lay on the ground in a pool of water.

18

✤

The Bronze Coffin

"I AM DEEPLY GRIEVED by his death, but I cannot help wondering whether it is not a good thing both for himself and for the monarchy. . . ."

Thus the Emperor Francis remarked to Captain Moll, who had traveled all day to carry the news to Linz, where the Court was in residence. With tears in his eyes, the Eaglet's grandfather continued his strange funeral oration:

"With his unfortunate character, we could have expected the worst. As long as I was alive, there would have been nothing to fear, but he might well have given my son a great deal of trouble. He was imbued with the most corrupt political principles, though no one has ever been able to discover who instilled them into him."

In mingled tones of horror and relief, the Emperor recalled a conversation at the Court Theater in which Reichstadt had defended "the sovereignty of the people."

"Just imagine!" the Emperor went on in retrospective alarm. "Think what would happen if my subjects came and told me they didn't want me any more!"

Moll tried to defend Francis's memory.

"You are right," concluded the Emperor. "He could be two people at one and the same time."

By the time Moll arrived back at Schönbrunn, the autopsy, which had been carried out by six doctors, was over.

"The liver large, but its substance normal." These seven words in the report which Malfatti and Wiehrer had to sign were a complete condemnation of their diagnosis. As Foresti remarked: "It is sad to see that the two greatest doctors in Vienna could go on insisting on the presence of a disease which did not exist, while at the same time denying that of another disease whose symptoms were only too obvious."

Dressed in his white uniform, Francis lay in the Salon des Laques on a table draped in black, surrounded by a dozen candelabra. They had had to put on his hat, because within a few hours of his death all his hair had been cut off by souvenir hunters. The public filed past. The silence was broken only by the sobs which many of those who had come to pay their last respects could not hold back.

Night fell.

"It was a dark, cloudy night," Baroness Sturmfeder tells us, "lit up from time to time by great flashes of lightning. The castle itself was dark and silent, although the courtyards were full of people. When the clock struck ten a long procession of priests, all carrying tapers, came out of the chapel and made their way to the mortuary chamber to bless the body. Silence and darkness descended again on the castle until the great doors leading to the outer staircase were thrown open. Then I saw the priests come out again, followed by the coffin. They went into the chapel. The long procession moved slowly along and finally disappeared behind the closed door."

The funeral procession, flanked by cavalrymen carrying lighted torches, finally set off on the road to Vienna. The body, lying in an open coffin, wrapped in a white taffeta shroud, had been placed in a litter. Hartmann, Moll and Standeisky, thinking of their future careers, followed in a carriage. All along the route, despite the lateness of the hour, the people of Vienna had gathered to watch.

The next morning—Tuesday the 24th—Marie Louise went to join the imperial family at the castle of Persenbeug. For the last time—though on this occasion etiquette required it of her—she left her son in the hands of mercenaries.

The body had been placed in its open coffin in the middle of the Court chapel. Three rows of silver candelabra shed their light on Francis's face. The chin had been bound up too late and the teeth could be seen between the half-open lips. Red-and-gold draperies hung down from the coffin, and on the steps covered with black velvet there shone the dead man's arms—leopards and chimeras on an ermine ground.

Chimeras . . .

At the four corners of the coffin four officers in the rich red-and-gold uniforms of the German and Hungarian Guard stood rigidly at attention. In the side chapels one Mass was celebrated after another. The crowds filed past. The Comte de Montbel, Charles X's Minister, and the Count of Paar found themselves next to each other.

"I was present at the Prince's baptism," murmured the Count of Paar, "and here I am at his funeral. You see the insignia of the Order of St. Stephen, there beside the coffin? Well, I was with the Prince Schwarzenberg when, on the Emperor's orders, he attached that same decoration to the King of Rome's cradle."

At two o'clock a chamberlain, escorted by two pages with lighted torches and followed by Hartmann and Moll, carried the silver bowl containing the Eaglet's heart to the Loretto Chapel.

Then Francis's three officers took the vase in which the entrails were preserved to St. Stephen's. They drove there in the famous glass state-coach, accompanied by a crowd of footmen, chamberlains, major-domos and lifeguards.

At five o'clock the coffin was closed and placed by the Prince's and the Emperor's valets on the hearse reserved for archdukes' funerals, an antiquated carriage covered with red morocco and drawn by six white horses harnessed in red. Lifeguards, lackeys and pages carrying torches hemmed it in on all sides. Slowly, preceded by grenadiers and a cavalry detachment, the procession moved off, crossed the Josephplatz and the Lobkowitzplatz, and made for the Capuchin church.

Wasa's regiment—which was of course Francis's regiment too—lined the route all the way, sounding a muffled roll on their crepe-covered drums. A huge crowd dressed in black watched the Court carriages go by with Hartmann, Moll and Standeisky inside. The harbingers of the chamber and the Court, and the imperial, royal and ducal valets came next, followed by the troops who brought up the rear of the slow procession.

In the Neue-Markt, the hearse came to a halt in front of the little Capuchin church. Another Mass—the last—was celebrated. Then, after the final prayers of intercession, the coffin was lowered into the crypt. In accordance with ancestral tradition, Count Czernin, the Grand Imperial Master, had the bier opened in order to show the body to the father in charge of the Kaisergruft. For the last time Captain Moll looked at Francis's emaciated features.

His heart started beating wildly . . . for Francis now bore such a hallucinating resemblance to his father that it was as if he had Napoleon's death mask before his eyes. . . .

Some time later the coffin was covered with copper and decorated with a trefoiled cross on which the following inscription was engraved in Latin:

IN PERPETUAL MEMORY

OF JOSEPH CHARLES FRANCIS, DUKE OF REICHSTADT,

SON OF NAPOLEON, EMPEROR OF THE FRENCH

AND

OF MARIE LOUISE, ARCHDUCHESS OF AUSTRIA,

BORN IN PARIS ON MARCH 20, 1811.

HAILED IN HIS CRADLE AS KING OF ROME.

IN THE PRIME OF LIFE,

ENDOWED WITH EVERY QUALITY OF MIND AND BODY

TALL STATURE, A HANDSOME FACE,

AND SINGULAR GRACE OF SPEECH;

NOTED FOR HIS MILITARY ACCOMPLISHMENTS AND APTITUDES;

STRICKEN BY PHTHISIS,

CARRIED OFF BY THE CRUELEST OF DEATHS

IN THE IMPERIAL PALACE OF SCHÖNBRUNN,

NEAR VIENNA,

ON JULY 22, 1832.

Son of Napoleon, Emperor of the French . . .
It did not matter now that the Eaglet was no longer given as born of a "father unknown."

Before leaving Schönbrunn, Moll went to see the Archduchess Sophia. She spoke to him of Francis, whom she had not seen since July 5, "with great simplicity" but "without any display of emotion." "I was touched," she said, "by the courtesy he always showed me."

Those were scarcely the words of a woman in love. With the same essential coldness she sent Marie Louise a letter in which she spoke at once of "her dear Reichstadt" and the death of her grandmother which had occurred the same day. "One night," she sighed, "was enough to rob me of two persons dear to my heart!" Her funeral oration was rather like the one the Emperor had pronounced in front of Captain Moll: "It is true that it is sad, very sad to die young, before being able to enjoy the pleasures of life, but with these passing pleasures he would have come to know great bitterness, for he was not young in spirit but serious and thoughtful, and he did not see the world as young people see it—adorned with illusion and hope—but in all its sorry reality. Oh no, I knew him too well not to feel that he is better off, much better off up there than he would have been on earth."

Dietrichstein, who had been away from Schönbrunn at the time of his pupil's death, could not refrain from a final grumble in the letter he wrote to Marie Louise: "His lack of confidence and trust, so natural at his age, has always distressed me; I hoped that he might open his heart to me in the midst of his suffering, but all in vain! God has called him and the only consolation which remains to me is the thought that he was fortunate to die young; I shall say no more about that! However, from another point of view, his death is an incalculable disaster, as I have often maintained and as the near future will show, alas, for we are standing on a volcano which he might well have been able to get under control. His disappearance is the subject of universal regret, for no prince has ever aroused greater interest and sympathy in every class of society; I am in a position to know that this is so, and the knowledge makes me deeply unhappy. Oh, if only he had listened to my advice, he would be in perfect health today and his glory would be assured! . . ."

Marie Louise had taken all her son's papers with her to Parma, and told Dietrichstein that she intended to burn them. The ex-tutor, writing to her on September 9, gave his approval, though not without an expression of regret: "If he had been willing to put a little order into his ideas, he would have written great things." It must be assumed that certain papers Francis had left concerned Marie Louise . . . unless Reichstadt had felt the need to commit to paper certain ideas of an excessively liberal character. For on November 9, 1832, Dietrichstein wrote to Parma: "I have read and reread the letter which Your

Majesty wrote to me on September 16 concerning the Prince's manuscripts. I cannot imagine what he can have written that was so blameworthy as to call forth such disturbing condemnation! Alas, he was an inveterate scribbler, and loved filling whole notebooks with incoherent and often rather mad ideas—but there was more than that in his manuscripts. . . ."

The only person who mourned the Eaglet with all his heart was Prokesch. It was at Bologna, on his way back to Austria, that he heard the news of Reichstadt's death, which "struck him like a thunderbolt." For the rest of his life he continued to live in imaginary communion with his dead friend. When Napoleon III came to the throne and the Powers recognized him by that name, Prokesch exclaimed: "Now at last Europe has granted the son sleeping in his tomb the title of Napoleon II which it refused to give him in his lifetime. . . . In a moment of prophecy the noble youth once declared: 'My birth and my death form my entire history'; but outside his own history there is another, and that history cannot but mourn his destiny and his death."

For more than a century nearly every Frenchman who went to Vienna visited the Capuchin vaults, where, in the midst of dusty disorder, the son of Napoleon slept in a copper coffin patinated by time. The attendant would pronounce his name—after that of the Emperor Francis—and tap the sarcophagus with his key, before going on to the next tomb, to which Marie Louise had come to rest at the end of 1847. Often, before leaving the crypt, someone would place a few Parma violets on the coffin. . . .

Napoleon III had tried to have his cousin's body sent back to Paris, but Francis Joseph—Sophia's son—had refused his permission. He could remember that July morning when, as a child, he had spent nearly an hour with Marie Louise by the Eaglet's deathbed. "Good Eichstadt isn't sleeping," he had said.

For some reason or other he persisted in his refusal . . . and the son of Napoleon remained a prisoner. It needed the terrible defeat of 1940 to set him free.

"Between the melancholy fate of the Duke of Reichstadt, a prisoner in his own family," declared Marshal Pétain in his message to the

French people, "and the cruel fate of France, exiled in her own country by the arbitrament of war, history will note a moving analogy. . . ."

And a hundred years to the day after the return from St. Helena came the return from Vienna.

It was bitterly cold on that night of December 14-15, 1940. Lying on a gun carriage, the coffin crossed a Paris wrapped in darkness and sleep, following the Seine, passing the Tuileries where the little King had been born, and going along the riverside terrace where he had often ridden in his little carriage drawn by Franconi's sheep. . . .

It was nearly one o'clock in the morning when the procession, preceded by a motorcycle escort, came to a halt on the esplanade in front of the Invalides. It had started snowing. In the huge courtyard stood a double line of Republican Guards holding lighted torches. Officials exchanged a few words outside the gate. But the German soldiers came no farther. Twenty Republican Guards took hold of the heavy bronze coffin, and it was on French shoulders that the remains of Napoleon's son slowly crossed the courtyard with its immaculate carpet of snow.

Bugles blared out. Then the drums beat a general salute as of old. . . . The body of the Duke of Reichstadt was carried round the marble balustrade and placed before the altar above the tomb where, for the past hundred years, the Emperor had been waiting for his son. A huge tricolor flag covered the gray coffin, hanging down in folds over the purple steps dotted with golden bees. Wreaths of incense rose into the air.

The few of us who were present went away deeply moved, leaving the little white ghost surrounded by ten Republican Guards with drawn swords, ten Guards in full dress, wearing a uniform which recalled that worn by the soldiers of the Grand Army. . . . In the half-light of the side chapels, Foch, Vauban and Turenne also watched over the colonel in the white uniform.

The King of Rome, in his long bronze coffin placed beside the red porphyry sarcophagus, was henceforth to rest beneath the gleaming golden dome "on the banks of the Seine, in the midst of the French people" whom he would so much have liked to know and love.

The Eaglet had come home to the Eagle.

Sources

The term *Archives of Marie Louise* refers both to the documents reproduced in the catalogue published by the House of Karl and Faber of Munich and to the letters which I have been able to copy myself, thanks to M. Castaing (Cf. Foreword). All these letters were addressed to Maria Louise between 1810 and 1832.

PART ONE

I

THE BEAUTIFUL HEIFER

(March, 1810)

Archives of Marie Louise: Letter from the Emperor Francis of Austria: 17-III-1810; Empress Maria Ludovica: 14-III, 15-III, 17-III, 28-III-1810; King Anthony, Clement, Theodore of Saxony: 26-II-1810.

Archives Nationales: 02.18; 02.19; 02.41; 02.203; 02.1217; AF IV-1453. Marie Louise's journey; delivery at Braunau; clothes; presents, etc., etc.

Memoirs, anecdotes, etc.: Queen Hortense, General Gourgaud, Mme. Durand, Grand Marshal Bertrand, Marchand, Pasquier, Bausset, Constant, Méneval, Ligne, Clary-et-Aldringen, Metternich, Archduke Rainer, etc.

Correspondence de Marie-Louise (1799-1847), Vienna, 1887: *Lettres inédites de Napoléon à Marie-Louise* (B.N. 1935). Letters from Metternich to the Emperor Francis. Letter from Schwarzenberg to Metternich.

Principal works consulted (list valid for the whole of Part One): Raymonde Bessard: *Marie-Louise intime;* Édouard Gachot: *Marie-Louise;* Jules Bertaut: *Marie-Louise;* Jean de Bourgoing: *Marie-Louise;* Léon Grégoire: *Le divorce de Napoléon;* Frédéric Masson: *Napoléon et son fils; L'impératrice Marie-Louise; Napoléon et sa famille;* Viktor Bibl: *François II; Napoléon II;* Jean Savant: *Tel fut le Roi de Rome;* Bernardine Melchior-Bonnet: *Le Pape et l'Empereur;* Édouard von Wertheimer: *Der Herzog von Reichstadt;* Metternich: *Nachgelassene Papiere;* French newspapers of the time and *Wiener Zeitung.*

II
THE AUSTRIAN WOMB
(April 1, 1810, to March 20, 1811)

Archives of Marie Louise: Letters from the Empress Maria Ludovica: 23-IV, 21-V, 20-VI, 2-VII, 1-IX, 30-IX-1810; 22-II-1811; Emperor Francis: 15-IV, 16-VII, 21-IX-1810; 11-I-1811; Countess Lazansky: 24-IV-1810, 20-II-1811.

Archives Nationales: AF IV-1453 (plans before birth); F.I. c. I.105 (summons to bishops, etc.); 02.519 (cradles, furnishings); 02.524 (cradles and layette); 02.815 and 816 (health service); 02.1219 (clothes, household); 02.1220 (layette).

Bibliothèque Thiers: Fonds Masson.

Bibliothèque Nationale: MSS. T. 6578. N.A. 5876.

Memoirs, newspaper, anecdotes (besides those already listed): Anatole de Montesquiou (*Revue de Paris,* V-48); Marie Louise's travel diary (*Revue de Paris,* II and III-1921); Coignet, Comtesse de Kielmansegge, Alfred Nettement, Las Cases, Stendhal, Frénilly, Comtesse de Boigne, Dr. Poumiès de la Siboutie, Rovigo.

Correspondences (besides those already listed): Letters from Marie Louise to her father. Vienna Archives (*Haus-Hof und Staatsarchiv*).

Principal works consulted (besides those already listed): Dr. Paul Ganière: *Corvisart;* Garros: *Quel roman que ma vie* (Napoleon's itinerary); Ravage: *Iphigénie ou la vie de Marie-Louise;* J.-L. Dubreton: *La France de Napoléon;* Roger Whal: *Le Palais du Roi de Rome;* Henri Welschinger: *Le Roi de Rome;* Octave Aubry: *Le Roi de Rome;* Helfert: *Marie-Louise;* Firmin Didot: *Le baptême du Roi de Rome;* newspapers of the time: *Le Moniteur, Journal de l'Empire,* etc.

III
THE KING OF ROME
(March 20 to June 23, 1811)

Archives of Marie Louise: Letters from the Austrian family on the occasion of the birth of the King of Rome: Emperor Francis, Empress Maria Ludovica, Archdukes Rudolph and Francis Charles, Joseph, Count Palatine, Archduchess Leopoldine, Queen Maria Theresa of Saxony and Countess Lazansky (March and April, 1811).

Archives Nationales: AF. IV-1453, 1685 and 1690, speeches and odes (cities of the Empire); 02.203 (illuminations); 02.215 (wet-nurses); 02.1219 (grants and cradle); 02.1218 (pawnshop) (the file of 02.1218 bears the words *Fils de Buonaparte* written under the Restoration); 02.18 (costs of hospitality); F. Ic. 105 and 02.816 (poems); 02.41 (presents); 02.20 and 02.41 (expenses); 02.29 (presents); 02.138 (expenses at Notre-Dame); 02.137 (baptism); 02.139 and 192 (Saint-Cloud); 02.137 (sprinkling); 02.815 and 816 (vaccination).

Memoirs and anecdotes (besides those already listed): Mameluk Ali, Mme. Blanchard and *Correspondance de Louis XVIII.*

Principal works consulted (besides those already listed): Alberto Lumbroso: *Napoléon II;* Henri Welschinger: *Le Roi de Rome;* and Jean de Bourgoing: *Le Fils de Napoléon,* a work of capital importance, especially for Part Two of this biography. *Souvenirs du Roi de Rome* (Catalogue of the 1832 Exhibition).

IV
"THE LITTLE FELLOW"
(June, 1811, to January, 1814)

Archives of Marie Louise: Letters from the Emperor Francis: 21-VII-1811; 4-III, 12-V, 13-IX-1813; 11-V, 28-VII, 7-XII and 20-XII-1813; Empress Maria Ludovica: 7-VII, 2-VIII, 23-XI-1811; 13-I, 30-IV, 31-X, 4-XII, 18-XII-1812; 16-I, 13-II, 20-III, 11-V, 14-VIII, 20-IX, 3-X-1813; letter from Maria Theresa, Queen of Saxony: 22-VII-1813; Archduchess Leopoldine: 27-III-1813; Archduke Louis: 14-XI-1812; Archduke Francis Charles: 6-VIII-1812, 16-II-1813; Countess Lazansky: 17-XI-1812, 15-I-1813.

Archives Nationales: 02.527 (furniture); 02.1219 and 1220 (expenses, toys); 02.519 (Meudon); 02.1218 (Household of King of Rome, toys); 02.816 (pharmacy); 02.1216 (payments).

Memoirs, anecdotes, etc. (besides those already listed): Mme. de Montet, Caulaincourt, vol. II.

Correspondence: Marie Louise (*op. cit.*) and letters from Marie Louise to Napoleon from the Archives of the King of Sweden (published by Baron Palmstierna). These important letters were made public only in 1955 and have not hitherto been used for a work on the King of Rome. I have made little use of them for this chapter, but I cite them on almost every page of the three following chapters.

Principal works consulted (besides those already listed): Saint-Amand: *Les jours heureux de Marie-Louise;* Alain Decaux: *La Conspiration du général Malet;* Louis Madelin: *Histoire du Consulat et de l'Empire,* vols. XI, XII and XIII.

V
THE IMP
(January 23 to April 3, 1814)

Archives of Marie Louise: Letters from the Emperor Francis: 9-II, 6-III-1814.

Memoirs, anecdotes, etc.: King Joseph; Savary-Rovigo; Talleyrand: *L'Impératrice à Orléans* (*Revue de Paris*, Nov., 1832); MS of Duchemin de la Chesnaye (Vendôme Municipal Library); Amédée Thierry (*Souvenirs fragmentaires*); *Voyage de Marie-Louise à Blois* (par un page de Bonaparte); Mémoires des la Société des Sciences et des Lettres de Loir-et-Cher; Méneval (*op. cit.*).

Correspondence: Marie Louise and Napoleon. Napoleon's correspondence.

Works consulted (besides those already listed): Madelin: *Histoire du Consulat et de l'Empire*, vol. XIV; Henri Houssaye: *1814*; Robert Milliat: *L'Aiglon à Vendôme*; Masson: *Napoléon et sa famille*.

VI
THE PRINCE OF PARMA
(April 3 to March 21, 1814)

Archives of Marie Louise: Letters from the Emperor Francis: 7-IV, 12-IV, 4-V-1814; Empress Maria Ludovica: 24-IV and 8-V-1814; Archduchess Leopoldine: 27-IV-1814.

Archives Nationales: 02.1216 and 02.230 (winding-up of the Household of the King of Rome).

Memoirs, anecdotes, etc.: *Revue des Deux Mondes* (Dec., 1938, and Jan., 1939); Marie Louise's *Notebooks*, presented by Jean Hanoteau and the Baron de Bourgoing (Dr. Glauco Lombardi's collection) and, in the same review, the Empress's confidences to her daughter Albertine; Caulaincourt, III; Marmont; Galbois; Belliard; Macdonald; A. de Montesquiou (*op. cit.*); Waldburg-Truchess; Campbell; Bausset (*op. cit.*); Méneval (*op. cit.*).

Correspondence. Marie Louise and Napoleon (*op. cit.*).

Works consulted. The Baron de Bourgoing's *Fils de Napoléon* for the police report dated May 22, 1814, taken from the Archives of the Ministry of the Interior in Vienna; *Aus dem Tagebuch des Erzherzogs Johann* (the Archduke John's diary), passage translated by Jean de Bourgoing; Pierre Saint-Marc: *Marmont*; Robert Christophe: *Marmont*; *Revue des Deux Mondes*, 15-IX-1902 (arrival at Schönbrunn); newspapers of the time: *Le Moniteur, Le Journal des Débats*.

VII
ASTYANAX
(May 22, 1814, to February, 1815)

Archives of Marie Louise: Letters from the Emperor Francis: 7-VIII, 9-IX, 1-X-1814; Empress Maria Ludovica: 8-IX-1814, 31-VII; Archduchess Leopoldine: 12-VII, 30-VII, 12-VII-1814; Archduke Francis Charles: 13-VIII-1814; letter from the Queen of Naples, 22-VIII-1814; Duchesse de Montebello, 7-XI, 31-XI-1814. These letters are replies to those from Marie Louise published by Édouard Gachot (*Marie-Louise intime*).

Memoirs, anecdotes, etc.: Villemin; Mme. de Montesquiou: *Récit* published as a sequel to the *Souvenirs* of Comte Anatole de Montesquiou (*Revue de Paris,* V-48); Marchand, vol. I; Méneval (*op. cit.*); Vitrolles; Metternich (*op. cit.*); Pons de L'Hérault.

Correspondence: Maria Ludovica to the Emperor Francis; Augustin de la Garde; Marie Louise and Napoleon (*op. cit.*).

Works consulted: Harold Nicolson: *Le Congrès de Vienne;* Jean Thiry: *La Première Restauration;* A. Elmer: *Schulmeister;* Jean de Bourgoing: *Le Fils de Napoléon* (police reports, diary of J. G. Eynard, State archives); Weil: *Les dessous du Congrès de Vienne;* Aubry (*op. cit.*); Angebery: *Le Congrès de Vienne.*

VIII
NAPOLEON II
(March 5 to September 3, 1815)

Archives of Marie Louise: Letters from the Emperor Francis: 6-VIII, II-VIII, 6-IX, 30-IX-1815; letters from the Empress Maria Ludovica: 7-III, 8-III, IV, VII, VIII and IX-1815 (35 letters for 1815); letter from the Archduke Rainer: 26-VII-1815; letter from the Archduke Charles: 11-VI-1815.

Memoirs, anecdotes, etc.: Thibeaudeau, Montholon, Lafayette, Marchand, Benjamin Constant, Fleury de Chaboulon, Fouché, General Thiébaut, Lucien Bonaparte, Boulay de la Meurthe, Bausset (*op. cit.*), Villemain, Gourgaud (*op. cit.*).

Correspondence: Marie Louise to her father; Louis XVIII and Talleyrand; letters intercepted by the Austrian police (Bourgoing: *Le Fils de Napoléon*); Comte de la Garde (*op. cit.*).

Works consulted: Observations of Count Maurice Dietrichstein (*Revue des Études Napoléoniennes,* 1932, Jean de Bourgoing); Madelin: *Histoire du Consulat et de l'Empire,* XVI; Houssaye: *1815;* Madelin: *Fouché;* Angelberg (*op. cit.*); Hippolyte Carnot: *Souvenirs sur Carnot;* Gentz (text published by Bourgoing: *Le Fils de Napoléon*); Comte de la Garde (*op. cit.*); *Le Moniteur* (June 22 and 23); *Le Journal des Débats*.

PART TWO
IX
FRANCIS CHARLES
(June 30, 1815, to March, 1817)

Archives of Marie Louise: Letters from the future Duke of Reichstadt: III, IV, V, VIII, XII-1816; Count Maurice Dietrichstein: 13-II, 20-III, 26-III, 6-V, 20-VI, 5-IV, 21-XI and 9-XII-1816, 4-I, 1-II-1817; Emperor Francis: 30-IX-1815, 15-II, 16-IV, 8-X-1816; Empress Maria Ludovica: 9-III-1816; Archduke Rainer: II-IX, 17-XI-1815, 10-III, 14-II, 12-V, 17-V, 21-VII-1816, 19-II-1817; Archduchess Leopoldine: 2-III, 7-III, 17-V, 18-VI, 20-VI, 26-VI, 9-VII, 2-VIII, 27-VIII, 30-VIII, 3-IX, 15-X, 20-X, 14-XI, 19-XI, 14-XII-1816, 4-I, 7-I, 21-IV, 20-IV-1817; letters from Archduke Louis: 21/22-III, 22-IV, 7-VII, 21-VIII, 18-X-1816; Archduke Louis: 16-XI-1817; Archduke Francis Charles: 26-V, 15-VIII, 3-XI-1816, 15-IV-1817; the future Emperor Ferdinand: summer, 1816; Maria Theresa of Austria, Queen of Saxony: 29-III-1817; Henrietta, Princess of Nassau, wife of the Archduke Charles: 19-VI-1816 and 2-I-1817; Mme. Lazansky: 21-VI- and 30-VIII-1816; Count Feodor Karaczay: 21-VI-1816.

Memoirs, anecdotes, etc.: The most important are the documents published by the Baron de Bourgoing in the *Revue des Etudes Napoléoniennes* (July and August, 1932). They consist of Count Maurice Dietrichstein's *Observations* (*Bemerkungen*), which go up to 1818, and Captain Foresti's *Notes*, which stop at January 21, 1818. Cf. also the Baronne de Montet's *Souvenirs* and the *Mémoires* of Napoleon's companions at St. Helena: Gourgaud, Las Cases, Montholon, Marchand.

Corrrespondence: Letters from Marie Louise to Comtesse de Créneville; letters from Marie Louise to Dietrichstein, preserved in Count Dietrichstein's archives and published by the Baron de Bourgoing (*Le Fils de Napoléon*); letters from Marie Louise to her father (Vienna archives); letters from Marie Louise to Mme. de Montebello (published by E. S. Édouard Gachot); *Dépêches inédites aux hospodars de Valachie* and *Correspondance* of Gentz.

Works consulted (list valid for most of the chapters in this work): Jean de Bourgoing: *Le Fils de Napoléon*; Édouard von Wertheimer: *Der Herzog von Reichstadt*; Viktor Bibl: *Napoléon II, François II*; Octave Aubry: *Le Roi de Rome, La Trahison de Marie Louise*; Frédéric Masson: *Le*

Fils de Napoléon; Montbel: *Le duc de Reichstadt;* Jean Savant: *Tel fut le Roi de Rome;* Henri Welschinger: *Le Roi de Rome;* Édouard Driault: *Le Roi de Rome;* Raymonde Bessart: *La vie privée de Marie-Louise;* Jules Bertaut: *Marie-Louise;* Jean de Bourgoing: *Marie-Louise;* Alberto Lumbroso: *Napoleon II; Souvenirs du Roi de Rome* (Catalogue of 1932 Exhibition, Preface by Jean de Bourgoing); Alexandre Mahan: *Marie-Louise.*

X
"SWEET REICHSTADT"
(March 20, 1817, to May 8, 1821)

Archives of Marie Louise: Letters from the Duke of Reichstadt: first letter in German (1817); three letters for December 1818, April 1819, summer 1819, 20-XI, XII-1819; one letter 1819 (21 in the catalogue), 29-III, IV, 17-V and 18-IX-1820; letters from Dietrichstein: 25-III, 8-IV, 1-V, 20-V, 13-VI, 16-VII, 7-VII, 23-VIII, 26-VIII, 5-X, 11-XII-1817; 17-I, 2-II, 13-II, 30-III, 9-V, 20-IX, 3-X, 10-X, 9-XII-1818; 24-II, 16-III, 24-III, 28-IV, 26-V, 23-VI, 24-VII, 28-VIII, 29-IX, 20-IX, 20-XI, 9-X-1819; 5-I, 4-III, 22-III, 29-III, 8-IV, 15-IV, 26-IV, 17-V, 7-X, 18-X, 18-XI, 9-XII-1820; 6-I, 17-I, 16-V-1821; Emperor Francis: 12-X-1817, 6-I-1819; Empress Caroline: 19-XI-1817, 19-IX-1818, 9-XII-1819; Archduke Rainer: 25-II-1817, 3-I, 15-IX, 24-IX, 8-X-1818; 18-V, 8-XI, 8-X, 25-XII-1819; Archduchess Leopoldine: 16-III-1817, 14-VII-1820; Archduke Charles: 3-I-1818; Archduke Francis Charles: 17-X-1818; Maria Anna, Grand Duchess of Tuscany: 28-XI-1819; Queen Maria Theresa of Saxony: 29-III-1817, 30-IX-1818, 19-VIII-1819; Henrietta, Princess of Nassau: 7-I-1818, 7-X-1819; Countess Lazansky: 18-X, 25-XII-1818, 2-II, 19-IV-1820, 12-VI-1821; Archduke John: 22-VII-1818, 22-XII-1819; Archduke Louis: 18-V, 22-IX, 8-X, 11-XI-1819; Victoire Folliot de Créneville: 24-X-1819; Archduke Ferdinand (future Emperor), 17-X-1818; Maria Clementine (Princess of Salerno), 22-IX-1818, 21-III, 25-XII-1819, 26-I-1820, 4-X-1820; *Archives of the Ministry of Foreign Affairs,* Vienna, 1818-1819.

Memoirs, anecdotes, etc.: Papiers intimes et Journal du duc de Reichstadt, published by Jean de Bourgoing, translated by Étienne Kruger; *Observations* by Dietrichstein (*op. cit.*); *Notes* by Foresti (*op. cit.*) (for 1817 and the beginning of 1818); Montet (*op. cit.*); Charles Auguste Petit: *Chronique du village de Theresienfeld; Meine Selbstbiographie,* by Archbishop Ladislas de Pyrker (translated by J. de Bourgoing; *Le Fils de Napoléon*); Pasquier: *Mémoires.*

XI
"TO MY SON . . ."
(March, 1821, to January, 1823)

Archives of Marie Louise: Letters from the Duke of Reichstadt: 15-VIII, late XI, XII-1821, 28-II, 20-VI, 18-VII, 20-XII-1822; Count Dietrichstein: 13-VI, 1-VIII, 11-VIII, 25-VIII (1822 missing); Emperor Francis: 29-V-1820; Leopoldine, Empress of Brazil: 8-VIII-1822; Maria Clementine, Princess of Salerno: 11-I-1822; Queen Maria Theresa of Saxony: 6-VIII and 2-IX-1821; Archduke Leopold: 8-VIII-1822; Mme. Amelin de Sainte-Marie: 16-VII-1821; Victoire de Créneville: 18-VII, 18-VIII-1821.

Archives Nationales: F 7.6704, 6705, 6995 (Bonapartist plots and demonstrations).

Memoirs, anecdotes, etc.: Montet (*op. cit.*); Dr. Hermann Rollet: *Neue Beiträge zur Chronik der Stadt Baden bei Wien*; Antommarchi: *Mémoires*; Grand Marshal Bertrand: *Cahiers de Sainte-Hélène*, deciphered by Paul Fleuriot de Langle; Marchand (*op. cit.*); Gourgaud (*op. cit.*); Montholon (*op. cit.*); *Dans l'ombre de l'Histoire*, Prince de Faucigny-Lucinge.

Correspondence: Letter from the Duke of Reichstadt to Collin (*Neue Freie Presse*, 5-III-1889), published by Schütz; letters from Marie Louise (*op. cit.*); letters from F. R. de Chateaubriand to the Duke de Caraman (private archives of Mme. Firrino-Martell).

Works consulted: Guillon: *Les complots militaires sous la Restauration*; Octave Aubry: *Sainte-Hélène* (vol. II); Max Billard: *Les maris de Marie-Louise*; Lumbroso: *Napoléon II* (*op. cit.*); Octave Aubry: *La trahison de Marie-Louise*; Imbert de Saint-Amand: *Marie-Louise et le duc de Reichstadt.*

XII
DIETRICHSTEIN'S PUPIL
(Summer, 1822, to January, 1827)

Archives of Marie Louise: Letters from the Duke of Reichstadt: 28-II, 20-VI, 20-VII, 20-XII-1822, 4-IX, 24-IX, 29-X, 3-XII-1823, 10-I, 1-V, 30-V, 27-XI, 21-XII-1824, 25-I, 27-II, 22-III, 29-V, 5-VI, 16-VIII, 29-IX, 3-XII-1825, 18-IV, 28-V, 14-X, 21-XI-1826, 3-III-1827; Dietrichstein: 22-I-1823, 10-I, 30-V, 5-VIII-1824, 15-I, 22-III, 5-VI, 16-VIII, 3-XII, 20-XII-1825, 28-V, 14-X, 3-VIII, 4-X, 25-XI-1826; Archduchess Sophia: 5-X-1826; Countess Lazansky: 18-II, 24-XI-1824; Clementine, Princess of Salerno: 10-V-1824; 8-VII-1825, n.d. (1825?); Archduke

Louis: 3-III, 21-XI-1824, 5-III-1825; Marchand (Napoleon's valet): 1-VII-1822.

The extract from the Duke of Reichstadt's letter of 10-I-1827 is taken from the *Revue des Deux Mondes* (coll. of Dr. Glauco Lombardi, *op. cit.*); *Archives of the Ministry of Foreign Affairs,* Vienna, 406, 409.

Malmaison Museum (papers of the Duke of Reichstadt).

Memoirs, anecdotes, etc.: Fragment of Obenaus's diary for 1825 (*Revue des Études Napoléoniennes*), July-August, 1832, published by J. de Bourgoing; Montet (*op. cit.*); Vitrolles (*op. cit.*); Metternich (*op. cit.*).

Papers of the Duke of Reichstadt: Journal de voyage, August, 1823; essay: *MM. les chefs de brigade,* etc.; *Biographie du prince Philippe de Schwarzenberg* (1826).

<h3 style="text-align:center">XIII</h3>
<h3 style="text-align:center">"NOT A PRISONER, BUT . . ."</h3>
(January, 1827, to June 12, 1830)

Archives of Marie Louise: Letters from the Duke of Reichstadt: 21-V, 30-VI, 17-XI, 4-XII, 22-XII-1827, 24-III, 6-X, 2-XII-1828, 7-II, 7-III, 11-IV, 14-VII, 6-VIII, 20-IX, 3-XII, 22-XII-1829, 23-I, 22-IV, 26-V, 30-V-1830; Dietrichstein: II, 24-II, 3-III, 20-III, 5-IV, 28-VIII-1827, 1-I, 9-II, 11-III, 1-X-1828 27-I, 7-II, 3-III, 24-III, 25-IV, 19-V, 14-VII, 6-VIII, 14-XI, 19-XI, 22-XII, 24-XII, 28-XII-1829, 23-I, 27-II, 13-III, 10-IV, 22-IV, 24-IV, 29-IV, 9-V, 30-V-1830; Empress Caroline: 13-III-1829, 17-IV-1829; Countess Lazansky: 30-VII-1827, 29-III-1828, 8-VIII-1829; Count Feodor Karaczay: 4-VII-1827, 25-III-1830; fragments of two letters from the Duke of Reichstadt dated 16-I-1827 and 25-III-1830 (*Revue des Deux Mondes,* collection of Dr. Glauco Lombardi).

Archives Nationales: F.7. 6993 (Marie Louise's stay in Switzerland). *Musée de l'Histoire de France:* Letter from the Duke of Reichstadt to General Neipperg (22-IX-1827).

Malmaison Museum: Exercise books, drafts of letters, essays, notes, written by the Duke of Reichstadt.

Correspondence: Marie Louise to Metternich; Metternich to Marie Louise (Vienna Archives, Bourgoing).

Memoirs, anecdotes, etc.: Papers of the Duke of Reichstadt (*op. cit.*); *Séjour à Weinzierl; Journal* written at Gratz (1830); *Journal* by Obenaus (1829), also *Portrait caractéristique du duc de Reichstadt (Revue des Études Napoléoniennes,* published by the Baron de Bourgoing); Wertheimer: *Neue Freie Presse;* letter from the Duke of Reichstadt (appointment as captain); *Lettres Viennoises* (Viktor Bibl, *Napoléon II*).

XIV
NAPOLEON'S SON
(June to December, 1830)

Archives of Marie Louise: Letters from the Duke of Reichstadt: 11-XI, 11-XII-1830; Dietrichstein: 30-XI-1830; Metternich: 8-I-1831.

Memoirs, anecdotes, etc.: For Chapters VI, VII and VIII chiefly Prokesch's various publications: *Mes relations avec le duc de Reichstadt*, newly translated with notes by Jean de Bourgoing; *Notes marginales* (published by Henri Welschinger and Jean de Bourgoing); Prokesch: *Lettre sur la mort du duc de Reichstadt et le Journal;* Reichstadt papers (*op. cit.*); *Journal* written at Gratz; Marshal de Castellane (*Journal*); Metternich (*op. cit.*), vol. 5; *Observations résumées et étendues, etc.,* by Prince Dietrichstein; (Bibl., *op. cit.*); Rollet (*op. cit.*); Comtesse de Boigne: *Mémoires;* Vitrolles III (*op. cit.*).

Correspondence: Metternich to Apponyi and Apponyi to Metternich (Bourgoing: *Le Fils de Napoléon*); Camerata to Felix Bacciochi (Vienna archives, Bourgoing).

Works consulted: *L'Histoire de Dix Ans* by Louis Blanc and other works already listed.

XV
THE EAGLET
(December, 1830, to May, 1931)

Archives of Marie Louise: Letters from the Duke of Reichstadt: 2-II, XI, 27-XI, 4-XII-1830, 22-I, 26-II, 25-V-1831; Metternich: 3-IX-1830, 22-II, 27-II-1831; Dietrichstein: 13-XI, 23-XI, 30-XI, 7-XII, 16-XII-1830, 4-I, 6-I, 8-I, 11-I, 20-I, 14-II, 19-II, 20-II, 24-II, 26-II, 3-III, 12-III, 15-III, 19-III, 2-IV, 9-IV, 14-V, 17-V-1831.

Memoirs, anecdotes, etc.: Obenaus: *Fragments du journal de l'année 1831; Portrait caractéristique* (*Revue des Études Napoléoniennes,* published by the Baron de Bourgoing); Marmont (*op. cit.*); Prokesch (*op. cit.*); *Journal* by Lulu Thurheim (Bibl., *op. cit.*).

Correspondence: Letters from Marshal Maison to Mme. Godard-Duvivier (*Revue des Deux Mondes,* February, 1957); the Duke of Reichstadt to Prokesch (*Mes relations avec le duc de Reichstadt, op. cit.*); the Duke of Reichstadt to Esterházy (*Revue des Études Napoléoniennes,* Bourgoing, *op. cit.*); instructions to General Hartmann; Metternich to Apponyi, Apponyi to Metternich (Bibl., *op. cit.*).

Works consulted: Robert Christophe: *Marmont;* Pierre Saint-Marc: *Marmont;* H. E. Jacob: *Les Strauss et l'histoire de la valse;* Fleischmann: *Le*

Roi de Rome et les femmes; Bourgoing (*op. cit.*); Bibl. (*op. cit.*); Chateaubriand: *De la nouvelle proposition relative au bannissement de Charles X et de sa famille.* Also other works already listed.

XVI
THE COLONEL
(June, 1831, to February, 1832)

Archives of Marie Louise: Letters from the Duke of Reichstadt: 16-VI, 17-VI, 16-VIII, 2-IX, 15-X-1831; 4-II-1832; letters from Dietrichstein: 11-VI, 16-VI, 23-VI, 5-VII, 12-VII, 16-VII, 19-VII, 26-VII, 28-VII, 30-VII, 6-VIII, 13-VIII, 16-VIII, 18-VIII, 23-VIII, 3-IX, 15-IX, 17-IX, 24-IX, 29-IX, 6-X, 24-XI, 26-XI, 29-XI, 8-XII, 13-XII, 28-XII-1831, 19-I, 26-I, 28-I, 31-I, 4-II-1832; Dr. Malfatti: 3-IX-1831, 31-I, 7-II-1832; Countess Lazansky: 17-IV, 4-X-1831; General Hartmann-Klarstein: 4-I, 16-VI-1831, 4-II-1832.

Revue des Deux Mondes (*op. cit.*): F. Glauco Lombardi, fragments of letters from the Duke of Reichstadt: 2-VIII and 3-XII-1831.

Correspondence: Letter from Prince Dietrichstein to Metternich (Bourgoing: *Le Fils de Napoléon,* note XII); letters from the Duke of Reichstadt to his friend Esterházy (*Revue des Études Napoléoniennes,* July-August, 1932), published by the Baron de Bourgoing.

Memoirs, anecdotes, etc.: Malfatti: *Confidences* (Montbel, *op. cit.*); *Mémoires* by Baroness Sturmfeder (Bibl., *op. cit.*); Obenaus: *Journal* (*Revue des Études Napoléoniennes, op. cit.*).

XVII
"THE TERRIFYING METEOR"
(February to July, 1832)

Archives of Marie Louise: Letters from Dietrichstein: 9-II, 23-II, 13-III, 17-III, 20-III, 27-III, 3-IV, 7-IV, 12-IV, 17-V, 19-V, 23-V, 30-V, 3-VI, 8-VI, 14-VI-1832; Dr. Malfatti: 28-II, 24-III, 3-IV, 14-IV, 18-IV, 21-IV, 3-V-1832; General Hartmann-Klarstein: 25-II, 1-III, 27-III, 31-III, 12-IV, 24-IV, 26-IV, 8-V-1832; Countess Lazansky: 10-II-1832.

Correspondence: Marie Louise to Dietrichstein (Bourgoing, *op. cit.*); Marie Louise to her daughter: *Revue des Études Napoléoniennes* (*op. cit.*); letter from the Duke of Reichstadt dated March 17 (published by Jean de Bourgoing, *Le Fils de Napoléon, op. cit.*); letters from Marshal Maison (*Revue des Deux Mondes, op. cit.*).

Memoirs, anecdotes, etc.: Chiefly Baron Moll's *Journal,* not published in France until 1947 (*La fin du Roi de Rome,* Pietro Pedrotti); Princess Melanie von Metternich: *Journal;* Faucigny-Lucinge (*op. cit.*); Montbel (*op. cit.*); Malfatti and Foresti: *Confidences;* Ladislas con Pyrker's unpublished *Mémoires* (Bourgoing, *op. cit.*).

XVIII
THE BRONZE COFFIN

Archives of Marie Louise: Letter from Sophia: 25-VIII-1831; Dietrichstein: 25-VII, 15-VIII, 9-IX, 9-XI-1832.

Works consulted: Those already listed. Particularly Alberto Lumbroso: *Napoléon II, Souvenirs du Roi de Rome* (*op. cit.*); M. de Marceley: *Meurtre à Schönbrunn;* Montbel (*op. cit.*); Moll (*op. cit.*); Aubry (*op. cit.*).

Index